Ships of the United States Navy and their Sponsors

1913—1923

Compiled by
Anne Martin Hall
Edith Wallace Benham

Edited by
Anne Martin Hall

Privately Printed

THE·PLIMPTON·PRESS
NORWOOD·MASS·U·S·A

U. S. BATTLESHIP "COLORADO," STEAMING FULL SPEED

FOREWORD

THIS volume is supplementary to "Ships of the United States Navy and their Sponsors, 1797–1913," published in 1913 to bring together from widely separated and inaccessible sources all obtainable facts relating to the launching and naming of the fighting craft of our Navy, old and new, and the bestowal of the names upon these vessels by sponsors. Records of Navy launchings and namings had been preserved nowhere in book form up to that time. Laborious research in many directions was necessary to collect and verify fragmentary data.

The present volume has been prepared primarily for the Society of Sponsors of the United States Navy, and also in response to requests for an up-to-date book, from non-members and from libraries. Full accounts of all launchings would be repetition. Typical accounts only are given.

Complete biographies of individuals, or complete histories of vessels are manifestly impossible in this volume. Historical notes are not given as complete histories. Biographical notes of patriots for whom Navy vessels have been named are not given as complete biographies. Conspicuous facts of biographies and of histories are set forth for the purpose of interesting and unmistakable identification and for the inspiration of every reader with patriotic pride in the achievements of our Navy. Authorities for biographical notes of naval officers and civilians for whom naval vessels have been named are Navy Department Records and the family records of the patriots thus honored. Grateful acknowledgements are made to Mrs. Annie H. Eastman, of the Navy Department Library, for assistance in biographical research, and to many friends who have encouraged and assisted the work.

ANNE MARTIN HALL
Editor

[v]

CONTENTS

PAGE

CUSTOM OF BESTOWING THE NAME ON U. S. NAVY VESSELS   xi

NOMENCLATURE AND U. S. STATUTE LAWS GOVERNING NAMES OF VESSELS xvi

SHIPS OF THE U. S. NAVY AND THEIR SPONSORS 1913–1923. ALPHABETICALLY ARRANGED 3

SOCIETY OF SPONSORS OF THE U. S. NAVY 273

THE BAPTISM OF SHIPS — A HISTORY OF THE CUSTOM AMONG VARIOUS NATIONS 283

ADDENDA TO "SHIPS OF THE U. S. NAVY AND THEIR SPONSORS 1797–1913" 293

INDEX OF NAMES OF SPONSORS OF U. S. NAVY VESSELS . 301

LIST OF ILLUSTRATIONS

PAGE

U. S. Battleship "Colorado" steaming full speed . . . . *Frontispiece*
Launching Stand, U. S. Battleship "Arizona," arrival of the Sponsor . . .   6
Ready! Named! Launched!   8
Launching Party, U. S. Torpedoboat Destroyer "Badger" 12
U. S. Torpedoboat Destroyer "Bainbridge" taking the water 16
U. S. Torpedoboat Destroyer "Brooks" steaming full speed 24
Launching Party, U. S. Torpedoboat Destroyer "Broome" 28
Bow of U. S. Scout Cruiser "Cincinnati" and launching party 32
U. S. Torpedoboat Destroyer "Cole," speeding 40
Launching Party, U. S. Battleship "Colorado" 48
U. S. Torpedoboat Destroyer "Converse" steaming full speed 56
U. S. Torpedoboat Destroyer "Du Pont" just off the ways 62
U. S. Torpedoboat Destroyer "Ellis" entering the water 76
Launch of the Steam Frigate "Fulton the First" in 1814 86
U. S. Torpedoboat Destroyer "Reuben James" going full speed 104
A Good Luck Shower! 110
U. S. Cruiser "Marblehead" about to leave the ways 122
U. S. Battleship "Maryland" launching stand 126
U. S. Battleship "Maryland" sliding down the launching ways 130
U. S. Torpedoboat Destroyer "McDermut" just leaving the ways 138
U. S. Scout Cruiser "Milwaukee" under way 148
Ready to launch U. S. Battleship "New York" 156
U. S. Battleship "Oklahoma" under way 160
Launching Party, U. S. Scout Cruiser "Omaha" 168
Naming the U. S. Torpedoboat Destroyer "Peary" 172
Launching Party, U. S. Torpedoboat Destroyer "Pillsbury" 174
Submarine coming to the surface 182
U. S. Submarine "R–14" going full speed on the surface 186
Launching of the U. S. Submarine "R–2" 190
Naming the U. S. Submarine "R–26" 194
U. S. Torpedoboat Destroyer "Reid" going full speed 198
U. S. Scout Cruiser "Richmond" making a record run 202
Naming the U. S. Submarine "S–15" 206
U. S. Submarine "S–42" launched 210
Indian Princess Sponsor for the U. S. Submarine "S–48," with her party... 214

U. S. Airship "Shenandoah" moored to the mast of the U. S. S. "Patoka".. 218

Sponsor of U. S. Airship "Shenandoah" pulling the cord to break the bottle 220

Naming the U. S. Torpedoboat Destroyer "Stewart 2nd" 230

Sponsor and party of the U. S. Torpedoboat Destroyer "Sturtevant" . . . 236

U. S. Torpedoboat Destroyer "Tatnall" taking the water 240

U. S. Battleship "Tennessee" leaving the New York Navy Yard fully completed 244

Just before the U. S. Torpedoboat Destroyer "Tracy" started down the ways 248

U. S. Cruiser "Trenton 2nd," sponsor breaking the bottle 254

U. S. Torpedoboat Destroyer "Truxton 2nd," breaking the bottle on the bow 258

U. S. Torpedoboat Destroyer "Wainwright" leaving the ways 262

U. S. Torpedoboat Destroyer "Waters" camouflaged 266

Launching Party, U. S. Torpedoboat Destroyer "Whipple 2nd" 270

Sponsors present at organization meeting of Society of Sponsors of U. S. Navy. 278

Presidents of the Society of Sponsors of the U. S. Navy, 1908–1923 . . . 282

Launching Party, U. S. S. "Chattanooga 1st," October 13th, 1865 294

BESTOWING THE NAME

THE launching of a Navy ship is an engineering feat of great magnitude, usually so successfully performed that the spectator thrills with enthusiasm entirely devoid of anxiety. Each succeeding battleship becomes larger and heavier, and careful calculation must be worked out bearing directly upon the launching even before a single rivet has been driven.

It is the usual custom in launching naval vessels to send them into the water stern first, the fuller form of the hull aft tending to make the vessel rise more quickly from her first plunge than would be the case were she sent into the water bow first, and it also makes the pivotal strain less at that instant when the bow on entering the water and the stern upon rising throw the burden of weight upon the forward poppets or timber shores.

In the earlier years of our Navy the name of a United States Navy ship was usually bestowed by an officer of the Navy. The naming party went on board to be launched with the ship, and the sponsor broke a bottle of wine or water over the bow of the vessel and pronounced the name at the moment that the bow struck the water.

The ceremony of bestowing the name upon a United States Navy ship has always been a civil ceremony and without intent of religious significance.

Examined records give only one instance of religious ceremony in connection with the launch of a United States Navy ship prior to 1914. Prayer, offered by a clergyman, preceded the civil ceremony of launching and naming "Princeton (1st)" in 1843.

Just before the vessel was released Captain Stockton, U. S. Navy, who was in charge, assembled those on board and a prayer was offered by the Reverend Doctor Suddards:

"Eternal God, Creator of the Universe, Governor of Nations. Humbly we prostrate ourselves before Thee and ask Thy blessing. Most humbly we beseech Thee with Thy favor to behold and bless Thy servant the President of the United States and all the officers of the Government. May the vessel about to be launched be guarded by Thy gracious Providence and care. May it not bear the sword in vain, but as the minister of God be a terror to those who do evil and a defense to those who do well. Graciously bless its officers and men. May love of country be engraven upon their hearts. Remember in mercy both arms of our National defense, and may virtue, honor and religion pervade all their ranks. Bless all nations and individuals on the earth and hasten the time when the benefits of holy religion shall have so prevailed that none shall wage war again for the purpose of aggression and none shall need it as a means of defense. All of which blessings we ask in the name of Him who taught us to say: 'Our Father who art in Heaven' . . ." — (U. S. Gazette)

In 1914 the custom of prayer at launchings of our battleships was established through the efforts of the Society of Sponsors. A copy of the historic prayer offered in 1843 was forwarded to the Secretary of the Navy with a petition that an adapted form of the prayer be offered at launchings of our Navy battleships.

Army and Navy Journal:

"At the launching of the battleship "Oklahoma" at Camden, N. J., on March 23, 1914, there was observed the custom which has always prevailed in other Christian countries of prayer preceding the civil ceremony of naming a battleship. This suggestion, made by Mrs. Reynold T. Hall, president of the Society of Sponsors, was most enthusiastically received by the Oklahoma delegation to the launching, and Bishop Hoss, of Oklahoma, was invited to offer the invocation. Prior to this occasion the United States had launched its battleships with civil ceremony only. In other countries this religious custom is always observed, and in England the special prayer at launchings is one of great beauty. This suggestion made by the Society of Sponsors was highly commended by the Secretary of the Navy and by the Oklahoma state officials. Secretary Daniels is so favorably impressed with the idea, that hereafter a prayer will be part of the exercises of launching a battleship."

The prayer used at the launching of British battleships was prepared by the Archbishop of Canterbury for the launching of H. M. S. "Alexandra" in 1875. An admiralty circular gives the form of service to be observed at launchings and the prayer. The service commences with the 107th psalm, beginning with verse twenty-three: "They that go down to the sea in ships . . ." The prayer follows:

"O Thou that sitteth above the water-floods and stilleth the raging of the sea, accept, we beseech Thee, the supplication of Thy servants for all who in this ship now and hereafter shall commit their lives unto the perils of the deep. In all their ways enable them truly and godly to serve Thee, and by their Christian lives, to set forth Thy glory throughout the earth. Watch over them in their going forth and in their coming in that no evil befall them nor mischief come nigh to hurt their souls, and so through all the changes and chances of this mortal life bring them of Thy mercy to the sure haven of Thine everlasting kingdom, through Jesus Christ our Lord. Amen." The Lord's Prayer concludes the ceremonial.

Early records of naming ceremonies are not complete owing to destruction of old records, and lack of newspaper space or enterprise, for the records discovered show that Navy launchings were occasions of great public interest and enthusiasm, and were attended by large numbers of people. Many prominent officials were present and were launched with the ship. Commodore John Paul Jones was aboard the "America," the first ship of the line launched in America, and in several instances the Secretary of the Navy has been launched with a Navy ship. The "America" built in 1782, was presented to the French Government.

The first record of a United States Navy naming or "christening" is that of the "Constitution," October 20, 1797, on which occasion Captain James Sever, U. S. Navy, "broke a bottle of wine over the bow of the frigate." When the frigate "Independence" was launched, June 20, 1814, "an officer of the 'Constitution' (Commodore Bainbridge) had the honor of christening her as she struck the water." The frigate "Brandywine," in 1825, "smote the water in fine style and Captain Dove stationed on her bow christened her with the usual ceremony."

In 1828 the first woman sponsor appears in print, but her identity may be forever shrouded in the mystery of the words: "The 'Concord' glided beautifully into her destined element and was christened by a young lady of Portsmouth." (Preble's History of the Portsmouth Navy Yard.) In those days it was not the fashion to put the names of ladies in the papers.

From that date up to the present time examined records give the names of few men who have participated in the naming of United States Navy ships. The ships were: the "Pennsylvania" in 1837; the "Dale" in 1839; the "Princeton (1st)" and the frigate "Raritan" in 1843; the "San Jacinto" and "Susquehanna" in 1850; the "New Ironsides" in 1862; the "Miantonomah" in 1863; the "Quinnebaug" in 1866; the "Mackenzie" in 1901.[1]

A bottle of wine has been broken upon the bow of the majority of our Navy vessels at the time of naming. Some vessels have been sprinkled with water, the bottle of water usually having

[1] See Vol. 1, 1797-1913.

been brought from the river for which the ship was named, or from a spring in the state or near the city for which the ship was named. In a few instances two bottles have been broken — one of wine, the other water.

There have been a few unique exceptions. A bottle of American whiskey was broken over the bow of "Princeton (1st)" and over the frigate "Raritan" in 1843; and a bottle of brandy upon "San Jacinto" in 1850, and "New Ironsides" in 1862, by the Naval officers who bestowed the names, — probably to stimulate their good luck as strongly as possible. A fair young woman sponsor broke a bottle of pure Irish whiskey over the bow of the "Shamrock" in 1863, bestowing the name. The "Germantown" and the "Pawtuxet" were sprinkled with wine and water commingled at the time of naming.

At several of our Navy launchings, according to a Japanese custom, three doves or carrier pigeons have been let loose at the moment of launching, with red, white and blue ribbons attached to their necks. In Japan doves were originally believed to be messengers of Hachiman, the patron god of the warriors, and their use at launchings of their warships meant wishing success in arms.

Some Navy ships have been launched without ceremony of any kind, notably the "Monitor" and the "Boston," and many of the submarine chasers launched during the World War.

Of late years it has become the custom for the launching party to stand upon a platform beside the ship's stem, and at the instant that the vessel starts to move toward the water the sponsor breaks a bottle of champagne against the bow and pronouncing the name of the ship says: "I name thee in the name of the United States."

NOMINATING THE SPONSOR

IN the old Navy it was the custom for Navy Yard officials to invite a sponsor to break the bottle of wine or water and bestow the name upon the vessel. Sometimes contestants for the honor were allowed to draw lots.

Of late years it has been the custom for the Navy Department to request the Governor of the State to nominate a sponsor for the vessel to be named for a State; or the Mayor or Council of a City to nominate a sponsor for the vessel to be named for a city.

When vessels are named for individuals it is customary for the Navy Department to nominate as sponsor some member of the family of the officer, enlisted man, or distinguished civilian for whom the vessel is named. If no member of the family is available, the Navy Department or the officials of the Shipbuilding Company designate a sponsor.

EDITOR

NOMENCLATURE OF VESSELS OF THE
U. S. NAVY

THE Continental Navy was a heterogeneous collection of vessels, partly vessels commissioned by the Continental Congress, partly vessels fitted out and commissioned by the Colonies, and many privateers.

The first government vessels were purchased by a Marine Committee appointed by Congress, and were re-named by that Committee. Among the first names were: "Columbus," for Christopher Columbus; "Alfred," for Alfred the Great; "Cabot," for the early explorer of America; "Andrea Doria," for the famous Genoese sailor; "Lexington," for the Battle of Lexington, the first Revolutionary conflict.

The thirteen ships authorized to be built December 13, 1775, were by resolution of Congress to be named: "Congress," "Randolph," "Hancock," "Washington," "Trumbull," "Raleigh," "Effingham," "Montgomery," "Warren," "Boston," "Providence," "Virginia" and "Delaware." Among the next names authorized were "Ranger," "Alliance," "Hornet," "America" and "Deane."

In 1794 Congress authorized six frigates to be built, to be named: "United States," "Constitution," "Constellation," "President," "Chesapeake," "Congress."

In 1798 the Navy Department was established, and Benjamin Stoddert was appointed the first Secretary of the Navy.

March 3, 1819, Congress passed the first statute law governing the naming of vessels of the Navy.

"Resolved by the Senate and House of Representatives of the United States of America, in Congress assembled, That all the ships of the Navy of the United States, now building, or hereafter to be built, shall be named by the Secretary of the Navy, under the direction of the President of the United States, according to the following rule: to wit: Those of the first class shall be called after the States of this Union, those of the second class after the rivers; and those of the third class after the principal cities and towns, taking care that no two vessels in the Navy shall bear the same name."

[xvi]

June 12, 1858, the following Act was approved:

"And be it further enacted, That all the steamships of the Navy of the United States now building, or hereafter to be built, shall be named by the Secretary of the Navy, under the direction of the President of the United States, according to the following rule, namely, All those of forty guns or more shall be considered of the first class, and shall be called after the States of the Union; those of twenty and under forty guns shall be considered as of the second class, and be called after the rivers and principal towns or cities; and all those of less than twenty guns shall be of the third class, and named by the Secretary of the Navy as the President may direct, care being taken that no two vessels in the Navy shall bear the same name."

At the commencement of the Civil War a large number of vessels were purchased for the Navy and an Act of Congress, August 5, 1861, authorized the Secretary of the Navy to change the names of purchased vessels.

A large number of vessels were hurriedly built for the Navy, and in some instances were somewhat indiscriminately named. The first vessels built were gunboats of the "Shawmut" class, to many of which were given Indian names, the name often being taken from an Indian-named town or village or creek near where the vessel was built. Next came sloops-of-war of the "Tuscarora" class, named after Indian-named rivers. Double-enders of the "Sassacus" class were also given Indian names. Some vessels were named after places of Naval engagements, such as "Vicksburg."

The "Harriet Lane" named for the niece of President Buchanan and transferred from the U. S. Treasury Department to the Navy, is the only fighting vessel on the Navy lists named for a woman.

The "Monitor," an entirely new type of vessel, was named by Ericsson himself at the request of the Navy Department. Ericsson, in his letter to the Secretary of the Navy, says:

"The impregnable and aggressive character of this structure will admonish the leaders of the Southern rebellion that the batteries on the banks of their rivers will no longer present barriers to the entrance of the Union's forces. But there are other leaders who will be admonished . . . 'Downing Street' will hardly view with indifference this last 'Yankee notion' — this Monitor . . . On this and many similar grounds, I propose the name of this battery — 'Monitor.'"

Ironclads of the "Monitor" type were classed as Monitors.

Many were given Indian names, such as "Canonicus," "Manhattan," "Miantonomah."

At the beginning of the Spanish War, Act of Congress, May 4, 1898, was passed:

"That hereafter all first-class battleships and monitors owned by the United States shall be named for the States and shall not be named for any city, place or person until the names of the States shall have been exhausted."

May 13, 1908, the Act of May 4, 1898, was superseded by an Act providing that "Monitors may be named as the President may direct."

The Act of March 3, 1901, provided

"That the President of the United States be, and is hereby authorized to establish, and from time to time to modify, as the needs of the service may require, a classification of the vessels of the Navy."

That was put into effect, and vessels of war were divided up as follows:

"Torpedo boat destroyers, torpedo boats, tugs, sailing ships, and receiving ships shall not be rated. Other vessels shall be rated by tons of displacement, as follows:

"First-rates, men-of-war only of 8,000 tons and above.

"Second-rates, men-of-war of 4,000 tons and under 8,000 tons, and converted yachts and auxiliary vessels of 6,000 tons and above, except colliers, refrigerating ships, distilling ships, tank steamers, repair ships, hospital ships, and other ships constructed or equipped for special purposes.

"Third-rates, men-of-war from 1,000 to 4,000 tons, and converted and auxiliary vessels from 1,000 to 6,000 tons."

The above changes of statute laws will explain the seeming inconsistency of Navy namings at different periods.

Under existing statute laws our battleships and armored cruisers are named for States of the Union; our cruisers for cities. Torpedo boat destroyers are named for distinguished Naval Officers, for heroic enlisted men, for Secretaries of the Navy, and in a few instances for U. S. Senators and Congressmen distinguished in the Naval Committees, and for distinguished inventors. Mine sweepers are named for the various birds. Submarines are designated by letters and numerals. The first airship to be named and christened was the "Shenandoah," the Indian name meaning "Daughter of the Stars."

At the present time, fuel ships, such as colliers, are given Greek mythological names. Oil carriers are being assigned Indian names of rivers of the country in which oil is produced, repair ships after distinguished engineers, and all ships that are not specified under the law are to be named according to their distinctive purpose.

In order that the names of the States, or the names of historic ships may be assigned to the new dreadnoughts, there have been changes in the names of some of our ships — notably: "North Carolina" renamed "Charlotte"; "Maryland" renamed "Frederick"; "West Virginia" renamed "Huntingdon"; "South Dakota" renamed "Huron"; "Montana" renamed "Missoula"; "Pennsylvania" renamed "Pittsburgh"; "Colorado" renamed "Pueblo"; "Washington" renamed "Seattle"; "New York the first," changed to "Saratoga," then to "Rochester."

Of the German ships taken over during the World War and added to our Navy, were: "Kronprinz Wilhelm," renamed "Baron von Steuben," after the Prussian General who aided in the development and organization of Washington's army in the Revolution; "Prince Eitel Friederich," renamed "Baron de Kalb," after the Bavarian General who came to this country with Lafayette in 1777 and gave valuable services until 1780, when he was wounded and died; "Geier," renamed "Schurz," after Carl Schurz, German-American soldier and statesman. The names chosen for the other vessels were generally of coast towns which have some connection with our Navy.

In 1915 the suggestion was made by the Society of Sponsors that the battle cruisers just authorized to be built, a new type of U. S. Navy vessel for the naming of which existing statute laws made no provision, should be named for the famous old fighting ships of our early Navy: "Constitution," "Constellation," "Saratoga," "Lexington," "Ranger" and others. Later other organizations urged these names.

The Navy had long urged the revival of these names of famous fighting ships of our early history.

The names of famous fighting ships: "Constitution," "Constellation," "Saratoga," "Lexington," "Ranger," and "United States" were assigned to our new battle cruisers. The "Lexington" and "Saratoga" were scheduled for conversion into aircraft carriers in 1922.

The "Constitution," launched in 1797, was the famous "Old Ironsides," which, under command of Isaac Hull, captured the British man-of-war "Guerriere," August 19, 1812.

The "Constellation" of the old navy, called "The Lucky Ship" because of her long record of victories and captures, was launched in 1797 and continued in commission during the days of the Civil War.

The "Ranger" was a ship of John Paul Jones, and received the first salute of a foreign war ship, from the French fleet in Quiberon Bay, February 14, 1778.

The "Lexington" was the flagship of Commodore John Barry, which, sailing from Philadelphia, captured the British sloop "Edward" and brought back to the Marine Committee of the Continental Congress the first prize of the war.

The "Saratoga" was the flagship of Commodore MacDonough at the battle of Lake Champlain, September 14, 1814, when an inferior American force decisively defeated a superior British force.

The "United States'" principal exploit occurred under Commodore Decatur's command, when the "Macedonian" was captured after a hot fight in 1812. The latter was taken into port and afterwards added to the American fleet.

In commemoration of glorious records, and as reminders of worthy deeds of our history, such names, if continued in association with the current national life, would be a constant inspiration to the country and the Navy.

EDITOR

Ships of the United States Navy and Their Sponsors

1913—1923

Ships of the United States Navy and Their Sponsors

1913—1923

ABBOT

TORPEDO BOAT DESTROYER

Length, 314 feet   *Beam, 30 feet, 11 inches*   *Draft, 9 feet, 3 inches*

NAMED FOR COMMODORE JOEL ABBOT, U. S. NAVY

Launched July 4, 1918, at Newport News S. B. & D. D. Company, Newport News, Virginia.

Sponsor: MISS LOUISE ABBOT COOKE, great-granddaughter of Commodore Joel Abbot, U. S. Navy.

COMMODORE JOEL ABBOT, U. S. Navy, was born in Westford, Massachusetts, 1793; died 1855. Appointed midshipman, 1812; his first cruise was under Commodore Rodgers on the frigate "President," who recommended him to Commodore Macdonough, then in command of the naval forces of Lake Champlain; he was given a mission to penetrate the British lines and destroy a quantity of masts and spars; this he accomplished, having assumed the disguise of a British officer, for which service he was promoted lieutenant and voted a sword by Congress. He was commissioned captain in 1848; in 1852 he commanded the frigate "Macedonian" on the Japan expedition, succeeding Commodore Perry as fleet officer of the squadron. During this critical period he often performed delicate diplomatic duties with complete satisfaction to our government.

[3]

ALAMEDA

FUEL SHIP

Length, 446 feet   *Beam, 58 feet*   *Draft, 25 feet, 6 inches*

NAMED FOR ALAMEDA, CALIFORNIA

Launched July 15, 1919, at William Cramp and Sons' S. and E. Company, Philadelphia, Pennsylvania.

Sponsor: MRS. RICHARD G. WIDDOWS (ETHEL MULL), daughter of Mr. J. H. Mull, President of the Company.

ALDEN

TORPEDO BOAT DESTROYER

Length, 314 feet   *Beam, 30 feet, 11 inches*   *Draft, 9 feet, 4 inches*

NAMED FOR REAR ADMIRAL JAMES ALDEN, U. S. NAVY

Launched June 7, 1919, at William Cramp & Sons' Company, Philadelphia, Pennsylvania.

Sponsor: MRS. VERNON M. DORSEY (Sarah Alden), great-niece of Rear Admiral James Alden, U. S. Navy.

REAR ADMIRAL JAMES ALDEN, U. S. Navy, was born in Portland, Maine, 1810, died 1877. Appointed midshipman 1828, rear admiral 1871. During the Mexican War — 1847–48 — he was attached to the home squadron and participated in the capture of Vera Cruz; Civil War — 1861, commanded the U. S. S. "South Carolina," which reinforced Fort Pickens. April, 1862, was actively engaged in operations on the Mississippi River and at Mobile Bay with Admiral Farragut; 1869–1871, Chief of Bureau of Navigation.

ALLEN

TORPEDO BOAT DESTROYER

Length, 315 feet   *Beam, 29 feet, 11 inches*   *Draft, 9 feet*

NAMED FOR COMMANDER WILLIAM HENRY ALLEN, U. S. Navy

Launched December 5, 1916, at Bath Iron Works, Bath, Maine.

Sponsors: MISS HARRIET ALLEN BUTLER AND MISS DORTHEA DIX ALLEN, great-grandnieces of Commander William Henry Allen, U. S. Navy.

COMMANDER WILLIAM HENRY ALLEN, U. S. Navy, was born in Providence, Rhode Island, 1784; appointed midshipman, U. S. Navy, 1800; lieutenant, 1807; master commandant (commander) 1813; died 1813. Served on the "George Washington," "Philadelphia," "John Adams," and "Congress"; third lieutenant of the "Chesapeake" 1807, when she struck her flag to H. B. M. S. "Leopard" and fired the only gun from the "Chesapeake"; first lieutenant on the "United States" in her engagement with the "Macedonian"; 1813 commanded the "Argus" and took U. S. Minister William Harris Crawford to France; after successful cruising was attacked and captured August 14, 1813, by H. B. M. S. "Pelican"; Allen was severely wounded in the early part of the action, but remained on deck until he fainted, was carried below, and his leg amputated; removed to Mill Prison Hospital, Plymouth, England, where he died August 18, 1813. He was included in the thanks of Congress to the officers and men of the "United States" in recognition of gallant conduct in the capture of the "Macedonian" and awarded silver medal January 29, 1813.

ANTHONY

TORPEDO BOAT DESTROYER

Length, 314 feet   *Beam, 30 feet, 11 inches*   *Draft, 9 feet, 2 inches*

NAMED FOR SERGEANT MAJOR WILLIAM ANTHONY, U. S. MARINE CORPS

Launched August 10, 1918, at Bethelehem Shipbuilding Corporation, San Francisco, California.

[5]

Sponsor: MISS GRACE HEATHCOTE, daughter of Mr. Bruce Heathcote, Manager, Canadian Bank of Commerce, San Francisco.

SERGEANT MAJOR WILLIAM ANTHONY, United States Marine Corps, was born in Albany, New York. Enlisted in Marine Corps 1875, and with short intervals between re-enlistments served almost continuously therein, until June 26, 1899. Capt. C. D. Sigsbee, called the attention of the Secretary of the Navy to the soldierly conduct of Private William Anthony on the occasion of the explosion of the "Maine," and stated as follows: "At the time of the explosion I was in the captain's cabin of the "Maine." The lights of the vessel were instantly obscured and the apartments were filled with smoke; there was immediate and intense darkness. On leaving my cabin through the usual passage forward, feeling my way along, I was met near the outer door of the superstructure by Private Anthony who was coming into the cabin to fulfill, on that dangerous occasion, the precise duties of his position by notifying me of the explosion. He ran against me in the darkness, apologized hastily, and reported to me that the ship had been blown up and was sinking. On an occasion when a man's instinct would lead him to seek safety outside the ship, he started into the superstructure and toward the cabin, irrespective of the danger. The action was a noble one, and I feel it an honor to call his conduct to the attention of the Navy Department with the recommendation that he be made a sergeant."

ARIZONA (3D.)

BATTLESHIP

| *Length, 608 feet* | *Beam, 97 feet* | *Draft, 28 feet, 10 inches* |

NAMED FOR THE STATE OF ARIZONA
(Admitted to the Union in 1912)

Launched June 19, 1915, at Navy Yard, New York, New York.

[6]

LAUNCHING STAND OF U.S. BATTLESHIP
"ARIZONA"
Arrival of The Sponsor

Sponsor: MISS ESTHER ROSS, Prescott, Arizona, daughter of Mr. W. W. Ross, a prominent pioneer citizen of Arizona. Miss Ross broke two bottles upon the ship, one containing American champagne and the other water procured at the risk of a man's life from the famous Roosevelt Dam of the Arizona River. Maids of honor were Miss Eva Behn, Miss Sallie King, and Miss Marie Farrell.

The Society of Sponsors' "Prayer for our Navy" was offered just before the launching by Bishop J. W. Atwood of Arizona.

Among those on the stand were Secretary of the Navy Josephus Daniels, Governor Hunt of Arizona, Senator Ashurst of Arizona, Mayor Mitchel of New York, Mr. and Mrs. W. W. Ross, General Leonard Wood, Rear Admiral F. F. Fletcher, Rear Admiral R. T. Hall, Vice Admiral H. T. Mayo, a large number of officials, and members of the Society of Sponsors. 75,000 spectators witnessed the launching.

After the launching and the banquet, Secretary and Mrs. Daniels entertained the visiting Arizonians, the Society of Sponsors, and prominent officials on board the U. S. S. "Dolphin," taking the party for a sail past the Statue of Liberty and down the bay.

THE battleship "Arizona" is the third Navy ship to bear the name. The second "Arizona" was a first-class screw frigate, launched in 1865 at Philadelphia Navy Yard. The first "Arizona" was an iron side-wheel steamer purchased by the Government in 1863.

ASHEVILLE

GUNBOAT

Length, 241 feet	*Beam, 41 feet*	*Draft, 11 feet, 4 inches*

NAMED FOR ASHEVILLE, NORTH CAROLINA

Launched July 4, 1918, at Navy Yard, Charleston, South Carolina.

[7]

Sponsor: Miss ALYNE J. REYNOLDS, daughter of Carl Vernon Reynolds, M. D., a prominent citizen of Asheville.

AUK

MINE SWEEPER

Length, 187 feet   *Beam, 35 feet*   *Draft, 9 feet, 9 inches*

NAMED FOR THE BIRD AUK

Launched September 28, 1918, at Todd Shipyard Corporation, New York.

Sponsor: Miss NAN McARTHUR BEATTIE, daughter of one of the foremen of the company.

AULICK

TORPEDO BOAT DESTROYER

Length, 314 feet   *Beam, 30 feet, 11 inches*   *Draft, 9 feet, 4 inches*

NAMED FOR COMMODORE JOHN H. AULICK, U. S. NAVY

Launched April 11, 1919, at Bethlehem Shipbuilding Company, Quincy, Massachusetts.

Sponsor: Mrs. PHILIP J. WILLETT (Elizabeth Sullivan), wife of Lieutenant Commander Willett, P. C., U. S. Navy.

COMMODORE JOHN H. AULICK, U. S. Navy, was born in Winchester, Virginia, 1787; died 1873. Appointed midshipman, 1809, and was made commodore on the retired list 1867. Served on the "Enterprise" in her victory over the "Boxer" September 4, 1813, and brought the "Boxer" into port after the engagement. Received thanks and a silver medal from Congress. In 1851–1853 commanded the East India Squadron and prepared the way for the treaty with Japan made by Commodore Perry.

AUSBURN

TORPEDO BOAT DESTROYER

Length, 314 feet   *Beam, 30 feet, 11 inches*   *Draft, 9 feet, 4 inches*

READY! NAMED! LAUNCHED!

Photo by New York Shipbuilding Corporation

NAMED FOR CHARLES L. AUSBURN, ELECTRICIAN
1ST CLASS, U. S. NAVY

Launched December 18, 1919, at Bethlehem Shipbuilding
Corporation, Quincy, Massachusetts.

Sponsor: MRS. DELLA E. AUSBURN, sister-in-law of
Charles L. Ausburn, U. S. N.

CHARLES L. AUSBURN, electrician, first class, United
States Navy, was born 1889, in New Orleans, Louisiana;
lost at sea October 17, 1917. Entered the United States
Navy February 25, 1908, as apprentice seaman; re-enlisted
as seaman, 1912; re-enlisted as quartermaster, third class
1916. On October 15, 1917, the U. S. S. "Antilles" left
Quiberon Bay, bound for America. Just after daylight
on the morning of October 17 she was struck by a torpedo
and went down in four and a half minutes. Radio Electrician Ausburn remained at his post in an effort to give warning, regardless of his personal safety, and went down with
the ship.

AVOCET

MINE SWEEPER

Length, 187 feet   *Beam, 35 feet*   *Draft, 9 feet, 9 inches*

NAMED FOR THE BIRD AVOCET

Launched March 9, 1918, at Baltimore Drydock and
Shipbuilding Company.

Sponsor: MISS FRANCES VIRGINIA IMBACH, daughter of
the superintendent of the upper plant of the company.

BABBITT

TORPEDO BOAT DESTROYER

Length, 314 feet   *Beam, 30 feet, 11 inches*   *Draft, 9 feet, 4 inches*

NAMED FOR LIEUTENANT FITZ HENRY BABBITT,
U. S. NAVY

Launched September 30, 1918, at New York Shipbuilding Corporation, Camden, New Jersey.

Sponsor: MISS LUCILLE BURLIN, niece of the Chief Engineer of the New York Shipbuilding Company.

THE "BABBITT," named in memory of Lieutenant Fitz Henry Babbitt, U. S. Navy, who was killed in action between the British ships of war "Endymion" and "Pomona" and the U. S. S. "Adams" on January 15, 1815. He was appointed a midshipman, 1804, and promoted to lieutenant 1810; served on the "Nautilus" from February 19, 1812 to November 29, 1812, and on the "Adams" from November 30, 1812 to April 6, 1813.

BADGER

TORPEDO BOAT DESTROYER

Length, 314 feet   *Beam, 30 feet, 11 inches*   *Draft, 9 feet, 4 inches*

NAMED FOR COMMODORE OSCAR C. BADGER, U. S. NAVY

Launched August 24, 1918, at New York Shipbuilding Corporation, Camden, New Jersey.

Sponsor: MRS. HENRY F. BRYAN (Elizabeth Badger), granddaughter of Commodore Oscar C. Badger, U. S. N.

COMMODORE OSCAR C. BADGER, U. S. Navy, was born in Connecticut; died 1899. Appointed midshipman, 1841; commissioned commodore, 1881. Cruised on the coast of Africa in the "Saratoga," 1843–44, and took part in the destruction of the Barbary villages. On the steam frigate "Mississippi," Gulf Squadron, Mexican War, and at first attack on Alvarado. Subsequently attached to the "Brazil," Pacific Squadron, until 1856. While attached to the "John Adams," 1856, commanded a party sent to attack and destroy the village of Vutia, Fiji Islands, and was engaged with these islanders on other occasions. 1858–1860 on the "Macedonian," Mediterranean Squadron. Civil War: 1861–62 commanded the "Anacostia" and other vessels of the Potomac Flotilla in attacks off Cockpit Point battery and other points on the Potomac River for which he was mentioned in dispatches from the commanding officer of the flotilla; took part also in the siege of Yorktown and defenses of Gloucester Point, Virginia, 1862 –63. Ordnance officer in charge of arming gunboats of the western rivers. 1863–64 attached to the South Atlantic Blockading Squadron, commanded the ironclad "Patapsco" in attacks on forts in Charleston Harbor. Commanded the ironclad "Montauk" in a night attack on Fort Sumter, August 22, 1863. Flag captain South Atlantic Blockading Squadron and was on the flagship "Weehawken," in attack of Fort Sumter, September 1, 1863, and was severely wounded in the right leg; mentioned by Rear Admiral Dahlgren in dispatches to the department for services during these operations.

GEORGE E. BADGER

TORPEDO BOAT DESTROYER

Length, 314 feet   *Beam, 30 feet, 11 inches*   *Draft, 9 feet, 4 inches*

NAMED FOR SECRETARY OF THE NAVY
GEORGE E. BADGER

Launched March 6, 1920, at Newport News Shipbuilding & Dry Dock Company, Newport News, Virginia.

Sponsor: MISS MARY BADGER WILSON, granddaughter of Secretary of the Navy George E. Badger.

SECRETARY OF THE NAVY GEORGE E. BADGER was born in Newbern, North Carolina, 1795; died 1866. He was graduated from Yale University in 1813, and studied law in Raleigh. In 1816 he was elected to the State Legislature; 1820–1825 judge of the North Carolina Superior Court at Raleigh. He was appointed Secretary of the Navy in 1841 and subsequently served in the Senate for two terms.

[11]

BAGLEY (2D)

TORPEDO BOAT DESTROYER

Length, 314 feet   *Beam, 30 feet, 11 inches*   *Draft, 9 feet, 3 inches*

NAMED FOR ENSIGN WORTH BAGLEY, U. S. NAVY

Launched October 19, 1918, at Newport News Shipbuilding & Dry Dock Company, Newport News, Virginia.

Sponsor: MRS. ADELAIDE WORTH BAGLEY, mother of Ensign Worth Bagley, U. S. Navy. Accompanying Mrs. Bagley were her daughter, Mrs. Josephus Daniels, her son-in-law, Secretary of the Navy Josephus Daniels, Miss Belle Bagley, and Miss Ethel Bagley.

ENSIGN WORTH BAGLEY, U. S. Navy, was born in Raleigh, North Carolina, in 1874. Appointed naval cadet in 1891; ensign, 1897. Ensign Bagley was the first naval officer killed in action during the Spanish-American War of 1898. He served on the U. S. Torpedo Boat "Winslow" and lost his life in its attack on batteries at Cardenas, Cuba, May 11, 1898.

BAILEY

TORPEDO BOAT DESTROYER

Length, 314 feet   *Beam, 30 feet, 11 inches*   *Draft, 9 feet, 4 inches*

NAMED FOR REAR ADMIRAL THEODORUS BAILEY, U. S. NAVY

Launched February 5, 1919, at Bethlehem Shipbuilding Corporation, Squantum, Massachusetts.

Sponsor: MISS ROSALIE FELLOWS BAILEY, great-granddaughter of Rear Admiral Theodorus Bailey, U. S. Navy.

REAR ADMIRAL THEODORUS BAILEY, U. S. Navy, was born at Chateaugay, New York, 1805; died 1877. Appointed midshipman, 1818; rear admiral, 1866; commended for energy, enterprise, and gallantry in fitting out and

LAUNCHING PARTY OF U.S. TORPEDO BOAT DESTROYER "BADGER",
The Sponsor With Her Father and Mother Rear Admiral C. J. Badger and Mrs. Badger

Photo by New York Shipbuilding Corporation

leading expedition against the enemy in the War with Mexico, 1847–48; 1861–1865 second in command and led attack on the forts and the capture of New Orleans; was included in the thanks of Congress to officers for distinguished service and successful operations on the lower Mississippi River. He afterwards was in command of the East Gulf Blockading Squadron and captured a large number of vessels.

BAINBRIDGE (3D)

TORPEDO BOAT DESTROYER

Length, 314 feet　　　*Beam, 30 feet, 11 inches*　　　*Draft, 9 feet, 4 inches*

NAMED FOR COMMODORE WILLIAM BAINBRIDGE,
U. S. NAVY

Launched June 12, 1920, at New York Shipbuilding Corporation, Camden, New Jersey.

Sponsor: MISS JULIET EDITH BERTRAM GREENE, great-great-granddaughter of Commodore William Bainbridge, U. S. Navy. Miss Greene was accompanied by her mother, Mrs. Louise Bainbridge Hoff Greene, sponsor for the U. S. S. "Bainbridge (2d)," launched in 1901.

COMMODORE WILLIAM BAINBRIDGE, U. S. Navy; born in Princeton, New Jersey, 1774; died 1833. Appointed lieutenant, United States Navy, August 3, 1798; promoted to captain May 20, 1800; distinguished service in War with France; March 7, 1803, ordered to command the frigate "Philadelphia," served in the Tripolitan War; captured on the "Philadelphia" in the harbor of Tripoli December 29, 1803; held prisoner by the Tripolitans until June 3, 1805; War of 1812, commanded the U. S. S. "Constitution," engaged and captured H. B. M. S. "Java" December 26, 1812; severely wounded in this engagement; awarded gold medal by Congress for gallantry, and received thanks of Congress; held position of Navy Commissioner 1824–1827.

BALLARD

TORPEDO BOAT DESTROYER
Length, 314 feet   Beam, 30 feet, 11 inches   Draft, 9 feet, 4 inches
NAMED FOR MIDSHIPMAN EDWARD J. BALLARD,
U. S. NAVY

Launched December 7, 1918, at Bethlehem Shipbuilding Corporation, Quincy, Massachusetts.

Sponsor: MISS ELOISE BALLARD, daughter of Mr. J. Edward Ballard, a descendant of Midshipman Edward J. Ballard, U. S. Navy.

MIDSHIPMAN EDWARD J. BALLARD, United States Navy. Appointed a midshipman, 1809; lieutenant, 1813. Ordered to the "Chesapeake" with Capt. James Lawrence. Killed in the early part of the engagement between that ship and H. B. M. S. "Shannon," June 1, 1813. Commission as lieutenant was issued before news of the battle had been received by the Navy Department.

BANCROFT (2D)

TORPEDO BOAT DESTROYER
Length, 314 feet   Beam, 30 feet, 11 inches   Draft, 9 feet, 4 inches
NAMED FOR GEORGE BANCROFT

Launched March 22, 1919, at Bethlehem Shipbuilding Corporation, Quincy, Massachusetts.

Sponsor: MISS MARY W. BANCROFT, great-granddaughter of George Bancroft.

NAMED for George Bancroft, American historian and statesman and founder of the United States Naval Academy at Annapolis, who was born at Worcester, Massachusetts, October 3, 1800. In 1845 he entered President Polk's Cabinet as Secretary of the Navy, with the determination of founding a Naval Academy. Served until 1846, when for a month he acted as Secretary of War. From 1846 to 1849 he was minister to Great Britain; 1867 minister to Prussia; to the North German Confederation, 1868; and to the new German Empire in 1871. From this post he was recalled at his own request in 1874. While minister at Berlin he assisted in the settlement of the Northwest boundary dispute between the United States and Great Britain.

BARKER

TORPEDO BOAT DESTROYER

Length, 314 feet   Beam, 30 feet, 11 inches   Draft, 9 feet, 4 inches

NAMED FOR REAR ADMIRAL ALBERT S. BARKER, U. S. NAVY

Launched September 11, 1919, at William Cramp & Sons' Company, Philadelphia, Pennsylvania.

Sponsor: MRS. ELLIN BARKER, widow of Rear Admiral Albert S. Barker, U. S. Navy.

REAR ADMIRAL ALBERT S. BARKER, United States Navy, was born in Hanson, Massachusetts, 1845; died 1916. Appointed midshipman 1859; commissioned rear admiral 1899. After graduating from the Naval Academy in 1862 he was ordered to the U. S. S. "Mississippi" and took part in the bombardment and passage of forts below New Orleans and the capture of that city; was on the "Mississippi" when she got ashore and was set on fire to prevent her capture; transferred to the "Monongahela" and took part in operations of the West Gulf Blockading Squadron until August 9, 1863, when ordered to the "Niagara" for special service. After the close of the Civil War held various prominent positions ashore. During the Spanish-American War commanded the "Newark" and participated in the bombardment of Santiago July 1, 1898; commanded the "Oregon" August 2, 1898, to May 29, 1899, on special service in the Pacific. His last duty afloat was commander-in-chief of the Atlantic Fleet, 1903-1905.

[15]

BARNEY

TORPEDO BOAT DESTROYER

Length, 314 feet   *Beam, 30 feet, 11 inches*   *Draft, 9 feet*

NAMED FOR COMMODORE JOSHUA BARNEY,
U. S. NAVY

Launched September 5, 1918, at William Cramp & Sons' Company, Philadelphia, Pennsylvania.

Sponsor: MISS NANNIE DORNIN BARNEY, great-granddaughter of Commodore Joshua Barney, U. S. Navy.

COMMODORE JOSHUA BARNEY, U. S. Navy, was born in Baltimore, Maryland, 1759; died 1818. At an early age he went to sea in the merchant service, and at the commencement of the Revolutionary War served as a volunteer on the "Hornet"; was transferred to the "Wasp," where he saw his first sea fight, and for gallantry on that occasion was promoted to lieutenant; awarded a medal by Congress. Owing to disagreement as to precedence, he declined a commission in the United States Navy in 1794; and served in the French Navy 1797-1800. At the outbreak of the War of 1812 he again entered the United States Navy and had command of a fleet of gunboats built for the defense of Chesapeake Bay.

BARRY (3D)

TORPEDO BOAT DESTROYER

Length, 314 feet   *Beam, 30 feet, 11 inches*   *Draft, 9 feet, 4 inches*

NAMED FOR COMMODORE JOHN BARRY, U. S. NAVY

Launched October 28, 1920, at New York Shipbuilding Corporation, Camden, New Jersey.

Sponsor: MRS. SHELTON E. MARTIN (Charlotte Barnes), great-grandniece of Commodore John Barry, U. S. Navy. The sponsor was sponsor for U. S. S. "Barry (2D)" in 1902.

COMMODORE JOHN BARRY, United States Navy, was born in Ireland in 1745. Died in Philadelphia in 1803.

[16]

Photo by New York Shipbuilding Corporation

U.S. TORPEDO BOAT DESTROYER "BAINBRIDGE"
TAKING THE WATER

He received one of the first commissions in the Navy. In 1776 commanded the "Lexington," the first cruiser to sail, and captured the British schooner "Edward," the first Navy prize. In 1781, returning from conveying to France our Minister Laurens in the "Alliance," he captured the "Atalanta" and "Trepassa," and was severely wounded. He held many important commands and was one of the bravest and most daring of officers. He was the third commander-in-chief of the Navy.

BELKNAP

TORPEDO BOAT DESTROYER

Length, 314 feet   *Beam, 30 feet, 11 inches*   *Draft, 9 feet, 4 inches*

NAMED FOR REAR ADMIRAL GEORGE EUGENE BELKNAP, U. S. NAVY

Launched January 14, 1919, at Bethlehem Shipbuilding Company, Quincy, Massachusetts.

Sponsor: MISS FRANCES GEORGIANA BELKNAP, granddaughter and namesake of Rear Admiral George E. Belknap, U. S. Navy.

REAR ADMIRAL GEORGE EUGENE BELKNAP, U. S. Navy, was born in Newport, New Hampshire, 1832; died 1903. Appointed midshipman, 1847; commissioned rear admiral, 1889. 1856–1857, East India squadron. Took prominent part in engagements with the Barrier Forts, Canton River, China, November, 1856. Actively engaged in the Civil War, 1861–65. Commanded a division of boats from the U. S. S. "St. Louis," in reinforcement of Fort Picken, Florida, April, 1861. Participated in the operations in Charleston Harbor; commanded the ironclad "Canonicus" in attacks on Fort Fisher, North Carolina, December 24–25, 1864, and January 13–15, 1865, resulting in their surrender. After this returned to Charleston, South Carolina, and fired the last gun against its defenses. In 1867–1868 commanded the U. S. S. "Hartford," Asiatic Station, and was in command of the expedition against Formosa. 1873–

1874 performed important duty, surveying, in the Pacific. Held important positions at sea and ashore from 1875 until retired, 1894.

BELL

TORPEDO BOAT DESTROYER
Length, 314 feet   *Beam, 30 feet, 11 inches*   *Draft, 9 feet*

NAMED FOR REAR ADMIRAL HENRY H. BELL, U. S. NAVY

Launched April 20, 1918, at Bethlehem Shipbuilding Company, Fore River, Massachusetts.

Sponsor: MRS. JOSEPHUS DANIELS (ADELAIDE BAGLEY), wife of Secretary of the Navy Josephus Daniels.

REAR ADMIRAL HENRY H. BELL, U. S. NAVY, was born in North Carolina about 1808; died January 11, 1868. Appointed midshipman, 1823; rear admiral, 1866; commanded a division in the West Gulf Blockading Squadron at the surrender of New Orleans and Forts Jackson and St. Philip, April, 1862 (Civil War). He was drowned by the capsizing of his barge while crossing the bar at the entrance to Osaka River, January 11, 1868.

BERNADOU

TORPEDO BOAT DESTROYER
Length, 314 feet   *Beam, 30 feet, 11 inches*   *Draft, 9 feet*

NAMED FOR COMMANDER JOHN BAPTISTE BERNADOU, U. S. NAVY

Launched November 7, 1918, at William Cramp & Sons' Company, Philadelphia, Pennsylvania.

Sponsor: MISS CORA WINSLOW BERNADOU, sister of Commander John Baptiste Bernadou, U. S. Navy

COMMANDER JOHN BAPTISTE BERNADOU, U. S. Navy, was born in Philadelphia, Pennsylvania, 1858; died 1908. Graduated from the Naval Academy in 1880; com-

[18]

missioned commander, 1906; 1884–1885 he was attached
to the Asiatic station and rendered most efficient service
during the first uprising in Seoul, Korea. For this service
he received the thanks of the Japanese Government. He
was promoted ten numbers for his gallantry in action off
Cardenas, Cuba, in 1898; in command of the torpedo boat
"Winslow," he ran in under the guns of Cardenas in one of
the first engagements of the Spanish-American War. During this engagement the "Winslow's" steering gear was
damaged by the enemy's fire, and five of her crew, including Ensign Worth Bagley, were killed. Bernadou,
then Lieutenant, was himself severely wounded. The torpedo boat was under the raking fire of the Spanish guns
for an hour, and was finally rescued by the revenue cutter
"Hudson." He was an expert ordnance officer, especially
in regard to explosives, and the discovery of the principles
of smokeless powder is credited to him. His last sea duty
was as executive officer of the "Kearsarge" and his last
shore duty naval attaché at Rome and Vienna.

BIDDLE (2D)

TORPEDO BOAT DESTROYER
Length, 314 feet   *Beam, 30 feet, 11 inches*   *Draft, 9 feet*

NAMED FOR CAPTAIN NICHOLAS BIDDLE, U. S. NAVY

Launched October 3, 1918, at William Cramp & Sons'
Company, Philadelphia, Pennyslvania.

Sponsor: MISS ELISE BIDDLE ROBINSON, great-granddaughter of Captain James S. Biddle, U. S. Navy, and
great-great-grandniece of Captain Nicholas Biddle, U. S.
Navy.

CAPTAIN NICHOLAS BIDDLE, United States Navy,
was born in Philadelphia in 1750. He was in command of
"Andrea Doria," 16 guns, in 1775, and captured so many
prizes that he had but five of his original crew when he returned to the Delaware River. Sailed not long after from
Charleston, South Carolina, and in a few days came back

with four prizes. In engagement with the "Yarmouth," 64 guns, March 1778, his ship, the "Randolph," 32 guns, blew up and the gallant Biddle and three hundred men perished.

BILLINGSLEY

TORPEDO BOAT DESTROYER

Length, 314 feet   *Beam, 30 feet, 11 inches*   *Draft, 9 feet, 4 inches*

NAMED FOR ENSIGN WILLIAM D. BILLINGSLEY, U. S. NAVY

Launched December 10, 1919, at Bethlehem Shipbuilding Corporation, Squantum, Massachusetts.

Sponsor: MISS IRENE BILLINGSLEY, sister of Ensign William D. Billingsley, U. S. Navy.

ENSIGN WILLIAM D. BILLINGSLEY, U. S. Navy, was born in Winona, Mississippi, April 24, 1887; killed in an aeroplane accident 1913. Appointed midshipman 1905; graduated in 1909; ensign, 1911. On June 20, 1913, started from the aviation station near Annapolis in a Wright biplane which had been converted into a hydroplane. When about 10 miles down the bay a gust of wind struck the hydroaeroplane and caused it to dive. Ensign Billingsley was thrown into the water. He was an officer of determination and fearless courage.

BITTERN

MINE SWEEPER

Length, 187 feet   *Beam, 35 feet*   *Draft, 9 feet, 9 inches*

NAMED FOR THE BIRD BITTERN

Launched February 15, 1919, at Alabama Drydock and Shipbuilding Company.

Sponsor: MRS. CHAUNCEY R. DOLL (Martha Braendlein), wife of Lieutenant C. R. Doll, U. S. Navy, Inspector of Machinery for the Navy at the works.

BLAKELEY (2D)

TORPEDO BOAT DESTROYER

Length, 314 feet   *Beam, 30 feet, 11 inches*   *Draft, 9 feet*

NAMED FOR CAPTAIN JOHNSTON BLAKELEY, U. S. NAVY

Launched September 19, 1918, at William Cramp & Sons' Company, Philadelphia, Pennsylvania.

Sponsor: MRS. CHARLES A. BLAKELEY (Virginia Lyons), wife of Commander C. A. Blakeley, U. S. Navy, a great-great-nephew of Captain Johnston Blakeley, U. S. Navy.

CAPTAIN JOHNSTON BLAKELEY, U. S. Navy, was born in Ireland, in 1781. Appointed Midshipman in 1800. In 1813, in command of the "Enterprise," captured the privateer "Fly." In 1814, in the "Wasp," captured H. B. M. S. "Reindeer" by superior gunnery. Congress voted him a gold medal. He cut out the "Mary" with military stores from under the guns of the "Armada," 74 guns. Sank the "Avon." Captured the "Atlanta." He was lost at sea in the "Wasp" in 1814.

BOBOLINK

MINE SWEEPER

Length, 187 feet   *Beam, 35 feet*   *Draft, 9 feet, 9 inches*

NAMED FOR THE BIRD BOBOLINK

Launched June 15, 1918, at Baltimore Drydock and Ship-building Company, Baltimore, Maryland.

Sponsor: MISS ELSIE JEAN WILLIS, daughter of Mr. J. M. Willis, Vice President and General Manager of the Company.

BOGGS

TORPEDO BOAT DESTROYER

Length, 314 feet   *Beam, 30 feet, 11 inches*   *Draft, 9 feet*

NAMED FOR REAR ADMIRAL CHARLES S. BOGGS,
U. S. NAVY

Launched April 25, 1918, at Mare Island Navy Yard, California.

Sponsor: MISS RUTH HASCAL, niece of the late Lieutenant William C. Turner, U. S. Marine Corps.

REAR ADMIRAL CHARLES S. BOGGS, United States Navy, was born in New Jersey, 1811; died 1888. Appointed midshipman November 1, 1826; commissioned rear admiral July 1, 1870. Took part in the Mexican War, 1846–1847; present at the siege of Vera Cruz; commanded a boat expedition against the Mexicans and re-took the brig "Truxtun" which had been captured by the Mexicans. Civil War, 1861–1865. Commanded the sloop-of-war "Varuna" of Admiral Farragut's squadron at the passage of Forts Jackson and St. Philip April 24, 1862. She was attacked by two Confederate rams and badly damaged, was obliged to run into the bank, and ably fought to the last. 1863 commanded the "Juniata," and special duty New York 1864–1866. 1867–1868 commanded the "De Soto" of the North Atlantic Squadron.

BORIE

TORPEDO BOAT DESTROYER

Length, 314 feet   *Beam, 30 feet, 11 inches*   *Draft, 9 feet, 4 inches*

NAMED FOR SECRETARY OF THE NAVY
ADOLPH EDWARD BORIE

Launched October 4, 1919, at William Cramp & Sons' Company, Philadelphia, Pennsylvania.

Sponsor: MISS PATTY BORIE, great-great-niece of Secretary of the Navy Adolph Edward Borie.

SECRETARY OF THE NAVY ADOLPH EDWARD BORIE was born in Philadelphia, 1809; died 1880. In 1826 he was graduated from the University of Pennsylvania and went to Paris to complete his education. After spending

[22]

several years abroad, he returned to the United States and entered into mercantile pursuits. He gave large sums toward the enlistment and care of soldiers during the Civil War. On March 5, 1869, he became Secretary of the Navy.

BRANCH

TORPEDO BOAT DESTROYER

Length, 314 feet   *Beam, 30 feet, 11 inches*   *Draft, 9 feet, 4 inches*

NAMED FOR SECRETARY OF THE NAVY JOHN BRANCH

Launched April 19, 1919, at Newport News Shipbuilding Company, Newport News, Virginia.

Sponsor: MISS LAURIE O'BRIEN BRANCH, grand-niece of Secretary of the Navy John Branch.

SECRETARY OF THE NAVY JOHN BRANCH, was born in Halifax, North Carolina, 1782. After graduation at the University of North Carolina in 1801 he studied law, became judge of the superior court, and was a State senator from 1811 to 1817, in 1822, and again in 1834. He was elected governor of his State in 1817, and from 1823 to 1829 was United States Senator, resigning in the latter year when he was appointed Secretary of the Navy, which office he held until 1831. 1844–1845 was governor of the Territory of Florida. Died 1863.

BRANT

MINE SWEEPER

Length, 187 feet   *Beam, 35 feet*   *Draft, 9 feet, 9 inches*

NAMED FOR THE BIRD BRANT

Launched May 30, 1918, at Sun Shipbuilding Company, Chester, Pennsylvania.

Sponsor: MISS LOIS GRAHAM, daughter of the Vice President of the company.

BRAZOS

FUEL SHIP

Length, 475 feet   *Beam, 56 feet*   *Draft, 26 feet, 8 inches*

NAMED FOR BRAZOS RIVER, TEXAS

Launched May 1, 1919, at Navy Yard, Boston, Massachusetts.

Sponsor: MISS CATHERINE RUSH, daughter of Captain William R. Rush, U. S. Navy, in command of the Boston Navy Yard.

BRECK

TORPEDO BOAT DESTROYER

Length, 314 feet   *Beam, 30 feet, 11 inches*   *Draft, 9 feet, 4 inches*

NAMED FOR ACTING VOLUNTEER LIEUTENANT COMMANDER JOSEPH B. BRECK, U. S. NAVY

Launched September 5, 1919, at Bethlehem Shipbuilding Corporation, Quincy, Massachusetts.

Sponsor: MRS. FOREST MACNEE (ELLEN BRECK), granddaughter of Lieutenant Commander Joseph B. Breck, U. S. Navy.

ACTING VOLUNTEER LIEUTENANT COMMANDER JOSEPH B. BRECK, United States Navy, was born in Maine in 1830; died 1865. Appointed acting ensign, 1863; acting master, 1863; acting lieutenant, 1863; acting volunteer lieutenant commander, 1864; on U. S. S. "Niphon" in the North Atlantic blockading squadron took part in the capture of six of the largest blockade runners off the New Inlet and Masonboro Inlet, North Carolina. An officer of pluck and resource, and won a brilliant name for himself by his successes on the Wilmington blockade, although his health was much impaired by his devotion to duty.

Photo by New York Shipbuilding Corporation

U.S. TORPEDO BOAT DESTROYER "BROOKS" STEAMING FULL SPEED

1

BRECKINRIDGE

TORPEDO BOAT DESTROYER

Length, 314 feet   *Beam, 30 feet, 11 inches*   *Draft, 9 feet*

NAMED FOR ENSIGN JOSEPH CABELL BRECKINRIDGE, U. S. NAVY

Launched August 17, 1918, at William Cramp & Sons' Company, Philadelphia, Pennsylvania.

Sponsor: MISS GENEVIEVE DUDLEY BRECKINRIDGE, niece of Ensign Joseph Cabell Breckinridge, U. S. Navy.

ENSIGN JOSEPH CABELL BRECKINRIDGE, United States Navy, was born 1872; appointed midshipman 1887; ensign 1897. Made his first cruise on the battleship "Texas." He displayed remarkable coolness and ability in time of peril, in storms, and in controlling the turret machinery at the peril of his life, especially on the occasion when the ammunition hoist gave way and the shot was falling into the powder, he sprang to the rescue, and by his presence of mind, saved the ship from probable instant destruction. His rescues of persons from drowning were many; and while serving on the "Cushing" he was washed overboard and drowned. The vessel gave a sudden roll, the life lines parted, his feet slipped on the wet deck and without a cry he went overboard.

BREESE

TORPEDO BOAT DESTROYER

Length, 314 feet   *Beam, 30 feet, 11 inches*   *Draft, 9 feet, 3 inches*

NAMED FOR CAPTAIN KIDDER RANDOLPH BREESE, U. S. NAVY

Launched May 11, 1918, at Newport News Shipbuilding Corporation, Newport News, Virginia.

Sponsor: MRS. GILBERT MCILVAINE (Elizabeth Breese), daughter of Captain Kidder Randolph Breese, U. S. Navy.

CAPTAIN KIDDER RANDOLPH BREESE, U. S. Navy, was born in Philadelphia, Pennsylvania, 1831; died 1881. Appointed midshipman, 1846; commissioned captain, 1874. Commanded the second division in the operations before Vicksburg in the summer of 1862. Commanded the flagship "Black Hawk," Mississippi Squadron, at Arkansas Post, 1862, and at the siege of Vicksburg, 1863; in charge of mortars a short time during the siege. Commanded the naval forces at feigned attacks on Haines Bluff in co-operation with Gen. Sherman, 1863; Red River Expedition, 1864, fleet captain of North Atlantic Squadron in both attacks on Fort Fisher; commanded the naval forces in assault on Fort Fisher, and was present at subsequent operations on Cape Fear River. Repeatedly received the thanks of Admiral Porter for his efficiency and zeal in the discharge of his important and responsible duties.

BRIDGE

SUPPLY SHIP

Length, 422 feet   *Beam, 55 feet*   *Draft, 20 feet, 8 inches*

NAMED FOR COMMODORE HORATIO BRIDGE, U. S. NAVY

Launched May 18, 1916, at Navy Yard, Boston, Massachusetts.

Sponsor: MRS. GRANVILLE SEARCY FLEECE (Pauline Bridge), grandniece of Commodore Horatio Bridge, U. S. Navy.

COMMODORE HORATIO BRIDGE, U. S. Navy, was born 1806, graduated from Bowdoin College in 1825. In 1838 appointed a Paymaster in the Navy; served on board the "Cyane" until 1841; after an interval of shore duty, was ordered to the "Saratoga," and visited the African Coast. He published "The Journal of an African Cruiser," which was edited by Nathaniel Hawthorne from Bridge's notes.

From 1846 to 1848 cruised in the frigate "United States."

From 1849 to 1851, stationed at the Portsmouth Navy Yard. In 1851 was assigned to duty as Chief of the Bureau of Provisions and Clothing.

In 1869 was assigned to duty as Chief Inspector of Provisions and Clothing until he retired with the rank of commodore.

He first employed in the American Navy the idea of comprehensive fleet supply, and under his direction the schedule for the systematic supply of the vessels of the Navy on the Atlantic and Gulf Coasts during the Civil War was established.

BROOKS

TORPEDO BOAT DESTROYER

Length, 314 feet   *Beam, 30 feet, 11 inches*   *Draft, 9 feet, 4 inches*

NAMED FOR FIRST LIEUTENANT JOHN BROOKS, U. S. MARINE CORPS

Launched April 24, 1919, at New York Shipbuilding Corporation, Camden, New Jersey.

Sponsor: MRS. GEORGE S. KEYES (Emma Reed), greatniece of Lieutenant John Brooks, U. S. Navy.

FIRST LIEUTENANT JOHN BROOKS, United States Marine Corps, was born in 1783. Appointed a second lieutenant October 1, 1807; promoted first lieutenant January 30, 1809. He served at various stations of the Marine Corps and was commanding officer of the marine guard aboard the vessel "Lawrence" during the War of 1812, and was killed in the engagement between the American and British fleets on Lake Erie, September 10, 1813.

BROOME

TORPEDO BOAT DESTROYER

Length, 314 feet   *Beam, 30 feet, 11 inches*   *Draft, 9 feet, 4 inches*

NAMED FOR LIEUTENANT COLONEL JOHN LLOYD BROOME, U. S. MARINE CORPS

[27]

Launched May 14, 1919, at William Cramp & Sons' Company, Philadelphia, Pennsylvania.

Sponsor: MISS MARY JOSEPHINE KEYWORTH BROOME, granddaughter of Lieutenant Colonel John Lloyd Broome, U. S. Marine Corps.

LIEUTENANT COLONEL JOHN LLYOD BROOME, U. S. Marine Corps, was born in New York in 1824; died 1898, Commissioned second lieutenant, U. S. Marine Corps, 1848; was made brevet lieutenant colonel for gallant and meritorious services in operations against Vicksburg; lieutenant colonel 1879. Served in the Mexican War and was commended for gallantry. In 1861 took part in the relief of Fort Pickens; 1862 ordered as fleet marine officer of Admiral Farragut's squadron; brevetted major for gallant service at the capture of New Orleans. Took part in all prominent engagements on the Mississippi River of Farragut's squadron from 1862 to May, 1863. Held important posts on shore stations until he was retired.

BRUCE

TORPEDO BOAT DESTROYER

Length, 314 feet   Beam, 30 feet, 11 inches   Draft, 9 feet, 4 inches

NAMED FOR LIEUTENANT FRANK BRUCE, U. S. NAVY

Launched May 20, 1920, at Bethlehem Shipbuilding Corporation, San Francisco, California.

Sponsor: MRS. ANNIE BRUCE, widow of Lieutenant Frank Bruce, U. S. Navy.

LIEUTENANT FRANK BRUCE, United States Navy, was born August 20, 1879, in Grand Island, Nebraska. Entered the Navy in 1896 as apprentice; appointed boatswain 1911; chief boatswain, 1917; ensign, 1917; lieutenant (j. g.), Feb. 1, 1918; lieutenant (T), July 1, 1918, in command of the mine sweeper "Bobolink." Killed

LAUNCHING PARTY OF U.S. TORPEDO BOAT DESTROYER "BROOME"
Sponsor With Attendants Wearing the War Service Uniform of the Emergency Aid

May 14, 1919, when a mine, which the "Bobolink" was heaving in, exploded.

BUCHANAN

TORPEDO BOAT DESTROYER

Length, 314 feet   *Beam, 30 feet, 11 inches*   *Draft, 9 feet*

NAMED FOR CAPTAIN FRANKLIN BUCHANAN, U. S. NAVY

Launched January 2, 1919, at Bath Iron Works, Bath, Maine.

Sponsor: MRS. CHARLES P. WETHERBEE (Katherine Brown), wife of the Vice President of Bath Iron Works.

CAPTAIN FRANKLIN BUCHANAN, United States Navy, was born in Baltimore, Maryland, 1800; died 1874. Entered the Navy as midshipman 1815; commissioned lieutenant 1825; commander 1841; captain 1855. He was the organizer and first superintendent of the United States Naval Academy (1845–1847). He co-operated in the landing of the troops at Vera Cruz under Gen. Scott, and was one of the leading spirits of the Navy there at the capture of San Juan d'Ulloa; was the first officer to step on the soil of Japan in the expedition of Commodore Perry. Resigned at the outbreak of Civil War. (Later he commanded the Confederate Squadron in the waters of Virginia on board the "Merrimac" in the engagement in Hampton Roads, Virginia, March 8, 1862, during which he was severely wounded. After the war he was president of the Maryland Agricultural College.)

BULMER

TORPEDO BOAT DESTROYER

Length, 314 feet   *Beam, 30 feet, 11 inches*   *Draft, 9 feet, 4 inches*

NAMED FOR CAPTAIN ROSCOE C. BULMER, U. S. NAVY

Launched January 22, 1920, at William Cramp & Sons' Company, Philadelphia, Pennsylvania.

Sponsor: MISS ANITA POOR BULMER, daughter of Captain Roscoe C. Bulmer, U. S. Navy.

CAPTAIN ROSCOE C. BULMER, United States Navy, was born in Virginia City, Nevada, 1874; died 1919, at Kirkwall, Scotland, from an automobile accident. Appointed naval cadet, 1890; ensign, 1896; lieutenant, (j. g.), 1899; lieutenant, 1902; lieutenant commander, 1908; commander, 1913; captain (T), 1918. In command of the U. S. S. "Black Hawk," December 18, 1917; was United States naval representative at a conference at the British Admiralty in London, October 31, 1918, which met to consider clearing the seas of mines after the war. Assumed command of mining operations with title of commander, Mine Sweeping Detachment, on January 5, 1919.

JOHN FRANCIS BURNES

TORPEDO BOAT DESTROYER

Length, 314 feet   *Beam, 30 feet, 11 inches*   *Draft, 9 feet, 4 inches*

NAMED FOR CAPTAIN JOHN FRANCIS BURNES, U. S. MARINE CORPS

Launched November 10, 1918, at Bethlehem Shipbuilding Corporation, San Francisco, California.

Sponsor: MRS. JULIUS KAHN (Florence Prag), wife of Honorable Julius Kahn, Member of Congress from San Francisco.

CAPTAIN JOHN FRANCIS BURNES, United States Marine Corps, was born in Binghamton, New York, 1883. Enlisted in the Marine Corps in 1904, served four enlistments, and shortly before the war was appointed a machine gunner, and was commissioned in June, 1917. Was sent to France, and while there was awarded the distinguished service cross posthumously for — "In the attack on the

[30]

Bois de Belleau, June 12, 1918, he was badly wounded, but completed the disposition of his platoon under violent fire. The injuries which he sustained in the performance of this self-sacrificing duty later caused his death."

BURNS

TORPEDO BOAT DESTROYER

Length, 314 feet   *Beam, 30 feet, 11 inches*   *Draft, 9 feet, 2 inches*

NAMED FOR CAPTAIN OTWAY BURNS, U. S. NAVY

Launched July 4, 1918, at Bethlehem Shipbuilding Corporation, San Francisco, California.

Sponsor: MISS ALICE H. PALMER, daughter of Mr. W. F. Palmer, president of the Northwestern Pacific Railroad.

CAPTAIN OTWAY BURNS, United States Navy, was born in Queen's Creek, North Carolina, 1775; died at Portsmouth, North Carolina, August 25, 1850. During the War of 1812 he commanded the letter of marque "Snap Dragon," and had several encounters with British men-of-war, taking 15 prizes, one of which had a cargo valued at $350,000; from 1821 to 1834 he served in the General Assembly of North Carolina; in 1835 was appointed by President Jackson as keeper of Brant Island Shoal light, and held the position until his death.

BUSH

TORPEDO BOAT DESTROYER

Length, 314 feet   *Beam, 30 feet, 11 inches*   *Draft, 9 feet, 2 inches*

NAMED FOR LIEUTENANT WILLIAM S. BUSH,
U. S. MARINE CORPS

Launched October 27, 1918, at Bethlehem Shipbuilding Corporation, Quincy, Massachusetts.

Sponsor: MISS JOSEPHINE T. BUSH, great-niece of Lieutenant William S. Bush, U. S. Navy.

First LIEUTENANT WILLIAM S. BUSH, United States Marine Corps. Appointed United States Marine Corps, July 3, 1809; promoted first lieutenant, 1811. He served during the War of 1812, and lost his life, August 19, 1812, while aboard the "Constitution" during its engagement with the British frigate "Guerriere." The vessels, after an engagement lasting for some time, were brought together, and Lieutenant Bush fell mortally wounded while attempting to board the British vessel. Capt. Hull, who commanded the "Constitution," said of him in his report to the Secretary of the Navy: "In him our country has lost a valuable and brave officer."

BUSHNELL

SUBMARINE TENDER

Length, 350 feet   *Beam, 45 feet*   *Draft, 19 feet, 5 inches*

NAMED FOR DAVID BUSHNELL

Launched February 9, 1915, at Seattle Dry Dock and Construction Company, Seattle, Washington.

Sponsor: MISS ESCULINE WARWICK BUSHNELL, great-great-niece of David Bushnell.

DAVID BUSHNELL, American Inventor. Born in Saybrook, Connecticut, in 1742; died 1824. Called the "Father of the Submarine." Graduated from Yale University in 1775. Made a study of submarine warfare. Constructed a diving boat and called it the "American Turtle." With it made a number of unsuccessful attempts to blow up the British ships of war, one of which was the "Eagle" lying in New York Harbor in 1776. Another attempt was on the "Cerebus" anchored off New London, in 1777. A schooner lying astern of the frigate was blown to pieces and a number of lives lost.

CALDWELL

TORPEDO BOAT DESTROYER

Length, 314 feet   *Beam, 30 feet, 8 inches*   *Draft, 8 feet*

BOW OF U.S. SCOUT CRUISER "CINCINNATI" AND
LAUNCHING PARTY

NAMED FOR LIEUTENANT JAMES R. CALDWELL, U. S. NAVY

Launched July 10, 1917, at Navy Yard, Mare Island, California.

Sponsor: MISS CHARLOTTE M. CALDWELL, great-great-grandniece of Lieutenant James R. Caldwell, U. S. Navy.

LIEUTENANT JAMES R. CALDWELL, U. S. Navy, was appointed midshipman May 22, 1798, and commissioned lieutenant November 1, 1800. He was killed in action August 7, 1804, during the war with Tripoli.

CALIFORNIA (3D)

BATTLESHIP

Length, 624 feet   *Beam, 97 feet, 3½ inches*   *Draft, 30 feet, 3 inches*

NAMED FOR THE STATE OF CALIFORNIA
(*Admitted to the Union in 1850*)

Launched November 20, 1919, at Mare Island Navy Yard, California.

Sponsor: MRS. BARBARA STEPHENS ZANE, daughter of Governor William D. Stephens of California, and widow of Major Randolph Talbott Zane, U. S. M. C., for whom the torpedo boat destroyer "Zane" is named.

Accompanying the sponsor were Governor W. D. Stephens, Mrs. W. D. Stephens, Captain Frank T. Clarke, U. S. N., Captain Edward L. Beach, U. S. N., Captain Milton Reed, and others.

The Society of Sponsors' Prayer for Our Navy was offered just before the launching by the Navy Yard Chaplain. The day before the launching a telegram from the Secretary of the Navy directed that the prayer be offered. The launching interested the entire State of California, and an immense crowd witnessed the event. A bottle of native California wine was broken upon the bow of the battleship.

The super dreadnaught "California" is the third to bear

the name. Her predecessor, the armored cruiser "California" launched in 1904, is now named "San Diego." The first "California" was a wooden screw sloop built in 1863.

CARDINAL

MINE SWEEPER

Length, 187 feet   *Beam, 35 feet*   *Draft, 9 feet, 9 inches*

NAMED FOR THE BIRD CARDINAL

Launched March 29, 1918, at Staten Island Shipbuilding Company, New York.

Sponsor: MISS ISABELLA NELSON, daughter of the Superintendent for the Company.

CASE

TORPEDO BOAT DESTROYER

Length, 314 feet   *Beam, 30 feet, 11 inches*   *Draft, 9 feet, 4 inches*

NAMED FOR REAR ADMIRAL AUGUSTUS LUDLOW CASE, U. S. NAVY

Launched September 21, 1919, at Bethlehem Shipbuilding Corporation, Quincy, Massachusetts.

Sponsor: MISS HELENA de St. PIERRE CASE, granddaughter of Rear Admiral Augustus Ludlow Case, U. S. Navy.

REAR ADMIRAL AUGUSTUS LUDLOW CASE, U. S. Navy, was born in Newburg, New York, 1813; died 1893. Appointed midshipman 1828; rear admiral 1872. South Sea Exploring Expedition 1837–1842. 1846–1848 Mexican war; took part in the captures of Vera Cruz, Alvarado, and Tabasco. After the capture of Laguna sent with 25 men to the Palisada River and held town of that name for two weeks against Mexican cavalry. On the Paraguay Expedition in 1859. Civil War, fleet captain of the North Atlantic Blockading Squadron at capture of Forts Clark and Hatteras, August 28, 29, 1861. Specially mentioned by Flag Officers Stringham and Goldsborough. North Atlantic Blockading Squadron until 1863; command of "Iroquois" in search of the C. S. S. "Alabama"; 1863, in charge of the blockade of New Inlet, North Carolina, and took part in the cutting out of the steamer "Kate" from under the batteries of Fort Fisher and New Inlet; 1869–1873. Chief of Bureau of Ordnance; 1873–1875, commanded European Squadron and combined North and South Atlantic Fleets.

CHAMPLIN

TORPEDO BOAT DESTROYER

Length, 314 feet   *Beam, 30 feet, 11 inches*   *Draft, 9 feet, 2 inches*

NAMED FOR CAPTAIN STEPHEN CHAMPLIN, U. S. NAVY

Launched April 7, 1918, at Bethlehem Shipbuilding Corporation, San Francisco, California.

Sponsor: MISS GEORGINA HINE ROLPH, daughter of Honorable James Rolph, Mayor of San Francisco.

CAPTAIN STEPHEN CHAMPLIN, U. S. Navy, was born in Kingston, Rhode Island, 1789; died 1870. Appointed sailing master 1812; captain 1867. In command of the "Scorpion" he fired the first shot on the American side of the battle of Lake Erie, and in capturing the "Little Belt" fired the last shot of the battle. He was placed in command of the captured vessels "Queen Charlotte" and "Detroit." In 1814 he commanded the "Tigress," and, with Captain Turner on the "Scorpion," blockaded Mackinac. Surprised by a superior force sent out from Mackinac on the night of September 3, 1814, he was dangerously wounded and taken prisoner and held at Mackinac for 38 days. He was finally paroled and sent to Erie and later to his home in Connecticut.

CHANDLER

TORPEDO BOAT DESTROYER

Length, 314 feet   *Beam, 30 feet, 11 inches*   *Draft, 9 feet, 4 inches*

NAMED FOR SECRETARY OF THE NAVY
WILLIAM EATON CHANDLER

Launched March 19, 1919, at William Cramp & Sons' Company, Philadelphia, Pennsylvania.

Sponsor: MRS. LLOYD H. CHANDLER (Agatha Edson), wife of Rear Admiral L. H. Chandler, U. S. Navy.

HON. WILLIAM EATON CHANDLER, was born in Concord, New Hampshire, 1835; died 1917. He was graduated from the Harvard law school in 1855. Member of New Hampshire House of Representatives, 1862–63–64. Elected Speaker of New Hampshire House of Representatives in 1864, at age of 27. Solicitor and Judge Advocate of Navy Department on March 9, 1865, and held this office until June 17, 1865, when he was appointed First Assistant Secretary of the Treasury, which office he held until his resignation on Nov. 30, 1867. Secretary of the Navy April 12, 1882, until March 4, 1885. U. S. Senator from New Hampshire from June 4, 1887, until Jan. 10, 1901. President Spanish Treaty War Claims Commission from March 6, 1901, until he resigned on Sept. 23, 1907.

CHASE

TORPEDO BOAT DESTROYER

Length, 314 feet   *Beam, 30 feet, 11 inches*   *Draft, 9 feet, 4 inches*

NAMED FOR MIDSHIPMAN REUBEN CHASE,
U. S. NAVY

Launched September 2, 1919, Bethlehem Shipbuilding Corporation, San Francisco, California.

Sponsor: MRS. JOHN ASKETT ANNEAR (Ray Eitel), great-granddaughter of Midshipman Reuben Chase, U. S. Navy.

MIDSHIPMAN REUBEN CHASE, United States Navy, was born in Nantucket, Massachusetts. Entered the Navy as seaman in 1777. Cruised on the "Ranger" in operations around the British Isles and the capture of H. B. M. S. "Drake" April 24, 1778. Transferred to the "Bonhomme Richard" March 18, 1779, as midshipman. His name is listed among those entitled to receive prize money for captures made by the "Bonhomme Richard" including the "Serapis."

CHAUNCEY (2D)

TORPEDO BOAT DESTROYER

Length, 314 feet   Beam, 30 feet, 11 inches   Draft, 9 feet, 4 inches

NAMED FOR COMMODORE ISAAC CHAUNCEY, U. S. NAVY

Launched September 29, 1918, at Bethlehem Shipbuilding Corporation, San Francisco, California.

Sponsor: MISS DOROTHY MAE TODD, great-great-granddaughter of Commodore Isaac Chauncey, U. S. Navy, and daughter of Mrs. Stanton W. Todd, sponsor for U. S. S. "Chauncey (1ST)" in 1901.

COMMODORE ISAAC CHAUNCEY, U. S. Navy, was born in Connecticut 1772; died 1840. Commissioned a lieutenant 1798; captain 1806; served on the "Constellation," War with France, 1798–1801; attacks on town and naval force of Tripolitans 1804; commanded the naval forces on Lake Ontario; rendered distinguished service in co-operating with Army defense of the Lakes, War of 1812; served as Navy commissioner 1820–1824 and 1833–1840; was included in the thanks of Congress to officers for service in the War with Tripoli and awarded a sword for his gallantry.

CHEW

TORPEDO BOAT DESTROYER

Length, 314 feet   *Beam, 30 feet, 11 inches*   *Draft, 9 feet, 2 inches*

NAMED FOR CAPTAIN SAMUEL CHEW, U. S. NAVY

Launched May 26, 1918, at Bethlehem Shipbuilding Corporation, San Francisco, California.

Sponsor: MRS. FELIX X. GYGAX (Estelle Ise), wife of Commander Gygax, U. S. Navy, on duty in San Francisco.

CAPTAIN SAMUEL CHEW, United States Navy, was born in Philadelphia, Pennsylvania. Appointed by the marine committee July 17, 1777, to command the Continental brigantine "Resistance." The "Resistance," carrying 10 four-pounders, on March 14, 1778, fell in with a British letter of marque of 20 guns, and in a hand-to-hand fight which ensued, Captain Chew fell gallantly fighting.

CHEWINK

MINE SWEEPER

Length, 187 feet   *Beam, 35 feet*   *Draft, 9 feet, 9 inches*

NAMED FOR THE BIRD CHEWINK

Launched December 21, 1918, at Todd Shipyard Corporation, New York.

Sponsor: MISS MARION SPERRIN, daughter of a foreman of the Company and selected by Mr. Todd.

CHILDS

TORPEDO BOAT DESTROYER

Length, 314 feet   *Beam, 30 feet, 11 inches*   *Draft, 9 feet, 4 inches*

NAMED FOR LIEUTENANT EARLE W. F. CHILDS, U. S. NAVY

Launched August 19, 1919, at New York Shipbuilding Corporation, Camden, New Jersey.

[38]

Sponsor: MRS. GERTRUDE B. CHILDS, widow of Lieutenant Earle W. F. Childs.

LIEUTENANT EARLE W. F. CHILDS, United States Navy, was born in Philadelphia, Pennsylvania, 1893; appointed midshipman 1911; ensign 1915; lieutenant (junior grade) 1917; lieutenant October 15, 1917. While attached to the U. S. S. "Al-2" he was selected from her officers for instructional patrol on board H. M. S. "H-5," which vessel was sunk in collision with the S. S. "Rutherglen" and all on board were lost March 7, 1918.

CINCINNATI (3D)

LIGHT CRUISER

Length, 555 feet, 6 inches *Beam, 55 feet* *Draft, 14 feet, 3 inches*

NAMED FOR THE CITY OF CINCINNATI, OHIO

Launched May 23, 1921, at the Todd Dry Dock & Construction Corporation, Tacoma, Washington.

Sponsor: MRS. CHARLES EDGAR TUDOR (Lillie Fogg), wife of the Director of Public Safety of Cincinnati, Ohio, christened the ship with champagne and Ohio River water.

The first "Cincinnati" was an iron clad gunboat, built in 1861. Sunk at Vicksburg, 1863.
The second "Cincinnati" was an unarmored protected cruiser launched in 1892.

CLAXTON

TORPEDO BOAT DESTROYER

Length, 314 feet *Beam, 30 feet, 11 inches* *Draft, 9 feet*

NAMED FOR MIDSHIPMAN THOMAS CLAXTON,
U. S. NAVY

Launched January 19, 1919, at Mare Island Navy Yard, California.

Sponsor: MRS. FREDERICK WILLIAM KELLOGG (Florence Scripps), wife of Mr. F. W. Kellogg, Business Manager and Publisher of the San Francisco Call.

MIDSHIPMAN THOMAS CLAXTON, United States Navy, was born in Baltimore, Maryland. Appointed a midshipman 1810; died of wounds received on board the "Lawrence" early in the Battle of Lake Erie. Congress awarded a sword to his nearest male relative and expressed deep regret for his loss and commended his name "to the recollection and affection of a grateful country and his conduct as an example to future generations."

CLEMSON

TORPEDO BOAT DESTROYER

Length, 314 feet   *Beam, 30 feet, 11 inches*   *Draft, 9 feet, 4 inches*

NAMED FOR PASSED MIDSHIPMAN
HENRY A. CLEMSON, U. S. NAVY

Launched September 5, 1918, at Newport News S. B. & D. D. Company, Newport News, Virginia.

Sponsor: MISS MARY CLEAVES DANIELS, niece of Secretary of the Navy Josephus Daniels.

PASSED MIDSHIPMAN HENRY A. CLEMSON, U. S. Navy, was born in New Jersey. Appointed midshipman 1836; passed midshipman 1846; ordered to the "St. Marys," Home Squadron; transferred to the brig "Somers," which capsized in a squall in the Gulf of Mexico off Vera Cruz; Midshipman Clemson insisted that the men should take the only available boat, and he clung to a spar, which he abandoned when he found it inadequate to support all who were hanging on it.

COGHLAN

TORPEDO BOAT DESTROYER

Length, 314 feet   *Beam, 30 feet, 11 inches*   *Draft, 9 feet, 4 inches*

U.S. TORPEDO BOAT DESTROYER "COLE" SPEEDING

NAMED FOR REAR ADMIRAL JOSEPH B. COGHLAN, U. S. NAVY

Launched June 16, 1920, at Bethlehem Shipbuilding Corporation, San Francisco, California.

Sponsor: MRS. GRAHAM COGHLAN (Elizabeth B.), daughter-in-law of Rear Admiral Joseph B. Coghlan, U. S. Navy.

REAR ADMIRAL JOSEPH BULLOCH COGHLAN, United States Navy, was born in Frankfort, Kentucky, 1844; died 1908. Appointed midshipman, 1860; rear admiral, 1902; served Civil War, 1863–1865, on the U. S. S. "Sacramento"; 1865–1897, cruised on Brazil, European, Pacific, North Atlantic, and Asiatic Stations. Spanish American War, 1898, commanded U. S. S. "Raleigh"; took prominent part in the battle of Manila Bay, May 1, 1898; commanded expedition for capture of batteries at Manila, May 2, 1898, and capture of Isla Grande, July 7, 1898, Subig Bay. Recommended by Admiral Dewey for his gallantry and skill; included in thanks of Congress to Admiral Dewey, officers and men for victory of May 1, 1898. Advanced six numbers by act of Congress for eminent and conspicuous conduct in battle. Commanded Caribbean squadron of North Atlantic fleet, 1902; held many important posts on shore.

COLE

TORPEDO BOAT DESTROYER

Length, 314 feet   *Beam, 30 feet, 11 inches*   *Draft, 9 feet*

NAMED FOR MAJOR EDWARD B. COLE, U. S. MARINE CORPS

Launched January 11, 1919, at William Cramp & Sons' Company, Philadelphia, Pennsylvania.

Sponsor: MRS. MARY WELSH COLE, widow of Major Edward B. Cole, U. S. M. C. Mrs. Cole was accompanied by her two small sons, Charles Cole and Edward Cole.

[41]

MAJOR EDWARD B. COLE, U. S. Marine Corps, was born in Boston, Massachusetts, 1879, and died June 18, 1918, from wounds received in action. Appointed from civil life, where he was regarded as one of the leading machine gun experts in the country. Major Cole was in the first contingent of marines to go to France during the world war. In the Bois de Belleau on June 10, 1918, he displayed such extraordinary heroism in organizing positions, rallying his men and disposing of his guns, that he was awarded the distinguished-service cross. During this battle he suffered the loss of his right hand and received wounds in the upper arm and both thighs, from which he died on June 18.

COLHOUN

TORPEDO BOAT DESTROYER

Length, 314 feet   *Beam, 30 feet, 11 inches*   *Draft, 9 feet, 2 inches*

NAMED FOR REAR ADMIRAL EDMUND R. COLHOUN, U. S. NAVY

Launched February 21, 1918, Bethlehem Shipbuilding Company, Quincy, Massachusetts.

Sponsor: MISS HELEN A. COLHOUN, daughter of Rear Admiral Edmund R. Colhoun, U. S. Navy.

REAR ADMIRAL EDMUND R. COLHOUN, U. S. Navy, was born in Chambersburg, Pennsylvania, 1821; died 1897. Appointed midshipman 1839; rear admiral 1882; Mexican War, under Commodores Conner and Perry at Alvarado and Tobasco; Civil War, North Atlantic Blockading Squadron, took part in engagements at Roanoke Island, Blackwater River, 1862; commanded monitor "Weehawken," South Atlantic Blockading Squadron; took part in bombardment and capture of Fort Fisher, North Carolina, December, 1864–January, 1865; commander-in-chief of the South Pacific Station, 1874–1875; commanded Mare Island Navy Yard 1877–1881. Retired 1883.

COLORADO (3D)

Length, 624 feet   *Beam, 97 feet, 3½ inches*   *Draft, 30 feet, 6 inches*

NAMED FOR THE STATE OF COLORADO
(*Admitted to the Union in 1876*)

Launched March 22, 1921, at New York Shipbuilding Corporation, Camden, New Jersey.

Sponsor: MRS. RUTH NICHOLSON MELVILLE (Mrs. Max Melville), daughter of Senator Samuel D. Nicholson of Colorado.

The sponsor broke a bottle of water from the Colorado River. The Society of Sponsors' Prayer for our Navy was offered by Chaplain C. H. Dickins just before the launching.

Among those present on the stand were Assistant Secretary of the Navy Theodore Roosevelt, Jr., and Mrs. Roosevelt, Rear Admiral Reynold T. Hall and Mrs. Hall, Colonel Russell C. Langdon, U. S. A., and Mrs. Langdon, Rear Admiral L. M. Nulton and Mrs. Nulton, Captain Lloyd Bankson, U. S. Navy, Captain T. G. Roberts, U. S. Navy, delegation of members of the Society of Sponsors. A vast concourse of spectators witnessed the launching.

The battleship "Colorado" is the third of that name and second named for the State.

"Colorado (2D)" launched in 1903, is an armored cruiser now re-named "Pueblo" for the Colorado City.

"Colorado (1ST)," a steam frigate, launched in 1856, was named for the Colorado River.

CONCORD (3D)

LIGHT CRUISER

Length, 555 feet, 6 inches   *Beam, 55 feet*   *Draft, 14 feet, 3 inches*

NAMED FOR THE CITY OF CONCORD,
MASSACHUSETTS

(*The scene of the Battle of Concord, in 1775*)

Launched December 15, 1921, at William Cramp & Sons' Shipbuilding Co., Philadelphia, Pennsylvania.

Sponsor: MISS HELEN BAGLEY BUTTRICK, daughter of Mr. Stedman Buttrick, a descendant of Captain John Buttrick, who led the Continental troops in the Battle of Concord.

The first "Concord" was a sloop of 700 tons, launched in 1828. The first woman sponsor appears in the records of her launching ceremonies.

The second "Concord" was a gunboat of 1700 tons, launched in 1890.

CONNER

TORPEDO BOAT DESTROYER

Length, 315 feet   *Beam, 30 feet, 8 inches*   *Draft, 8 feet*

NAMED FOR COMMODORE DAVID CONNER, U. S. NAVY

Launched August 21, 1917, at William Cramp & Sons' Company, Philadelphia, Pennsylvania.

Sponsor: MISS ELSA DIEDERICH, great-great-granddaughter of Commodore David Conner, U. S. Navy.

COMMODORE DAVID CONNER, U. S. Navy, was born at Harrisburg, Pennsylvania, in 1792, and died 1856. He was appointed midshipman January 16, 1809; commissioned captain 1835; was Navy commissioner 1841, to 1842; served on "Hornet" in chase of British ship "Belvidera" and on "Hornet" in action with British ship "Peacock" February 24, 1813, and action with British ship "Penguin" March 23, 1815, being wounded during the latter action. Commander of Home Squadron during War with Mexico, 1846–1847.

CONVERSE

TORPEDO BOAT DESTROYER

Length, 314 feet   Beam, 30 feet, 11 inches   Draft, 9 feet, 4 inches

NAMED FOR REAR ADMIRAL GEORGE A. CONVERSE, U. S. NAVY

Launched November 28, 1919, at Bethlehem Shipbuilding Corporation, Quincy, Massachusetts.

Sponsor: MISS J. EDITH CONVERSE COLT, granddaughter of Rear Admiral George A. Converse, U. S. Navy.

REAR ADMIRAL GEORGE A. CONVERSE, U. S. Navy, was born in Norwich, Vermont, 1844; died 1909. Appointed midshipman 1861; commissioned rear admiral 1903. Rear Admiral Converse was one of the first officers connected with the introduction of electricity aboard men-of-war. He was probably the pioneer in the experimentation and introduction of smokeless powder in the Navy; was instrumental in obtaining the first torpedo boat called "Lightning," built for the United States Navy in 1876 by the Herreschoffs; was chief of Bureaus of Equipment, Ordnance, and Navigation in turn. He was well known as a naval expert on ordnance, especially in regard to torpedoes.

CONYNGHAM

TORPEDO BOAT DESTROYER

Length, 315 feet   Beam, 30 feet, 11 inches   Draft, 9 feet, 4 inches

NAMED FOR CAPTAIN GUSTAVUS CONYNGHAM, U. S. NAVY

Launched July 8, 1915, at William Cramp & Sons' Company, Philadelphia, Pennsylvania.

Sponsor: MISS ANNA CONYNGHAM STEVENS, great-great-granddaughter of Captain Gustavus Conyngham, U. S. Navy.

[45]

CAPTAIN GUSTAVUS CONYNGHAM, U. S. Navy, was born in Ireland, in 1747; died 1819. In 1775 commanded a privateer and sailed from Philadelphia for Dunkirk to obtain supplies "necessary for War for the Colonies." March 1, 1777, commissioned captain in the Continental Navy. Commanded the "Surprise," "Revenge," and "Experiment." Made a number of valuable prizes. Was himself taken prisoner on two or three occasions; had extraordinary escapes; became a terror to the British coasting vessels. During the Naval War with France commanded the armed brig "Maria." At the outbreak of the War of 1812 he took part for a brief period.

CORMORANT

MINE SWEEPER

Length, 187 feet *Beam, 35 feet* *Draft, 9 feet, 9 inches*

NAMED FOR THE BIRD CORMORANT

Launched February 5, 1919, at Todd Shipyard Corporation, New York.

Sponsor: MISS MARIE ELIZA VILLAIRE, daughter of one of the foremen of Robin's Dry Dock Company.

CORRY

TORPEDO BOAT DESTROYER

Length, 314 feet, 4 inches *Beam, 31 feet* *Draft, 9 feet, 4 inches*

NAMED FOR LIEUTENANT COMMANDER WILLIAM MERRILL CORRY, JR., U. S. NAVY

Launched March 28, 1921, at Bethlehem Shipbuilding Corporation, San Francisco, California.

Sponsor: MRS. WILLIAM MERRILL CORRY (Sarah Wiggins), mother of Lieutenant Commander William Merrill Corry, U. S. Navy.

LIEUTENANT COMMANDER WILLIAM MERRILL CORRY, U. S. Navy, was born in Quincy, Florida, 1889;

died October 7, 1920. Midshipman 1906; lieutenant commander 1918; served on U. S. S. "Kansas" 1911–1915; naval aviator with U. S. S. "North Carolina" and "Washington" 1916; August 22, 1917, assigned to duty in Europe with U. S. Naval Aviation Forces; later was ordered to command naval air station at Le Croisic, Loire, France, the first United States operating unit of the World War; his success and skill as an air pilot won for him the cross of Chevalier of the Legion of Honor from France; June 7, 1918, until end of the demobilization was in command of naval air station, Brest, Finisterre; June 5, 1919, represented the United States in aeronautic Interallied Commission of Control; June 1, 1920–October 7, 1920 was aid for aviation staff of Commander in Chief of the Atlantic Fleet. His death was caused by inhaling flame from a burning airplane after its crash, when though badly wounded he was endeavoring to rescue his companion from the burning flame.

COWELL

TORPEDO BOAT DESTROYER

Length, 314 feet   *Beam, 30 feet, 11 inches*   *Draft, 9 feet, 2 inches*

NAMED FOR MASTER JOHN G. COWELL, U. S. NAVY

Launched November 23, 1918, at Bethlehem Shipbuilding Corporation, Quincy, Massachusetts.

Sponsor: MISS EMILY P. GARNEY, great-granddaughter of Master John G. Cowell, U. S. Navy.

MASTER JOHN G. COWELL, U. S. Navy, was appointed a master in the United States Navy January 21, 1809; and died of wounds, April 18, 1814, received near Valparaiso in the action between the United States frigate "Essex" and his British Majesty's frigate "Phoebe" and the sloop-of-war "Cherub," April 18, 1814. The conduct of this brave and heroic officer who lost a leg during the action, excited the admiration of every man on the ship.

[47]

After being wounded, he would not consent to be taken below until loss of blood rendered him insensible. He was at the time of the action an acting lieutenant.

CRANE

TORPEDO BOAT DESTROYER

Length, 314 feet   *Beam, 30 feet, 11 inches*   *Draft, 9 feet, 2 inches*

NAMED FOR CAPTAIN WILLIAM M. CRANE, U. S. NAVY

Launched July 4, 1918, at Bethlehem Shipbuilding Corporation, San Francisco, California.

Sponsor: MRS. MAY McGUIRE, wife of Mr. M. J. McGuire, San Francisco, California, who was head of one of the Labor organizations and active in influencing maximum production during the World War.

CAPTAIN WILLIAM M. CRANE, United States Navy, was born in Elizabethtown, New Jersey, 1776; died 1846. Appointed midshipman 1799; captain 1814. As a lieutenant on the "Congress," he participated in the operations and attacks on Tripoli, 1804, and was included in the thanks of Congress for his gallantry, and awarded a sword. July 16, 1812, commanding the "Nautilus," he was captured by H. B. M. S. "Southampton" off New York. In 1827 he commanded the Mediterranean squadron and acted as one of the commissioners in the negotiations with the Ottoman Empire. 1842–1846, he was the first chief of the Bureau of Ordnance and Hydrography of the Navy Department.

T. A. M. CRAVEN (2D)

TORPEDO BOAT DESTROYER

Length, 315 feet   *Beam, 30 feet, 8 inches*   *Draft, 8 feet*

NAMED FOR CAPTAIN TUNIS AUGUSTUS MACDONOUGH CRAVEN, U. S. NAVY

LAUNCHING PARTY OF U.S. BATTLESHIP "COLORADO"

Launched June 29, 1918, at Navy Yard, Norfolk, Virginia.

Sponsor: MRS. FRANK LEARNED (Ellin Craven), daughter of Captain T. A. M. Craven, U. S. Navy.

In naming the ship the sponsor said:

"May God bless thee, God lead thee, and speed thee; and may all who sail on thee serve God and country with the same brave and faithful spirit as he did whose name is now given unto thee."

Prayer was offered by the Rt. Rev. Arthur C. Thomson, Suffragan Bishop of Southern Virginia.

CAPTAIN TUNIS AUGUSTUS MACDONOUGH CRAVEN, U. S. Navy, was born in Portsmouth, New Hampshire, 1813. Appointed midshipman 1829; commissioned Commander April 24, 1861. Served with distinction in the Mexican War. From 1850 to 1857 in command of the "Corwin" on Coast Survey duty. In 1857 in command of the Atrato Expedition, surveyed a route for a proposed ship canal through the Isthmus of Darien via the Atrato and Truando rivers. In 1861, in command of the "Crusader" performed conspicuous blockade service off the Florida Coast. In the "Tuscarora," 1861–1863, performed with distinction special blockade service in European waters. In command of the "Tecumseh," April, 1864, joined Admiral Lee's squadron in the James River. Joined Admiral Farragut's fleet August 4, 1864, at sunset for the attack on Mobile. On August 5, 1864, the fleet steamed up Mobile Bay, the "Tecumseh" leading the attack. The first gun was fired by the "Tecumseh" at 6:47. At 7:15 the "Tecumseh" was struck by a torpedo and sank almost immediately, carrying down her gallant commander.

CROSBY

TORPEDO BOAT DESTROYER

Length, 314 feet   *Beam, 30 feet, 11 inches*   *Draft, 9 feet, 2 inches*

NAMED FOR REAR ADMIRAL PIERCE CROSBY, U. S. NAVY

[49]

Launched September 28, 1918, at Bethlehem Shipbuilding Company, Fore River, Massachusetts.

Sponsor: MRS. CHARLES TITTMAN (Jean Crosby), daughter of Rear Admiral Pierce Crosby, U. S. Navy.

REAR ADMIRAL PIERCE CROSBY, United States Navy, was born in Delaware County, Pennsylvania. Was appointed a midshipman in 1838; rear admiral in 1872. In the Mexican War he took part in the attack and capture of Tuxpan and Tobasco. At the outbreak of the Civil War his first duty was to keep open the communication between Annapolis, Maryland, the Chesapeake Bay and Havre de Grace. Prior to the battle of Big Bethel he volunteered to take a converted canal boat, the "Fannie," with her boilers held down to the decks by chains and proceeded with her to the attack on Forts Hatteras and Clarke in order to have a light draft vessel for landing troops. When the sea had swamped the troop boats, Lieutenant Crosby took a ship's heavy launch and continued the landing of 300 men. The following day the squadron closed in from sea and captured a garrison of 700 men, which by Crosby's picket line had been prevented from making a reconnoisance and learning the exact strength of the Federal troops. In 1863, while in command of the "Florida," he destroyed two blockade runners and in 1864 in command of the "Keystone State" captured five more blockaders. In 1864–1865 in command of the "Metacomet" in attack in Mobile Bay, he planned and directed the construction of torpedo nets on the Blakely River and superintended the removal of 140 torpedoes, clearing the way so as to allow the squadron to pass safely to Mobile.

CROWNINSHIELD

TORPEDO BOAT DESTROYER

Length, 314 feet   *Beam, 30 feet, 11 inches*   *Draft, 9 feet*

NAMED FOR SECRETARY OF THE NAVY
BENJAMIN WILLIAMS CROWNINSHIELD

Launched July 24, 1919, at Bath Iron Works, Bath, Maine.

Sponsor: MISS EMILY CROWNINSHIELD DAVIS, great-great-granddaughter of Secretary of the Navy Benjamin Williams Crowninshield.

HON. BENJAMIN WILLIAMS CROWNINSHIELD, Secretary of the Navy, 1814–1818. Born in Boston, Massachusetts, December 27, 1772; died 1851. He was State Senator in 1811, and on December 17, 1814, was appointed Secretary of the Navy by President Madison. He held the same office in the Monroe Cabinet and resigned in November, 1818. He was presidential elector in 1820; was again State senator in 1822–1823 and a member of Congress from 1823 to 1831.

CURLEW

MINE SWEEPER

Length, 187 feet   *Beam, 35 feet, 6 inches*   *Draft 9 feet, 9 inches*

NAMED FOR THE BIRD CURLEW

Launched August 29, 1918, at Staten Island Shipbuilding Company, New York.

Sponsor: MRS. GERTRUDE CAROL RHODES, who was serving as yeoman (F) 1st Class, U. S. N. R. F., in the office of the Inspector of Machinery of Mine Sweepers, Third Naval District during the World War.

CUSHING (2D)

TORPEDO BOAT DESTROYER

Length, 305 feet   *Beam, 30 feet, 4 inches*   *Draft, 9 feet, 5 inches*

NAMED FOR COMMANDER WILLIAM BARKER CUSHING, U. S. NAVY

Launched January 16, 1915, at Fore River Shipbuilding Company, Quincy, Massachusetts.

Sponsor: MISS MARIE L. CUSHING, daughter of Commander W. B. Cushing, U. S. Navy.

COMMANDER WILLIAM BARKER CUSHING, U. S. Navy, was born in Delafield, Wisconsin, in 1842. His career was filled with daring planning and clever execution. He was especially distinguished for the destruction of the Confederate ram "Albermarle." He undertook the attack with a steam launch carrying a spar torpedo and towing an armed cutter. When near the "Albermarle" he was detected but pushed forward under a shower of bullets and fire of howitzers. He had time to drive the steam launch over the baulks and to explode the torpedo against the "Albermarle," sinking her, before his launch was destroyed. Cushing and one other escaped, the rest were captured. For destroying the "Albermarle" he received the thanks of Congress and promotion to Lieutenant Commander.

CUYAMA

FUEL SHIP

Length, 475 feet   *Beam, 56 feet*   *Draft, 26 feet, 2 inches*

NAMED FOR CUYAMA MOUNTAINS

Launched June 16, 1917, at Navy Yard, Mare Island, California.

Sponsor: MISS MARGARET OFFLEY, daughter of Commander Cleland N. Offley, U. S. Navy, Engineer Officer of the Navy Yard.

DAHLGREN (2D)

TORPEDO BOAT DESTROYER

Length, 314 feet   *Beam, 30 feet, 11 inches*   *Draft, 9 feet, 4 inches*

NAMED FOR REAR ADMIRAL JOHN A. DAHLGREN, U. S. NAVY

Launched November 20, 1918, at Newport News S. B. & D. D. Company, Newport News, Virginia.

Sponsor: MRS. JOSIAH PIERCE (Ulrica Dahlgren), daughter of Rear Admiral John A. Dahlgren, U. S. Navy.

REAR ADMIRAL JOHN A. DAHLGREN, U. S. Navy, was born in Philadelphia in 1809. Died in 1870. Appointed midshipman in 1826. Rear admiral 1863. In 1847–1857 invented the famous Dahlgren gun, introduced howitzers afloat and ashore, and wrote important works on ordnance. In 1861 when ordnance officer at the Washington Navy Yard, Congress promoted him to command of the yard for conspicuous services after all other officers had resigned and left him alone with Lieutenant Wainwright to defend the yard. In 1863, in command of South Atlantic Blockading Squadron, he co-operated with General Gillmore in the occupation of Morris Island and destruction of Fort Sumter, South Carolina. In 1864 his squadron co-operated with General Sherman in the occupation of Savannah. In 1865 his squadron occupied Charleston, South Carolina, after the evacuation, and Georgetown. He was twice Chief of Bureau of Ordnance.

DALE (3D)

TORPEDO BOAT DESTROYER

Length, 314 feet   *Beam, 30 feet, 11 inches*   *Draft, 9 feet, 4 inches*

NAMED FOR COMMODORE RICHARD DALE,
U. S. NAVY

Launched November 19, 1919, at Bethlehem Shipbuilding Corporation, Squantum, Massachusetts.

Sponsor: MRS. ANDREW J. PETERS (Martha Phillips), wife of Hon. A. J. Peters, Mayor of Boston, Massachusetts.

CAPTAIN RICHARD DALE, United States Navy. Born near Norfolk, Virginia, 1756. Died 1826. Appointed midshipman, 1776; captured on the U. S. S. "Lexington," 1777. Imprisoned in Mill Prison, England; escaped to France. Appointed master's mate under John Paul Jones, 1778; first lieutenant, "Bonhomme Richard"; engagement and capture of the "Serapis," September 23, 1779; 1781–

[53]

1782, commanded "Queen Of France"; made several captures. Commissioned Captain No. 4 on list June 4, 1794. Commanded the Mediterranean squadron in operations against Tripoli, 1801. Resigned, December 17, 1802. After the death of John Paul Jones, the sword presented to John Paul Jones by Louis XVI was conveyed to Commodore Dale by request of Commodore Jones.

DALLAS

TORPEDO BOAT DESTROYER

Length, 314 feet   *Beam, 30 feet, 11 inches*   *Draft, 9 feet, 4 inches*

NAMED FOR CAPTAIN ALEXANDER J. DALLAS, U. S. NAVY

Launched May 31, 1919, at Newport News S. B. & D. D. Company, Newport News, Virginia.

Sponsor: MISS WATHEN DALLAS STRONG, great-granddaughter of Captain Alexander J. Dallas, U. S. Navy.

CAPTAIN ALEXANDER J. DALLAS, U. S. Navy, was born in Philadelphia, Pennsylvania, in 1791; died 1844. Appointed midshipman 1805; captain 1828. Fired the first shot of the War of 1812 in the engagement between the "President" and the "Little Belt," June 23, 1812. Commanded the "Spitfire" in operations against Algiers, 1815. Commanded the "John Adams" operating against pirates in the West Indies, 1824. From 1832–1834 was employed in laying out the Pensacola Navy Yard, and was commended for the good work accomplished. In 1835–1837 commanded the West Indian Squadron and co-operated with General Scott in suppressing the Seminole Indians. In recognition of this service, Fort Dallas was named for him. In 1843 was in command of the Pacific Squadron, and died on the "Savannah" in the harbor of Callao, Peru.

DAVIS (2D)

TORPEDO BOAT DESTROYER

Length, 315 feet   *Beam, 30 feet*   *Draft, 9 feet, 2 inches*

NAMED FOR REAR ADMIRAL CHARLES H. DAVIS,
U. S. NAVY

Launched August 15, 1916, at Bath Iron Works, Bath, Maine.

Sponsor: MISS ELIZABETH DAVIS, granddaughter of Rear Admiral Charles H. Davis, U. S. Navy.

REAR ADMIRAL CHARLES H. DAVIS, U. S. Navy, was born in Boston, Massachusetts, January 16, 1807. Appointed midshipman 1823; passed midshipman 1829; lieutenant 1831; commander 1854; captain 1861; commodore 1862; rear admiral 1863; died 1877. He did valuable coast survey work and wrote valuable works on Tides and Currents of the Ocean; also translated many valuable works. In the Civil War he was fleet captain in du Pont's expedition against Port Royal, South Carolina. He was flag officer at naval engagements at Fort Pillow and at Memphis in 1862, which effected the destruction of the Confederate iron clad fleet. He was with Farragut at Vicksburg and successfully co-operated with General Curtis in the Yazoo in 1862. First chief of Bureau of Navigation in 1862. On February 7, 1863, Commander Davis received the thanks of Congress for distinguished services at Fort Pillow, at Memphis, and for successful operations at other points on the Mississippi River and became a rear admiral on the date of the approval of this vote of thanks.

DECATUR (3D)

TORPEDO BOAT DESTROYER

Length, 314 feet, 4 inches *Beam, 31 feet* *Draft, 9 feet, 4 inches*

NAMED FOR COMMODORE STEPHEN DECATUR,
U. S. NAVY

Launched October 29, 1921, at Navy Yard, Mare Island, California.

Sponsor: MRS. JOSIAH S. McKEAN (Julie McHawxhurst), wife of Rear Admiral J. S. McKean, U. S. Navy, Commandant of the Navy Yard.

COMMODORE STEPHEN DECATUR was born in Maryland, 1779; died in 1820. In 1803 was in command of the "Enterprise" in Commodore Preble's Mediterranean Squadron and in 1804 led a daring expedition into the harbor of Tripoli for the purpose of burning the U. S. frigate Philadelphia, which had fallen into Tripolitan hands. He succeeded and made his escape under the fire of the batteries. This brilliant exploit earned him a captain's commission and a sword of honor from Congress. During the War of 1812 in the "United States" captured the "Macedonian." In the "President" he fought a superior fleet until his own decks were covered with the dead and wounded.

DE LONG (2D)

Length, 314 feet   *Beam, 30 feet, 11 inches*   *Draft, 9 feet, 4 inches*

NAMED FOR LIEUTENANT COMMANDER
GEORGE W. DeLONG, U. S. NAVY

Launched October 29, 1918, at New York Shipbuilding Corporation, Camden, New Jersey.

Sponsor: MISS EMMA DeLONG MILLS, granddaughter of Lieutenant Commander George W. DeLong, U. S. Navy, and daughter of Mrs. Sylvie DeLong Mills, sponsor for the U. S. S. DeLong (1st) in 1900.

LIEUTENANT COMMANDER GEORGE W. DE-LONG, U. S. Navy, was born in New York in 1844. Appointed midshipman in 1861. He commanded the Arctic exploration steamer "Jeanette" in an expedition for the discovery of the North Pole 1879–1881. The "Jeanette" was crushed in the ice. Three months later after discovering three islands, and dragging boats and provisions over shifting ice and open water, he died from exposure and starvation when almost within reach of help.

[56]

U.S. TORPEDO BOAT DESTROYER "CONVERSE," STEAMING FULL SPEED

DELPHY

TORPEDO BOAT DESTROYER

Length, 314 feet   *Beam, 30 feet, 11 inches*   *Draft, 9 feet, 4 inches*

NAMED FOR MIDSHIPMAN RICHARD DELPHY,
U. S. NAVY

Launched July 18, 1918, at Bethlehem Shipbuilding Corporation, Squantum, Massachusetts.

Sponsor: MRS. WILLIAM SOWDEN SIMS (Anne Hitchcock), wife of Rear Admiral Sims, U. S. Navy, in command of U. S. Naval forces in European waters in the War with Germany.

MIDSHIPMAN RICHARD DELPHY, U. S. Navy, was appointed a midshipman May 18, 1809. Served with ability on the "United States" in the engagement with the "Macedonian" October 25, 1812. Killed in the fight between the U. S. S. "Argus" and H. B. M. S. "Pelican," August 14, 1813.

DENT

TORPEDO BOAT DESTROYER

Length, 314 feet   *Beam, 30 feet, 11 inches*   *Draft, 9 feet*

NAMED FOR COMMODORE JOHN H. DENT,
U. S. NAVY

Launched March 23, 1918, at William Cramp & Sons' Company, Philadelphia, Pennsylvania.

Sponsor: MISS AMY WHIPPLE COLLINS, great granddaughter of Commodore John H. Dent, U. S. Navy.

COMMODORE JOHN H. DENT, U. S. Navy, was born in Maryland in 1779. Entered the Navy in 1793. Died in 1823. Appointed midshipman March 16, 1798; captain 1811. Served on board the "Constellation" when she captured the French frigate "Insurgente" 1799. He was first lieutenant of the frigate "Constitution" in the battle of Tripoli under Commodore Edward Preble. After the battle he was placed in command of the U. S. brig "Enterprise," whose captain, James Decatur, had been killed in the battle. Congress presented all the officers engaged in the battle of Tripoli with a bronze medal. In the war of 1812, Commodore Dent commanded the U. S. S. "Alligator" on the southern coast. Was stationed at Newport, Rhode Island, in 1815.

DETROIT (4TH)

LIGHT CRUISER

Length, 555 feet, 6 inches   *Beam, 55 feet*   *Draft, 14 feet, 3 inches*

NAMED FOR THE CITY OF DETROIT, MICHIGAN

Launched June 29, 1922, at Bethlehem Shipbuilding Corporation, Quincy, Massachusetts.

Sponsor: MISS MADELEINE COUZENS, daughter of Honorable James Couzens, Mayor of Detroit.

The first "Detroit" was a vessel of 400 tons, captured from the British at the Battle of Lake Erie, 1813.
The second "Detroit" was a screw steamer of 1380 tons, built during the Civil War but never completed.
The third "Detroit" was a protected cruiser, of 2072 tons, launched in 1891. Named for the city of Detroit.

DICKERSON

TORPEDO BOAT DESTROYER

Length, 314 feet   *Beam, 30 feet, 11 inches*   *Draft, 9 feet, 4 inches*

NAMED FOR SECRETARY OF THE NAVY
MAHLON DICKERSON

Launched March 12, 1919, at New York Shipbuilding Corporation, Camden, New Jersey.

Sponsor: MRS. JOHN STILES DICKERSON (Amelia Wagner), wife of the nearest relative of Secretary of the Navy Mahlon Dickerson.

SECRETARY OF THE NAVY MAHLON DICKERSON was born in Hanover, New Jersey, 1770; died 1853. Graduated at Princeton in 1789, was admitted to the bar in 1793. In 1805–1808 he was quartermaster general of Pennsylvania. He returned to New Jersey, became judge of the Supreme court and chancellor, and was elected a member of the legislature, 1811–1813. In 1815 he was elected governor of New Jersey, and at the close of his term was sent to the United States Senate. He was repeatedly re-elected, serving from December 1, 1817, till March 2, 1833. President Jackson appointed him Secretary of the Navy June 30, 1834, in which post he was continued by President Van Buren, serving till June 30, 1838.

DOBBIN

DESTROYER TENDER

Length, 483 feet   *Beam, 61 feet*   *Draft, 21 feet*

NAMED FOR HONORABLE JAMES
COCHRANE DOBBIN

Launched May 5, 1921, at Philadelphia Navy Yard.

Sponsor: MRS. H. H. JAMES (Louisa Dobbin), granddaughter of Hon. James Cochrane Dobbin.

HON. JAMES COCHRANE DOBBIN was Secretary of the Navy from 1853 to 1857. He was born in North Carolina in 1814. In 1832 he was graduated from the University of North Carolina, and practiced law. He was a member of Congress from 1845 to 1847, and also of the North Carolina Legislature from 1848 to 1852. In 1853 he became Secretary of the Navy, and during his administration he set about reform in all its branches. He was a firm believer in a strong Navy, and regarded the increase of Naval strength not as a war but as a peace measure, and during his administration there were built eighteen of the finest ships of their class that were in the world. He instituted the present apprentice system, the inauguration of a retired list for officers unable to perform active duty, the law for increased pay to seamen, and honorable discharges for good conduct. Under his auspices the Perry Expedition was carried to a successful termination and the treaty with Japan made. He died in 1857.

DORSEY

TORPEDO BOAT DESTROYER

Length, 314 feet   *Beam, 30 feet, 11 inches*   *Draft, 9 feet*

NAMED FOR MIDSHIPMAN JOHN DORSEY, U. S. NAVY

Launched April 9, 1918, at William Cramp & Sons' Company, Philadelphia, Pennsylvania.

Sponsor: MISS AGNES MEANS, first cousin, thrice removed, of Midshipman John Dorsey, U. S. Navy.

MIDSHIPMAN JOHN DORSEY, United States Navy, was born in Maryland. Killed in engagement with the enemy August 7, 1804. Appointed midshipman April 28, 1801. Ordered to the "Siren," Mediterranean Squadron, under Commodore Edward Preble operating against Tripoli. One of the officers of Gunboat No. 9 in attack on Tripolitan batteries August 7, 1804. Killed by explosion of a hot shot which struck her magazine. Commended in Commodore Preble's report to the Secretary of the Navy.

DOWNES

TORPEDO BOAT DESTROYER

Length, 305 feet   *Beam, 30 feet, 7 inches*   *Draft, 9 feet, 7 inches*

NAMED FOR CAPTAIN JOHN DOWNES, U. S. NAVY

Launched November 8, 1913, at New York Shipbuilding Company, Camden, New Jersey.

Sponsor: MRS. MANLEY H. SIMONS (Katherine Nazro), wife of Lieutenant Commander Simons, U. S. Navy, and great-granddaughter of Captain John Downes, U. S. Navy.

CAPTAIN JOHN DOWNES, United States Navy, was born 1784, in Massachusetts; died 1854. Appointed midshipman 1802; commissioned lieutenant 1807; master commandant (commander) 1813; captain 1817. Served: Distinguished service in the operations against Tripoli in 1804; executive officer of the "Essex," War of 1812, in action with British ships "Cherub" and "Phoebe," March 28, 1814; 1815 commanding U. S. S. "Epervier," Mediterranean Squadron, captured an Algerine frigate and a brig, June 15–17, 1815; 1819–1821 commanded the "Macedonian," Pacific Squadron; 1828–1829, "Java," Mediterranean Squadron, and 1832–1834 in the "Potomac," commanded the Pacific Squadron; last duty was commanding Charlestown Navy Yard, 1850–1852.

DOYEN

TORPEDO BOAT DESTROYER

Length, 314 feet   *Beam, 30 feet, 11 inches*   *Draft, 9 feet, 4 inches*

NAMED FOR BRIGADIER GENERAL CHARLES A. DOYEN, U. S. MARINE CORPS

Launched July 28, 1919, at Bethlehem Shipbuilding Corporation, Squantum, Massachusetts.

Sponsor: MISS FAY ELIZABETH DOYEN, daughter of Brigadier General Charles A. Doyen, U. S. M. C.

BRIGADIER GENERAL CHARLES A. DOYEN, United States Marine Corps, was born in New Hampshire, 1859. Awarded the distinguished service medal posthumously for distinguished services rendered; commander of the Fifth Regiment of Marines from the time of its organization in the United States throughout its period of training in France until the arrival there of the Sixth Regiment of Marines, when he commanded the Fourth Brigade, which consisted of the Fifth and Sixth Regiments and the Sixth Machine Gun Battalion. By his ability and personal effort he brought this brigade to a very high state of efficiency which enabled it to successfully resist the German Army and be victorious in Chateau-Thierry sector and Belleau Woods. The strong efforts on his part undermined his health and necessitated his being invalided to the United States before having the opportunity to command the brigade in action; but his work was shown by the excellent service rendered by his brigade. He died October 6, 1918.

DU PONT

TORPEDO BOAT DESTROYER

Length, 314 feet   *Beam, 30 feet, 11 inches*   *Draft, 9 feet*

NAMED FOR REAR ADMIRAL SAMUEL FRANCIS DU PONT, U. S. NAVY

Launched October 22, 1918, at William Cramp & Sons' Company, Philadelphia, Pennsylvania.

Sponsor: MISS CONSTANCE SIMONS DU PONT, great-grandniece of Rear Admiral Samuel Francis du Pont U. S. Navy.

REAR ADMIRAL SAMUEL FRANCIS DU PONT, U. S. Navy, was born at Bergen Point, New Jersey, 1803; died 1865. Appointed midshipman 1815; rear admiral 1862. Commanded U. S. S. "Cyane" 1846–1848, and rendered conspicuously gallant service at San Diego, Mazatlan, San Jose, and other ports, and was included in the thanks of Congress to officers for service in the war with Mexico.

DYER

TORPEDO BOAT DESTROYER

Length, 314 feet   *Beam, 30 feet, 11 inches*   *Draft, 9 feet, 2 inches*

NAMED FOR CAPTAIN N. MAYO DYER, U. S. NAVY

Launched April 13, 1918, at Bethlehem Shipbuilding Corporation, Quincy, Massachusetts.

Sponsor: MISS VIRGINIA BLACKMUR, daughter of Paul Rupert Blackmur of Quincy, Massachusetts.

[62]

U.S. DUPONT.
JUST OFF THE WAYS.
CRAMPS PHILA. PA.
OCT. 22-1918. C.159.

U.S. TORPEDO BOAT DESTROYER "DU PONT," JUST OFF THE
WAYS WITH A TRANSPORT ALONGSIDE

CAPTAIN N. MAYO DYER, U. S. Navy, was born in Massachusetts 1839; died 1910. Entered volunteer Navy as master's mate; promoted to acting ensign and acting master for gallant service; served in U. S. S. "Metacomet" at battle of Mobile Bay; entered Regular Navy as lieutenant commander December 18, 1868; captain, commanding the "Baltimore" at the battle of Manila Bay. May 1, 1898, in Commodore George Dewey's Squadron.

EDSALL

TORPEDO BOAT DESTROYER

Length, 314 feet   *Beam, 30 feet, 11 inches*   *Draft, 9 feet, 4 inches*

NAMED FOR NORMAN E EDSALL, SEAMAN, U. S. NAVY

Launched July 29, 1920, at William Cramp & Sons' Company, Philadelphia, Pennsylvania.

Sponsor: MRS. BESSIE EDSALL BRACEY, sister of Norman E. Edsall, U. S. Navy.

NORMAN E. EDSALL, SEAMAN, U. S. Navy, was born in Kentucky in 1873; killed by hostile natives near Apia, Samoa, April 1, 1899, while attached to the U. S. S. "Philadelphia." Enlisted in the United States Navy as seaman 1898. On April 1, 1899, while attached to the U. S. S. "Philadelphia," he went ashore with a party under command of Lieut. Lansdale, U. S. Navy, to suppress the hostile natives near Apia, Samoa. The thicket was so dense that when the order to retreat was sounded it was not possible for the different parts of the expedition to render each other mutual support. Lieut. Lansdale was wounded below the knee and was incapable of marching. Edsall was mortally wounded while assisting Lieut. Lansdale to a place of safety, showing a spirit of bravery and self-sacrifice in keeping with the standards of the Navy.

EDWARDS

TORPEDO BOAT DESTROYER

Length, 314 feet   *Beam, 30 feet, 11 inches*   *Draft, 9 feet, 4 inches*

NAMED FOR MIDSHIPMAN WILLIAM W. EDWARDS,
U. S. NAVY

Launched October 10, 1918, at Bethlehem Shipbuilding Corporation, Squantum, Massachusetts.

Sponsor: MISS JULIA EDWARDS NOYES, daughter of Mr. Edward A. Noyes. Midshipman William W. Edwards, U. S. Navy, was a nephew of the sponsor's great-grandfather, Thomas Edwards.

MIDSHIPMAN WILLIAM W. EDWARDS, United States Navy, was born in Petersburg, Virginia. Appointed a midshipman September 1, 1811; 1813 attached to the "Argus," on which ship he was killed in action with the "Pelican" August 14, 1813.

JOHN D. EDWARDS

TORPEDO BOAT DESTROYER

Length, 314 feet   *Beam, 30 feet, 11 inches*   *Draft, 9 feet, 4 inches*

NAMED FOR LIEUTENANT JOHN DAVIS EDWARDS,
U. S. NAVY

Launched October 18, 1919, at William Cramp and Sons' Company, Philadelphia, Pennsylvania.

Sponsor: MRS. JOHN D. EDWARDS (Mae Marshall), widow of Lieutenant John Davis Edwards, U. S. Navy. Mrs. Edwards was accompanied by her two small children.

LIEUTENANT JOHN DAVIS EDWARDS, United States Navy. Born in Isle of Wight County, Virginia, 1885; died at sea, October 9, 1918. Appointed warrant machinist, December 31, 1908; ensign, July 30, 1914; lieutenant, October 15, 1917. Attached to U. S. S. "Shaw," cruising in British waters. Killed when the "Shaw" was rammed in collision with the British troopship "Aquitania." The "Shaw" had just sighted a German submarine and in going for her crossed the path of the giant transport.

EIDER

MINE SWEEPER

Length, 187 feet   *Beam, 35 feet*   *Draft, 9 feet, 9 inches*

NAMED FOR THE BIRD EIDER

Launched May 26, 1918, at Pusey & Jones Company.

Sponsor: MISS MAREN LYSHOLM, daughter of Mr. Henry Lysholm, vice president of the Company.

ELLIOT

TORPEDO BOAT DESTROYER

Length, 314 feet   *Beam, 30 feet, 11 inches*   *Draft, 9 feet*

NAMED FOR LIEUTENANT COMMANDER
RICHARD McCALL ELLIOT

Launched July 4, 1918, at William Cramp & Sons' Company, Philadelphia, Pennsylvania.

Sponsor: MRS. JOAN PACKARD ELLIOT, widow of Lieutenant Commander Richard McCall Elliot, U. S. Navy.

LIEUTENANT COMMANDER RICHARD McCALL ELLIOT, U. S. Navy, was born in Philadelphia in 1888. Was killed on board the "Manley" March 20, 1918. The "Manley" while performing escort duty in the war zone, came in contact with one of the convoy. An explosion of depth charges located on the after end of the vessel occurred causing serious damage and loss of life. Lieut. Commander Elliot, who was on the bridge, immediately started aft to take charge of the situation. He was killed by flying pieces of wreckage as he gained the deck.

[65]

ELLIS

TORPEDO BOAT DESTROYER

Length, 314 feet   *Beam, 30 feet, 11 inches*   *Draft, 9 feet*

NAMED FOR CHIEF YEOMAN GEORGE HENRY ELLIS,
U. S. NAVY

Launched November 30, 1918, at Wm. Cramp & Sons' Company, Philadelphia, Pennsylvania.

Sponsor: MRS. EDWARD T. STOTESBURY (Eva Roberts), wife of a prominent citizen of Philadelphia.

CHIEF YEOMAN GEORGE HENRY ELLIS, U. S. Navy, was killed in the Battle of Santiago, July 3, 1898, while serving on board the flagship of Commodore Schley, the U. S. S. "Brooklyn." He was born in Peoria, Illinois, 1875, and enlisted in the Navy as an apprentice seaman 1892. He served on the "Minnesota," "Richmond," "Mononga-hela," "Chicago," "Vermont," "Dolphin," "Columbia," and "Brooklyn." During the battle he was stationed to give the ranges shown by the stadimeter to the captain, who communicated them from time to time to the different divisions. Ellis was struck in the face by a large shell, and instantly killed.

ERICSSON (2D)

TORPEDO BOAT DESTROYER

Length, 305 feet   *Beam, 30 feet, 7 inches*   *Draft, 9 feet, 9 inches*

NAMED FOR JOHN ERICSSON

Launched August 22, 1914, at New York Shipbuilding Company, Camden, New Jersey.

Sponsor: MRS. J. WASHINGTON LOGUE (Mary Barry), wife of Representative in Congress J. W. Logue of Philadelphia, Pennsylvania.

JOHN ERICSSON, engineer and inventor, was born in Sweden, in 1812. After serving in the Swedish Army, he moved to England. In 1839 came to United States where he furnished designs for U. S. S. "Princeton" and brought out numerous inventions. In 1861, during the Civil War, he designed and finished in 100 days the Ironclad Monitor and built a number of similar vessels for our Navy. In 1883 he erected a "Sun Motor" in New York, for developing power from direct rays of the sun. He died in New York in 1889. Buried in the place of his birth, a U. S. Navy vessel conveying his body in 1890.

EVANS

TORPEDO BOAT DESTROYER

Length, 314 feet   *Beam, 30 feet, 11 inches*   *Draft, 9 feet*

NAMED FOR REAR ADMIRAL ROBLEY D. EVANS,
U. S. NAVY

Launched October 30, 1918, at Bath Iron Works, Bath, Maine.

Sponsor: MISS DOROTHY NEVILLE SEWALL, granddaughter of Rear Admiral Robley D. Evans, U. S. Navy.

REAR ADMIRAL ROBLEY D. EVANS, U. S. Navy, was born in Floyd County, Virginia, in 1846; died 1912. Appointed midshipman 1860; commissioned rear admiral 1901; participated in Civil War and severely wounded twice in attack on Fort Fisher, January, 1865; in 1891–1892 commanded the "Yorktown," Pacific station, where he became known as "Fighting Bob" by his vigorous action in upholding the honor of the United States during strained relations with Chile; commanded "Iowa" during War with Spain, taking prominent part in battle of Santiago; commander in chief of Atlantic Fleet from east to west coast on trip around world in 1907–1908.

FAIRFAX

TORPEDO BOAT DESTROYER

Length, 314 feet   *Beam, 30 feet, 11 inches*   *Draft, 9 feet*

NAMED FOR REAR ADMIRAL DONALD MCNEILL FAIRFAX, U. S. NAVY

Launched December 15, 1917, at Navy Yard, Mare Island, California.

Sponsor: MISS ELIZABETH GEORGE, daughter of Captain Harry George, U. S. Navy, Commandant of the Navy Yard.

REAR ADMIRAL DONALD McNEILL FAIRFAX, U. S. Navy. Born in Virginia, 1821; died 1894; appointed midshipman August 12, 1837; rear admiral, July 11, 1880; executive officer of the "San Jacinto," November 8, 1861, when the British steamer "Trent" was seized by Captain Charles Wilkes; boarded that vessel and took off the Confederate commissioners; retired at own request, September 30, 1881.

FALCON

MINE SWEEPER

Length, 187 feet   *Beam, 35 feet*   *Draft, 9 feet, 9 inches*

NAMED FOR THE BIRD FALCON

Launched September 7, 1918, at Consolidated Shipbuilding Corporation, New York City.

Sponsor: MRS. WILLIAM J. PARSLOW (Cora Pendleton), wife of the vice president of the Consolidated S. B. Corporation.

FARENHOLT

TORPEDO BOAT DESTROYER

Length, 314 feet, 4 inches   *Beam, 30 feet, 11 inches*   *Draft, 9 feet*

NAMED FOR REAR ADMIRAL OSCAR W. FARENHOLT, U. S. NAVY

Launched March 9, 1921, at Bethlehem Shipbuilding Corporation, San Francisco, California.

Sponsor: MRS. J. STEWART FAIRWEATHER (Rachael Hovey), whose father had been a close friend of Rear Admiral Farenholt, U. S. Navy.

REAR ADMIRAL OSCAR W. FARENHOLT, U. S. Navy, born in San Antonio, Texas, in 1843; died 1920. Entered the Navy as a seaman in 1861; served on the flagship Wabash under Admiral du Pont in engagements at Fort Hatteras, Port Royal, and Fort Pulaski 1861–1862. Discharged and re-enlisted in 1863; on board the monitor "Catskill" participated in engagements with the defenses at Charleston Harbor and the storming of Fort Sumter 1863–1864; appointed acting ensign 1864; took part in operations of the north Atlantic blockading squadron until after the surrender of Fort Fisher 1865; March 1868 commissioned ensign; rear admiral 1901. After being commissioned in the regular service he held important positions on shore; his last sea service was in command of the Monocacy, Asiatic Station.

FARQUHAR

TORPEDO BOAT DESTROYER

Length, 314 feet   *Beam, 30 feet, 11 inches*   *Draft, 9 feet, 4 inches*

NAMED FOR REAR ADMIRAL NORMAN H. FARQUHAR, U. S. NAVY

Launched January 18, 1919, at Bethlehem Shipbuilding Corporation, San Francisco, California.

Sponsor: MRS. JAMES REED (Laura Maltby), wife of Commander James Reed, C. C., U. S. Navy.

REAR ADMIRAL NORMAN H. FARQUHAR, U. S. Navy, was born at Pottsville, Pennsylvania, 1840; died 1907. Appointed a midshipman 1859; commissioned rear admiral 1899. First cruise on the coast of Africa for the suppression of the slave trade, and brought to the United

States (while still a midshipman) the captured slaver "Triton." During the Civil War served on the "Mahaska" and other vessels of the North Atlantic blockading squadron, and was executive officer of the "Santiago de Cuba" in both attacks on Fort Fisher, December, 1864, and January, 1865. Commanded the "Trenton," Pacific station, and received commendation for the manner in which he handled his ship during the memorable hurricane at Apia, Samoa, 1889; served as Chief of the Bureau of Yards and Docks from 1890 to 1894. Held various important shore stations and commanded the North Atlantic squadron 1899–1901.

FARRAGUT

TORPEDO BOAT DESTROYER

Length, 314 feet   *Beam, 30 feet, 11 inches*   *Draft, 9 feet, 4 inches*

NAMED FOR ADMIRAL DAVID GLASGOW FARRAGUT, U. S. NAVY

Launched November 21, 1918, at Bethlehem Shipbuilding Corporation, San Francisco, California.

Sponsor: MRS. TEMPLIN M. POTTS (Marie Charlier), wife of Captain T. M. Potts, U. S. Navy.

ADMIRAL DAVID GLASGOW FARRAGUT, United States Navy, was born at Campbells Station, Tennessee, 1801; died 1870. Appointed midshipman 1810; vice admiral 1864; admiral 1866. Ordered to the "Essex" in 1812, under the command of Captain David Porter, and was with him in his memorable cruise in the Pacific. When but twelve years of age was given command of a prize and took her safely into Valparaiso. In January, 1862, he was given command of the West Gulf Blockading Squadron. On the flagship "Hartford" he opened up the Mississippi River by taking the forts below New Orleans and receiving the surrender of the city April 24–25, 1862. On August 5, 1864, he attacked and passed the defenses of Mobile Bay and received, after a gallant fight, the surrender of the Confederate fleet in those waters. He received the thanks of Congress. The grade of vice admiral was created for him by President Lincoln and that of admiral by Congress.

FINCH

MINE SWEEPER

Length, 187 feet   *Beam, 35 feet*   *Draft, 9 feet, 9 inches*

NAMED FOR THE BIRD FINCH

Launched March 30, 1918, at Standard Shipbuilding Corporation, New York.

Sponsor: MRS. FREDERIC G. PEABODY (Gertrude Douglas).

FLAMINGO

MINE SWEEPER

Length, 187 feet   *Beam, 35 feet*   *Draft, 9 feet, 9 inches*

NAMED FOR THE BIRD FLAMINGO

Launched August 25, 1918, at New Jersey D. D. & T. Company.

Sponsor: MISS FANNY CAROLINE MORITZ, daughter of Commander Albert Moritz, U. S. Navy.

FLUSSER (2d)

TORPEDO BOAT DESTROYER

Length, 314 feet   *Beam, 30 feet, 11 inches*   *Draft, 9 feet, 4 inches*

NAMED FOR LIEUTENANT COMMANDER CHARLES
W. FLUSSER, U. S. NAVY

Launched November 7, 1919, at Bethlehem Shipbuilding Corporation, Squantum, Massachusetts.

Sponsor: MRS. HENRY WILLIAMS (Maud Steers), wife of Captain H. Williams, C. C., U. S. Navy, Superintending Naval Constructor.

LIEUTENANT COMMANDER CHARLES W. FLUS-SER, United States Navy, was born in Maryland, 1832; died 1864; appointed midshipman 1847; lieutenant commander, 1862; cruised on various stations; at the commencement of the Civil War was assigned to the command of the U. S. S. "Commodore Perry," and took part in the attack on Roanoke Island, February 7, 1862, and other operations in North Carolina waters. Served in the North Atlantic Blockading Squadron during 1862, 1863, and 1864. He commanded the U. S. S. "Miami," operating in the Sounds of North Carolina, and was killed in the battle with the Confederate States ironclad "Albemarle," Plymouth, North Carolina.

FOOTE (2D)

TORPEDO BOAT DESTROYER

Length, 314 feet   *Beam, 30 feet, 11 inches*   *Draft, 9 feet, 2 inches*

NAMED FOR REAR ADMIRAL ANDREW HULL FOOTE, U. S. Navy

Launched December 14, 1918, at Bethlehem Shipbuilding Corporation, Quincy, Massachusetts.

Sponsor: MRS. FRANCIS E. CADY (Leila Foote), granddaughter of Rear Admiral Andrew Hull Foote, U. S. Navy.

REAR ADMIRAL ANDREW HULL FOOTE, U. S. Navy, was born at New Haven, Connecticut, 1806; died 1863; distinguished himself in engagements with barrier forts, Canton River, China, finally carrying them by storm; Chief of Bureau of Equipment and Recruiting; received thanks of Congress for gallant service during the Civil War; appointed to command the South Atlantic Blockading Squadron in 1863, but died en route.

JOHN D. FORD

TORPEDO BOAT DESTROYER

Length, 314 feet   *Beam, 30 feet, 11 inches*   *Draft, 9 feet, 4 inches*

NAMED FOR REAR ADMIRAL JOHN DONALDSON
FORD, U. S. NAVY

Launched September 2, 1920, at William Cramp & Sons'
Company, Philadelphia, Pennsylvania.

Sponsor: MISS FLORENCE FAITH FORD, daughter of
Rear Admiral John Donaldson Ford, U. S. Navy.

REAR ADMIRAL JOHN DONALDSON FORD, U. S.
Navy, was born in Baltimore, Maryland, 1840; died 1918.
Appointed third assistant engineer 1863; first assistant
engineer 1868; passed assistant engineer 1874; chief
engineer 1890; commander 1899; captain 1902; rear
admiral 1902. Served during the Civil War: 1862–1865
West Gulf Blockading Squadron; recapture of Baton Rouge,
passage of Port Hudson, and engagements at other points
on the Mississippi River. Second assistant engineer of the
U. S. S. "Richmond" at the battle of Mobile Bay. Attached to the "Sacramento" when she was wrecked off the
coast of India in June, 1867. Cruised on various stations
and held important posts on shore. As fleet engineer took
part in the Battle of Manila Bay, May, 1898, and operations
at Cavite, Sangley Point, capture of forts at Corregidor and
Manila. Advanced three numbers for "eminent and
conspicuous service in battle." Retired in May, 1902,
but retained on active duty as inspector of machinery and
ordnance until 1908.

FOX (2D)

TORPEDO BOAT DESTROYER

Length, 314 feet   *Beam, 30 feet, 11 inches*   *Draft, 9 feet, 4 inches*

NAMED FOR ASSISTANT SECRETARY OF THE NAVY
GUSTAVUS V. FOX

Launched June 12, 1919, at New York Shipbuilding
Corporation, Camden, New Jersey.

Sponsor: MISS VIRGINIA BLAIR, grandniece of Assistant
Secretary Gustavus V. Fox.

[73]

Hon. GUSTAVUS V. FOX, Assistant Secretary of the Navy, was born in Saugus, Massachusetts, 1821; died 1883. Appointed midshipman, 1838; was given the rank of lieutenant and resigned July 10, 1852. During the Mexican War served on the brig "Washington" and took active part in the second expedition against Tabasco, in which the town was captured. At the commencement of the Civil War volunteered for service and was given a temporary appointment in the Navy. August 1, 1861, appointed Assistant Secretary of the Navy by President Lincoln; held the position until the close of the war.

FULLER

TORPEDO BOAT DESTROYER

Length, 314 feet   *Beam, 30 feet, 11 inches*   *Draft, 9 feet, 4 inches*

NAMED FOR CAPTAIN EDWARD C. FULLER, U. S. MARINE CORPS

Launched December 5, 1918, at Bethlehem Shipbuilding Corporation, San Francisco, California.

Sponsor: MISS GLADYS SULLIVAN, niece of U. S. Senator Phelan, of San Francisco.

CAPTAIN EDWARD C. FULLER, U. S. Marine Corps, was born in Hamilton, Virginia, 1893; was graduated from the Naval Academy in 1916, and immediately requested overseas duty in the Marine Corps. He was awarded the distinguished service cross posthumously for: "While fearlessly exposing himself in an artillery barrage for the purpose of getting his men into a position of security in the attack on the Bois de Belleau, on June 12, where he was killed, and thereby gave his life in an effort to protect his men."

FULTON (2D)

SUBMARINE TENDER

Length, 226 feet   *Beam, 35 feet*   *Draft, 13 feet*

NAMED FOR ROBERT FULTON

Launched June 6, 1914, at Fore River Shipbuilding Company, Quincy, Massachusetts.

Sponsor: MRS. ARTHUR TAYLOR SUTCLIFFE (Alice Crary), great-granddaughter of Robert Fulton.

ROBERT FULTON, artist and inventor, was born November 14, 1765, in Little Britain, now "Fulton" Township, Pennsylvania; died, 1815.

In 1782, went to Philadelphia and became a painter of miniatures. Four years later he sailed for England to study art, where he painted historical scenes and many portraits, exhibiting several in the Royal Academy. From 1794 to 1799 he invented machines for cutting marble, spinning flax and twisting ropes; a double inclined plane for canal navigation and an earth scoop for aqueducts. He crossed to France in 1797, where he painted and patented an Historic Panorama, and continued his scientific studies. His chief inventions, the submarine torpedo and the steamboat, although proved effective in France, were rejected by Napoleon as impracticable. In 1804, Fulton returned to England and offered his submarine to the British Government which desired its suppression but declined its use. Two years later Fulton returned to America and immediately set about to demonstrate his two inventions, blowing up a brig, July 20th, 1807, in the harbor of New York; and on August 17th of the same year, accomplishing the voyage from New York to Albany in his steamboat, the Clermont, a distance of 150 miles, in 32 hours. Thereafter Fulton built more than twenty steamboats, and established them upon the Hudson, Raritan, Mississippi and Potomac Rivers. He also built the first steam ferries and the first steam war frigate, "Demologus" (The Voice of the People) later named the "Fulton." His motto, frequently quoted in his numerous writings, was "The Liberty of the Seas will be the Happiness of the Earth."

"Fulton 1st" (originally "Demologus") was the first steam frigate of the U. S. Navy, and was named for her inventor.

From New York Evening Post, Saturday, Oct. 29th, 1814:

"STEAM FRIGATE LAUNCH

"This morning at a quarter before 9 o'clock, the Steam Frigate 'Fulton the First' was launched from the shipyards of Adam and Noah Brown, at Corlear's Hook, amidst the roar of cannon and the shouts and acclamations of upwards of twenty thousand people who had assembled to witness the event. The ground adjacent was crowded, as was also the wharves and housetops, and the river covered with gun boats and water craft of every description. She took leave of her bed a quarter of an hour earlier than was intended, owing to the jarring produced by the discharge of a 32 pounder on deck to give warning to the spectators. She measures 145 feet on deck and 55 feet breadth of beam, draws only 8 feet of water and is to mount 32 pound carronades and 2 Columbiads, the latter to carry each a 100 pound red hot ball. She is to be commanded by Commodore Porter and from appearances she bids fair to become a formidable weapon in harbor warfare."

GAMBLE

TORPEDO BOAT DESTROYER

Length, 314 feet   *Beam, 30 feet, 11 inches*   *Draft, 9 feet, 3 inches*

NAMED FOR LIEUTENANT COLONEL JOHN M. GAMBLE, U. S. M. C., AND LIEUTENANT PETER GAMBLE, U. S. NAVY

Launched May 11, 1918, at Newport News Shipbuilding Company, Newport News, Virginia.

Sponsor: MISS EVELYN H. JACKSON, daughter of Mr. Herbert Worth Jackson, a relative of Secretary of the Navy Josephus Daniels.

LIEUTENANT COLONEL JOHN M. GAMBLE, U. S. M. C., was appointed a second lieutenant in the Marine

U. S. TORPEDO BOAT DESTROYER "ELLIS" ENTERING THE WATER

Corps, 1809; was promoted first lieutenant 1811; captain 1814; and major 1834. He was promoted major, by brevet, 1816, and lieutenant colonel, by brevet, 1827. Died 1836. He served during the War of 1812 and while in command of the marine guard of the "Essex" he was temporarily placed in command of three prize vessels, the "Seringapatam," "Sir Andrew Hammond," and the "Greenwich," also a fort at Nooaheevah, during the absence of the "Essex." Despairing of the return of the "Essex" he rigged up the prize vessels with the intention of quitting the Marquesas. During a fight with mutineers of his command, who took the "Seringapatam," Lieut. Gamble was badly wounded in the foot, and later in an engagement with the natives, one officer, and three men of his command were killed, and one other severely wounded. With but four men on board the "Sir Andrew Hammond" fit for duty Lieut. Gamble put to sea, and without a chart made his way to the Sandwich Islands, in 17 days, only to fall into the hands of the enemy, being later released.

LIEUTENANT PETER GAMBLE, U. S. Navy, was appointed midshipman January 16, 1809; commissioned lieutenant 1814. On duty at Providence, R. I., until October 9, 1813, when transferred to the U. S. S. "Enterprise." Ordered to Lake Champlain May 4, 1814, and killed in action September 11, 1814.

GANNET

MINE SWEEPER

Length, 187 feet   *Beam, 35 feet*   *Draft, 9 feet, 9 inches*

NAMED FOR THE BIRD GANNET

Launched March 19, 1919, at Todd Shipyard Corporation, New York.

Sponsor: MISS EDNA MAE FRY, daughter of a foreman of the Todd Shipyard Corporation.

GILLIS

TORPEDO BOAT DESTROYER

Length, 314 feet   *Beam, 30 feet, 11 inches*   *Draft, 9 feet, 4 inches*

NAMED FOR COMMODORE JOHN P. GILLIS, U. S. NAVY,
AND REAR ADMIRAL JAMES H. GILLIS, U. S. NAVY

Launched May 29, 1919, at Bethlehem Shipbuilding Corporation, Quincy, Massachusetts.

Sponsors: MRS. JOSEPHINE T. SMITH, niece of Commodore John P. Gillis, U. S. Navy, and MISS HELEN IRVING MURRAY, granddaughter of Rear Admiral James H. Gillis, U. S. Navy.

COMMODORE JOHN P. GILLIS, U. S. Navy, was born in Wilmington, Delaware, 1803; died 1873. Appointed midshipman, 1825; commodore, retired list, 1866. Served with distinction during the Mexican War. In 1853–1854 was on the Japan expedition under Commodore Perry. Commanded the U. S. S. "Monticello" and the U. S. S. "Seminole" during the Civil War and took part in many attacks. Held positions of importance on shore.

REAR ADMIRAL JAMES H. GILLIS, U. S. Navy, was born at Ridgway, Pennsylvania, 1831; died 1910. Appointed midshipman, 1848; rear admiral (acting) 1888–1890. While attached to the store ship "Supply," lying in the harbor of Montevideo rescued the crew of a foundered vessel and received the thanks of the Argentine minister and a valuable medal. Held a brilliant record during the Civil War. Served in the Pacific Squadron, 1866. Received thanks of the British subjects for services rendered at the time of the tidal wave at Arica. Subsequently served on various stations ashore and afloat until retired in 1893.

GILMER

TORPEDO BOAT DESTROYER

Length, 314 feet   *Beam, 30 feet*   *Draft, 9 feet, 4 inches*

NAMED FOR SECRETARY OF THE NAVY
THOMAS WALKER GILMER

Launched May 24, 1919, at New York Shipbuilding Corporation, Camden, New Jersey.

Sponsor: MRS. ALFRED H. MILES (Elizabeth Gilmer), granddaughter of Secretary of the Navy Thomas Walker Gilmer, and wife of Commander A. H. Miles, U. S. Navy.

SECRETARY OF THE NAVY Thomas Walker Gilmer was born in Virginia; died near Washington, D. C., February 28, 1844. Served for many years in the Virginia State Legislature and for two sessions as speaker. In 1840–1841 he was governor of Virginia. On February 15, 1844, he was appointed Secretary of the Navy, and ten days later he was killed by the bursting of a gun on board the U. S. S. "Princeton."

GOFF

TORPEDO BOAT DESTROYER
Length, 314 feet   Beam, 30 feet, 11 inches   Draft, 9 feet, 4 inches

NAMED FOR SECRETARY OF THE NAVY
NATHAN GOFF

Launched June 2, 1920, at New York Shipbuilding Corporation, Camden, New Jersey.

Sponsor: MRS. NATHAN GOFF (Katherine Penney), widow of Secretary of the Navy Nathan Goff.

SECRETARY OF THE NAVY Nathan Goff was born in Clarksburg, West Virginia, 1843; died 1920. Educated at the Northwestern Virginia Academy, Georgetown College, and the University of New York. In 1861 he enlisted in the National Army in the 3d Regiment of Virginia Volunteer Infantry, served as lieutenant and then adjutant of this regiment, and in 1863 was promoted to major of the 4th Virginia Cavalry. In 1865 he was admitted to the bar and elected to the West Virginia Legislature. In 1868 appointed district attorney, which office he resigned in

[79]

1880 to accept the Secretaryship of the Navy under President Hayes to fill out the unexpired term of Richard W. Thompson, who had vacated it. In March, 1881, he was re-appointed district attorney of West Virginia, which office he again resigned on July 1, 1882. He was elected to Congress in 1884 and re-elected in 1886.

GOLDSBOROUGH (2D)

TORPEDO BOAT DESTROYER

Length, 314 feet   *Beam, 30 feet, 11 inches*   *Draft, 9 feet, 4 inches*

NAMED FOR REAR ADMIRAL LOUIS M. GOLDSBOROUGH, U. S. NAVY

Launched November 20, 1918, at Newport News Shipbuilding and Dry Dock Company, Newport News, Virginia.

Sponsor: MISS LUCETTA PENNINGTON GOLDSBOROUGH, niece of Rear Admiral Louis M. Goldsborough, U. S. Navy.

REAR ADMIRAL LOUIS M. GOLDSBOROUGH, United States Navy, was born in Washington, D. C., 1805; died 1877; warranted midshipman when only a little more than seven years of age, June 18, 1812; was commissioned rear admiral 1862. In September, 1827, while convoying a fleet of merchant vessels, one of the convoy, an English vessel named "Comet," was attacked and carried off by Greek pirates. After a fierce fight, in which 90 of the pirates were killed, the "Comet" was rescued, and he received the thanks of the British Government. He was appointed flag officer at the outbreak of the Civil War; and September, 1861, planned and took part in the joint Army and Navy expedition to the sounds of North Carolina, and participated in the capture of Roanoke Island February 5, 1862.

GRAHAM

TORPEDO BOAT DESTROYER

Length, 314 feet   *Beam, 30 feet, 11 inches*   *Draft, 9 feet, 4 inches*

NAMED FOR SECRETARY OF THE NAVY WILLIAM A. GRAHAM

Launched March 22, 1919, at Newport News Shipbuilding Company, Newport News, Virginia.

Sponsor: MRS. ROBERT F. SMALLWOOD (Annie Graham), granddaughter of Secretary of the Navy William A. Graham.

SECRETARY OF THE NAVY WILLIAM A. GRAHAM was born in Lincoln County, North Carolina, in 1804; died 1875. He was graduated from the University of North Carolina in 1824, was admitted to the bar in 1826. From 1833 he was repeatedly elected to the House of Commons, of which in 1839–1840 he was speaker. In 1840–1843 he was in the United States Senate, in 1844 and 1846 he was elected Whig governor of North Carolina, and declined a third term, and from 1850–1852 was Secretary of the Navy, in which capacity he organized Perry's expedition to Japan.

GREBE

MINE SWEEPER

Length, 187 feet   *Beam, 35 feet*   *Draft, 9 feet, 9 inches*

NAMED FOR THE BIRD GREBE

Launched December 17, 1918, at Staten Island S. B. Co., New York.

Sponsor: MISS EMMA GRACE YOUMANS, who was serving as Yeoman (F) 1st class, attached to the office of the Inspector of Machinery of Mine Sweepers, Third Naval District, during the World War.

GREENE

TORPEDO BOAT DESTROYER

Length, 314 feet   *Beam, 30 feet, 11 inches*   *Draft, 9 feet, 4 inches*

NAMED FOR COMMANDER SAMUEL DANA GREENE, U. S. NAVY

Launched November 2, 1918, at Bethlehem Shipbuilding Corporation, Squantum, Massachusetts.

Sponsor: MRS. JOHN STEVENS CONOVER (Mary Greene), daughter of Commander Samuel Dana Greene, U. S. Navy.

COMMANDER SAMUEL DANA GREENE, United States Navy, was born in 1840 in Cumberland, Maryland; died 1884. Appointed acting midshipman 1855; midshipman 1859; commander 1872; served 1859–1861 on the "Hartford" in the East Indies; served as executive officer of the "Monitor" during her fight with the Confederate steamship "Merrimac" March 9, 1862; took command after her commander, Worden, was wounded; was executive officer of the "Monitor" in the engagements in the James River, Virginia, April–May, 1862, and when she foundered in a gale. Particularly commended by Commander Bankhead for his good conduct during the gale, and called to the attention of the admiral commanding the squadron and to the Secretary of the Navy.

GREER

TORPEDO BOAT DESTROYER

Length, 314 feet   *Beam, 30 feet, 11 inches*   *Draft, 9 feet, 4 inches*

NAMED FOR REAR ADMIRAL JAMES A. GREER, U. S. NAVY

Launched August 1, 1918, at William Cramp & Sons' Company, Philadelphia, Pennsylvania.

Sponsor: MISS EVELINA PORTER GLEAVES, daughter of Rear Admiral Albert Gleaves, U. S. Navy, was sponsor by request of the family of Rear Admiral Greer. The sponsor brought with her two flags formerly flown by Rear Admiral Greer, and the Destroyer was launched with these flags flying.

REAR ADMIRAL JAMES A. GREER, U. S. Navy, was born in Ohio in 1833. Died 1904. Appointed midshipman January 10, 1848; commissioned rear admiral April 3, 1892;

1848–1860 cruised on the home, Pacific, Paraguay expedition and African Squadron; Civil War, 1861–1865, on the "San Jacinto" when the Confederate commissioners were taken off the English steamer "Trent" by direction of Capt. Wilkes; special service on the "St. Louis" 1862–1863; 1863–1865 attached to the Mississippi Squadron; commanded the ironclads "Carondelet" and "Benton" and a division of the squadron at the passage of Vicksburg April 16, 1863; fought the batteries at Grand Gulf for five hours April 29, 1863, took part in the Red River expedition May, 1863; engaged in the combined attack on Vicksburg May 19, 1863, and almost constantly under fire during the 45 days' siege of Vicksburg; Red River expedition of March and April, 1864; commanded naval station at Mound City October and November, 1864; commanded the flagship "Black Hawk" until February, 1865; had charge of convoying Army transports up the Tennessee River February, 1865; 1866–1867 commanded the "Mohongo," North Pacific station; commended by State Department for course pursued in defending American interests in Mexico; 1873 commanded "Tigress" on "Polaris" relief expedition; 1874–1877 cruised on the Pacific station; 1878 special service on the "Constitution" to Paris Exposition; 1887–1889 commanding European station; held important shore stations until retired, 1895.

GREGORY

TORPEDO BOAT DESTROYER

Length, 314 feet   Beam, 30 feet, 11 inches   Draft, 9 feet, 2 inches

NAMED FOR REAR ADMIRAL FRANCIS
HOYT GREGORY, U. S. NAVY

Launched January 27, 1918, at Bethlehem Shipbuilding Corporation, Quincy, Massachusetts.

Sponsor: MRS. GEORGE S. TREVOR (Alice Haven), great-granddaughter of Rear Admiral Francis Hoyt Gregory, U. S. Navy.

[83]

REAR ADMIRAL FRANCIS HOYT GREGORY, U. S. Navy, was born in Norwalk, Connecticut, 1789; died 1866. Appointed midshipman 1808; commissioned rear admiral 1862; attached to bomb brig "Vesuvius" in 1810, and while in charge of one of the boats of that vessel captured a British slaver off Balize; 1811, in command of gun-boat No. 162; in her, between August 7 and September 7, 1811, he captured five piratical vessels and put to flight a British privateer in the West Indies; served with distinction under Commodore Chauncey in the squadron on Lake Ontario.

GRIDLEY

TORPEDO BOAT DESTROYER

Length, 315 feet   *Beam, 30 feet, 11 inches*   *Draft, 9 feet, 2 inches*

NAMED FOR CAPTAIN CHARLES VERNON
GRIDLEY, U. S. NAVY

Launched July 4, 1918, at Bethlehem Shipbuilding Corporation, San Francisco, California.

Sponsor: MRS. FRANCIS P. THOMAS (Ruth Gridley), daughter of Captain Charles Vernon Gridley, U. S. Navy.

CAPTAIN CHARLES VERNON GRIDLEY, U. S. Navy, was born in Logansport, Indiana, 1844; died 1898. Appointed midshipman 1860; captain 1897; was especially commended for gallant and conspicuous service in the Battle of Mobile Bay August 6, 1864; selected to command the U. S. S. "Olympia," flagship of the Asiatic Squadron; took command July 28, 1897; though ill at the time, refused to be relieved from duty and directed in person the movements of this vessel in the battle of Manila Bay, May 1, 1898; recommended to be advanced six numbers, for eminent and conspicuous conduct in battle. Died at Kobe, Japan, June 5, 1898, en route home after the battle. Death directly due to the strain of battle on his already depleted strength.

Dewey's memorable command "You may fire when ready, Gridley" was addressed to him.

GWIN

TORPEDO BOAT DESTROYER

Length, 314 feet   *Beam, 30 feet, 8 inches*   *Draft, 8 feet*

NAMED FOR LIEUTENANT COMMANDER
WILLIAM GWIN, U. S. NAVY

Launched December 22, 1917, at Seattle Construction & Dry Dock Company.

Sponsor: MRS. JAMES STERRETT WOODS (Dorothy Day), wife of Lieutenant Commander J. S. Woods, U. S. Navy.

LIEUTENANT COMMANDER WILLIAM GWIN, United States Navy, was born in Indiana, 1832; appointed midshipman 1847; commissioned lieutenant commander 1862; was mortally wounded in attack on Haines Bluff December 27, 1862, while in command of division of vessels, and died January 3, 1863. Rendered distinguished service in western waters and in the Mississippi Squadron.

Dimensions of Submarines H–3 to H–9, inclusive, are:

Length, 150 feet   *Beam, 15 feet, 9 inches*   *Draft, 12 feet, 4 inches*

H–3

SUBMARINE

Launched July 3, 1913, at Seattle D. D. & S. B. Company, Seattle, Washington.

Sponsor: MISS HELEN McEWAN, daughter of Mr. B. H. McEwan, of Seattle.

H–4

SUBMARINE

Launched October 9, 1918, at Puget Sound Navy Yard.

Sponsor: MRS. RALPH OTIS DAVIS (Anita Cresap), wife of Lieutenant R. O. Davis, U. S. Navy, the prospective commanding officer.

[85]

H-5
SUBMARINE

Launched September 24, 1918, at Puget Sound Navy Yard.

Sponsor: MISS MARY INGRAM HOOPES, daughter of Commander Edward T. Hoopes, U. S. Navy, Supply Corps.

H-6
SUBMARINE

Launched August 26, 1918, at U. S. Navy Yard, Puget Sound.

Sponsor: MISS CATHERINE ELY, daughter of Commander C. F. Ely, M. C., U. S. Navy. Medical Aide to the Commandant of the 13th Naval District.

H-7
SUBMARINE

Launched October 17, 1918, at Navy Yard, Puget Sound, Washington.

Sponsor: MISS JULIA FIELD, daughter of Captain Harry A. Field, U. S. Navy, in command of the Navy Yard.

H-8
SUBMARINE

Launched November 14, 1918, at Navy Yard, Puget Sound, Washington.

Sponsor: MRS. RALPH W. HOLT (Fay Sly), wife of Lieutenant R. W. Holt, U. S. Navy, prospective commanding officer.

H-9
SUBMARINE

Launched November 23, 1918, at Navy Yard, Puget Sound, Washington.

LAUNCH OF STEAM FRIGATE "FULTON"
THE FIRST IN 1814

Sponsor: Mrs. Vincendon L. Cottman (Elizabeth Klink), widow of Rear Admiral Cottman, U. S. Navy, formerly in command of the Navy Yard.

HALE

TORPEDO BOAT DESTROYER

Length, 314 feet   *Beam, 30 feet, 11 inches*   *Draft, 9 feet*

NAMED FOR UNITED STATES SENATOR
EUGENE HALE

Launched May 29, 1919, at Bath Iron Works, Bath, Me.

Sponsor: Miss Mary Cameron Hale, granddaughter of United States Senator Eugene Hale.

Hon. EUGENE HALE, Member of the United States Senate, 1881–1911. Born in Turner, Maine, 1836; died 1918. Admitted to the bar in 1857. For nine successive years was attorney for Hancock county. In 1867, 1868, and 1880 was member of the State (Maine) Legislature, and was elected to Congress from that State 1869, and served until 1879. Elected to the United States Senate March 4, 1881, and served in that body until March, 1911. He declined the position of Postmaster General offered him by President Grant and also declined the portfolio of Secretary of the Navy offered him by President Hayes. He was greatly interested in naval affairs and served for a number of years on the Naval committee; for some time as its chairman.

HAMILTON

TORPEDO BOAT DESTROYER

Length, 314 feet   *Beam, 30 feet, 11 inches*   *Draft, 9 feet*

NAMED FOR LIEUTENANT ARCHIBALD HAMILTON,
U. S. NAVY

Launched January 19, 1919, at Mare Island Navy Yard, California.

Sponsor: MISS DOLLIE HAMILTON HAWKINS, great-grandniece of Lieutenant Archibald Hamilton, U. S. Navy.

LIEUTENANT ARCHIBALD HAMILTON, U. S. Navy, appointed a midshipman, 1809; acting lieutenant, 1812; lieutenant, 1813. He was attached to the "United States" October 25, 1812, and served gallantly in the engagement and capture of H. B. M. S. "Macedonian" by that vessel. Was chosen to bear the flags captured on that occasion to the Navy Department. Killed January 15, 1815, on board the "President," in the action between that vessel and the British ships of war "Endymion" and "Pomona."

PAUL HAMILTON

TORPEDO BOAT DESTROYER
Length, 314 feet   *Beam, 30 feet, 11 inches*   *Draft, 9 feet, 4 inches*

NAMED FOR SECRETARY OF THE NAVY PAUL HAMILTON

Launched February 21, 1919, at Bethlehem Shipbuilding Corporation, San Francisco, California.

Sponsor: MISS JUSTINE McGRATH, daughter of Mr. Justin McGrath, editor of the "San Francisco Examiner."

HON. PAUL HAMILTON, who was Secretary of the Navy during the years 1809–1813, was born in St. Paul's Parish, South Carolina, 1762; died 1816. He rendered important services during the Revolution; was comptroller of South Carolina from 1799–1804, improving the financial system of the State; was governor of South Carolina 1804–1806, Secretary of the Navy 1809–1813.

HARADEN

TORPEDO BOAT DESTROYER
Length, 314 feet   *Beam, 30 feet, 11 inches*   *Draft, 9 feet, 3 inches*

NAMED FOR CAPTAIN JONATHAN HARADEN, U. S. NAVY

Launched July 4, 1918, at Newport News Shipbuilding Company, Newport News, Virginia.

Sponsor: MISS MABEL BEATRICE STEPHENS, nearest relative of Captain Jonathan Haraden, U. S. Navy.

CAPTAIN JONATHAN HARADEN, U. S. Navy, was born in Gloucester, Massachusetts, 1745; died in Salem, Massachusetts, 1803; was in command of the U. S. S. "General Pickering" in 1780, when he met and defeated the English privateer "Achilles," in an engagement lasting three hours. Farragut said of his fight with the "Achilles": "I would rather have fought that fight than any ever fought on the ocean." Captured 1000 guns during the war of 1812.

HARDING

TORPEDO BOAT DESTROYER

Length, 314 feet   *Beam, 30 feet, 11 inches*   *Draft, 9 feet, 2 inches*

NAMED FOR CAPTAIN SETH HARDING,
U. S. NAVY

Launched July 4, 1918, at Bethlehem Shipbuilding Corporation, San Francisco, California.

Sponsor: MRS. GEORGE A. ARMES (Katherine M.), wife of Mr. George A. Armes, Engineer-in-Chief at Union Iron Works for fifteen years.

CAPTAIN SETH HARDING, United States Navy, was born at Norwich, Connecticut. Appointed to command the Connecticut brigantine "Defence," February 3, 1776; captured a number of British vessels while in command of this ship; September 25, 1778, commissioned captain by Continental Congress, and given command of frigate "Confederacy"; 1779 convoyed the returning minister, M. Gerard, to France, and took Hon. John Jay, United States Minister, to Spain.

HART

TORPEDO BOAT DESTROYER
Length, 314 feet   *Beam, 30 feet, 11 inches*   *Draft, 9 feet, 2 inches*

NAMED FOR CAPTAIN EZEKIEL B. HART, U. S. NAVY, AND
LIEUTENANT COMMANDER JOHN E. HART, U. S. NAVY

Launched July 4, 1918, at Bethlehem Shipbuilding Corporation, San Francisco, California.

Sponsor: MRS. DANIEL C. NUTTING (Priscilla Dew), wife of Captain D. C. Nutting, C. C., U. S. Navy, Superintending Constructor at the shipyard at the time.

CAPTAIN EZEKIEL B. HART, U. S. Navy, entered the Navy as a midshipman April 30, 1814, and was killed in the action of Commodore Chauncey's squadron on Lake Ontario, August 26, 1814.

LIEUTENANT COMMANDER JOHN E. HART, U. S. Navy, was appointed a midshipman February 23, 1841; lieutenant commander July 16, 1862; distinguished himself in the engagements of the West Gulf blockading squadron, and died of fever contracted on duty in the Mississippi River while in command of the "Albatross," June 11, 1863.

HATFIELD

TORPEDO BOAT DESTROYER
Length, 314 feet   *Beam, 30 feet, 11 inches*   *Draft, 9 feet, 4 inches*

NAMED FOR MIDSHIPMAN JOHN HATFIELD,
U. S. NAVY

Launched March 17, 1919, at New York Shipbuilding Corporation, Camden, New Jersey.

Sponsor: MRS. J. EDMOND HAUGH (Helen Brooks), who served for nearly two years as chief yeoman, U. S. N. R. F., during the World War.

[90]

Midshipman JOHN HATFIELD, U. S. Navy. Appointed a midshipman, June 18, 1812. Volunteered for duty on Lake Ontario under Commodore Isaac Chauncey. Killed in the attack on York, Canada. He was in the detachment of officers and men from the U. S. S. "Lady of the Lake."

HAZELWOOD

TORPEDO BOAT DESTROYER

Length, 314 feet   *Beam, 30 feet, 11 inches*   *Draft, 9 feet, 2 inches*

NAMED FOR COMMODORE JOHN HAZELWOOD,
U. S. NAVY

Launched June 22, 1918, at Bethlehem Shipbuilding Corporation, San Francisco, California.

Sponsor: MISS MARION LOUISE NEITZEL, daughter of the Superintendent of Construction at the Shipbuilding Company.

Commodore JOHN HAZELWOOD, U. S. Navy, born in England about 1726; died 1800; appointed by the Pennsylvania Committee of Safety to superintend the building of fire rafts for the protection of Philadelphia; 1777, placed by the Continental Congress in command of the Continental vessels in the Delaware River, in conjunction with the vessels already under his command. He forced the British fleet below the American defenses in that river to retire, and drove H. B. M. S. "Augusta" and "Merlin" ashore, where they were burned. Congress voted him a handsome sword in recognition of his services in the Delaware River.

HENSHAW

TORPEDO BOAT DESTROYER

Length, 314 feet   *Beam, 30 feet, 11 inches*   *Draft, 9 feet, 4 inches*

NAMED FOR SECRETARY OF THE NAVY
DAVID HENSHAW

Launched June 28, 1919, at Bethlehem Shipbuilding Corporation, Quincy, Massachusetts.

Sponsor: MISS ETHEL HANLEY DEMPSEY, daughter of Mr. George C. Dempsey, Boston, Massachusetts.

SECRETARY OF THE NAVY DAVID HENSHAW was born in Leicester, Massachusetts, 1791; died 1852. He acquired note as a political writer and was elected to the State senate in 1826 and to the House of Representatives in 1839, after holding the post of collector of customs at Boston since 1830. He was very active in promoting the earlier railroad enterprises in Massachusetts. On July 24, 1843, he was appointed Secretary of the Navy.

HERBERT

TORPEDO BOAT DESTROYER

Length, 314 feet   *Beam, 30 feet, 11 inches*   *Draft, 9 feet, 4 inches*

NAMED FOR SECRETARY OF THE NAVY
HILARY ABNER HERBERT

Launched May 8, 1919, at New York Shipbuilding Corporation, Camden, New Jersey.

Sponsor: MRS. BENJAMIN MICOU (Ella Herbert), daughter of Secretary of the Navy Hilary Abner Herbert.

SECRETARY OF THE NAVY HILARY ABNER HERBERT was born in Laurensville, South Carolina, 1834. Educated at the universities of Alabama and Virginia; was admitted to the bar, and practiced in Greenville, Alabama. Was elected to Congress in 1877 and re-elected seven times. He was chairman of the Naval Committee in three Congresses. Appointed Secretary of the Navy on March 6, 1893, and held that office until 1897. Died 1919.

HERNDON

TORPEDO BOAT DESTROYER

Length, 314 feet   *Beam, 30 feet, 11 inches*   *Draft, 9 feet, 4 inches*

NAMED FOR COMMANDER WILLIAM LEWIS HERNDON,
U. S. NAVY

Launched May 31, 1919, at Newport News S. B. & D. D. Company, Newport News, Virginia.

Sponsor: MISS LUCY TAYLOR HERNDON, niece of Commander William Lewis Herndon, U. S. Navy.

COMMANDER WILLIAM LEWIS HERNDON, U. S. Navy, was born in Fredericksburg, Virginia, 1813. Appointed midshipman 1828; in 1847–1848 commanded the "Iris" and was actively employed in the Gulf of Mexico during the war with Mexico. In 1855 he was granted leave by the Navy Department to take command of the Pacific Mail steamer "George Law," afterwards the "Central America," running between New York and Aspinwall. This line of steamers at the time was required to be commanded by officers of the Navy. On September 7, 1857, when off Cape Hatteras, a heavy gale was encountered lasting almost a week. The steamer sprung a leak which extinguished the fires and left the vessel at the mercy of the waves. On September 12, the brig "Marine" of Boston was sighted; boats were lowered and Capt. Herndon remained on board directing the rescue work until the vessel went down. The last order of this gallant officer was to an approaching boat to "Keep off"; to have gone nearer would have swamped her.

HERON

MINE SWEEPER

Length, 187 feet	*Beam, 35 feet*	*Draft, 9 feet, 9 inches*

NAMED FOR THE BIRD HERON

Launched May 18, 1918, at Standard Shipbuilding Corporation, New York.

Sponsor: MISS ASTRID RUNDQUIST, daughter of Lieutenant K. Rundquist, U. S. Navy, prospective commanding officer.

[93]

HOGAN

TORPEDO BOAT DESTROYER

Length, 314 feet   *Beam, 30 feet, 11 inches*   *Draft, 9 feet, 2 inches*

NAMED FOR SEAMAN DANIEL HOGAN, U. S. NAVY

Launched April 12, 1919, at Bethlehem Shipbuilding Corporation, San Francisco, California.

Sponsor: MRS. MAGNUS A. ANDERSON (Maude Lane), sister of Secretary of the Interior, Hon. Franklin K. Lane.

SEAMAN DANIEL HOGAN, U. S. Navy, entered the United States Navy from Boston, Massachusetts, 1811, on the United States schooner "Revenge," commanded by Lieut. O. H. Perry; transferred to the U. S. S. "Constitution" February 18, 1811. On the "Constitution" during the engagement with the British frigate "Guerriere," and when the flag was shot away from the foretop-gallant masthead he climbed up and lashed it in place in the face of the firing. Remained on the "Constitution" and, in the fight between that ship and the "Java," January 3, 1813, was severely wounded, losing the fingers of both hands. He died September 1, 1818.

HOPEWELL

TORPEDO BOAT DESTROYER

Length, 314 feet   *Beam, 30 feet, 11 inches*   *Draft, 9 feet, 3 inches*

NAMED FOR MIDSHIPMAN POLLARD HOPEWELL,
U. S. NAVY

Launched June 8, 1918, Newport News Shipbuilding Co., Newport News, Virginia.

Sponsor: MRS. GROTE HUTCHESON (Rosalie St. George), wife of General Grote Hutcheson, U. S. Army.

MIDSHIPMAN POLLARD HOPEWELL, U. S. Navy, was appointed a midshipman, June 4, 1812. Served on the "Chesapeake" from August 21, 1812, until killed in action between that vessel and the British frigate "Shannon," June 1, 1813.

HOPKINS (2D)

TORPEDO BOAT DESTROYER

Length, 314 feet   *Beam, 30 feet, 11 inches*   *Draft, 9 feet, 4 inches*

NAMED FOR COMMODORE ESEK HOPKINS,
U. S. NAVY

Launched June 26, 1920, at New York Shipbuilding Corporation, Camden, New Jersey.

Sponsor: MISS SARAH A. H. BABBITT, great-great-great granddaughter of Commodore Esek Hopkins, U. S. Navy.

COMMODORE ESEK HOPKINS, U. S. Navy, was born in Scituate, Rhode Island, in 1718; died in 1802. He was the first commander-in-chief of the Continental Navy and the only officer in the Navy who has had that title, which is now borne by the president. He successfully harassed the British, although not strong enough to meet the enemy's fleets victoriously. Sailed with his fleet for the West Indies March 3, 1776, landed on the east end of the island of New Providence; captured the forts, secured cannon and supplies, captured the governor and lieutenant governor and took them as prisoners to the United States.

HOVEY

TORPEDO BOAT DESTROYER

Length, 314 feet   *Beam, 30 feet, 11 inches*   *Draft, 9 feet, 4 inches*

NAMED FOR ENSIGN CHARLES EMERSON HOVEY,
U. S. NAVY

Launched April 26, 1919, at William Cramp & Son's Company, Philadelphia, Pennsylvania.

Sponsor: MRS. AUSTIN KAUTZ (Louise Hovey), sister of Ensign Charles Emerson Hovey, U. S. Navy.

ENSIGN CHARLES EMERSON HOVEY, U. S. Navy, was born in Portsmouth, New Hampshire, January 10, 1885; died in the Philippines in 1911. Graduated from the United States Naval academy in 1907. A detachment of men from the U. S. S. "Pampanga," of which Ensign Hovey was in charge, September 11, 1911, was attacked by hostile natives on the Island of Basilan, Philippine Islands, and he was shot by one of the natives.

HOWARD

TORPEDO BOAT DESTROYER

Length, 314 feet   *Beam, 30 feet, 11 inches*   *Draft, 9 feet, 2 inches*

NAMED FOR ACTING ENSIGN CHARLES W. HOWARD, U. S. NAVY

Launched April 26, 1919, at Bethlehem Shipbuilding Corporation, San Francisco, California.

Sponsor: MISS MARION FILMER, daughter of Mr. W. P. Filmer, and appointed at the suggestion of Congressman William Kettner of California.

ACTING ENSIGN CHARLES W. HOWARD, U. S. Navy; appointed master's mate October 7, 1862; acting ensign, 1863; master, 1863. Died October 6, 1863, of wounds received in action at Charleston, South Carolina. Served on the ironclad "New Ironsides," South Atlantic Blockading Squadron, and took part in operations against defenses of Charleston Harbor. Dangerously wounded by rifle shot from the "David" that attacked the "New Ironsides," and attempted to blow her up in Charleston Harbor on the night of October 5, 1863. Promoted for his conspicuously brave conduct while in charge of the deck when the "Ironsides" was attacked.

HULBERT

TORPEDO BOAT DESTROYER

Length, 314 feet   *Beam, 30 feet, 11 inches*   *Draft, 9 feet, 4 inches*

NAMED FOR FIRST LIEUTENANT HENRY L. HULBERT,
U. S. MARINE CORPS

Launched June 28, 1919, at Navy Yard, Norfolk, Virginia.

Sponsor: MRS. VICTORIA C. HULBERT (Victoria Akelitys), widow of Lieutenant Henry L. Hulbert, U. S. Navy.

FIRST LIEUTENANT HENRY L. HULBERT, U. S. Marine Corps, was born 1867, in England; killed in action near Mount Blanc, October 5, 1918. Served over 20 years in the Marine Corps; held congressional medal of honor for bravery and distinguished service in Samoa in 1899; awarded the distinguished service cross for extraordinary heroism displayed at Chateau-Thierry June 6, 1918, where he displayed coolness and courage in directing his platoon in attack during which he was badly wounded but refused assistance until wounded men near him had been treated.

Awarded Croix de Guerre with palm, October 3, 1918, when he coolly and courageously led his men under enemy fire. Awarded decoration of Navy Cross posthumously.

HULL (3D)

TORPEDO BOAT DESTROYER

Length, 314 feet, 4 inches   Beam, 30 feet, 11 inches   Draft, 9 feet, 4 inches

NAMED FOR COMMODORE ISAAC HULL
U. S. NAVY

Launched February 18, 1921, at Bethlehem Shipbuilding Corporation, San Francisco, California.

Sponsor: MISS ELIZABETH HULL, a direct descendant of Commodore Isaac Hull, U. S. Navy.

COMMODORE ISAAC HULL, U. S. Navy, was born in Connecticut in 1775. His father was an officer in the revolutionary army and was captured and died aboard a British prison ship. Young Hull's first service of note was when he sailed in a small vessel "Sally" into the Harbor of

[97]

Port Platte, Haiti, in broad daylight, captured the fort, spiked the guns and succeeded in getting away with a French letter of marque. He served under Commodore Preble at Tripoli. His most noted command was the "Constitution" in 1811. He displayed brilliant seamanship when he escaped the British Squadron under Admiral Blake in 1812.

HUMPHREYS

TORPEDO BOAT DESTROYRE

Length, 314 feet   *Beam, 30 feet, 11 inches*   *Draft, 9 feet, 4 inches*

NAMED FOR NAVAL CONSTRUCTOR JOSHUA HUMPHREYS, U. S. NAVY

Launched July 28, 1919, New York Shipbuilding Corporation, Camden, New Jersey.

Sponsor: MISS LETITIA A. HUMPHREYS, great-granddaughter of Naval Constructor Joshua Humphreys, U. S. Navy.

NAVAL CONSTRUCTOR JOSHUA HUMPHREYS was born in Haverford, Pennsylvania, 1751; died 1838. In the Revolutionary War was commissioned by the Pennsylvania Committee of Safety to build a "galley," which is said to have been the first armed vessel built during that war. When the Navy was reorganized by act of Congress, March 27, 1784, he was appointed to prepare plans for six ships to be built for the Government. Was commissioned naval constructor June 28, 1794. He was constructor for the "Constitution," "Chesapeake," "Congress," "President," "Constellation," and "United States."

HUNT

TORPEDO BOAT DESTROYER

Length, 314 feet   *Beam, 30 feet, 11 inches*   *Draft, 9 feet, 4 inches*

NAMED FOR SECRETARY OF THE NAVY, WILLIAM HENRY HUNT

Launched February 14, 1920, Newport News S. B. & D. D. Company, Newport News, Virginia.

Sponsor: MISS VIRGINIA LIVINGSTON HUNT, granddaughter of Secretary of the Navy William Henry Hunt.

SECRETARY OF THE NAVY WILLIAM HENRY HUNT was born in Charleston, South Carolina, in 1823; died 1884; was educated at Yale College and removed to New Orleans, where he was admitted to the bar. In 1876 he was appointed attorney general of the State of Louisiana, 1878 judge of the Court of Claims, 1881 Secretary of the Navy. In 1882 was U. S. Minister to Russia where he died at St. Petersburg on February 17, 1884.

IDAHO (3D)

BATTLESHIP

Length, 624 feet   *Beam, 97 feet, 4½ inches*   *Draft, 30 feet*

NAMED FOR THE STATE OF IDAHO

(Admitted to the Union in 1890)

Launched June 30, 1917, at New York Shipbuilding Corporation, Camden, New Jersey.

Sponsor: MISS HENRIETTA AMELIA SIMONS, Boise, Idaho, granddaughter of Governor Moses Alexander of Idaho. At her side stood Miss Honora Dever. "I name thee 'Idaho,'" said Miss Simons as she sent a bottle of champagne crashing against the side of the warship.

As the champagne struck the vessel Miss Dever broke a bottle of water from the Snake River, Idaho, over the opposite side, and the "Idaho" had been formally christened with both wine and water. The Society of Sponsors' "Prayer for our Navy" was offered by Chaplain Dickins, U. S. Navy, just before the launching: "May they not bear the sword in vain, but as a minister of God be a terror to those who do evil and a defense to those who do good," sounded the solemn key note of this launching of a battle ship in war time.

The greatest secrecy surrounded the launching. Only seven persons composed the governor's party. They were

Governor Alexander; his granddaughter, the sponsor; Mrs. Simons; T. A. Walters, Attorney General of Idaho; Colonel Dolphin of the Governor's staff; Miss Honora Dever, and Mrs. Gerson L. Levi.

The super dreadnaught "Idaho" is the third vessel to bear the name. Her predecessor, the battleship "Idaho," launched in 1905, was the second ship to bear the name. The first "Idaho" was a wooden sloop of the first rate launched in 1864.

INGRAHAM

TORPEDO BOAT DESTROYER

Length, 314 feet　　　*Beam, 30 feet, 11 inches*　　　*Draft, 9 feet, 1 inch*

NAMED FOR CAPTAIN DUNCAN N. INGRAHAM, U. S. NAVY

Launched July 4, 1918, at Bethlehem Shipbuilding Corporation, San Francisco, California.

Sponsor: MRS. ALFRED S. GUNN (Esther Roberts), wife of the Assistant General Manager of the Shipbuilding plant.

CAPTAIN DUNCAN N. INGRAHAM, United States Navy, was born in Charlestown, South Carolina, 1802; died 1891. Appointed midshipman 1812; captain 1855. While in command of the sloop of war "St. Louis" in the Mediterranean in July, 1853, he interfered at Smyrna with the detention by the Austrian consul of Martin Koszta, a Hungarian, who had declared in New York his intention of becoming an American citizen, and who had been seized and confined on board the Austrian ship "Hussar." For his conduct in the matter, he was voted thanks and a medal by Congress. Chief of the Bureau of Ordnance and Hydrography of the Navy Department from 1856 to 1860.

INGRAM

TORPEDO BOAT DESTROYER

Length, 314 feet　　　*Beam, 30 feet, 11 inches*　　　*Draft, 9 feet, 2 inches*

NAMED FOR OSMOND KELLEY INGRAM, GUNNER'S MATE, U. S. NAVY

Launched February 28, 1919, at Bethlehem Shipbuilding Corporation, Quincy, Massachusetts.

Sponsor: MRS. BETTY INGRAM (Mrs. N. E. Ingram), mother of Osmond Kelley Ingram.

OSMOND KELLEY INGRAM, Gunner's Mate, First Class, U. S. Navy, was born in Pratt City, Alabama, 1887. Killed when the destroyer "Cassin" was torpedoed in European waters October 16, 1917. Ingram, who saw a torpedo coming from a German submarine toward the stern of the "Cassin," and realized that, if the torpedo struck that part of the vessel where certain high explosives were placed the vessel would be blown up, instead of saving himself, deliberately went aft to throw these charges overboard before the torpedo struck, and while doing this was blown overboard and his body was not recovered. He sacrificed his life to save his ship and the lives of the officers and men on board.

ISHERWOOD

TORPEDO BOAT DESTROYER

Length, 314 feet   *Beam, 30 feet, 11 inches*   *Draft, 9 feet, 4 inches*

NAMED FOR REAR ADMIRAL BENJAMIN FRANKLIN ISHERWOOD, U. S. NAVY

Launched September 10, 1919, at Bethlehem Shipbuilding Company, Quincy, Massachusetts.

Sponsor: MRS. RALPH G. WALLING (Norma R.), wife of Commander Walling, U. S. Navy, Assistant Inspector of Machinery at Squantum Works.

REAR ADMIRAL BENJAMIN FRANKLIN ISHERWOOD, U. S. Navy, was born in New York, 1822; died, 1915. Appointed a first assistant engineer in the Navy, 1844; served during the Mexican War on the U. S. S.

"Princeton," and as senior engineer of the "Spitfire"; chief engineer of the "San Jacinto." Immediately after the outbreak of the Civil War was appointed engineer-in-chief of the Navy, and so important were his services considered that the Bureau of Steam Engineering was created for him. In the production of fast cruisers he was a pioneer, producing this class against most violent opposition. After leaving the Bureau of Steam Engineering, he became chief engineer of the Mare Island Navy Yard. President of the Experimental Board under the Bureau of Steam Engineering, which position he held up to the time of his retirement on October 6, 1884.

ISRAEL

TORPEDO BOAT DESTROYER

Length, 314 feet   *Beam, 30 feet, 11 inches*   *Draft, 9 feet, 1 inch*

NAMED FOR MIDSHIPMAN JOSEPH ISRAEL

Launched June 22, 1918, at Bethlehem Shipbuilding Corporation, Quincy, Massachusetts.

Sponsor: MISS DOROTHY BROWN, daughter of Mr. Harry Brown of Bethlehem, Pennsylvania.

MIDSHIPMAN JOSEPH ISRAEL, United States Navy, was appointed midshipman January 15, 1801; blown up by explosion on the ketch "Intrepid," September 4, 1804, having volunteered his services for expedition against Tripolitan ships in the harbor of Tripoli.

REUBEN JAMES

TORPEDO BOAT DESTROYER

Length, 314 feet   *Beam, 30 feet, 11 inches*   *Draft, 9 feet, 4 inches*

NAMED FOR BOATSWAIN'S MATE, REUBEN JAMES, U. S. NAVY

Launched October 4, 1919, at New York Shipbuilding Corporation, Camden, New Jersey.

Sponsor: MISS HELEN LIVINGSTON STRAUSS, daughter of Rear Admiral Joseph Strauss, U. S. Navy.

REUBEN JAMES, boatswain's mate, United States Navy, was born in Delaware about 1776; served under Commodore Truxtun on the "Constellation," 1779-1800, and took part in engagements with "L'Insurgente" and "La Vengeance;" saw active service in the operations against Tripoli, 1803-1805; volunteered and was one of the party that boarded the "Philadelphia," in the harbor of Tripoli, and assisted in her destruction after capture; was wounded in the fierce fight; took part in the engagement of August 3, 1804, between the Tripolitan boats and the gunboats of the United States; saved the life of Capt. Decatur when, in the hand-to-hand fight, he was knocked down by a Tripolitan and the scimiter of another was about to fall upon him, James interposed his own body and received the blow intended for his commander. He recovered from this and other wounds and followed Capt. Decatur to other ships. Took part in the battle with and capture of the "Macedonian"; was wounded on the "President" in her running fight of six hours with the British squadron January 15, 1915; made prisoner until close of the war, then returned to the United States.

JACOB JONES (1ST)

TORPEDO BOAT DESTROYER

Length, 310 feet　　　　*Beam, 30 feet*　　　　*Draft, 9 feet, 8 inches*

NAMED FOR COMMODORE JACOB JONES, U. S. NAVY

Launched May 29, 1915, at the New York Shipbuilding Company, Camden, New Jersey.

Sponsor: MRS. JEROME PARKER CRITTENDON (Pauline Cazenove Jones), great-granddaughter of Commodore Jacob Jones, U. S. Navy.

COMMODORE JACOB JONES, United States Navy, was born in Delaware in 1768; died 1850. Appointed midshipman, 1799; commissioned captain, 1813. His first cruise was with Capt. John Barry in the "United States," carrying commissioners Ellsworth and Davies to France; 1803 assigned to the "Philadelphia," commanded by Capt. William Bainbridge. This frigate struck on a rock in the harbor of Tripoli, could not get off, and was taken possession of by the Tripolitans, who held her officers prisoners for 20 months. Upon his release, Jones returned to the United States. In 1810 in command of the "Wasp," and was in command of her when the war with England broke out. His first prize was the brig "Dolphin." The "Wasp" sailed from the capes of Delaware, and October 18, 1812, encountered the British ship of war "Frolic"; a severe engagement followed, lasting 43 minutes, when the "Frolic" surrendered. He was ordered to assist Commodore Chauncey on Lake Ontario, where he rendered valuable service until the close of the war. Commanded the "Macedonian," and joined the squadron under Commodore Decatur in the Mediterranean, operating against the Algerines. He captured an Algerine brig and took part in securing the permanent peace with the Barbary powers. In 1821–1824 he commanded the Mediterranean Squadron; 1824–1826 was one of the Board of Navy Commissioners; 1826–1830 he commanded the Pacific station.

JACOB JONES (2D)

TORPEDO BOAT DESTROYER

Length, 314 feet   *Beam, 30 feet, 11 inches*   *Draft, 9 feet, 4 inches*

NAMED FOR COMMODORE JACOB JONES, U. S. NAVY

Launched November 20, 1918, New York Shipbuilding Corporation, Camden, New Jersey.

Sponsor: MRS. CAZENOVE DOUGHTEN (Florence Cazenove Jones), great-granddaughter of Captain Jacob Jones. NOTE: See "Jacob Jones (1ST)."

PAUL JONES (4TH)

TORPEDO BOAT DESTROYER

Length, 314 feet   *Beam, 30 feet, 11 inches*   *Draft, 9 feet, 4 inches*

U. S. TORPEDO BOAT DESTROYER "REUBEN JAMES" GOING FULL SPEED

NAMED FOR COMMODORE JOHN PAUL JONES,
U. S. NAVY

Launched September 30, 1920, at William Cramp & Sons' Company, Philadelphia, Pennsylvania.

Sponsor: MISS ETHEL BAGLEY, sister-in-law of Secretary of the Navy Josephus Daniels.

COMMODORE JOHN PAUL JONES, United States Navy, was born in Scotland in 1747. In 1775 was appointed first lieutenant of the "Alfred," the first American flagship. He hoisted the first Continental flag afloat, the yellow flag with rattlesnake and pine tree. In 1776, in command of the "Alfred" and "Providence," captured many prizes.

In command of the "Ranger," at Quiberon Bay, February 14, 1778, he received from the French fleet the first salute to the Stars and Stripes. In the "Ranger," captured the British sloop-of-war, "Drake." Jones was the terror of British shipping and seaport towns.

In 1779, in the "Bon Homme Richard," whipped the "Serapis," after his own ship was practically a wreck. He moved his men to the "Serapis" just before his own ship went down, saying, "I have not yet begun to fight."

Commodore Jones was knighted by France and presented with a sword by the king. Congress gave him a vote of thanks and command of the "America," then building. The "America" was the first ship-of-the-line launched in America and Paul Jones was aboard.

WILLIAM JONES

TORPEDO BOAT DESTROYER

Length, 314 feet   *Beam, 30 feet, 11 inches*   *Draft, 9 feet, 4 inches*

NAMED FOR SECRETARY OF THE NAVY
WILLIAM JONES

Launched April 19, 1919, at Bethlehem Shipbuilding Corporation, San Francisco, California.

[105]

Sponsor: MRS. ERNEST P. McRITCHIE (Isabel R.), wife of Assistant Naval Architect E. P. McRitchie, of the Bethlehem Shipbuilding Corporation.

HON. WILLIAM JONES, Secretary of the Navy during the years 1813–1814, was born in Pennsylvania in 1760; died 1831. He joined a volunteer company at the age of 16 and was present at the battles of Trenton and Princeton. Afterwards he entered the Continental naval service and served gallantly under Commodore Truxtun on the James River when that officer encountered and beat off a British ship. He then entered the merchant service, but in 1790–1793 lived in Charleston, South Carolina. He returned to Philadelphia in the latter year and was elected to Congress, serving one term in 1801–1803.

Dimensions of Submarines K–1 to K–8, inclusive, are:
Length, 153 feet, 6 inches   Beam, 16 feet, 8 inches   Draft, 13 feet, 1 inch

K–1
SUBMARINE

Launched September 3, 1913, at Fore River Shipbuilding Corporation, Quincy, Massachusetts.

Sponsor: MRS. ALBERT WARE MARSHALL (Mabel Flinn), wife of Lieutenant Commander A. W. Marshall, U. S. Navy, on duty at the ship yard.

K–2
SUBMARINE

Launched October 4, 1913, at Fore River Shipbuilding Corporation, Quincy, Massachusetts.

Sponsor: MISS RUTH CHAMBERLAIN McENTEE, daughter of Naval Constructor William McEntee, U. S. Navy.

K–3
SUBMARINE

Launched March 14, 1914, at Union Iron Works, San Francisco, California.

[106]

Sponsor: MRS. CLARENCE MEIGS ODDIE (Alice Treanor), sister-in-law of Governor Tasker L. Oddie of Nevada.

K-4
SUBMARINE

Launched March 19, 1914, at Seattle Construction Company.

Sponsor: MRS. JAMES P. OLDING (Ethelyn Hofer), wife of Lieutenant J. P. Olding, U. S. Navy, on duty at the shipyard at the time.

K-5
SUBMARINE

Launched March 17, 1914, at Fore River Shipbuilding Corporation, Quincy, Massachusetts.

Sponsor: MRS. WARREN G. CHILD (Julie McGuire), wife of Lieutenant W. G. Child, U. S. Navy, on duty at the shipyard at the time.

K-6
SUBMARINE

Launched March 26, 1914, at Fore River Shipbuilding Corporation, Quincy, Massachusetts.

Sponsor: MRS. THOMAS GAINES ROBERTS (Ethel Trowbridge), wife of Naval Constructor T. G. Roberts, U. S. Navy, superintending constructor at the shipyard at the time.

K-7
SUBMARINE

Launched June 20, 1914, at Union Iron Works, San Francisco, California.

Sponsor: MISS KATIE-BEL McGREGOR, daughter of the president of the Union Iron Works.

[107]

K–8
SUBMARINE

Launched July 11, 1914, at Union Iron Works, San Francisco, California.

Sponsor: Mrs. John William Lewis (Lenore Musto), wife of Lieutenant J. W. Lewis, U. S. Navy.

KALK

TORPEDO BOAT DESTROYER

Length, 314 feet   *Beam, 30 feet, 11 inches*   *Draft, 9 feet*

Named for Lieutenant Stanton F. Kalk, U. S. Navy

Launched December 21, 1918, at Bethlehem Shipbuilding Corporation, Quincy, Massachusetts.

Sponsor: Mrs. Frank G. Kalk (Flora Stanton), mother of Lieutenant Stanton F. Kalk, U. S. Navy.

Lieutenant STANTON F. KALK, U. S. Navy, was born in Alabama, 1894. Appointed a midshipman, 1912. Graduated 1916, and assigned to the battleship "Florida" as junior lieutenant. Died December 6, 1917, when the destroyer "Jacob Jones" was torpedoed by a German submarine, from exposure while endeavoring to save the lives of others. He was praised in the official report of the disaster to the "Jacob Jones" for his promptness in measures taken to avoid the enemy's weapon of destruction and for his general ability as an officer.

KANAWHA

FUEL SHIP

Length, 475 feet   *Beam, 56 feet*   *Draft, 26 feet, 2 inches*

Named for Kanawha River

Launched July 11, 1914, at Mare Island Navy Yard, California.

Sponsor: MISS DOROTHY BENNETT, daughter of Captain Frank M. Bennett, U. S. Navy Commandant of the Navy Yard.

KANE

TORPEDO BOAT DESTROYER

Length, 314 feet   Beam, 30 feet, 11 inches   Draft, 9 feet, 4 inches

NAMED FOR SURGEON ELISHA KENT KANE, U. S. NAVY

Launched August 12, 1919, at New York Shipbuilding Corporation, Camden, New Jersey.

Sponsor: MISS FLORENCE BAYARD KANE, niece of Surgeon Elisha Kent Kane, U. S. Navy.

SURGEON ELISHA KENT KANE, U. S. Navy, was born in Philadelphia, Pennsylvania, 1820; died 1857. Appointed assistant surgeon, 1843. Served in the East India Squadron, African and Home Squadrons. Saw active service with the marines in the Mexican War and was wounded. On May 22, 1850, on the "Advance," went on Arctic expedition in search of Sir John Franklin and companions. In 1853 sailed on the second Grinnell expedition to the Arctic regions; attained the highest latitude up to that period and made valuable discoveries; was highly honored by many scientific associations. The United States presented him with Arctic medals and the English Government gave him the Queen's medal.

KENNEDY

TORPEDO BOAT DESTROYER

Length, 314 feet   Beam, 30 feet, 11 inches   Draft, 9 feet, 4 inches

NAMED FOR SECRETARY OF THE NAVY JOHN PENDLETON KENNEDY

Launched February 15, 1919, Bethlehem Shipbuilding Corporation, San Francisco, California.

Sponsor: MRS. EUGENE F. ESSNER (Dora T.), wife of the Superintendent of Machinery at the works.

HON. JOHN PENDLETON KENNEDY, who was Secretary of the Navy 1852–1856, was born in Baltimore, Maryland, 1795; died in 1870. He was graduated at Baltimore College (now the University of Maryland) in 1812. He was admitted to the bar in 1816. In 1820 and for two successive years he was elected to the Maryland House of Delegates. In 1838 he was elected to Congress and was a member of that body during practically all of the succeeding years until he was appointed Secretary of the Navy in 1852. It was under his administration that Commander Perry's expedition visited Japan and that Dr. Kane's second Arctic voyage was made.

KENNISON

TORPEDO BOAT DESTROYER

Length, 314 feet *Beam, 30 feet, 11 inches* *Draft, 9 feet*

NAMED FOR ACTING VOLUNTEER LIEUTENANT WILLIAM W. KENNISON, U. S. NAVY

Launched June 8, 1918, at Mare Island Navy Yard, California.

Sponsor: MISS ELIZABETH RINER, sister of Major Clarence C. Riner, U. S. M. C.

ACTING VOLUNTEER LIEUTENANT WILLIAM W. KENNISON, U. S. Navy; appointed acting master's mate August 28, 1861; acting volunteer lieutenant March 26, 1862. Honorably discharged May 4, 1866; reappointed acting master August 20, 1866; mustered out November 16, 1868. Promoted for gallant conduct in action between the C. S. S. "Merrimac" and the U. S. S. "Cumberland" March 8, 1862.

A GOOD LUCK SHOWER!

KIDDER

TORPEDO BOAT DESTROYER

Length, 314 feet　　*Beam, 30 feet, 11 inches*　　*Draft, 9 feet, 4 inches*

NAMED FOR LIEUTENANT HUGH P. KIDDER,
U. S. MARINE CORPS

Launched July 10, 1919, at Bethlehem Shipbuilding Corporation, San Francisco, California.

Sponsor: MISS ETHEL MURRAY JOHNSTONE, daughter of Mr. Robert M. Johnstone, of the Woodwork Department of the Shipbuilding Company.

FIRST LIEUTENANT HUGH P. KIDDER, U. S. Marine Corps, was born in Waukon, Iowa, 1897; awarded the croix de guerre with palm and star for courage and endurance displayed in carrying orders to advanced positions for a period of nine days under violent machine gun and artillery fire. Awarded distinguished service cross for extraordinary heroism in action near Blanc Mont, France, October 2–3, 1918, when he led a small patrol into enemy trenches and captured two strong machine gun positions; killed in action October 3, 1918, while attempting to better his position in the face of a heavy machine gun and artillery fire.

KILTY

TORPEDO BOAT DESTROYER

Length, 314 feet　　*Beam, 30 feet, 11 inches*　　*Draft, 9 feet*

NAMED FOR REAR ADMIRAL AUGUSTUS H. KILTY,
U. S. NAVY

Launched April 25, 1918, at Mare Island Navy Yard, California.

Sponsor: MISS ELIZABETH HARRISON SHAPLEY, daughter of Commander Lloyd S. Shapley, U. S. Navy.

REAR ADMIRAL AUGUSTUS H. KILTY, U. S. Navy, was born in Maryland; died 1879. Appointed midshipman, 1821; commissioned rear admiral, 1870. Served on the Pacific, Asiatic, Mediterranean, and African Stations. Took part in operations of the squadron under Commodore George Reid against Quallah Battoo, February, 1832, in defense of American merchantmen. During the Civil War was conspicuous for his activity and bravery on the western waters; at Island No. 10, and Fort Pillow; commanded an expedition to White River, Arkansas, and during an action of June 17, 1862, was severely wounded, causing the loss of his left arm.

KIMBERLY

TORPEDO BOAT DESTROYER

Length, 314 feet   *Beam, 30 feet, 11 inches*   *Draft, 9 feet, 2 inches*

NAMED FOR REAR ADMIRAL LEWIS ASHFIELD KIMBERLY, U. S. NAVY

Launched December 4, 1917, at Fore River Shipbuilding Company, Quincy, Massachusetts.

Sponsor: MISS ELSIE S. KIMBERLY, daughter of Rear Admiral Lewis Ashfield Kimberly, U. S. Navy.

REAR ADMIRAL LEWIS ASHFIELD KIMBERLY was born in Troy, New York, 1830; died 1902. Appointed midshipman, 1846; commissioned rear admiral, 1887; 1847 to 1860 in the African, Pacific and East India squadrons; Civil War, served on "Potomac" in west blockading squadron; took part in operations on Mississippi River at Port Hudson, Grand Gulf, Vicksburg, and other places; executive officer of "Hartford" at battle of Mobile Bay, and warmly commended for gallant and efficient service; 1866 to 1889 cruised in European, Atlantic, Pacific, and East India Stations; commanded land forces in attack on Korean ports, June 10–11, 1871.

KING

TORPEDO BOAT DESTROYER

Length, 314 feet   *Beam, 30 feet, 4 inches*   *Draft, 9 feet, 4 inches*

NAMED FOR COMMANDER FRANK R. KING, U. S. NAVY

Launched October 14, 1920, at New York Shipbuilding Corporation, Camden, New Jersey.

Sponsor: MRS. ALLENE A. KING, widow of Commander Frank R. King, U. S. Navy.

COMMANDER FRANK R. KING, United States Navy, was born at Montevallo, Alabama, 1884; died 1919, when the United States trawler "Richard Buckley" was sunk by an exploding mine. Appointed midshipman 1903; ensign 1909; lieutenant (j. g.) 1912; lieutenant 1915; lieutenant commander 1917; commander 1918; command of the trawler "Richard Buckley" July 7, 1919; lost at sea July 12, 1919, when that vessel struck a mine which exploded near the stern, sinking the ship in seven minutes. Commander King exerted himself to see that all were saved, and remained on the bridge until the last, going down with the ship.

KINGFISHER
MINE SWEEPER
Length, 187 feet *Beam, 35 feet* *Draft, 9 feet, 9 inches*
NAMED FOR THE BIRD KINGFISHER

Launched March 30, 1918, at Navy Yard, Puget Sound, Washington.

Sponsor: MISS NANCY GRISWOLD, daughter of Commander R. M. Griswold, U. S. Navy, on duty at the yard.

Dimensions of Submarines L-1 to L-4, inclusive, are:
Length, 168 feet, 5 inches *Beam, 17 feet, 5 inches* *Draft, 13 feet, 7 inches*

L–1
SUBMARINE

Launched January 20, 1915, at Fore River Shipbuilding Corporation, Quincy, Massachusetts.

Sponsor: MRS. FREELAND A. DAUBIN (Elizabeth Scott), wife of Lieutenant F. A. Daubin, U. S. Navy, first to command the L–1.

L–2
SUBMARINE

Launched February 11, 1915, at Fore River Shipbuilding Corporation, Quincy, Massachusetts.

Sponsor: MRS. RUSSELL GRAY (Amy Heard), mother of Lieutenant Commander Augustine H. Gray, U. S. Navy, first to command the L–2.

L–3
SUBMARINE

Launched March 15, 1915, at Fore River Shipbuilding Corporation, Quincy, Massachusetts.

Sponsor: MRS. LEW MORTON ATKINS (Charlotte Steele), wife of Naval Constructor L. W. Atkins, U. S. Navy, Assistant Superintending Constructor at Fore River S. B. Corporation.

L–4
SUBMARINE

Launched April 3, 1915, at Fore River Shipbuilding Corporation, Quincy, Massachusetts.

Sponsor: MRS. STEPHEN AYRAULT GARDNER (Florence Loomis), wife of the Quincy Manager of the Electric Boat Company.

Dimensions of Submarines L–5 to L–8, inclusive, are:

Length, 165 feet   *Beam, 14 feet, 9 inches*   *Draft, 13 feet, 3 inches*

L–5
SUBMARINE

Launched May 1, 1916, at Lake Torpedo Boat Company, Bridgeport, Connecticut.

Sponsor: MISS ROSALIND ROBINSON, daughter of former Naval Constructor R. H. M. Robinson, the General Manager of the Lake Torpedo Boat Company.

L–6
SUBMARINE

Launched August 31, 1916, at California Shipping Company, Long Beach, California.

Sponsor: MRS. WILLIAM ROBERT MUNROE (Katherine Johnson), wife of Lieutenant W. R. Munroe, U. S. Navy, Inspector of Machinery for the Navy at Long Beach.

L–7
SUBMARINE

Launched September 28, 1916, at California Shipping Company, Long Beach, California.

Sponsor: MRS. WILLIAM B. FOGARTY (Sarah Lloyd), wife of Naval Constructor W. B. Fogarty, U. S. Navy, Superintending Constructor.

L–8
SUBMARINE

Launched April 23, 1917, at Navy Yard, Portsmouth, New Hampshire.

Sponsor: MISS NANCY GILL, daughter of Lieutenant Charles C. Gill, U. S. Navy, and granddaughter of Rear Admiral W. L. Howard, U. S. Navy.

Dimensions of Submarines L–9 to L–11, inclusive, are:
Length, 168 feet, 5 inches   Beam, 17 feet, 5 inches   Draft, 13 feet, 7 inches

L–9
SUBMARINE

Launched October 27, 1915, at Fore River Shipbuilding Corporation, Quincy, Massachusetts.

[115]

Sponsor: MISS HEATHER PATTISON BAXTER, daughter of Naval Constructor W. J. Baxter, U. S. Navy, Chief Constructor at Navy Yard, Boston, Massachusetts.

L–10
SUBMARINE

Launched March 16, 1916, at Fore River Shipbuilding Corporation, Quincy, Massachusetts.

Sponsor: MISS CATHERINE RUSH, daughter of Captain William R. Rush, U. S. Navy, in command of Navy Yard, Boston, Massachusetts.

L–11
SUBMARINE

Launched May 16, 1916, at Fore River Shipbuilding Corporation, Quincy, Massachusetts.

Sponsor: MISS MARY RICHARDS LATIMER, daughter of Commander J. L. Latimer, U. S. Navy.

LAMBERTON
TORPEDO BOAT DESTROYER
Length, 314 feet   Beam, 30 feet, 11 inches   Draft, 9 feet, 3 inches

NAMED FOR REAR ADMIRAL BENJAMIN P. LAMBERTON, U. S. NAVY

Launched March 30, 1918, at Newport News Shipbuilding Company, Newport News, Virginia.

Sponsor: MISS ISABEL STEDMAN LAMBERTON, granddaughter of Rear Admiral Benjamin P. Lamberton, U. S. Navy.

REAR ADMIRAL BENJAMIN P. LAMBERTON, U. S. Navy, was born in Pennsylvania, 1844; died, 1912. Appointed a midshipman, 1861; commissioned rear admiral, 1903. Served, 1865–1898, on the "Brazil," South Atlantic, Pacific and North Atlantic stations, and held important positions on shore. In 1898 he was ordered to the Asiatic Fleet to command the "Boston," but Captain Wilde who was in command did not wish to give up command in the face of battle and Commander Lamberton was then made Chief of Staff to Admiral Dewey. After the battle of Manila Bay he went in and negotiated the terms of surrender of Cavite, and after the stars and stripes were hoisted he took the surrender flag which was later placed at the Naval Academy, Annapolis. When Captain Gridley was ordered to the hospital he was made commander of the "Olympia" bringing home Admiral Dewey. He was later advanced seven numbers for conspicuous gallantry during the battle of Manila Bay May 1, 1898.

LAMSON (2D)

TORPEDO BOAT DESTROYER

Length, 314 feet   *Beam, 30 feet, 11 inches*   *Draft, 9 feet, 4 inches*

NAMED FOR LIEUTENANT ROSWELL H. LAMSON, U. S. NAVY

Launched September 1, 1920, at Bethlehem Shipbuilding Company, San Francisco, California.

Sponsor: MISS ANNETTE REID ROLPH, daughter of Hon. James Rolph, Mayor of San Francisco.

LIEUTENANT ROSWELL H. LAMSON, United States Navy, was appointed midshipman in 1858. He was commended by Admiral du Pont for conduct in the battle of Port Royal and captures of Forts Walker and Beauregard in 1861. Commanded the "Mount Washington" in joint Army and Navy operations in Nansemond River. Took prominent and leading part in capture of batteries at Hills Point. Congratulated by Admiral Lee for performance of this duty. Commanding the "Gettysburg," took prominent part in attack on Fort Fisher and gallantly piloted powder-boat "Louisiana" in under the fort. He resigned in 1866. In 1895 in recognition of splendid Civil War service he was reappointed lieutenant and placed on the retired list.

[117]

LANGLEY (JUPITER)

AIRCRAFT CARRIER

Length, 542 feet   *Beam, 65 feet*   *Draft, 18 feet, 10 inches*

NAMED ORIGINALLY "JUPITER" FOR JUPITER THE
CHIEF GOD OF THE ROMANS. RENAMED LANGLEY
FOR PROFESSOR SAMUEL PIERPONT LANGLEY

Launched August 24, 1912, at Mare Island Navy Yard.
Rebuilt at Norfolk Navy Yard in 1920.

Sponsor: MRS. THOMAS F. RUHM (Edana Collins), wife
of Naval Constructor T. F. Ruhm, U. S. Navy.

PROF. SAMUEL PIERPONT LANGLEY, born in Rox-
bury, near Boston, Massachusetts, in August, 1834; died
in Aiken, South Carolina, February 27, 1906. Distinguished
American astronomer and physicist; received degrees from
Oxford, Cambridge, England; Harvard, Princeton, Yale,
and many other universities and colleges; 1865 assistant
in Harvard Observatory; 1866 assistant professor of mathe-
matics, United States Naval Academy; 1867 director
Allegheny Observatory; founded the system of railway
time service from observatories; devised the bolometer
and other scientific apparatus; 1881 organized a successful
scientific expedition to Mount Whitney, California; made
extended experiments to solve mechanical flying.

LANSDALE

TORPEDO BOAT DESTROYER

Length, 314 feet   *Beam, 30 feet, 11 inches*   *Draft, 9 feet, 2 inches*

NAMED FOR LIEUTENANT PHILIP VAN HORNE
LANSDALE, U. S. NAVY

Launched July 21, 1918, at Bethlehem Shipbuilding
Corporation, Fore River, Massachusetts.

Sponsor: MRS. PHILIP VAN HORNE LANSDALE (Ethel
Sidney Smith), widow of Lieutenant Philip Van Horne
Lansdale, U. S. Navy.

[118]

LIEUTENANT PHILIP VAN HORNE LANSDALE, United States Navy, was born 1858; killed at Apia, Samoan Islands, April 1, 1899. Appointed cadet midshipman 1873; lieutenant 1893. Served on the Asiatic, Mediterranean, North Atlantic, and Pacific stations, and held important positions on shore from 1879 to 1898, and on June 29, 1898, was ordered to the "Philadelphia," flagship of the Pacific station. He commanded the American detachment of joint American and British Expedition against hostile Samoans, and was killed in action with them at Apia, April 1, 1899.

LAPWING

MINE SWEEPER

Length, 187 feet   *Beam, 35 feet*   *Draft, 9 feet, 9 inches*

NAMED FOR THE BIRD LAPWING

Launched March 14, 1918, at Todd Shipyard Corporation, New York.

Sponsor: MISS AGNES FORSHEW SCHLEGEL, granddaughter of Commodore Robert Pierpont Forshew, New York Naval Militia.

LARDNER

TORPEDO BOAT DESTROYER

Length, 314 feet   *Beam, 30 feet, 11 inches*   *Draft, 9 feet, 4 inches*

NAMED FOR REAR ADMIRAL JAMES L. LARDNER, U. S. NAVY

Launched September 29, 1919, at Bethlehem Shipbuilding Corporation, Quincy, Massachusetts.

Sponsor: MISS MARGARET LARDNER LARGE, granddaughter of Rear Admiral James L. Lardner, U. S. Navy.

REAR ADMIRAL JAMES L. LARDNER, U. S. Navy, was born in Philadelphia, Pennsylvania, 1802; died 1881. Appointed midshipman, 1820; rear admiral, 1866. Served 1821–1824, Pacific Squadron; 1825–1826, Mediterranean

Squadron; joined this squadron after escorting Gen. Lafayette in the "Brandywine" back to France after his last visit to the United States. Civil War, September, 1861, ordered to command the frigate "Susquehanna"; took prominent part in the battle of Port Royal and capture of Forts Walker and Beauregard. Commended for gallantry in action by Rear Admiral du Pont and his name sent to Congress for a vote of thanks by President Lincoln. May, 1862, assumed command of the East Gulf Blockading Squadron, with rank of acting rear admiral. May, 1863, to October, 1864, commanded the West India Squadron.

LARK

MINE SWEEPER

Length, 187 feet   *Beam, 35 feet*   *Draft, 9 feet, 9 inches*

NAMED FOR THE BIRD LARK

Launched August 10, 1918, at Baltimore Dry Dock Company.

Sponsor: MRS. HENRY A. STANLEY (Gladys Curry), wife of Lieutenant H. A. Stanley, U. S. Navy, prospective commander of the "Lark."

LAUB

TORPEDO BOAT DESTROYER

Length, 314 feet   *Beam, 30 feet, 11 inches*   *Draft, 9 feet, 4 inches*

NAMED FOR MIDSHIPMAN HENRY LAUB, U. S. NAVY

Launched August 25, 1918, at Bethlehem Shipbuilding Corporation, Squantum Works.

Sponsor: MISS MARJORIE MOHUN, daughter of Mr. John Laub Mohun, grandnephew of Midshipman Henry Laub, U. S. Navy. The sword voted by Congress to the nearest male relative of Midshipman Laub is in the possession of the sponsor's father.

Mᴵᴰꜱʜᴵᴾᴹᴬᴺ HENRY LAUB, United States Navy, was born in York, Pennsylvania. Appointed a midshipman October 1, 1809, under Commodore O. H. Perry. Wounded in the early part of the battle of Lake Erie, September 10, 1813, carried below and struck by a round shot that crashed through the cockpit, killing him instantly. Congress expressed deep regret at his loss, commended his gallantry, and ordered that a sword be presented to his nearest male relative.

LA VALLETTE

TORPEDO BOAT DESTROYER

Length, 314 feet   *Beam, 30 feet, 11 inches*   *Draft, 9 feet, 4 inches*

Nᴀᴹᴇᴅ ꜰᴏʀ Rᴇᴀʀ Aᴅᴍᴵʀᴀʟ E. A. F. LᴀVᴀʟʟᴇᴛᴛᴇ, U. S. Nᴀᴠʏ

Launched July 15, 1919, at Bethlehem Shipbuilding Corporation, San Francisco, California.

Sponsor: Mᴵꜱꜱ Nᴀᴺᴄʏ Lᴀᴺᴇ, daughter of Honorable Franklin K. Lane, Secretary of the Interior.

Rᴇᴀʀ ADMIRAL ELIE A. F. LᴀVALLETTE, United States Navy, was born in Virginia in 1790; died 1862. Appointed acting lieutenant, 1814, and detailed to the "Saratoga." While on that vessel he took a conspicuous part in the battle of Lake Champlain; was awarded a silver medal, included in the thanks of Congress October 20, 1814, and promoted for his gallantry. 1821–1822 commanded the "Peacock" and the "Flag" and rendered efficient service in the suppression of piracy in the West Indies. Appointed commander, 1831; captain, 1840; rear admiral, 1862.

"Don't give up the ship." — Lᴀᴡʀᴇᴺᴄᴇ

LAWRENCE (4ᴛʜ)

TORPEDO BOAT DESTROYER

Length, 314 feet   *Beam, 30 feet, 11 inches*   *Draft, 9 feet, 4 inches*

NAMED FOR CAPTAIN JAMES LAWRENCE, U. S. NAVY

Launched July 10, 1920, at New York Shipbuilding Corporation, Camden, New Jersey.

Sponsor: MISS RUTH LAWRENCE, daughter of Supreme Court Justice Abraham Lawrence, of New York.

CAPTAIN JAMES LAWRENCE, U. S. Navy, was born in New Jersey in 1787; appointed midshipman in 1798. In 1803, on the "Enterprise," he distinguished himself in an attack on boats in Tripoli harbor led by Admiral Porter. In 1804, while on the "Intrepid" he engaged in the destruction of the "Philadelphia" in the harbor of Tripoli. While in command of the "Hornet" he captured the British ship "Peacock," in 1813. For this service he was promoted to captain and awarded a medal, and given the command of the frigate, "Chesapeake." Died on board the "Chesapeake" after her memorable fight with the "Shannon," June 1, 1813. His dying words were, "Don't give up the ship."

LEA

TORPEDO BOAT DESTROYER

Length, 314 feet   *Beam, 30 feet, 11 inches*   *Draft, 9 feet*

NAMED FOR COMMANDER EDWARD LEA, U. S. NAVY

Launched April 29, 1918, at William Cramp & Sons' Company, Philadelphia, Pennsylvania.

Sponsor: MRS. HARRY ELLIS COLLINS (Hester Borden), wife of Commander H. E. Collins, P. C., U. S. Navy.

COMMANDER EDWARD LEA, U. S. Navy; born in Maryland; appointed a midshipman, October, 1851; lieutenant commander, July 16, 1862; participated in the Civil War, and as executive officer of the "Harriet Lane" was killed in an action with the Confederate batteries at Gal-

U.S. CRUISER "MARBLEHEAD" ABOUT TO LEAVE
THE WAYS

veston, Texas, January 1, 1863. The burial service was performed by his father, Major Lea, of the Confederate Army.

LEARY

TORPEDO BOAT DESTROYER

Length, 314 feet   *Beam, 30 feet, 11 inches*   *Draft, 9 feet, 4 inches*

NAMED FOR LIEUTENANT CLARENCE F. LEARY, U. S. N. R. F.

Launched December 18, 1918, at New York Shipbuilding Corporation, Camden, New Jersey.

Sponsor: MRS. C. FREDERICK LEARY (Mary Hocken), mother of Lieutenant Clarence F. Leary, U. S. N. R. F.

LIEUTENANT CLARENCE F. LEARY, U. S. N. R. F., was born in England, 1894; died on the "Charlton Hall" July 20, 1918. Commissioned a lieutenant in the Naval Reserve June 12, 1918, and ordered to the U. S. S. "Charlton Hall" as executive officer. On July 20, when that vessel caught fire, he entered the hold in an effort to save the vessel and crew, and died as a result of smoke inhalation.

S. P. LEE

TORPEDO BOAT DESTROYER

Length, 314 feet   *Beam, 30 feet, 11 inches*   *Draft, 9 feet, 4 inches*

NAMED FOR REAR ADMIRAL SAMUEL PHILLIPS LEE, U. S. NAVY

Launched April 22, 1919, at Bethlehem Shipbuilding Corporation, San Francisco, California.

Sponsor: MRS. THOMAS J. WYCHE (Phillippa Ludwell), a relative of Rear Admiral Samuel Phillips Lee, U. S. Navy.

REAR ADMIRAL SAMUEL PHILLIPS LEE, U. S. Navy, was born in Fairfax County, Virginia, 1812; died 1897. In the Civil War he commanded the "Oneida" and took part in the passage of Forts Jackson and St. Philip,

[123]

April 24, 1862. July 16, 1862, ordered to command the North Atlantic Squadron. He held various prominent positions ashore. He was retired in 1873.

LITCHFIELD

TORPEDO BOAT DESTROYER

Length, 314 feet   *Beam, 30 feet, 11 inches*   *Draft, 9 feet, 4 inches*

NAMED FOR JOHN RUSSELL LITCHFIELD, U. S. NAVY

Launched August 12, 1919, at Navy Yard, Mare Island, California.

Sponsor: MRS. WILLIAM R. LITCHFIELD (Martha D.), mother of John R. Litchfield, U. S. Navy.

JOHN RUSSELL LITCHFIELD, pharmacist's mate, third class, United States Navy, who gave his life while serving as a member of the Hospital Corps of the Sixth Regiment, United States Marine Corps, in France. Born in Flanagan, Illinois, 1899; died September 15, 1918. He was awarded the distinguished service cross posthumously for extraordinary heroism in action. He displayed exceptional bravery in giving first aid to the wounded under shell fire near Thiacourt, France, and was killed while taking a wounded soldier out of a trench to the rear. Received citation from the French Government for bravery.

LITTLE

TORPEDO BOAT DESTROYER

Length, 314 feet   *Beam, 30 feet, 11 inches*   *Draft, 9 feet, 2 inches*

NAMED FOR CAPTAIN GEORGE LITTLE, U. S. NAVY

Launched November 11, 1917, at Bethlehem Shipbuilding Company, Quincy, Massachusetts.

Sponsor: MRS. SAMUEL W. WAKEMAN (Edith Vickery), wife of the General Manager of the Company at Quincy.

CAPTAIN GEORGE LITTLE, U. S. Navy, was born in Marshfield, Massachusetts, 1754; died, 1809; appointed first lieutenant of the Massachusetts ship "Protector" in 1779; in 1781, after a running fight of several hours, escaped from the British ship "Thames," but in a later engagement was captured by the same vessel; was made prisoner and escaped; returned to United States and was given command of Massachusetts ship "Winthrop," with which he captured two British privateers, the armed brig "Meriam," and a number of other vessels; commissioned captain, March 4, 1799, and given command of the United States frigate "Boston"; during the war with France captured the French ship "Le Berceau" and a number of other vessels.

LONG

TORPEDO BOAT DESTROYER
Length, 314 feet   *Beam, 30 feet, 11 inches*   *Draft, 9 feet, 4 inches*

NAMED FOR SECRETARY OF THE NAVY JOHN DAVIS LONG

Launched April 26, 1919, at William Cramp & Sons' Company, Philadelphia, Pennsylvania.

Sponsor: MRS JULIA JAMES LONG KNAPP, a cousin of Secretary of the Navy John D. Long.

SECRETARY OF THE NAVY JOHN DAVIS LONG was born in Buckfield, Oxford County, Maine, October 27, 1838; died August 28, 1915. Graduated from Harvard in 1857 and admitted to the bar in 1861. He was governor of Massachusetts in 1880–1882. In 1897 he became Secretary of the Navy. He ably administered the affairs of the Navy from 1897 to 1907, which included the period of the Spanish-American War.

LUCE

TORPEDO BOAT DESTROYER
Length, 314 feet   *Beam, 30 feet, 11 inches*   *Draft, 9 feet, 2 inches*

NAMED FOR REAR ADMIRAL STEPHEN B. LUCE, U. S. NAVY

Launched June 29, 1918, at Bethlehem Shipbuilding Corporation, Fore River, Massachusetts.

Sponsor: MRS. BOUTELLE NOYES (Charlotte Luce), daughter of Rear Admiral Stephen B. Luce, U. S. Navy.

REAR ADMIRAL STEPHEN BLEECKER LUCE, U. S. Navy, was born in New York, 1827; died 1917. Appointed midshipman, 1841; commissioned rear admiral, 1885. During the Civil War he took part in the engagements at Hatteras Inlet and Port Royal Ferry, 1861; in command of the monitor "Nantucket" he engaged the batteries in Charleston Harbor in 1863; 1864, in command of the "Canandaigua," North Atlantic Blockading Squadron; 1865 in command of the "Pontiac," he co-operated with the Army in the Savannah River; 1865–1868, commandant of midshipman at the Naval Academy; 1868–1869, cruising in the Pacific and Mediterranean Squadrons; 1878–1881, in command of the United States naval training ship "Minnesota"; 1881–1884, in command of the training squadron; 1884–1885, president of the Naval War College; and from 1886–1889 he was in command of the naval forces of the North Atlantic Squadron. He was the founder of the Naval War College at Newport, Rhode Island, and was on special duty in connection with it from 1901 to 1910.

LUDLOW

TORPEDO BOAT DESTROYER

Length, 314 feet   *Beam, 30 feet, 11 inches*   *Draft, 9 feet, 2 inches*

NAMED FOR LIEUTENANT AUGUSTUS C. LUDLOW, U. S. NAVY

Launched June 9, 1918, at Bethlehem Shipbuilding Corporation, San Francisco, California.

Sponsor: MISS ELIZABETH LUDLOW CHRYSTIE, great-great-grandniece of Lieutenant Augustus C. Ludlow, U. S. Navy.

U.S. BATTLESHIP "MARYLAND" LAUNCHING STAND

Secretary of the Navy Josephus Daniels, the Sponsor, Governor Ritchie, Mrs. Cabell, Mrs. Daniels

LIEUTENANT AUGUSTUS C. LUDLOW, U. S. Navy, born in Newburgh, New York, 1792; appointed a midshipman, April 2, 1804; lieutenant, June 3, 1810; died of wounds received while directing the fighting in the engagement of the "Chesapeake" and the "Shannon."

M-1

SUBMARINE

Length, 196 feet   *Beam, 19 feet*   *Draft, 11 feet*

Launched September 14, 1915, at Fore River S. B. Corporation, Quincy, Massachusetts.

Sponsor: MISS SARA DEAN ROBERTS, daughter of Congressman Ernest W. Roberts of Massachusetts, member of the Naval Committee of the House of Representatives.

MACDONOUGH (2D)

TORPEDO BOAT DESTROYER

Length, 314 feet, 4 inches   *Beam, 30 feet, 11 inches*   *Draft, 9 feet, 4 inches*

NAMED FOR COMMODORE THOMAS MACDONOUGH, U. S. NAVY

Launched December 15, 1920, at Bethlehem S. B. Corporation, San Francisco, California.

Sponsor: MRS. CHARLES W. DABNEY (Lucy Russell), great-granddaughter of Commodore Thomas Macdonough, U. S. Navy.

COMMODORE THOMAS MACDONOUGH, U. S. Navy, was born in Middletown, Delaware, in 1783; died in 1825. Appointed midshipman 1800; captain 1814; first cruised in the Ganges in 1800 during the war with France; in 1803–1804 was actively engaged in operations before Tripoli; one of the midshipman selected by Decatur to go in the "Intrepid" for the recapture and destruction of the U. S. S. "Philadelphia" in Tripoli harbor 1804. During the war of 1812 commanded the United States squadron on Lake

Champlain; September 11, 1814, he gained a brilliant victory over the British squadron; received the thanks of Congress and a gold metal; 1818–1820 cruised in the Mediterranean and again in 1824 the same squadron commanding the "Constitution." Severe illness obliged him to give up his command and return home in the merchant brig "Edward." He died before reaching the United States.

MACKENZIE

TORPEDO BOAT DESTROYER

Length, 314 feet   Beam, 30 feet, 11 inches   Draft, 9 feet, 2 inches

NAMED FOR LIEUTENANT COMMANDER ALEXANDER SLIDELL MACKENZIE, U. S. NAVY

Launched September 29, 1919, at Bethlehem Shipbuilding Corporation, San Francisco, California.

Sponsor: MRS. PERCY J. COTTON (Henrietta Macdonald), wife of the superintendent of Hull Construction of the Union Works.

LIEUTENANT COMMANDER ALEXANDER SLIDELL MACKENZIE was appointed midshipman in 1855. Served in the "Kineo" and "New Ironsides" during the Civil War. Was killed in Formosa, June 13, 1867, while leading a party against the savages who had murdered the whole crew of the American bark "Rover" some time before.

MACLEISH

TORPEDO BOAT DESTROYER

Length, 314 feet   Beam, 30 feet, 11 inches   Draft, 9 feet, 4 inches

NAMED FOR LIEUTENANT KENNETH MACLEISH, U. S. NAVAL RESERVE FORCE

Launched December 18, 1919, at William Cramp & Sons' Company, Philadelphia, Pennsylvania.

[128]

Sponsor: Miss Ishbel M. MacLeish, sister of Lieutenant Kenneth MacLeish, U. S. N. R. F.

Lieutenant KENNETH MACLEISH, U. S. Naval Reserve Force, was born in Glencoe, Illinois, 1894. After serving in the United States Naval Reserve Force as an enlisted man since March 24, 1917, he was appointed ensign in the Naval Reserve Flying Corps August 31, 1917. On October 13, 1917, he was ordered to aviation duty in France; commissioned lieutenant (junior grade) March 23, 1918; lieutenant July 1, 1918. Detached from duty at Clermond Ferrand July 2, 1918, and ordered to Dunkerque; on August 18, 1918, ordered to duty with Northern Bombing Group, Dunkerque, France, where he took part in many air raids over the enemy's lines. Early in September he was ordered to Eastleigh, England, as Chief of the Assembly Department at the U. S. Naval Aviation Station. On October 13 he flew to Dunkerque with a convoy of planes. While on a raid there with the R. A. F. Squadron No. 213, October 14, 1918, the squadron was attacked by a large number of enemy planes. In the engagement which ensued MacLeish's plane was shot down and he was instantly killed. He was considered one of the best pilots of this group. On Armistice Day, 1920, was posthumously awarded the Navy Cross for "distinguished service and extraordinary heroism."

MADDOX

TORPEDO BOAT DESTROYER

Length, 314 feet   *Beam, 30 feet, 11 inches*   *Draft, 9 feet, 2 inches*

Named for Captain William A. T. Maddox, U. S. Marine Corps

Launched October 27, 1918, at Bethlehem Shipbuilding Corporation, Quincy, Massachusetts.

Sponsor: Mrs. C. N. Hinkamp (Frances Miller), granddaughter of Captain William A. T. Maddox, U. S. Navy.

CAPTAIN WILLIAM A. T. MADDOX, United States Marine Corps, was born in Maryland. Appointed second lieutenant in the Marine Corps 1837. The previous year he had served in the war with the Creeks and Seminole Indians as first lieutenant, commanding a company of volunteers under Gen. Jessup; 1845–1847, while serving on the sloop "Cyane," Pacific Squadron, he landed at Monterey July 7, 1846, when the American flag was hoisted, thereby assisting in taking possession of the country, and hoisted the American flag at San Diego July 29, 1846; August 15, 1846, was appointed by Commodore Stockton to take command of two companies of mounted riflemen to proceed against Gen. Alvarado; 1846, was appointed for services rendered, military commandant of the middle district of California, headquarters at Monterey; attached to the frigate "Columbus" 1847–1848; at headquarters, Washington, 1848–1850; brevetted captain, for gallant and meritorious conduct at the Battle of Santa Clara, and in suppressing an insurrection at Monterey during the time he was commandant of the middle district of California; died 1889.

MAHAN

TORPEDO BOAT DESTROYER

Length, 314 feet   *Beam, 30 feet, 11 inches*   *Draft, 9 feet, 2 inches*

NAMED FOR REAR ADMIRAL ALFRED T. MAHAN,
U. S. NAVY

Launched August 4, 1918, at Bethlehem Shipbuilding Corporation, Quincy, Massachusetts.

Sponsor: MISS ELLEN K. MAHAN, daughter of Rear Admiral Alfred T. Mahan, U. S. Navy.

REAR ADMIRAL ALFRED T. MAHAN, U. S. Navy, was born in 1840, at West Point, New York; died 1914. Appointed midshipman, 1856; rear admiral, 1906; Civil War, participated in the operations of the South Atlantic and West Gulf blockading squadrons; president of the

U.S. BATTLESHIP "MARYLAND" SLIDING
DOWN THE LAUNCHING WAYS

Naval War College, 1886–1889; delegate to the Hague Convention, 1909. His treatises on naval matters are standard the world over and are translated into many foreign languages.

MALLARD

MINE SWEEPER

Length, 187 feet   *Beam, 35 feet*   *Draft, 9 feet, 9 inches*

NAMED FOR THE BIRD MALLARD

Launched December 17, 1918, at Staten Island Shipbuilding Company, New York.

Sponsor: MRS. ANNE FALES BRAYTON, wife of Lieutenant Harry R. Brayton, U. S. Navy, prospective commanding officer.

MANLEY

TORPEDO BOAT DESTROYER

Length, 314 feet   *Beam, 30 feet, 8 inches*   *Draft, 8 feet*

NAMED FOR CAPTAIN JOHN MANLEY, U. S. NAVY

Launched August 23, 1917, at Bath Iron Works, Bath, Maine.

Sponsor: MISS DOROTHY S. SEWALL, daughter of Mr. William T. Sewall, a prominent citizen of Bath, Maine.

CAPTAIN JOHN MANLEY, U. S. Navy, was born in Torquay, England, in 1733, and died February 12, 1793. He was appointed by Gen. Washington on October 24, 1775, captain of the "Lee," the first continental ship to get to sea. On April 17, 1776, he was commissioned captain by the Continental Congress, in the Continental Navy; commanded the "Hancock" in 1776; was captured, imprisoned in Old Mill Prison, and escaped; commanded a number of privateers, and made many prizes and captured a number of British transports. In January, 1783, he received the surrender of the last transport captured during the Revolution.

MARBLEHEAD (3D)

LIGHT CRUISER

Length, 555 feet, 6 inches   *Beam, 55 feet*   *Draft, 14 feet, 3 inches*

NAMED FOR THE CITY OF MARBLEHEAD, MASSACHUSETTS

Launched October 9, 1923, at the William Cramp & Sons' Shipbuilding Company, Philadelphia, Pennsylvania.

Sponsor: MRS. JOSEPH EVANS (Hannah Martin), selected by the city of Marblehead, being the mother of the first man from Marblehead killed in the World War. Among those present were Rear Admiral Scales, U. S. Navy, Mr. Joseph Evans, Captain and Mrs. W. P. Robert, Rear Admiral R. T. Hall, Mrs. Hall, Mrs. Russell Langdon, President of the Society of Sponsors, Captain Lloyd Bankson, and others.

The first "Marblehead" was a 570 ton gunboat, launched in 1861. The second "Marblehead" was a protected cruiser of 2072 tons, launched in 1892.

MARCUS

TORPEDO BOAT DESTROYER

Length, 314 feet   *Beam, 30 feet, 11 inches*   *Draft, 9 feet, 4 inches*

NAMED FOR LIEUTENANT ARNOLD MARCUS, U. S. NAVY

Launched August 22, 1919, at Bethlehem Shipbuilding Corporation, San Francisco, California.

Sponsor: MRS. HELEN COWLES MARCUS, widow of Lieutenant Arnold Marcus, U. S. Navy.

LIEUTENANT (JUNIOR GRADE) ARNOLD MARCUS, U. S. Navy, was born in Atlantic City, New Jersey, 1892; appointed midshipman 1909; ensign 1913; lieutenant (junior grade) 1916; command of U. S. S.

"A–7" March 13, 1917; died July 27 from the effects of an explosion on the U. S. S. "A–7" while that vessel was engaged in patrol duty in Manila Bay, Philippine Islands. With one exception, all who were in the interior of the boat died from the explosion. Lieutenant Marcus upheld the best traditions of the service in that, although terribly burned and wounded, he did everything possible to save his ship and men. He remained at his post until ordered to a hospital by his Division Commander, where he died a few hours later.

MARYLAND (3D)

BATTLESHIP

Length, 624 feet   *Beam, 97 feet, 3¾ inches*   *Draft, 30 feet, 6 inches*

NAMED FOR THE STATE OF MARYLAND
(Ratified the Constitution in 1788)

Launched March 20, 1920, at Newport News Shipbuilding & Dry Dock Company, Newport News, Virginia.

Sponsor: MRS. BROOKE LEE (Elizabeth Wilson), Silver Spring, Maryland, wife of Mr. Brooke Lee, Comptroller of the State, and daughter-in-law of former U. S. Senator Blair Lee, was appointed sponsor by Governor Ritchie of Maryland.

THE official party were invited by Secretary of the Navy Josephus Daniels to go to Newport News on board the U. S. S. "Mayflower." After the launching a large party of Marylanders who had come down on other boats were invited to luncheon on board the "Mayflower." In the official party were Governor Ritchie, Adjutant General Milton Reckerd, Mrs. Henry L. Cabell, the Governor's aunt, Mr. Blair Lee, Doctor Hugh Young of Baltimore, and Major Brooke Lee.

U. S. S. "Maryland 1st" was a 380 ton sailing ship purchased in 1799.

"Maryland 2d" is an armored cruiser launched in 1903 and now renamed "Frederick" for that city in Maryland.

[133]

MASON

TORPEDO BOAT DESTROYER

Length, 314 feet   *Beam, 30 feet, 11 inches*   *Draft, 9 feet, 4 inches*

NAMED FOR SECRETARY OF THE NAVY
JOHN YOUNG MASON

Launched March 8, 1919, at Newport News S. B. & D. D. Company, Newport News, Virginia.

Sponsor: MISS MARY MASON WILLIAMS, great-granddaughter of Secretary of the Navy John Young Mason.

HONORABLE JOHN YOUNG MASON, Secretary of the Navy, 1844–1845, 1846–1849, was born in Greene County, Virginia, 1799; died 1859. He was successively a member of the legislature of Virginia and of the State constitutional convention of 1829, a member of Congress from 1831 to 1837, and chairman of Committee on Foreign Affairs, and judge of the United States District Court, and of the circuit court of Virginia. In 1844 he was appointed Secretary of the Navy by President Tyler, and in 1845 President Polk made him Attorney General of the United States, but in the next year he was again placed at the head of the Navy Department. He was president of the Virginia constitutional convention of 1850. In 1853 he was appointed United States minister to France, and he was reappointed by President Buchanan, remaining in that post until his death.

MAUMEE

FUEL SHIP

Length, 475 feet   *Beam, 56 feet*   *Draft, 26 feet, 2 inches*

NAMED FOR MAUMEE RIVER

Launched April 17, 1915, at Navy Yard, Mare Island, California.

Sponsor: MISS JANET CROSE, daughter of Captain William M. Crose, U. S. Navy, on duty at the Navy Yard.

MAURY

TORPEDO BOAT DESTROYER

Length, 314 feet   *Beam, 30 feet, 11 inches*   *Draft, 9 feet, 2 inches*

NAMED FOR COMMANDER MATTHEW F. MAURY,
U. S. NAVY

Launched July 4, 1918, at Bethlehem Shipbuilding Corporation, Quincy, Massachusetts.

Sponsor: MISS ANNA HAMLIN, daughter of Honorable Charles S. Hamlin, member of the Federal Reserve Board.

COMMANDER MATTHEW FONTAINE MAURY, United States Navy, astronomer and hydrographer, was born in Spottsylvania County, Virginia, 1806; died 1873. Appointed midshipman, 1825; commander, 1855. He was appointed superintendent of the department of charts and instruments in 1842, and upon the organization of the Naval Observatory in 1844 he was appointed its superintendent and held that position until his resignation, April, 1861. He published some of the best known scientific works, and his "Wind and Current Charts," "Sailing Directions," and "Physical Geography of the Sea," are the standard works on those subjects for nearly all nations. (At outbreak of Civil War he resigned and joined the Confederate Navy, where he attained the rank of commodore. Afterwards occupied the chair of Physics in Virginia Military Institute.)

McCALLA

TORPEDO BOAT DESTROYER

Length, 314 feet   *Beam, 30 feet, 11 inches*   *Draft, 9 feet, 4 inches*

NAMED FOR REAR ADMIRAL BOWMAN H. McCALLA,
U. S. NAVY

Launched February 18, 1919, at Bethlehem Shipbuilding Corporation, Fore River, Massachusetts.

Sponsor: MRS. ELIZABETH MCCALLA MILLER, daughter of Rear Admiral Bowman H. McCalla, U. S. Navy.

REAR ADMIRAL BOWMAN H. McCALLA, U. S. Navy, was born in Camden, New Jersey, 1844; died 1910. Appointed midshipman, 1861; rear admiral, 1903; retired 1906. He saw much sea duty from 1866–1881. Assistant to Chief of Bureau of Navigation from 1882 until 1884, and from 1885 to 1887. In command of the U. S. S. "Enterprise" 1887 to 1890; in command of the U. S. S. "Marblehead" September 11, 1897 to September 16, 1898 (advanced six numbers from August 10, 1898, for eminent and conspicuous conduct in battle); commanded the U. S. S. "Newark" from September 1st, 1899 to July 5, 1901, and while in command was advanced three numbers for eminent and conspicuous conduct in battle; engaged in the relief column under Vice Admiral Seymour, with meritorious mention for service in Cuban waters during the War with Spain.

McCAWLEY

TORPEDO BOAT DESTROYER

Length, 314 feet   *Beam, 30 feet, 11 inches*   *Draft, 9 feet, 4 inches*

NAMED FOR COLONEL CHARLES GRYMES McCAWLEY, U. S. MARINE CORPS

Launched June 14, 1919, at Bethlehem Shipbuilding Corporation, Quincy, Massachusetts.

Sponsor: MISS ELEANOR LAURIE McCAWLEY, granddaughter of Colonel Charles Grymes McCawley, U. S. M. C.

COLONEL CHARLES GRYMES McCAWLEY, United States Marine Corps, was born in Philadelphia, Pennsylvania, 1827; died 1891. Appointed second lieutenant in the Marine Corps, 1847; lieutenant colonel, 1867. Served with the Army in Mexico and was brevetted first lieutenant September 13, 1847, for gallantry in action during the capture of the city of Mexico. In 1862 was sent to reoccupy the Norfolk Navy Yard with a force of 200 men, and hoisted the national flag. In July, 1863, was brevetted major for bravery in an attack on Fort Sumter. In 1876 became colonel in command of the Marine Corps with headquarters at Washington.

McCOOK

TORPEDO BOAT DESTROYER

Length, 314 feet   *Beam, 30 feet, 11 inches*   *Draft, 9 feet, 4 inches*

NAMED FOR COMMANDER RODERICK S. McCOOK, U. S. NAVY

Launched January 31, 1919, at Bethlehem Shipbuilding Corporation, Quincy, Massachusetts.

Sponsor: MRS. HENRY C. DINGER (Gertrude Mack), wife of Commander H. C. Dinger, U. S. Navy, Assistant to Inspector of Machinery for U. S. Navy.

COMMANDER RODERICK S. McCOOK, United States Navy, was born in New Lisbon, Ohio, in 1839; died 1886. Appointed midshipman 1854; commander 1873. Civil War: On the "Minnesota" at capture of forts at Hatteras Inlet. On the "Stars and Stripes" at battle of Roanoke Island, February 7–8, 1862; commanded the naval howitzer battery on shore at the battle of Newbern, North Carolina; commanded the "Stars and Stripes" in sounds of North Carolina and Wilmington blockade. 1863, executive officer of the ironclad "Canonicus"; December 24–25, 1864, and January 13–15, 1865, executive officer of the "Canonicus" at attacks on and surrender of Fort Fisher, and mentioned in reports for gallant service. Included in the thanks of Congress to Capt. L. M. Goldsborough, his officers and men, for victory at Roanoke Island, February 7, 8, 10, 1861; and thanks to Admiral Porter, officers and men for victory at Fort Fisher, December 24, 25, and January 13, 15, 1865.

[137]

McCORMICK

TORPEDO BOAT DESTROYER

Length, 314 feet   *Beam, 30 feet, 11 inches*   *Draft, 9 feet, 4 inches*

NAMED FOR LIEUTENANT (J. G.) ALEXANDER A. McCORMICK, JR., U. S. NAVAL RESERVE FORCE

Launched February 14, 1920, at William Cramp & Sons' Company, Philadelphia, Pennsylvania.

Sponsor: MISS KATHERINE McCORMICK, sister of Lieutenant Alexander A. McCormick, Jr., U. S. N. R. F.

LIEUTENANT (J. G.) ALEXANDER A. McCORMICK, U. S. Naval Reserve Force. Born in Chicago, Illinois, 1897; enrolled in the United States Naval Reserve Force as ensign, November 2, 1917; detached from duty at the Naval Aviation Station, Pensacola, Florida, May 28, 1918, to duty with aviation forces in France. Died September 24, 1918, at Calais, France, from injuries received in battle when acting as an aerial gunner on Handley Page Plane with a British Squadron. He had been detailed to that squadron for training over the lines. Buried in Military Cemetery, Calais, France. Posthumously awarded the Navy Cross.

McDERMUT

TORPEDO BOAT DESTROYER

Length, 314 feet   *Beam, 30 feet, 11 inches*   *Draft, 9 feet, 4 inches*

NAMED FOR COMMANDER DAVID A. McDERMUT, U. S. NAVY

Launched August 6, 1918, at Bethlehem Shipbuilding Corporation, Quincy, Massachusetts.

Sponsor: MRS. EUGENE G. GRACE (Marion Brown), wife of the president of the shipbuilding corporation. As it started down the ways a shower of roses was dropped on the deck from aloft.

[138]

U.S. TORPEDO BOAT DESTROYER "McDERMUT"
JUST LEAVING THE WAYS

Lieutenant COMMANDER DAVID A. McDERMUT U. S. Navy, was born in New York. Appointed a midshipman, 1841; passed midshipman, 1847; master, 1855; lieutenant, 1855; lieutenant commander, 1862. During the Civil War he served on the receiving ship at New York from January 18, 1861, until May 31, 1861; served on the U. S. S. "Potomac" until June 5, 1861; on the "Marion" until December 1, 1862; in command of the "Cayuga" from December 2, 1862, until killed, April 18, 1863, in boat expedition in Sabine Pass, by the Confederates.

McDOUGAL

TORPEDO BOAT DESTROYER

Length, 305 feet   *Beam, 30 feet, 7 inches*   *Draft, 9 feet, 3 inches*

NAMED FOR REAR ADMIRAL DAVID S. McDOUGAL, U. S. NAVY

Launched April 22, 1914, at Bath Iron Works, Bath, Maine.

Sponsor: MISS MARGUERITE S. LeBRETON, granddaughter of Rear Admiral David S. McDougal.

Rear ADMIRAL DAVID S. McDOUGAL, U. S. Navy, was born 1809, in Ohio. Died August 7, 1882. Appointed midshipman April 1, 1828; lieutenant, 1841; captain, 1864; rear admiral, 1873. Cruised on the various stations. During the Mexican War was attached to the "Mississippi" and took part in capture of Vera Cruz and other places. Commanded the "Wyoming" at the battle of Shimonoseki Straits, Japan, July 16, 1863.

McFARLAND

TORPEDO BOAT DESTROYER

Length, 314 feet   *Beam, 30 feet, 11 inches*   *Draft, 9 feet, 3 inches*

NAMED FOR SEAMAN JOHN McFARLAND, U. S. NAVY

Launched March 30, 1920, at New York Shipbuilding Corporation, Camden, New Jersey.

Sponsor: MISS LOUISA HUGHES, daughter of Rear Admiral Charles F. Hughes, U. S. N., in command at Navy Yard, Philadelphia, Pennsylvania.

SEAMAN JOHN McFARLAND, U. S. Navy. Entered the Navy as seaman December 24, 1861. Was attached to the West Gulf Blockading Squadron, on board the U. S. S. "Hartford." Was rated captain of the forecastle. Had the station at the wheel in every engagement in which the "Hartford" participated. Displayed great coolness and intelligence and was commended by his commanding officers. Was awarded the medal of honor for his gallant and meritorious service.

McKEAN

TORPEDO BOAT DESRTOYER

Length, 314 feet   *Beam, 30 feet, 11 inches*   *Draft, 9 feet, 4 inches*

NAMED FOR COMMODORE WILLIAM WISTER McKEAN, U. S. NAVY

Launched July 4, 1918, at Bethlehem Shipbuilding Corporation, San Francisco, California.

Sponsor: MISS HELEN L. ELY, daughter of Mr. Joseph Ely, and great-granddaughter of Commodore William Wister McKean, U. S. Navy.

COMMODORE WILLIAM WISTER McKEAN, United States Navy, was born in Huntington County, Pennsylvania, in 1800; died 1865. Appointed midshipman 1814; appointed commodore 1862; rendered valuable service with Commodore David Porter's squadron in the West Indies in suppressing piracy; lieutenant on the "Dale" during Mexican War, and at the time of his death member of the naval board.

[140]

McKEE (2d)

TORPEDO BOAT DESTROYER

Length, 314 feet   *Beam, 30 feet, 11 inches*   *Draft, 9 feet*

NAMED FOR LIEUTENANT HUGH W. McKEE,
U. S. NAVY

Launched March 23, 1918, at Bethlehem Shipbuilding Corporation, San Francisco, California.

Sponsor: MRS. JOSEPH J. TYNAN (Margaret McGinty), wife of the General Manager of the Shipbuilding Company.

LIEUTENANT HUGH W. McKEE, U. S. Navy, born in Lexington, Kentucky; died on board the "Colorado," in Korea, June 11, 1871; appointed midshipman September 25, 1861; commissioned lieutenant March 21, 1870; was mortally wounded while leading the attack on the Korean forts on Kango-Hoa Island, June 11, 1871.

McLANAHAN

TORPEDO BOAT DESTROYER

Length, 314 feet   *Beam, 30 feet, 11 inches*   *Draft, 9 feet, 4 inches*

NAMED FOR PASSED MIDSHIPMAN TENANT
McLANAHAN, U. S. NAVY

Launched September 22, 1918, at Bethlehem Shipbuilding Corporation, Quincy, Massachusetts.

Sponsor: MRS. CHARLES M. HOWE (Virginia N), wife of Lieutenant Commander C. M. Howe, U. S. N., Assistant Inspector of Machinery at Quincy.

PASSED MIDSHIPMAN TENANT McLANAHAN, U. S. Navy, was born in Louisiana; appointed a midshipman December 12, 1839, passed midshipman 1845. Midshipman McLanahan served on the sloop of war "Preble" in the Mediterranean squadron and on various ships in the Brazil, African, and East Indian Squadrons, from 1840 to 1845. While serving on the "Cyane," he was one of the party besieged with Lieut. Heywood. He was killed by a rifle shot in the neck. Capt. du Pont in his report mentioned McLanahan as "gallant, unflinching and devoted."

MEADE

TORPEDO BOAT DESTROYER
Length, 314 feet   *Beam, 30 feet, 11 inches*   *Draft, 9 feet, 4 inches*

NAMED FOR REAR ADMIRAL RICHARD W. MEADE, U. S. NAVY, AND FOR BRIGADIER GENERAL ROBERT L. MEADE, U. S. MARINE CORPS

Launched May 24, 1919, at Bethlehem Shipbuilding Corporation, Quincy, Massachusetts.

Sponsor: MISS ANNIE PAULDING MEADE, daughter of Rear Admiral Richard W. Meade, U. S. Navy.

REAR ADMIRAL RICHARD W. MEADE, U. S. Navy, was born in New York City 1837; died 1897. Appointed midshipman, 1850; rear admiral, 1894. Civil War, 1862, was commended by Admiral Porter in official dispatches for breaking up guerrilla warfare on the Mississippi River; 1863–1864 commanded the "Marblehead" and co-operated with the Army in operations in Stono River and Johns Island; thanked by Admiral Dahlgren and recommended for promotion; January 22, 1865, destroyed the blockade runner "Delphina" in the face of a greatly superior force; was officially thanked by Commodore Palmer. From 1865 to 1868 on duty at the Naval Academy. Held many important shore stations.

BRIGADIER GENERAL ROBERT L. MEADE, U. S. Marine Corps, was born in the District of Columbia; died 1910. Commissioned second lieutenant June 14, 1862; brevetted first lieutenant for gallant and meritorious service, 1863, during a night attack on Fort Sumter; commissioned first lieutenant, 1864; commissioned captain, 1876. Fleet marine officer South Atlantic Station 1877–1879. Took part in the expedition to Panama, 1885; commanded marine barracks, navy yard, Washington, 1890–1892. Commissioned major September 6, 1892. Commissioned colonel March 3, 1899. Retired December 26, 1903. Brigadier general, 1905. Brother of Rear Admiral Meade.

MEDUSA

REPAIR SHIP

Length, 483 feet, 10 inches   *Beam, 70 feet*   *Draft, 18 feet, 11 inches*

NAMED FOR MEDUSA, ONE OF THE GORGONS IN ANCIENT GREEK LITERATURE

Launched April 16, 1923, at Navy Yard, Puget Sound, Washington.

Sponsor: MRS. BURNS POE (Elsie Grumbling), selected by United States Senator Miles Poindexter, of Washington.

MELVILLE

DESTROYER TENDER

Length, 417 feet   *Beam, 54 feet*   *Draft, 20 feet*

NAMED FOR REAR ADMIRAL GEORGE W. MELVILLE, U. S. Navy

Launched March 2, 1915, at New York Shipbuilding Corporation, Camden, New Jersey.

Sponsor: MISS HELEN WOOLSTON NEEL, granddaughter of Rear Admiral George W. Melville, U. S. Navy.

REAR ADMIRAL GEORGE WALLACE MELVILLE, U. S. Navy; born in New York City 1841; died 1912. Appointed third assistant engineer July 19, 1861; commissioned chief engineer March 4, 1881; Chief of Bureau of Steam Engineering, with rank of rear admiral, 1887–1903; served throughout the Civil War, 1861–1865, in different squadrons and commended for his ability and zeal; cruised on various stations from 1866 to 1879, when he was selected as one of the officers to accompany the "Jeannette Arctic Expedition"; advanced fifteen numbers for his heroism in endeavoring to rescue Lieutenant Commander De Long and his party, who were lost in the ice in the Lena Delta, Siberia; commanded the party which finally discovered the remains of the unfortunate men; highly honored by scientific societies at home and abroad.

MELVIN

TORPEDO BOAT DESTROYER

Length, 314 feet, 4 inches   Beam, 30 feet, 11 inches   Draft, 9 feet, 4 inches

NAMED FOR LIEUTENANT (J. G.) JOHN T. MELVIN, U. S. Navy

Launched April 11, 1921, at Bethlehem Shipbuilding Corporation, San Francisco, California.

Sponsor: MISS LAURA LIVINGSTON MCKINSTREY, daughter of Honorable Elisha W. McKinstrey, Judge of Supreme Court of California.

LIEUTENANT (J. G.) JOHN T. MELVIN, U. S. Navy, was born in Selma, Alabama, in 1887; died November 5, 1917. Appointed midshipman 1907; ensign 1911; lieutenant (j. g.) 1915; resigned 1915. Appointed lieutenant (j. g.) United States Naval Reserve Force, February 9, 1917, and assigned to duty at New Haven, Connecticut; attached to the patrol boat "Alcedo" and lost his life when that vessel was sunk by a German submarine in the war zone.

MEREDITH

TORPEDO BOAT DESTROYER

Length, 314 feet   Beam, 30 feet, 11 inches   Draft, 9 feet, 2 inches

NAMED FOR SERGEANT JONATHAN MEREDITH, U. S. MARINE CORPS

Launched September 22, 1918, at Bethlehem Shipbuilding Corporation, Fore River, Massachusetts.

Sponsor: MRS. WILLIAM F. MEREDITH (Julia D.) took

[144]

the place of her small daughter, Mary R. Meredith, great-great-granddaughter of Sergeant Jonathan Meredith.

SERGEANT JONATHAN MEREDITH, United States Marine Corps, enlisted in 1803 — promoted to the rank of sergeant 1803. On August 3, 1804, during an engagement in the harbor before Tripoli, he saved the life of Lieut. John Trippe, of the "Vixen." In close combat with a Tripolitan ship, Lieut. Trippe and nine men boarded the vessel, and before the rest of the crew could follow, the wash of the ship separated the two boats and Trippe and his men found themselves face to face with five times their number of the enemy. A conflict of the fiercest description ensued. Trippe singled out the Tripolitan commander and engaged him in a hand-to-hand fight. The Mohammedan was a gigantic man and accustomed to this method of fighting. In the battle that ensued he wounded Trippe no less than eleven times, finally breaking his sword and beating him to his knees. Before he could be cut down by the man, the gallant American, who was a small, slender man, seized a hand pike from the deck and by a desperate upward thrust impaled his huge antagonist, just as Sergeant Meredith, by a vicious bayonet thrust, pinned to the mast another corsair, who was about to finish him. Three days after this Sergeant Meredith was blown up in a gunboat.

MERVINE

TORPEDO BOAT DESTROYER

Length, 314 feet   *Beam, 30 feet, 11 inches*   *Draft, 9 feet, 4 inches*

NAMED FOR REAR ADMIRAL WILLIAM MERVINE,
U. S. NAVY

Launched August 11, 1919, at Bethlehem Shipbuilding Corporation, San Francisco, California.

Sponsor: MISS EILEEN DOLORES McCARTHY, daughter of former Mayor McCarthy, of San Francisco.

REAR ADMIRAL WILLIAM MERVINE, United States Navy, was born in Pennsylvania in 1790; died in 1868. Appointed a midshipman 1809; captain 1841; rear admiral (retired) 1866; served during the War of 1812 on Lake Ontario. Cruised 1819–1853 on Africa, West Indies, Mediteranean, Brazil and Pacific Stations. Mexican War, 1846–1847, commanded the "Savannah" in operations against Mexico. Commanded a detachment of 250 sailors and marines; landed at Monterey July 7, 1847, took possession of that place, hoisted the American flag and erected a block house for its defense, which was named in his honor Fort Mervine. Civil War: May 6, 1861, commanded the Gulf Squadron until obliged to give up the command on account of ill health. Held many important positions on shore between his sea cruises.

MEYER

TORPEDO BOAT DESTROYER

Length, 314 feet   *Beam, 30 feet, 11 inches*   *Draft, 9 feet, 4 inches*

NAMED FOR SECRETARY OF THE NAVY
GEORGE VON L. MEYER

Launched July 18, 1919, at Bethlehem Shipbuilding Company, Quincy, Massachusetts.

Sponsor: MRS. CHRISTOPHER R. P. RODGERS (Alice Meyer), wife of Commander Rodgers, U. S. Navy, and daughter of Secretary of the Navy George von L. Meyer.

SECRETARY OF THE NAVY GEORGE VON L. MEYER was born in Boston, 1858; died 1918. He was graduated from Harvard University in 1879. Served as member of the Massachusetts House of Representatives 1892–1897, being speaker during the last three years. In 1900–1905 was ambassador to Italy, and from 1905–1907 was ambassador to Russia; 1907–1909 Postmaster General; 1909–1913 Secretary of the Navy.

MILWAUKEE (3D)

LIGHT CRUISER

Length, 555 feet, 6 inches   *Beam, 55 feet*   *Draft, 14 feet, 3 inches*

NAMED FOR THE CITY OF MILWAUKEE, WISCONSIN

Launched March 24, 1921, at Todd D. D. & C. Company, Tacoma, Washington.

Sponsor: MRS. RUDOLPH PFEIL (Josephine Schultz), appointed by the Mayor of Milwaukee in recognition of work during the World War for American soldiers and sailors.

THE first "Milwaukee" was an iron clad monitor of 970 tons, built in 1863, sunk by a torpedo in 1865. Named for Milwaukee River.

The second "Milwaukee" was a cruiser of 9700 tons, launched in 1904. Named for the city of Milwaukee.

MISSISSIPPI (3D)

BATTLESHIP

Length, 624 feet   *Beam, 97 feet, 4½ inches*   *Draft, 30 feet*

NAMED FOR THE STATE OF MISSISSIPPI
(*Admitted to the Union in 1817*)

Launched January 25, 1917, at Newport News S. B. & D. D. Company, Newport News, Virginia.

Sponsor: MISS CAMILLE MCBEATH, Meridian, Mississippi, daughter of the Chairman of the Mississippi State Highway Commission.

THE dreadnaught "Mississippi" is the third ship to bear the name. The battleship "Mississippi," launched in 1905 and sold to Greece in 1914, was the second of the name, but was the first to be named after the State of Mississippi. The first "Mississippi," the side wheel steam frigate of Civil War fame, was named for the Mississippi River.

[147]

MONOCACY (2D)

GUNBOAT

Length, 160 feet *Beam, 24 feet* *Draft, 2 feet, 5 inches*

NAMED FOR MONOCACY RIVER

Launched April 27, 1914, at Shanghai Dock & Engine Company, Shanghai, China.

Sponsor: MRS. ANDREW F. CARTER (Augusta Heacock), wife of Lieutenant A. F. Carter, U. S. Navy, Inspector of Machinery for the vessel.

"Monocacy 1st" was a "Double Ender" launched in 1864.

MONTGOMERY (2D)

TORPEDO BOAT DESTROYER

Length, 314 feet *Beam, 30 feet, 11 inches* *Draft, 9 feet, 3 inches*

NAMED FOR REAR ADMIRAL JOHN BERRIEN
MONTGOMERY, U. S. NAVY

Launched March 23, 1918, at Newport News Shipbuilding Company.

Sponsor: MRS. ANDREW JONES (Julia Montgomery Wood), great-granddaughter of Rear Admiral John B. Montgomery, U. S. Navy, and daughter of Captain E. P. Wood, U. S. Navy.

REAR ADMIRAL JOHN BERRIEN MONTGOMERY, United States Navy, was born in Allentown, New Jersey, 1794; died 1873. Appointed midshipman 1812; rear admiral 1866. Participated in the attack on Little York, Canada, and Fort George, 1813. Volunteered for service with Commodore O. H. Perry and one of the midshipman of the "Niagara" in the battle of Lake Erie, September 10, 1813. He received the thanks of Congress and a sword for gallantry on that occasion. Took part in the blockade and attack upon "Mackinaw," August, 1814. Served with Commodore Stephen Decatur in operations against Algiers, 1815. Commanded the sloop-of-war "Portsmouth" 1845–

U.S. SCOUT CRUISER "MILWAUKEE" UNDER WAY

1847 on the Pacific, and took prominent part in operations against the Mexicans on that side of the coast. Captured many vessels and aided the Army in taking possession of prominent Mexican towns.

MOODY

TORPEDO BOAT DESTROYER

Length, 314 feet　　　*Beam, 30 feet, 11 inches*　　　*Draft, 9 feet, 4 inches*

NAMED FOR SECRETARY OF THE NAVY WILLIAM HENRY MOODY

Launched June 28, 1919, at Bethlehem Shipbuilding Corporation, Quincy, Massachusetts.

Sponsor: MISS MARY E. MOODY, sister of Secretary of the Navy William Henry Moody.

HON. WILLIAM HENRY MOODY, Secretary of the Navy 1902–1904. Born in Newberry, Massachusetts, 1853; died 1917. He was graduated from Phillips Academy, Andover, Massachusetts, in 1872, and from Harvard University in 1876. In 1895 he was elected to the House of Representatives, and during his three terms there made a reputation by his knowledge of parliamentary procedure and by his perseverance in debate. In 1902 he became Secretary of the Navy and continued in that capacity until 1904, when he was made Attorney General. He subsequently was appointed Associate Justice of the Supreme Court.

MORRIS

TORPEDO BOAT DESTROYER

Length, 314 feet　　　*Beam, 30 feet, 11 inches*　　　*Draft, 9 feet, 4 inches*

NAMED FOR COMMODORE CHARLES MORRIS, U. S. NAVY

Launched April 12, 1919, at Bethlehem Shipbuilding Company, Quincy, Massachusetts.

[149]

Sponsor: MRS. GEORGE EMLEN ROOSEVELT (Julia Morris Addison), great-granddaughter of Commodore Charles Morris, U. S. Navy.

COMMODORE CHARLES MORRIS, U. S. Navy, was born in Woodstock, Connecticut, 1784; died 1856. Appointed midshipman 1799; captain 1813; as one of the officers of the "Intrepid" he took part in the recapture and destruction of the "Philadelphia" in the harbor of Tripoli February 17, 1804; took prominent part in the engagement between the "Constitution" and "Guerriere," being severely wounded while in the act of boarding the latter vessel; for his gallantry on this occasion he was advanced one grade by the President; in 1825 commanded the "Brandywine," taking Gen. Lafayette back to France; 1851–1856 was Chief of Bureau of Ordnance.

MUGFORD

TORPEDO BOAT DESTROYER

Length, 314 feet   *Beam, 30 feet, 11 inches*   *Draft, 9 feet, 2 inches*

NAMED FOR CAPTAIN JAMES MUGFORD, U. S. NAVY

Launched April 14, 1918, at Bethlehem Shipbuilding Corporation, San Francisco, California.

Sponsor: MRS. GEORGE H. FORT (Edythe McQuade), wife of Lieutenant Commander G. H. Fort, U. S. Navy, prospective executive officer of the "Mugford."

CAPTAIN JAMES MUGFORD, United States Navy. Commanding the continental schooner "Franklin," he captured the British ship "Hope" with a large cargo of military stores and powder, and took his prize into Boston, running past the British fleet lying in the harbor. The "Franklin" was attacked at night, however, by a greatly surperior force, in which action Captain Mugford was killed.

[150]

MULLANY

TORPEDO BOAT DESTROYER

Length, 314 feet   *Beam, 30 feet, 11 inches*   *Draft, 9 feet, 4 inches*

NAMED FOR REAR ADMIRAL J. R. MADISON MULLANY, U. S. Navy

Launched July 9, 1919, Bethlehem Shipbuilding Corporation, San Francisco, California.

Sponsor: MISS ALICE Lee HALL, daughter of Lieutenant Colonel Dickinson P. Hall, U. S. Marine Corps.

REAR ADMIRAL J. R. MADISON MULLANY, United States Navy, was born in New York City, 1818; died 1887. Appointed midshipman 1832; rear admiral 1874. Served on various stations; 1847–1848 attached to the home squadron, and took part in the capture of Tobasco and other engagements of the Mexican War; 1861 commanded the "Wyandotte" at Pensacola; 1862–1864 attached to the "Bienville" in the North Atlantic and West Gulf Blockading Squadrons; volunteered for service in Mobile Bay; was assigned to the "Oneida"; exposed to the most destructive fire; displayed great heroism, and was wounded. He was obliged to have his arm amputated; received the thanks of Congress for his gallantry; 1874–1875 commanded the North Atlantic station and protected American interests on the Isthmus of Panama.

MURRAY

TORPEDO BOAT DESTROYER

Length, 314 feet   *Beam, 30 feet, 11 inches*   *Draft, 9 feet, 1 inch*

NAMED FOR CAPTAIN ALEXANDER MURRAY, U. S. NAVY
AND
REAR ADMIRAL ALEXANDER MURRAY, U. S. NAVY

Launched June 8, 1918, at Bethlehem Shipbuilding Corporation, Quincy, Massachusetts.

[151]

Sponsor: MISS ALICE S. GUTHRIE, daughter of Mr. Robert Walker Guthrie, and grand-niece of Rear Admiral Alexander Murray, U. S. Navy.

CAPTAIN ALEXANDER MURRAY, U. S. Navy, was born in Chestertown, Maryland, July 12, 1755; commanded "Constellation," 1800–1802, in operations against the Barbary Powers; 1805, commanded the "John Adams." Last duty was in command of the Philadelphia Navy Yard.

REAR ADMIRAL ALEXANDER MURRAY, U. S. Navy, was born in Pittsburgh, Pennsylvania, January 2, 1816; died November 10, 1884; served with distinction in the Mexican War; prominently engaged in the North Atlantic Blockading Squadron, 1861–1863; included in thanks of Congress for gallantry at Roanoke Island, 1862; special service to Russia, 1866–1867; member of Lighthouse Board, 1873–1876.

Dimensions of Submarines N-1 to N-3 inclusive are:
Length, 147 feet, 3 inches   Beam, 15 feet, 9 inches   Draft, 12 feet, 5¾ inches

N–1
SUBMARINE

Launched December 30, 1916, at Seattle C. & D. D. Company.

Sponsor: MRS. GUY E. DAVIS (Mabel Matheson), wife of Lieutenant G. E. Davis, U. S. Navy, supervising construction for the Government.

"In the name of the United States I name thee. May you bring peace," were the words of the sponsor.

N–2
SUBMARINE

Launched January 16, 1917, at Seattle C. & D. D. Company.

Sponsor: MRS. WHITFORD DRAKE (Evelyn R.), wife of Naval Constructor W. Drake, U. S. Navy.

N-3
SUBMARINE

Launched February 21, 1917, at Seattle C. & D. D. Company.

Sponsor: MISS BERTHA COONTZ, daughter of Captain Robert E. Coontz, U. S. Navy, in command of Puget Sound Navy Yard.

Dimensions of Submarines N-4 to N-7 inclusive are:
Length, 155 feet   Beam, 14 feet, 7 inches   Draft, 12 feet, 4 inches

N-4
SUBMARINE

Launched November 27, 1916, at Lake Torpedo Boat Company, Bridgeport, Connecticut.

Sponsor: MISS DOROTHY HASTINGS ELLIOTT, Reynoldsville, Pennsylvania, appointed by request of Honorable W. B. Wilson, Secretary of Labor.

N-5
SUBMARINE

Launched March 22, 1917, at Lake Torpedo Boat Company, Bridgeport, Connecticut.

Sponsor: MRS. GEORGE E. BEVANS (Ida Miller), niece of Mr. H. S. Miller, president of the shipbuilding company.

N-6
SUBMARINE

Launched April 21, 1917, at Lake Torpedo Boat Company, Bridgeport, Connecticut.

Sponsor: MRS. JOHN A. KISSICK (Irene Gauthier), wife of an official of the shipbuilding company.

N-7
SUBMARINE

Launched May 19, 1917, at Lake Torpedo Boat Company, Bridgeport, Connecticut.

Sponsor: MRS. FRANK MILLER (Anne Hallock), wife of the Treasurer of the Lake Torpedo Boat Company.

NECHES

FUEL SHIP

Length, 475 feet   *Beam, 56 feet*   *Draft, 26 feet, 8 inches*

NAMED FOR NECHES RIVER, TEXAS

Launched June 2, 1920, at Navy Yard, Boston, Massachusetts.

Sponsor: MISS HELEN GRIFFIN, daughter of Rear Admiral Robert S. Griffin, U. S. Navy, Chief of Bureau of Steam Engineering at the time.

NEREUS

FUEL SHIP

Length, 522 feet   *Beam, 62 feet*   *Draft, 27 feet*

NAMED FOR THE GREEK MYTHOLOGICAL SEA GOD NEREUS

Launched April 26, 1913, at Newport News S. B. & D. D. Company, Newport News, Virginia.

Sponsor: MISS ANNE SEYMOUR JONES, daughter of Congressman W. A. Jones, of Virginia.

NEVADA (3D)

BATTLESHIP

Length, 583 feet   *Beam, 95 feet, 2½ inches*   *Draft, 28 feet, 6 inches*

NAMED FOR THE STATE OF NEVADA
(Admitted to the Union in 1864)

Launched July 11, 1914, at Fore River Shipbuilding Company, Quincy, Massachusetts.

Sponsor: MISS ELEANOR ANNE SIEBERT, Reno, Nevada, niece of Governor Tasker L. Oddie of Nevada, and great-great-great-granddaughter of Benjamin Stoddert, the first Secretary of the Navy.

AMONG those present on the stand were Assistant Secretary of the Navy, Franklin D. Roosevelt, Governor Oddie, and officers of the Army and Navy and also the Argentine Navy.

Her predecessor, the Monitor "Nevada," launched in 1900, is now renamed "Tonopah." "Nevada (1st)," launched in 1865, bore successively the names "Neshaminy," "Nevada" and "Arizona."

NEW MEXICO

BATTLESHIP

Length, 624 feet   *Beam, 97 feet, 4½ inches*   *Draft, 30 feet*

NAMED FOR THE STATE OF NEW MEXICO

(Admitted to the Union in 1912)

Launched April 23, 1917, at Navy Yard, New York, New York.

Sponsor: MISS MARARET C. DEBACA, daughter of former Governor DeBaca of New Mexico, and chosen for the honor by Governor William C. McDonald.

JUST before the launching the Sponsors' "Prayer for our Navy" was offered.

After the sponsor had broken a bottle of champagne and named the ship, Miss Virginia M. Carr, maid of honor, broke against the bow a jug made by New Mexican Indians and containing water from the Rio Grande and Pecos rivers. There were fifty residents of New Mexico on the stand.

The launching was private because the United States was at war with Germany. From the small launching stand built near her bow, only the ship's bow could be seen. This was one of many war precautions. The Navy Yard was strictly guarded.

NICHOLAS

TORPEDO BOAT DESTROYER

Length, 314 feet   *Beam, 30 feet, 11 inches*   *Draft, 9 feet, 4 inches*

[155]

NAMED FOR MAJOR SAMUEL NICHOLAS,
U. S. MARINE CORPS

Launched May 1, 1919, at Bethlehem Shipbuilding Corporation, San Francisco, California.

Sponsor: MISS EDITH BARRY, daughter of James H. Barry, Naval Officer of the Port, San Francisco, and editor of "*The Star.*"

MAJOR SAMUEL NICHOLAS, U. S. Marine Corps; appointed by the marine committee in 1775. June 6, 1776, appointed major by the Continental Congress and placed at the head of the Marines. Served with Commodore Esek Hopkins in the fleet that attacked New Providence, West Indies, March 3, 1776. Landed in command of 200 marines, and about 50 sailors at Fort Nassau. Captured 88 cannon, 15 mortars, and the landing party captured the governor, lieutenant governor, and a number of other prominent persons and brought them to the United States. The officials were immediately returned. Major Nicholas remained in the service throughout the War of the Revolution.

NICHOLSON (2D)

TORPEDO BOAT DESTROYER

Length, 300 feet   *Beam, 30 feet*   *Draft, 9 feet, 5½ inches*

NAMED FOR CAPTAIN SAMUEL NICHOLSON,
U. S. NAVY

Launched August 19, 1914, at William Cramp & Sons' Company, Philadelphia, Pennsylvania.

Sponsor: MRS. CHARLES T. TAYLOR (Sophie Davis), wife of the Treasurer of the Shipbuilding Company, and granddaughter of William Cramp, founder of the company.

CAPTAIN SAMUEL NICHOLSON, U. S. Navy, was born in Maryland 1743; died at Charlestown, Massachusetts, December 29, 1811. Commissioned captain December 10,

READY TO LAUNCH THE U.S. BATTLESHIP
"NEW YORK"

1776. Cruised in command of the "Deane" from 1777 to 1782; made many valuable prizes.

Upon the reorganization of the Navy commissioned captain June 10, 1794, and ordered to superintend the building of the "Constitution." Was the first to command this vessel in 1798.

NITRO

AMMUNITION SHIP

Length, 482 feet   *Beam, 60 feet, 11 inches*   *Draft, 20 feet, 11 inches*

NAME "NITRO" INDICATES THE PRESENCE OF
NITROGEN IN AMMUNITION

Launched December 16, 1919, at Puget Sound Navy Yard.

Sponsor: MRS. HENRY SUZZALO (Edith Moore), wife of the president of the University of Washington.

NOA

TORPEDO BOAT DESTROYER

Length, 314 feet   *Beam, 30 feet, 11 inches*   *Draft, 9 feet, 4 inches*

NAMED FOR MIDSHIPMAN LOVEMAN NOA,
U. S. NAVY

Launched June 28, 1919, at Norfolk Navy Yard.

Sponsor: MRS. ALBERT MOREHEAD (Bianca Noa), sister of Midshipman Loveman Noa, U. S. Navy.

MIDSHIPMAN LOVEMAN NOA, U. S. Navy, was born in Chattanooga, Tennessee, October 5, 1878; killed by natives on the Island of Samar, Philippine Islands, October 26, 1901. Appointed cadet 1896; graduated in 1900; sent to Asiatic Station on board the "Mariveles." On October 26, 1901, Midshipman Noa, with an armed crew of six men, put off in a small boat from the "Mariveles" to watch for boats engaged in smuggling contraband of war from the Island of Leyte to Samar Island. The wind turning against them, they were obliged to land in a small cove on the Island of Samar, and while scouting the nearby woods Midshipman Noa was stabbed by Filipino insurgents and died before aid could reach him.

Dimensions of Submarines O–1 to O–10 inclusive are:
Length, 172 feet, 4 inches   *Beam, 18 feet*   *Draft, 14 feet, 5 inches*

O–1
SUBMARINE

Launched October 9, 1918, at U. S. Navy Yard, Portsmouth, New Hampshire.

Sponsor: MRS. CORA ISABEL ADAMS, wife of Captain L. S. Adams, C. C., U. S. Navy, Industrial Manager of the Navy Yard.

O–2
SUBMARINE

Launched May 24, 1918, at Navy Yard, Puget Sound, Washington.

Sponsor: MRS. FRANCIS T. CHEW (Mary Hoge), wife of Lieutenant Commander F. T. Chew, U. S. Navy.

O–3
SUBMARINE

Launched September 29, 1917, at Bethlehem Shipbuilding Corporation, Quincy, Massachusetts.

Sponsor: MRS. GEORGE L. DICKSON (Alma Hodges), wife of Lieutenant G. L. Dickson, U. S. Navy, the prospective commanding officer.

O–4
SUBMARINE

Launched October 20, 1917, at Bethlehem Shipbuilding Corporation, Quincy, Massachusetts.

Sponsor: MRS. HENRY WILLIAMS (Maud Steers), wife of Naval Constructor Henry Williams, U. S. Navy, Superintending Construction.

O–5
SUBMARINE

Launched November 11, 1917, at Bethlehem Shipbuilding Corporation, Quincy, Massachusetts.

Sponsor: MRS. FRANK T. CABLE (Nettie Hungerford), wife of the vice president and general manager of the New London S. & E. Company.

O–6
SUBMARINE

Launched November 25, 1917, at Bethlehem Shipbuilding Corporation, Quincy, Massachusetts.

Sponsor: MRS. CARROL Q. WRIGHT (Dessaline Shepard), wife of Lieutenant C. Q. Wright, U. S. Navy, prospective commanding officer of the vessel.

O–7
SUBMARINE

Launched December 16, 1917, at Bethlehem Shipbuilding Corporation, Quincy, Massachusetts.

Sponsor: MISS CONSTANCE SEARS, daughter of Hon. Russell A. Sears, formerly Mayor of Quincy.

O–8
SUBMARINE

Launched December 31, 1917, at Bethlehem Shipbuilding Corporation, Quincy, Massachusetts.

Sponsor: MRS. ROBERT A. BURG (Alice Claire), wife of Lieutenant R. A. Burg, U. S. Navy, prospective commanding officer.

O–9
SUBMARINE

Launched January 27, 1918, at Bethlehem Shipbuilding Corporation, Quincy, Massachusetts.

Sponsor: MRS. FREDERICK C. SHERMAN (Fanny Jessop), wife of Lieutenant Commander F. C. Sherman, first commanding officer of the vessel.

O–10
SUBMARINE

Launched February 21, 1918, at Bethlehem Shipbuilding Corporation, Quincy, Massachusetts.

SPONSOR: MRS. JOHN ELIOT BAILEY (Bertha Martin), wife of Captain J. E. Bailey, C. C., U. S. Navy, on duty at Boston Navy Yard.

Dimensions of Submarines O–11 to O–16, inclusive, are:
Length, 175 feet   *Beam, 16 feet*   *Draft, 13 feet, 10 inches*

O–11
SUBMARINE

Launched October 29, 1917, at Lake Torpedo Boat Company, Bridgeport, Connecticut.

Sponsor: MRS. BERNARD M. BARUCH (Anne Griffen), wife of Mr. B. M. Baruch, Chairman of the War Industries Board during the World War.

O–12
SUBMARINE

Launched September 29, 1917, at Lake Torpedo Boat Company, Bridgeport, Connecticut.

Sponsor: MRS. HOMER S. CUMMINGS (Marguerite Owings), wife of the Democratic National Chairman at the time.

U.S. BATTLESHIP "OKLAHOMA" UNDER WAY

O–13

SUBMARINE

Launched December 27, 1917, at Lake Torpedo Boat Company, Bridgeport, Connecticut.

Sponsor: MISS MARGARET ARLETTA ADAMS, niece of Mr. Simon Lake, submarine boat inventor, and daughter of Mr. Clement E. Adams, Secretary and Assistant Treasurer of the Company.

O–14

SUBMARINE

Launched May 6, 1918, at California Shipbuilding Company, Long Beach, California.

Sponsor: MISS ELEANOR N. HATCH, daughter of Mr. P. E. Hatch, President of the National Bank of Long Beach and Treasurer of the Company.

O–15

SUBMARINE

Launched February 12, 1918, at California Shipbuilding Company, Long Beach, California.

Sponsor: MRS. JAMES J. MURPHY, wife of Lieutenant (T) J. J. Murphy, C. C., U. S. Navy.

O–16

SUBMARINE

Launched February 9, 1918, at California Shipbuilding Company, Long Beach, California.

Sponsor: MRS. IRVING HALL MAYFIELD (Juliet Borden), wife of Lieutenant Commander I. H. Mayfield, U. S. Navy, Inspector of Machinery for the Navy at the works.

O'BANNON

TORPEDO BOAT DESTROYER

Length, 314 feet   *Beam, 30 feet, 11 inches*   *Draft, 9 feet, 2 inches*

[161]

NAMED FOR LIEUTENANT PRESLEY NEVILLE O'BANNON,
U. S. MARINE CORPS

Launched February 28, 1919, at Bethlehem Shipbuilding
Corporation, San Francisco, California.

Sponsor: MRS. HENRY O'BANNON COOPER (Katharine
Low), wife of great-great-nephew of Lieutenant Presley Neville O'Bannon, U. S. Navy.

FIRST LIEUTENANT PRESLEY N. O'BANNON, U. S.
Marine Corps. Appointed second lieutenant, 1801; first
lieutenant, 1802; resigned 1807. During the war with
Tripoli, an expedition was started out from Alexandria,
Egypt, to Derne. The force consisted of mercenaries, together with Lieut. O'Bannon, one sergeant, and six privates
of the Marine Corps. A march of 600 miles was made, and
the force, which had been augmented by additional marines,
arrived before Derne April 26, 1805. The works were shelled
by the "Hornet," "Nautilus," and "Argus" on April 27,
and the principal work was stormed by a force led by Lieut.
O'Bannon and Midshipman Mann. The Tripolitan ensign
was hauled down, and for the first time in the history of the
country the flag of the Republic was hoisted on a fortress of
the Old World. Gen. Eaton was wounded and Lieut.
O'Bannon, with a detachment under his command, took
possession of the battery, planted the American flag upon
its ramparts, and turned its guns upon the enemy.

O'BRIEN (2D)

TORPEDO BOAT DESTROYER

Length, 305 feet   *Beam, 30 feet, 4 inches*   *Draft, 9 feet, 5½ inches*

NAMED FOR CAPTAIN JEREMIAH O'BRIEN,
U. S. NAVY

Launched July 20, 1914, at William Cramp & Sons'
Company, Philadelphia, Pennsylvania.

Sponsor: MISS MARCIA BRADBURY CAMPBELL, great-
great-grandniece of Captain Jeremiah O'Brien, U. S. Navy.

CAPTAIN JEREMIAH O'BRIEN, United States Navy, was born in Kittery, Maine, 1744; died 1818 at Machias, Maine. June 12, 1775, in a small sloop called the "Unity" manned by six volunteers, armed with a few muskets and some pitchforks, boarded and captured after a sharp fight the British schooner "Margaretta." O'Brien put the "Margaretta's" guns on the "Unity" which he renamed the "Machias Liberty" and with her captured the British coast-guard "Diligence" and her tender, which had been sent from Halifax to protect the "Margaretta," whose capture was the first of an enemy's vessel in the Revolutionary War. He later commanded the privateer "Hannibal," in which he was captured, imprisoned on the Jersey prison ship in New York harbor, afterwards taken to Mill Prison, England, from which he escaped.

OKLAHOMA

BATTLESHIP

Length, 583 feet   *Beam, 95 feet, 2½ inches*   *Draft, 28 feet, 6 inches*

NAMED FOR THE STATE OF OKLAHOMA

(Admitted to the Union in 1907)

Launched March 23, 1914, at New York Shipbuilding Corporation, Camden, New Jersey.

Sponsor: MISS LORENA JANE CRUCE, daughter of Governor Lee Cruce, of Oklahoma.

THE sponsor and maids of honor carried bouquets of mistletoe, the State flower of Oklahoma. A huge bunch of mistletoe was suspended over the bow of the vessel and the name of the ship was outlined in the same flowers.

The launching party consisted of Secretary of the Navy Josephus Daniels, Mrs. Daniels, Assistant Secretary Franklin J. Roosevelt, Colonel Hunter Craycroft, Senators Owen and Gore of Oklahoma, Rear Admiral Reynold T. Hall, members of the Society of Sponsors, and some 600 invited guests. Vice President Marshall, as representative of President Wilson, headed the government officials. Governor

[163]

Tenner of Pennsylvania, Governor Glynn of New York, and Governor Baldwin of Connecticut were present. An enormous concourse of spectators witnessed the launching.

"At the launching of the battleship 'Oklahoma' at Camden, New Jersey, on March 23, there was observed the custom which has always prevailed in other Christian countries of prayer preceding the civil ceremony of naming a battleship. This suggestion, made by Mrs. Reynold T. Hall, president of the Society of Sponsors, was most enthusiastically received by the Oklahoma delegation to the launching, and Bishop Hoss of Oklahoma, was invited to offer the invocation. Prior to this occasion the United States has launched its battleships with civil ceremony only. In other countries this religious custom is always observed, and in England the special prayer at launchings is one of great beauty. This suggestion made by the Society of Sponsors was highly commended by the Secretary of the Navy and by the Oklahoma state officials. Secretary Daniels is so favorably impressed with the idea, that hereafter a prayer will be part of the exercises of launchings of battleships."—*Army and Navy Journal.*

OMAHA (2D)

LIGHT CRUISER

Length, 555 feet   *Beam, 55 feet*   *Draft, 13 feet, 6 inches*

NAMED FOR OMAHA, NEBRASKA

Launched December 14, 1920, at Todd Dry Dock and C. Company, Tacoma, Washington.

Sponsor: MISS LOUISE BUSHNELL WHITE, daughter of the Mayor of Omaha, Victor White.

The first "Omaha" was a sloop of war, launched in 1869 and named for Omaha River.

ORIOLE

MINE SWEEPER

Length, 187 feet   *Beam, 35 feet*   *Draft, 9 feet, 9 inches*

NAMED FOR THE BIRD ORIOLE

Launched July 3, 1918, at Staten Island Shipbuilding Corporation, New York.

Sponsor: MISS DOROTHY LEAVERTON, daughter of an employee of the Engineering Department of the Company.

ORTOLAN

MINE SWEEPER

Length, 187 feet   *Beam, 35 feet*   *Draft, 9 feet, 9 inches*

NAMED FOR THE BIRD ORTOLAN

Launched January 30, 1919, at Staten Island Shipbuilding Company, New York.

Sponsor: MISS THERESA MARION FINN, telephone operator at the contractor's plant.

OSBORNE

TORPEDO BOAT DESTROYER

Length, 314 feet   *Beam, 30 feet, 11 inches*   *Draft, 9 feet, 4 inches*

NAMED FOR LIEUTENANT WEEDEN E. OSBORNE, U. S. NAVY

Launched December 29, 1919, at Bethlehem Shipbuilding Company, Quincy, Massachusetts.

Sponsor: MRS. HARRY HUTCHINS FISHER (Elizabeth Osborne), sister of Lieutenant Weeden Edward Osborne, U. S. Navy. Mrs. Fisher was assisted by Mrs. Channing H. Cox, wife of Lieutenant Governor Cox, of Massachusetts.

LIEUTENANT WEEDEN E. OSBORNE, dental surgeon, U. S. Navy, was born in Chicago, Illinois, 1892. Killed in action with the Sixth Regiment Marines, June 6, 1918, at Chateau Thierry, France. Appointed dental surgeon in the Navy with the rank of lieutenant (junior grade) May 8, 1917. Detailed to duty with the Sixth Regiment Marines March 26, 1918. Posthumously awarded the distinguished service cross and the Navy medal of honor for extraordinary heriosm under fire during the advance on

Bouresches, France. The nature of his professional duties gave him every justification for remaining in the rear, but he threw himself into the general rescue work and performed heroic deeds in aiding the wounded. While carrying a wounded officer to a place of safety he was struck by a shell and instantly killed. He was the first commissioned officer of the United States Navy to meet death during the land fighting overseas.

OSPREY

MINE SWEEPER

Length, 187 feet   *Beam, 35 feet*   *Draft, 9 feet, 9 inches*

NAMED FOR THE BIRD OSPREY

Launched November 19, 1918, at Consolidated Shipbuilding Corporation, New York City.

Sponsor: MRS. JOHN J. AMORY (Mary S.), wife of the president of the corporation.

OVERTON

TORPEDO BOAT DESTROYER

Length, 314 feet   *Beam, 30 feet, 11 inches*   *Draft, 9 feet, 4 inches*

NAMED FOR CAPTAIN MACON C. OVERTON, U. S. MARINE CORPS

Launched July 10, 1919, at New York Shipbuilding Corporation, Camden, New Jersey.

Sponsor: MRS. MARGARET C. OVERTON, mother of Captain Macon C. Overton, U. S. M. C.

CAPTAIN MACON C. OVERTON, U. S. Marine Corps, was born in Union Point, Georgia, 1890; died in France November 1, 1918. On June 13, 1918, he was recommended for reward by his regimental commander for successfully carrying out an assault on a supposedly impregnable machine-gun nest in the Bois de Belleau. This assault was made under heavy fire of machine guns and grenades, and its success against tremendous odds gave the enemy the severest single blow that it suffered throughout the operations in the Bois de Belleau. Awarded croix de guerre with palm for remarkable bravery and tenacity in an engagement, July 19, 1918, near Vierzy. Awarded croix de guerre with silver star and palm for brilliantly leading his men on a machine-gun nest. Awarded distinguished-service cross for extraordinary heroism in action near Mount Blanc, October 2–10, 1918, where his gallantry was an inspiration to his men. Awarded oak-leaf cluster for displaying remarkable courage at St. George, November 1, 1918, where he was fatally wounded while guiding a tank forward against an enemy machine gun position.

OWL

MINE SWEEPER

Length, 187 feet   *Beam, 35 feet*   *Draft, 9 feet, 9 inches*

NAMED FOR THE BIRD OWL

Launched May 4, 1918, at Todd Shipyard Corporation, New York.

Sponsor: MISS RUTH REBECCA DODD, daughter of the foreman shipfitter of the company.

PALMER

TORPEDO BOAT DESTROYER

Length, 314 feet   *Beam, 30 feet, 11 inches*   *Draft, 9 feet, 2 inches*

NAMED FOR REAR ADMIRAL JAMES SHEDDEN PALMER, U. S. Navy

Launched August 18, 1918, at Bethlehem Shipbuilding Corporation, Quincy, Massachusetts.

Sponsor: MRS. ROBERT B. HILLIARD (Grace Powell), wife of Naval Constructor R. B. Hilliard, U. S. Navy, on duty at Fore River.

REAR ADMIRAL JAMES SHEDDEN PALMER, U. S. Navy, was born in New Jersey, 1810; died 1867. Appointed a midshipman 1825; rear admiral 1866. Took part in the attack on Quallah Battoo and Mushie, island of Sumatra, and commanded the "Flirt" in the blockade of the Mexican ports during the war with Mexico. Commanded the U. S. S. "Iroquois." May, 1862, joined the West Gulf Blockading Squadron and took prominent part in engagements against Baton Rouge, Grand Gulf, Natchez, passage of Vicksburg batteries, June 28, 1862. Attack on the ram "Arkansas." Farragut's commander on the "Hartford" when he ran the batteries at Port Hudson March, 1863. 1864 commanded the naval station at New Orleans. Commanded the West Gulf Squadron, after the battle of Mobile Bay, until Feb. 21, 1865; commanded West India Squadron 1866.

PALOS (2D)

GUNBOAT

Length, 160 feet   *Beam, 24 feet*   *Draft, 2 feet, 5 inches*

NAMED FOR PALOS, SPAIN, THE PORT FROM WHICH COLUMBUS SAILED

Launched April 23, 1914, at Shanghai Dock and Engineering Company, Shanghai, China.

Sponsor: MRS. LEE SCOTT BORDER (Chetanna Nesbitt), wife of Naval Constructor L. S. Border, U. S. Navy, who superintended the construction of the vessel.

PALOS 1st" was a steam vessel which under Commodore Beardsley, was the first vessel to carry the flag through the Suez Canal in 1868, en route to China.

PARROTT

TORPEDO BOAT DESTROYER

Length, 314 feet   *Beam, 30 feet, 11 inches*   *Draft, 9 feet, 4 inches*

LAUNCHING PARTY OF U.S. SCOUT CRUISER "OMAHA"

NAMED FOR LIEUTENANT GEORGE FOUNTAIN PARROTT, JR.,
U. S. Navy

Launched November 25, 1919, at William Cramp and
Sons' Company, Philadelphia, Pennsylvania.

Sponsor: MISS JULIA BIZZELL PARROTT, sister of Lieutenant George Fountain Parrott, Jr.

LIEUTENANT GEORGE FOUNTAIN PARROTT, Jr.,
United States Navy. Born in North Carolina, 1887; died
at sea, October 9, 1918. Appointed midshipman, July 3,
1906; lieutenant (j. g.), March 7, 1915; attached to the
U. S. S. "Shaw." The "Shaw" had just sighted a German
submarine and was going for her when she crossed the bow
of the British troopship "Squitania." Lieutenant Parrott
died in the performance of duty.

PARTRIDGE

MINE SWEEPER

Length, 187 feet   *Beam, 35 feet, 6 inches*   *Draft, 9 feet, 9 inches*

NAMED FOR THE BIRD PARTRIDGE

Launched October 15, 1918, at Sun Shipbuilding Company, Chester, Pennsylvania.

Sponsor: MISS CAROLYN HEWES McCAY, daughter of
Commander H. K. McCay, U. S. Navy.

JAMES K. PAULDING

TORPEDO BOAT DESTROYER

Length, 314 feet   *Beam, 30 feet, 11 inches*   *Draft, 9 feet, 4 inches*

NAMED FOR SECRETARY OF THE NAVY
JAMES KIRKE PAULDING

Launched April 20, 1920, at New York Shipbuilding
Corporation, Camden, New Jersey.

Sponsor: MISS MARY HUBBARD PAULDING, great-granddaughter of Secretary of the Navy James Kirke Paulding.

SECRETARY OF THE NAVY JAMES KIRKE PAULD-ING was born in Nine Partners, Dutchess County, New York, August 27, 1778; died 1860. From 1815 to 1823 he was secretary of the first Board of Navy Commissioners. After having filled the office of Navy agent at the port of New York for twelve years, he resigned to become Secretary of the Navy, July 1, 1838.

PEACOCK

MINE SWEEPER

Length, 187 feet   *Beam, 35 feet*   *Draft, 9 feet, 9 inches*

NAMED FOR THE BIRD PEACOCK

Launched April 8, 1919, at Staten Island Shipbuilding Company, New York.

Sponsor: MISS ANNA MARIAN DANNER, daughter of Lieutenant John Danner, U. S. Navy, prospective commanding officer.

PEARY

TORPEDO BOAT DESTROYER

Length, 314 feet   *Beam, 30 feet, 11 inches*   *Draft, 9 feet, 4 inches*

NAMED FOR REAR ADMIRAL ROBERT EDWIN PEARY, U. S. NAVY

Launched April 6, 1920, at William Cramp & Sons' Company, Philadelphia, Pennsylvania.

Sponsor: MRS. EDWARD STAFFORD (Marie Ahnighito Peary), daughter of Rear Admiral Robert Edwin Peary, U. S. Navy.

The launching took place on the eleventh anniversary of Rear Admiral Peary's discovery of the North Pole. The sponsor carried a flag he had carried to the North Pole.

REAR ADMIRAL ROBERT EDWIN PEARY, United States Navy, C. E. Corps, was born in Cresson, Pennsylvania, 1856; died 1920; graduate of Bowdoin, Edinburgh, and Tufts colleges; promoted to rear admiral and given the thanks of Congress by special act of March 30, 1911. Assistant engineer of Nicaragua Ship Canal Company under Government orders, 1884–1885; in charge of Nicaragua Canal survey, 1887–1888; invented rolling lock gates for the canal. His first Arctic expedition was in 1886; chief of the Arctic expedition sent by the Academy of Science, Philadelphia, Pennsylvania, 1891; commanded Arctic expedition, 1898–1902; named the most northerly land in the world Cape Morris Jessup; July, 1905, sailed on the S. S. "Roosevelt" for the Arctic regions; returned in October, 1906, having reached "highest north." July, 1908, sailed on eighth Arctic expedition. In April, 1909, made his final dash of 130 miles to the North Pole in five days, reaching it April 6, 1909. Received honors from the scientific societies of Europe and America for his distinguished services in Arctic explorations and discoveries; was the author of numerous books on the North Pole and polar travel.

PECOS

FUEL SHIP

Length, 475 feet   *Beam, 56 feet*   *Draft, 26 feet, 8 inches*

NAMED FOR PECOS RIVER, IN NEW MEXICO AND TEXAS

Launched May 1, 1921, at the Navy Yard, Boston, Massachusetts.

Sponsor: MISS ANNA S. HUBBARD, granddaughter of Commodore Thomas Laurens Swann, U. S. Navy.

PELICAN

MINE SWEEPER

Length, 187 feet   *Beam, 35 feet*   *Draft, 9 feet, 9 inches*

NAMED FOR THE BIRD PELICAN

Launched June 15, 1918, at Consolidated Shipbuilding Corporation, New York City.

Sponsor: MISS ELIZABETH BACHE PATTERSON, daughter of Mr. H. W. Patterson, chief designer for the corporation.

PENGUIN

MINE SWEEPER

Length, 187 feet   *Beam, 35 feet*   *Draft, 9 feet, 9 inches*

NAMED FOR THE BIRD PENGUIN

Launched June 12, 1918, at New Jersey D. D. & T. Company.

Sponsor: MISS LILLIAN RAE, daughter of Mr. James Rae, foreman iron worker for the contractor.

PENNSYLVANIA (5TH)

BATTLESHIP

Length, 608 feet   *Beam, 97 feet*   *Draft, 28 feet, 10 inches*

NAMED FOR THE STATE OF PENNSYLVANIA
(Ratified the Constitution in 1787)

Launched March 16, 1915, at Newport News Shipbuilding and Dry Dock Company, Newport News, Virginia.

Sponsor: MISS ELIZABETH KOLB, Philadelphia, Pennsylvania, daughter of Mr. Louis J. Kolb, a friend of Governor Brumbaugh of Pennsylvania.

JUST before the launching, Bishop Joseph F. Berry offered the Society of Sponsors' "Prayer for our Navy," the Secretary of the Navy having directed that this prayer be offered. Prayer marked a Navy launching ceremony for the second time since 1843, the custom having been revived at the launching of the battleship "Oklahoma" in 1914 at the suggestion of the Society of Sponsors.

An enormous concourse of people witnessed the launching. Among those on the sponsor's stand were Secretary of the Navy Josephus Daniels, Mrs. Daniels, Governor Brumbaugh, Governor Stuart of Virginia, Honorable Mitchell Palmer

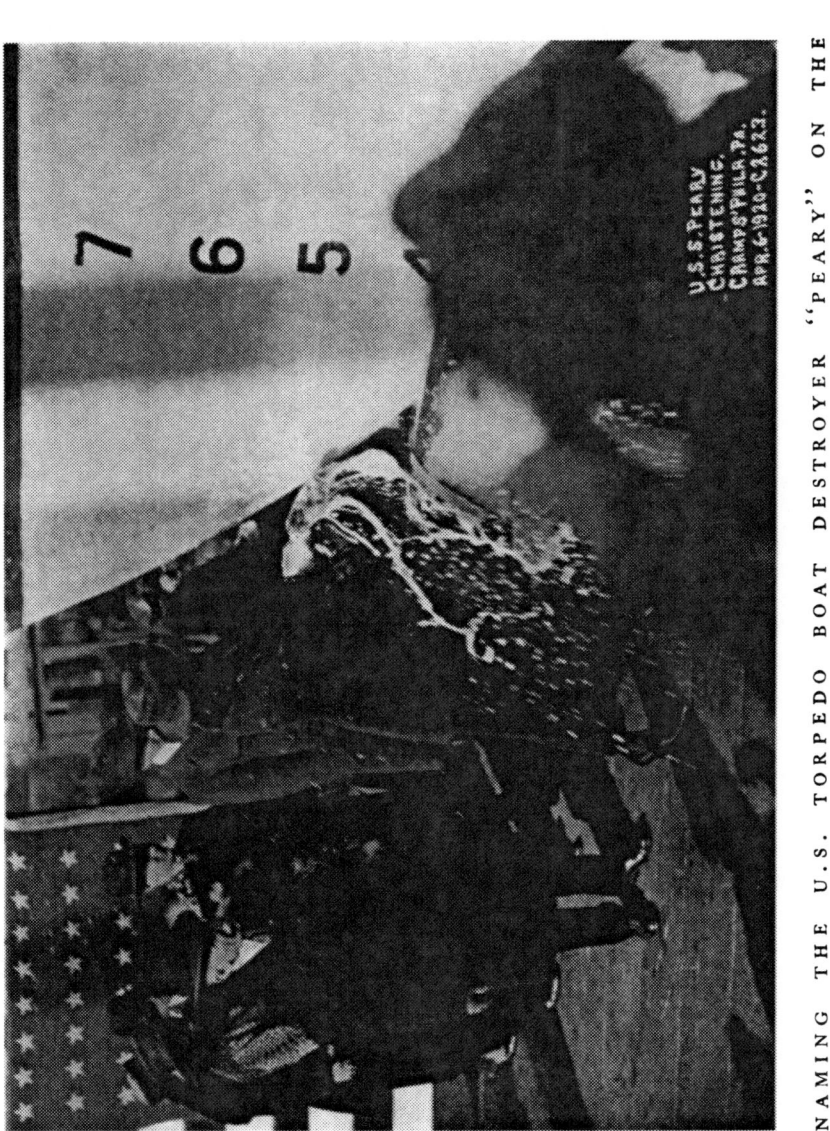

U.S.S.PEARY
CHRISTENING.
CRAMPS PHILA.PA.
APR.6-1920-CA623.

NAMING THE U.S. TORPEDO BOAT DESTROYER "PEARY" ON THE
ELEVENTH ANNIVERSARY OF THE DISCOVERY OF THE NORTH POLE

of Pennsylvania, Senator Swanson of Virginia, Mr. John Gribbel, Attorney General Francis Shunk Brown, Senator George T. Oliver, Congressman Wm. E. Vare, Admiral F. E. Beatty, Commandant of Norfolk Navy Yard, Colonel Haines, Commandant of Fort Monroe, and a large party of Pennsylvanians.

Mrs. Reynold T. Hall, President of the Society of Sponsors, and Miss Edith Benham, Secretary, accompanied Mrs. Daniels from Washington on board the U. S. S. "Mayflower."

After the launching the sponsor's party and invited guests boarded the U. S. S. "Mayflower," and landing at Fort Monroe, were entertained at a luncheon at the Hotel Chamberlin. Speeches were made by Governor Brumbaugh of Pennsylvania, Governor Stuart of Virginia, Secretary Daniels, and other officials. The sponsor responded to the toast "The Sponsor" in a graceful speech.

The super dreadnaught "Pennsylvania" is the fifth to bear the name of the State. Her predecessor, the armored cruiser "Pennsylvania," launched in 1903, is now renamed "Pittsburgh."

"Pennsylvania (3d)" was a coast line battleship authorized in 1899. For two years she bore the name "Pennsylvania" but in 1901 was renamed "Nebraska."

"Pennsylvania (2d)" was a screw sloop built in 1863, but never completed.

The first "Pennsylvania" was a 120 gun ship of the line, launched in 1837.

PERCIVAL

TORPEDO BOAT DESTROYER

Length, 314 feet   *Beam, 30 feet, 11 inches*   *Draft, 9 feet, 4 inches*

NAMED FOR CAPTAIN JOHN PERCIVAL, U. S. NAVY
Launched December 5, 1918, at Bethlehem Shipbuilding Corporation, San Francisco, California.

Sponsor: MISS ELEANOR WURTSBAUGH, daughter of Captain Daniel W. Wurtsbaugh, U. S. Navy.

[173]

CAPTAIN JOHN PERCIVAL, U. S. Navy, was born 1779 in Barnstable, Massachusetts; died 1862. Appointed a master's mate in 1799, and a midshipman in 1800; discharged under the peace establishment act of 1801. Entered the Merchant Service. Was captured and impressed into the British Service but escaped. In 1809 was appointed a sailing master and ordered to duty in the New York flotilla under Capt. Jacob Lewis; July 4, 1813, he borrowed a fishing smack named the "Yankee," and manning her with 36 volunteers, well armed, he concealed in the cabin all but 3 of the party, filled the deck with produce, and running toward the "Eagle," tender for the 74 gun line of battleship "Poictiers," at a given signal the concealed crew rose from their hiding, fired upon the "Eagle's" men, who were so taken by surprise that they took refuge below decks, not even waiting to haul down their colors; Percival took possession of the "Eagle" and carried her into New York, where he was received with great demonstrations of joy; April 29, 1814, he again distinguished himself in the action between the "Peacock" and the "Epervier," and was promoted by President Madison to lieutenant upon the recommendation of Capt. Warrington, his commanding officer in that engagement, and was also awarded a sword by Congress for his gallantry.

PERRY (4TH)

TORPEDO BOAT DESTROYER

Length, 314 feet, 4 inches   Beam, 30 feet, 11 inches   Draft, 9 feet, 4 inches

NAMED FOR COMMODORE OLIVER H. PERRY,
U. S. NAVY, AND CAPTAIN MATTHEW C. PERRY,
U. S. NAVY

Launched October 29, 1921, at the Navy Yard, Mare Island, California.

Sponsor: MISS ANNE RANDOLPH SCUDDER, daughter of Commander R. P. Scudder, U. S. Navy, and great-great-granddaughter of Commodore Oliver H. Perry, U. S. Navy.

[174]

LAUNCHING PARTY OF U.S. TORPEDO BOAT DESTROYER
''PILLSBURY''

COMMODORE OLIVER HAZARD PERRY, U. S. Navy, was born in Rhode Island in 1785; appointed midshipman in 1799; served in the Tripolitan War and was promoted to acting lieutenant at the age of seventeen. His most conspicuous service was in the War of 1812. He led the ships in Commodore Chauncey's attack on Fort George in 1813. Later he commanded the forces on Lake Erie, and defeated the British squadron in the Battle of Lake Erie. For this victory he was awarded a gold medal.

CAPTAIN MATTHEW C. PERRY, U. S. Navy, was born in 1795; appointed midshipman in 1809; served in the War of 1812 and commanded the Gulf Fleet in the Mexican War; rendered distinguished service at Tobasco and Vera Cruz. In 1853, as commodore of the East India squadron he went to Japan and after many difficulties negotiated a treaty safeguarding the rights of American commerce in Japanese waters.

Commodore Oliver H. Perry and Captain Matthew C. Perry were sons of Captain Christopher R. Perry, U. S. Navy, a distinguished officer of the Revolutionary War.

PHILIP

TORPEDO BOAT DESTROYER

Length, 314 feet   *Beam, 30 feet, 11 inches*   *Draft, 9 feet*

NAMED FOR REAR ADMIRAL JOHN WOODWARD PHILIP, U. S. NAVY

Launched July 25, 1918, at Bath Iron Works, Bath, Maine.

Sponsor: MRS. BARRETT PHILIP (Mazie F.), daughter-in-law of Rear Admiral John Woodward Philip, U. S. Navy.

REAR ADMIRAL JOHN WOODWARD PHILIP, United States Navy, was born in Kinderhook, Columbia County, New York, 1840; died in New York, June 30, 1900. Appointed midshipman September 20, 1856; commissioned rear admiral March 3, 1899; served in Civil War, and wounded in operations against Charleston, South Carolina;

[175]

1865–1867 distinguished in defense of Americans against attacks of Chinese and capture of the rebel Hon; in the war with Spain, commanded "Texas" at battle of Santiago, and was advanced five numbers for distinguished service.

PIGEON

MINE SWEEPER

Length, 187 feet   *Beam, 35 feet*   *Draft, 9 feet, 9 inches*

NAMED FOR THE BIRD PIGEON

Launched January 29, 1919, at Baltimore D. D. & S. B. Company.

Sponsor: MRS. JOSEPH B. PROVANCE, wife of one of the supervisors of the shipbuilding company.

PILLSBURY

TORPEDO BOAT DESTROYER

Length, 314 feet   *Beam, 30 feet, 11 inches*   *Draft, 9 feet, 4 inches*

NAMED FOR REAR ADMIRAL JOHN E. PILLSBURY, U. S. NAVY

Launched August 3, 1920, at William Cramp & Sons' Company, Philadelphia, Pennsylvania.

Sponsor: MISS HELEN LANGDON RICHARDSON, granddaughter of Rear Admiral John E. Pillsbury, U. S. Navy. The sponsor was accompanied by her mother, Mrs. Edward Bridge Richardson, sponsor for the U. S. S. "Smith" in 1909.

REAR ADMIRAL JOHN E. PILLSBURY, U. S. Navy, was born in Lowell, Massachusetts, 1846; died 1919. Appointed midshipman, 1862; ensign, 1868; master, 1870; lieutenant, 1872; lieutenant commander, 1892; commander, 1898; captain, 1902; rear admiral, 1908. Served on various stations afloat and ashore. From 1884 to 1891 commanded the coast steamer "Blake" and did excellent scientific work, using in some of his researches instruments of his own invention. In the Spanish-American War commanded the dynamite cruiser "Vesuvius" operating around the Island of Cuba and in the vicinity of Morro Castle. In 1905 he served as chief of staff of the North Atlantic Fleet; 1908-1909, was Chief of the Bureau of Navigation. Although Admiral Pillsbury's attainments as a sailor and fighting man were noteworthy, he was perhaps best known as being one of the foremost geographers of the world. He was actively identified with the National Geographic Society for many years, and was president of this society at the time of his death. His best known work was in connection with the investigation of the Gulf Stream, and his writings on that subject are accepted as the most authoritative in the world.

POPE

TORPEDO BOAT DESTROYER

Length, 314 feet   *Beam, 30 feet, 11 inches*   *Draft, 9 feet, 4 inches*

NAMED FOR COMMODORE JOHN POPE, U. S. NAVY

Launched March 23, 1920, at William Cramp & Sons' Company, Philadelphia, Pennsylvania.

Sponsor: MRS. WILLIAM SHEPHERD BENSON (Mary Wyse), wife of Rear Admiral Benson, U. S. Navy, and granddaughter of Commodore John Pope, U. S. Navy.

COMMODORE JOHN POPE, U. S. Navy, was born in Sandwich, Massachusetts, 1798; died 1876. Appointed midshipman, 1816; commodore, 1862. Served in the Mediterranean, West Indian, Brazil, African, and East India Squadrons. Civil War: Commanded the U. S. S. "Richmond," Gulf Squadron, from July 1, 1861, to October 24, 1861. Assisted in the blockade of the Passes of the Mississippi. Took part in the engagement with Confederate States vessels at the head of the Passes, October 12, 1861. Held position of prize commissioner, Boston, Massachusetts, 1864–1865, and lighthouse inspector, 1866. Detached from this duty in May, 1869, which terminated his active service at the age of seventy-one.

[177]

PORTER (2D)

TORPEDO BOAT DESTROYER
Length, 315 feet   *Beam, 30 feet*   *Draft, 9 feet, 4 inches*

NAMED FOR COMMODORE DAVID PORTER, U. S. NAVY,
AND FOR HIS SON,
ADMIRAL DAVID DIXON PORTER, U. S. NAVY

Launched August 26, 1915, at William Cramp & Sons' Company, Philadelphia, Pennsylvania.

Sponsor: MISS GEORGIANA PORTER CUSACHS, daughter of Lieutenant Carlos V. Cusachs, U. S. Navy, and great-granddaughter of Admiral David Dixon Porter, U. S. Navy.

COMMODORE DAVID PORTER, United States Navy, was born in Massachusetts, in 1780. Appointed midshipman in 1798. In 1799 took part in the fight between the "Constellation" and "L'Insurgente." In 1803 was captured in the "Philadelphia" at Tripoli. In 1812, in command of frigate "Essex," had a most adventurous career, making many captures of British packets and crippling British commerce. In 1813 cruised in the Pacific and captured many vessels. In 1814, at Valparaiso, surrendered the "Essex" to superior force of British frigates "Phoebe" and "Cherub" only when his own ship was too disabled to offer resistance longer, the contest having been unequal in every way.

ADMIRAL DAVID DIXON PORTER, United States Navy, was born in 1813. Appointed midshipman in U. S. Navy in 1829. In the Mexican War served with distinction in the "Spitfire." Engaged in every action on the coast. In the Civil War rose from Lieutenant to Admiral in two years. In 1862 Commander Porter commanded the mortar boat flotilla under Farragut at the passage of Forts Jackson and St. Philip. Bombarded forts at Vicksburg. Commanded the Mississippi Squadron as Acting Rear Admiral. In 1863 co-operated with General Sherman in capture of

[178]

Arkansas Port, for which he received a vote of thanks of Congress. Co-operated with General Grant in the capture of Vicksburg. Received thanks of Congress and promotion to Rear Admiral. In command of North Atlantic Blockading Squadron bombarded forts at Cape Fear River. Commanded Naval forces at Fort Fisher and for his brilliant work received thanks of Congress for the fourth time. In 1866 was made Vice Admiral. In 1870 was made Admiral of the Navy.

PREBLE (4TH)

TORPEDO BOAT DESTROYER

Length, 314 feet   *Beam, 30 feet, 11 inches*   *Draft, 9 feet, 4 inches*

NAMED FOR COMMODORE EDWARD PREBLE, U. S. NAVY

Launched March 8, 1920, at Bath Iron Works, Bath, Maine.

Sponsor: MISS SALLIE MACINTOSH TUCKER, great-granddaughter of Commodore Edward Preble, U. S. Navy.

COMMODORE EDWARD PREBLE, United States Navy. Born in Falmouth, Maine, 1761. Died 1807. When about 16 years of age he shipped on a letter of marque and sailed for Europe. Upon his return to America in 1779, he received an appointment in the Provincial Marine of Massachusetts and was attached to the "Protector." January 17, 1799, commissioned lieutenant in the United States Navy, and ordered to the "Constitution"; commissioned captain, May 15, 1799; ordered to the "Pickering," June 7, 1799. In command of the "Essex" he sailed for the East Indies to convoy to the United States a large fleet of merchantmen and had the honor of being the first naval officer to fly the American flag east of the Cape of Good Hope. Ordered to the "Constitution" in 1803 to command the squadron being fitted out to act against the Barbary powers. He established a treaty of peace with the Emperor of Morocco; had several engagements with

the Tripolitan gunboats and forts and endeavored to secure a treaty for the establishment of a permanent peace
upon honorable terms with the Bashaw.

PRESTON (2D)

TORPEDO BOAT DESTROYER

Length, 314 feet   *Beam, 30 feet, 11 inches*   *Draft, 9 feet, 4 inches*

NAMED FOR LIEUTENANT SAMUEL W. PRESTON,
U. S. NAVY

Launched October 15, 1919, at Bethlehem Shipbuilding
Corporation, San Francisco, California.

Sponsor: MRS. JOSEPHUS DANIELS (Adelaide Bagley),
wife of Secretary of the Navy, Josephus Daniels.

LIEUTENANT SAMUEL W. PRESTON, United States
Navy, was born in Canada and appointed midshipman
from the State of Illinois 1858. Graduated first in his class
1861. From 1861 to 1865 served on various vessels of the
South Atlantic blockading squadron. In an assault on Fort
Sumter, September 8, 1863, he was made prisoner and sent
to Libby Prison, where he was kept until exchanged in the
fall of 1864. Took part in the attacks on Fort Fisher,
December 24, 25, 1864, and January 15, 1865, when he
was killed while leading his men.

WILLIAM B. PRESTON

TORPEDO BOAT DESTROYER

Length, 314 feet   *Beam, 30 feet, 11 inches*   *Draft, 9 feet, 4 inches*

NAMED FOR SECRETARY OF THE NAVY,
WILLIAM B. PRESTON

Launched August 7, 1919, at U. S. Navy Yard, Norfolk,
Virginia.

Sponsor: MRS. WILLIAM RADFORD BEALE (Lucy Preston), daughter of Secretary of the Navy William B. Preston.

[180]

SECRETARY OF THE NAVY WILLIAM B. PRES-TON was born in Smithfield, Virginia, November 25, 1805; died 1862; was educated at the University of Virginia; adopted law as a profession and achieved signal success in its practice; served several times in the Virginia House of Delegates and Senate; appointed Secretary of the Navy in 1849; was subsequently sent by the Government on a mission to France, 1858–1859, the object of which was to establish a line of steamers between that country and Virginia and a more extended commercial relation between the two countries.

PRUITT

TORPEDO BOAT DESTROYER

Length, 314 feet   *Beam, 30 feet, 11 inches*   *Draft, 9 feet, 4 inches*

NAMED FOR CORPORAL JOHN H. PRUITT,
U. S. MARINE CORPS

Launched August 2, 1920, Bath Iron Works, Bath, Maine.

Sponsor: MRS. BELLE PRUITT, mother of Corporal John H. Pruitt, U. S. M. C.

CORPORAL JOHN H. PRUITT, United States Marine Corps, was born in Fadeville, Arkansas, 1896. Killed in action October 4, 1918. Posthumously awarded Navy medal of honor for conspicuous gallantry and courage above and beyond the call of duty in action with the enemy at Blanc Mont Ridge, France, October 3, 1918. Single handed he attacked two machine guns, capturing them and killing two of the enemy. He later captured forty prisoners in a dugout nearby. This gallant soldier was killed soon afterwards by shell fire while he was sniping at the enemy.

PUTNAM

TORPEDO BOAT DESTROYER

Length, 314 feet   *Beam, 30 feet, 11 inches*   *Draft, 9 feet, 4 inches*

NAMED FOR MASTER CHARLES FLINT PUTNAM,
U. S. Navy

Launched September 3, 1919, at Bethlehem Shipbuilding Corporation, Quincy, Massachusetts.

Sponsor: MISS KATHERINE BROWN (Mrs. Andrew Irwin McKee), fiancee of Lieutenant McKee, C. C., U. S. Navy.

MASTER CHARLES FLINT PUTNAM, U. S. Navy, was born in Illinois; died in the Arctic region in 1883. Appointed midshipman, 1869; master, 1880. 1881–1882, U. S. S. "Rodgers," Behring Sea, in search of the "Jeannette." While in command of a shore depot at Cape Serdze, Master C. F. Putnam learned of the burning of the "Rodgers." He set out for the relief of her officers and men in St. Lawrence Bay. Returning to Cape Serdze, missed his way in a blinding snowstorm, January 10, 1882, and drifted out to sea on an ice floe. Careful search was made for him by parties from the "Rodgers," officers and men, and at one time he was seen, but those trying to reach him were cut off by breaking ice. May 20, 1882, his body was seen by native hunters on a floating ice floe.

PYRO

AMMUNITION SHIP

Length, 482 feet	*Beam, 60 feet, 11 inches*	*Draft, 20 feet, 11 inches*

NAMED "PYRO," FIRE (GREEK)

Launched December 16, 1919, at Puget Sound Navy Yard.

Sponsor: MRS. GUY A. BISSET (Harriet Caperton), wife of Commander G. A. Bisset, C. C., U. S. Navy, Superintending Constructor.

QUAIL

MINE SWEEPER

Length, 187 feet	*Beam, 35 feet*	*Draft, 9 feet, 9 inches*

SUBMARINE COMING TO THE SURFACE

NAMED FOR THE BIRD QUAIL

Launched October 6, 1918, at Chester Shipbuilding Company.

Sponsor: MISS MARGARET CUNNINGHAM BAXTER, daughter of Captain William J. Baxter, Construction Corps, U. S. Navy.

Dimensions of Submarines R-1 to R-20, inclusive, are:
Length, 186 feet   *Beam, 18 feet*   *Draft, 14 feet, 6 inches*

R-1
SUBMARINE

Launched August 24, 1919, at Bethlehem Shipbuilding Corporation, Quincy, Massachusetts.

Sponsor: MRS. GEORGE W. DASHIELL (Margaret Rowe), wife of Lieutenant Commander G. W. Dashiell, U. S. Navy, prospective Commanding Officer.

R-2
SUBMARINE

Launched September 23, 1918, at Bethlehem Shipbuilding Corporation, Fore River, Massachusetts.

Sponsor: MRS. CHARLES M. COOKE (Sarah Bleecker), mother of Lieutenant Commander Charles M. Cooke, U. S. Navy, in command of the vessel.

R-3
SUBMARINE

Launched January 18, 1919, at Bethlehem Shipbuilding Corporation, Quincy, Massachusetts.

Sponsor: MRS. CHARLES G. MCCORD (Florence Christian), wife of Lieutenant Commander C. G. McCord, U. S. Navy, Inspector of Machinery for the Navy at the works.

R-4
SUBMARINE

Launched October 26, 1918, at Bethlehem Shipbuilding Corporation, Quincy, Massachusetts.

Sponsor: MRS. ALBERT W. STAHL (Blanche Vinton), wife of Captain Albert W. Stahl, Construction Corps, U. S. Navy.

R-5
SUBMARINE

Launched November 24, 1918, at Bethlehem Shipbuilding Corporation, Quincy, Massachusetts.

Sponsor: MISS MARGARETTA WOOD, daughter of Rear Admiral Spencer S. Wood, U. S. Navy, in command of the First Naval District.

R-6
SUBMARINE

Launched March 1, 1919, at Bethlehem Shipbuilding Corporation, Quincy, Massachusetts.

Sponsor: MISS KATHARINE LANGDON HILL, daughter of former Governor John F. Hill, of Maine.

R-7
SUBMARINE

Launched April 5, 1919, at Bethlehem Shipbuilding Corporation, Quincy, Massachusetts.

Sponsor: MRS. IVAN E. BASS (Florence Bouché), wife of Commander I. E. Bass, U. S. Navy, the Engineer Officer of Boston Navy Yard.

R-8
SUBMARINE

Launched April 17, 1919, at Bethlehem Shipbuilding Corporation, Quincy, Massachusetts.

Sponsor: MISS PENELOPE POTTER, daughter of Mrs. Albert B. Potter of New London, Connecticut.

R-9
SUBMARINE

Launched May 24, 1919, at Bethlehem Shipbuilding Corporation, Quincy, Massachusetts.

Sponsor: MRS. IRVING E. STOWE (Mary Ingalls), wife of Lieutenant I. E. Stowe, U. S. N. R. F., resident physician at the works.

R-10
SUBMARINE

Launched June 28, 1919, at Bethlehem Shipbuilding Corporation, Quincy, Massachusetts.

Sponsor: MRS. PHILIP C. RANSOM (Mary Sheafe), wife of Lieutenant Commander P. C. Ransom, U. S. Navy, prospective commanding officer.

R-11
SUBMARINE

Launched July 22, 1919, at Bethlehem Shipbuilding Corporation, Quincy, Massachusetts.

Sponsor: MISS DOROTHY BATCHELDER, daughter of Lieutenant George Batchelder, Supply Corps, U. S. N. Reserve.

R-12
SUBMARINE

Launched August 15, 1919, at Bethlehem Shipbuilding Corporation, Quincy, Massachusetts.

Sponsor: MISS HELEN MACK, sister-in-law of Commander H. S. Dinger, U. S. Navy, on duty at the works.

[185]

R-13
SUBMARINE

Launched August 27, 1919, at Bethlehem Shipbuilding Corporation, Quincy, Massachusetts.

Sponsor: MISS FANNIE BEMIS CHANDLER, daughter of Dr. Norman F. Chandler, Medford, Massachusetts.

R-14
SUBMARINE

Launched October 10, 1919, at Bethlehem Shipbuilding Corporation, Quincy, Massachusetts.

Sponsor: MISS FLORENCE LOOMIS GARDNER, daughter of Mr. Stephen A. Gardner, the General Manager of the Electric Boat Company.

R-15
SUBMARINE

Launched December 10, 1917, at Union Iron Works, San Francisco, California.

Sponsor: MRS. THALES STEWART BOYD (Lillian Martin), wife of Lieutenant Commander T. S. Boyd, U. S. Navy, prospective commanding officer.

R-16
SUBMARINE

Launched December 15, 1917, at Union Iron Works, San Francisco, California.

Sponsor: MRS. EDWARD R. WILSON (Alice Baer), wife of Passed Assistant Paymaster E. R. Wilson, U. S. Navy.

R-17
SUBMARINE

Launched December 24, 1917, at Union Iron Works, San Francisco, California.

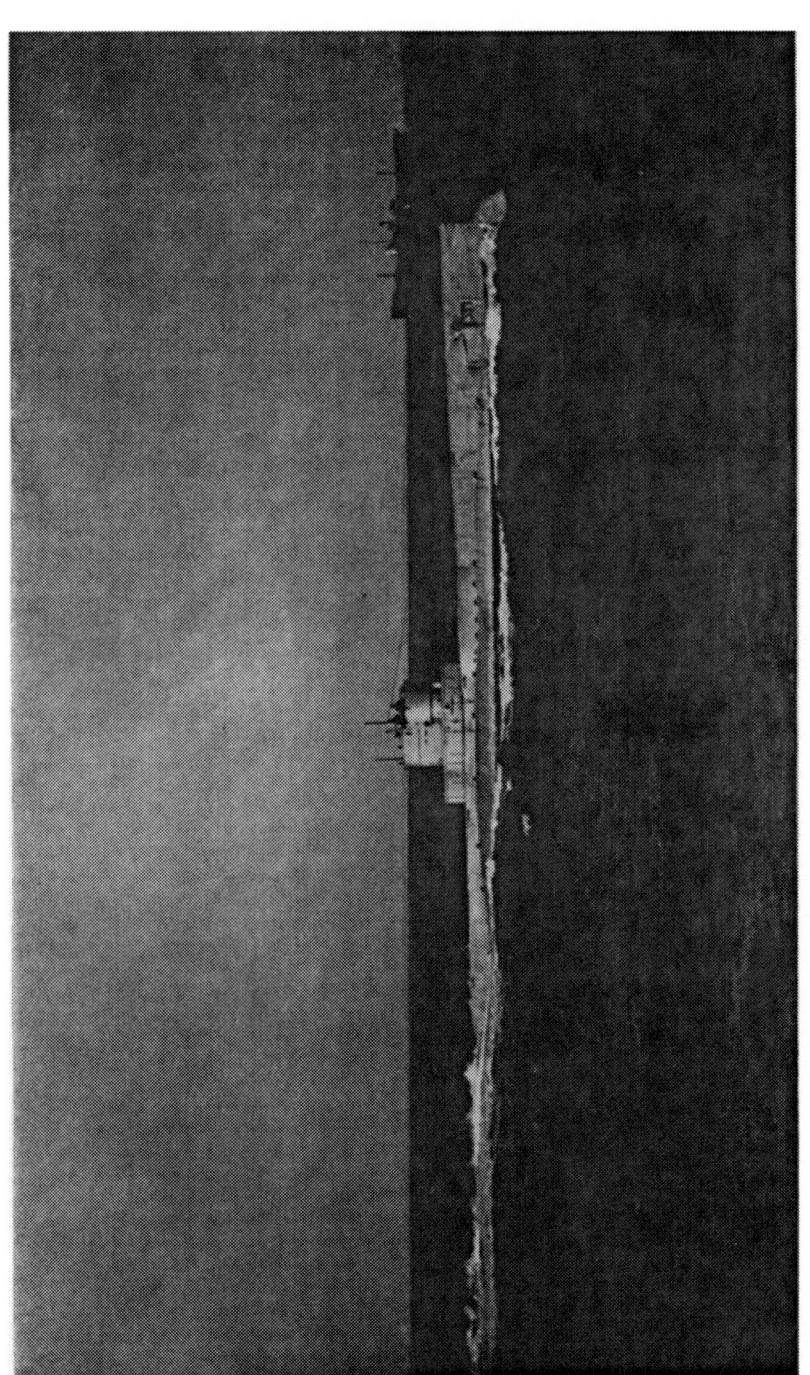

U.S. SUBMARINE "R-14" GOING FULL SPEED ON THE SURFACE

Sponsor: MISS BERTHA FRANCES DEW, sister-in-law of Captain D. C. Nutting, C. C., U. S. Navy, Superintending Constructor at the works.

R–18
SUBMARINE

Launched January 7, 1918, at Bethlehem Shipbuilding Corporation, San Francisco, California.

Sponsor: MISS MARION SOLEY RUSSELL, daughter of Captain Robert L. Russell, U. S. Navy, Commandant Third Naval District.

R–19
SUBMARINE

Launched January 28, 1918, at Bethlehem Shipbuilding Corporation, San Francisco, California.

Sponsor: MRS. ROBERT L. IRVINE (Janet Klink), wife of Commander R. L. Irvine, U. S. Navy, Inspector of Machinery at Bethlehem Shipbuilding Corporation.

R–20
SUBMARINE

Launched January 21, 1918, at Bethlehem Shipbuilding Corporation, San Francisco, California.

Sponsor: MRS. ARNOLD FOSTER (Maud Beatrice), wife of the Secretary and Treasurer of the Union Plant, Bethlehem Shipbuilding Corporation.

Dimensions of Submarines R–21 to R–27, inclusive, are:
Length, 175 feet   *Beam, 16 feet, 7 inches*   *Draft, 13 feet, 11 inches*

R–21
SUBMARINE

Launched July 10, 1918, at Lake Torpedo Boat Company, Bridgeport, Connecticut.

Sponsor: MRS. DALLAS CHARLES LAIZURE (May Morgan), wife of Lieutenant Commander D. C. Laizure, U. S. Navy, Inspector of Machinery at Lake Torpedo Boat Company.

R–22
SUBMARINE

Launched September 23, 1918, at Lake Torpedo Boat Company, Bridgeport, Connecticut.

Sponsor: MRS. ERICK A. EKLUND (Agnes Simpson), wife of the General Superintendent of Lake Torpedo Boat Company.

R–23
SUBMARINE

Launched November 5, 1918, at Lake Torpedo Boat Company, Bridgeport, Connecticut.

Sponsor: MISS RUTH JANE HARRIS, daughter of Mr. James R. Harris, General Manager of the Diesel Engine Co., St. Louis, Missouri.

R–24
SUBMARINE

Launched August 21, 1918, at Lake Torpedo Boat Company, Bridgeport, Connecticut.

Sponsor: MRS. EDMUND R. NORTON (Elizabeth Knowles), wife of Commander E. R. Norton, C. C., U. S. Navy, Superintending Constructor.

R–25
SUBMARINE

Launched May 15, 1919, at Lake Torpedo Boat Company, Bridgeport, Connecticut.

Sponsor: MRS. RICHARD H. M. ROBINSON (Rosalind Smith), wife of the Managing Director of the Lake Torpedo Boat Company, and formerly of the U. S. Navy Construction Corps.

R-26
S U B M A R I N E

Launched June 28, 1919, at Lake Torpedo Boat Company, Bridgeport, Connecticut.

Sponsor: MRS. J. WALTER BARNETT (Mary Serpell), wife of the Assistant General Manager of the Company.

R-27
S U B M A R I N E

Launched September 23, 1918, at Lake Torpedo Boat Company, Bridgeport, Connecticut.

Sponsor: MISS MARY LOUISE FOSTER, daughter of Judge Carl Foster, Bridgeport, Connecticut.

RADFORD
T O R P E D O   B O A T   D E S T R O Y E R

Length, 314 feet   Beam, 30 feet, 11 inches   Draft, 9 feet, 3 inches

NAMED FOR REAR ADMIRAL WILLIAM RADFORD, U. S. NAVY

Launched April 5, 1918, at Newport News S. B. & D. D. Company, Newport News, Virginia.

Sponsor: MISS MARY LOVELL RADFORD, granddaughter of Rear Admiral William Radford, U. S. Navy.

REAR ADMIRAL WILLIAM RADFORD was born in Fincastle, Virginia, 1808; died 1890. Appointed midshipman 1825; rear admiral 1866. During the Mexican War he commanded the party from the U. S. S. "Warren" that cut out and captured the Mexican man-of-war "Malek Adhel" at Mazatlan, and took part in the operations at Mazatlan and other places in Lower California, 1846–1847. Commanded the U. S. S. "Cumberland" at the time she was sunk by the C. S. S. "Merrimack" in Hampton Roads, but was by order of the Secretary of the Navy on board the U. S. S. "Roanoke" in Hampton Roads, at a Naval Court of Inquiry. He immediately rode to Newport News reaching there only in time to see the "Cumberland" sunk by being rammed by the "Merrimac." Commanded the "New Ironsides" in attacks on Fort Fisher December 24–25, 1864, and January 13–15, 1865, and was highly praised for the high order of ability displayed on that occasion. He was included in the thanks of Congress to Admiral Porter, his officers and men, for their gallant conduct on those occasions. Commanded the European Squadron 1869–1870.

RAIL

MINE SWEEPER

Length, 187 feet　　　*Beam, 35 feet*　　　*Draft, 9 feet, 9 inches*

NAMED FOR THE BIRD RAIL

Launched April 25, 1918, at Puget Sound Navy Yard, Washington.

Sponsor: MRS. ROBERT MORGAN (Elizabeth Mahan), wife of Lieutenant R. Morgan, C. C., U. S. Navy.

RALEIGH (3D)

LIGHT CRUISER

Length, 555 feet　　　*Beam, 55 feet*　　　*Draft, 14 feet, 3 inches*

NAMED FOR RALEIGH, THE CAPITAL OF
NORTH CAROLINA

Launched October 25, 1922, at Bethlehem Shipbuilding Corporation, Quincy, Massachusetts.

Sponsor: MISS JENNIE M. PROCTOR, daughter of Mr. Ivan M. Proctor, selected by Honorable T. B. Eldridge, Mayor of Raleigh.

THE first "Raleigh" was a frigate of 697 tons, authorized by the Continental Congress in 1775 and launched at Portsmouth, New Hampshire, May 21, 1775, and was actively engaged in the Revolutionary War.

The second "Raleigh" was a protected cruiser of 3183 tons,

LAUNCH OF U.S. SUBMARINE "R-2"

launched March 31, 1892, at Navy Yard, Norfolk, Virginia; was one of Commodore George Dewey's squadron in the battle of Manila Bay, May 1, 1898.

RAMSAY

TORPEDO BOAT DESTROYER

Length, 314 feet   *Beam, 30 feet, 11 inches*   *Draft, 9 feet, 3 inches*

NAMED FOR REAR ADMIRAL FRANCIS M. RAMSAY, U. S. Navy

Launched June 8, 1918, at Newport News S. B. & D. D. Company, Newport News, Virginia.

Sponsor: MISS MARY VIRGINIA RAMSAY, granddaughter of Rear Admiral Francis M. Ramsay, U. S. Navy.

REAR ADMIRAL FRANCIS M. RAMSAY, United States Navy, was born 1835; died 1914. Appointed midshipman 1850; commissioned rear admiral 1894. Served on "Preble," "St. Lawrence," "Falmouth," "Merrimac," and on ordnance duty at Washington Navy Yard, 1850–1860. Commanded "Choctaw," Mississippi Squadron 1863–1864. Engagements at Haines Bluff, Yazoo River, 1863. Expedition up the Yazoo River to Yazoo City, destroying the Confederate navy yard and vessels, May, 1863. Engagement at Liverpool Landing, Yazoo River, May, 1863. Engagement at Millikens Bend, Mississippi River, June 7, 1863. Siege of Vicksburg, May, June, and July, 1863. Commanded a battery of three heavy guns, mounted on scows, in front of Vicksburg, from June 19 to July 4, 1863. Commanded the third division, Mississippi Squadron, July, 1863, to September, 1864. Commanded the expedition up the Black and Ouachita Rivers, March, 1864. Engagement at Trinity, Louisiana, March, 1864. Engagement at Harrisonburg, Louisiana, Ouachita River, 1864. Red River Expedition, March, April, May, 1864. Expedition up the Black and Ouachita Rivers, April, 1864. Commanded the third and fourth divisions, Mississippi Squadron, May to September, 1864. Commanded the expeditions into the Atchafalaya River, June, 1864. Commanded "Unadilla," North Atlantic Squadron, 1864–1865. Engagements with Fort Fisher, North Carolina, December 24 and 25, 1864, January, 1865. Engagements with Fort Anderson and with other forts on the Cape Fear River, January, February, 1865. Promoted one grade by special Act of Congress for Civil War Service. Held important positions afloat and ashore 1865–1889. Chief of Bureau of Navigation 1889–1897.

RATHBURNE

TORPEDO BOAT DESTROYER

Length, 314 feet   *Beam, 30 feet, 11 inches*   *Draft, 9 feet*

NAMED FOR CAPTAIN JOHN PECK RATHBURNE, U. S. NAVY

Launched December 27, 1917, at William Cramp & Sons' Company, Philadelphia, Pennsylvania.

Sponsor: MISS MALINDA BENNETT MULL, daughter of Mr. J. Harry Mull, Vice President and General Manager of the Shipbuilding Company.

CAPTAIN JOHN PECK RATHBURNE, U. S Navy; appointed captain in the Continental Navy; January 27, 1778, commanding the "Providence," landed on the island of New Providence, West Indies, took possession of Fort Nassau, spiked the guns, removed a quantity of ammunition and small arms, beat off the British sloop of war "Grayton" and five other vessels, two of which he burned, and on the 29th of January sailed away with the remainder of his prizes and 20 released American prisoners; July 15, 1779, in company with two other Continental ships, captured 11 large vessels and valuable cargoes.

RED WING

MINE SWEEPER

Length, 187 feet   *Beam, 35 feet*   *Draft, 9 feet, 9 inches*

NAMED FOR THE BIRD RED WING

Launched June 7, 1919, at Baltimore D. D. & S. B. Company.

Sponsor: MRS FRED A. PLAGEMANN (Nellie Cloak), wife of the prospective commanding officer, Lieutenant F. A. Plagemann, U. S. Navy.

REID (2D)

TORPEDO BOAT DESTROYER

Length, 314 feet   Beam, 30 feet, 11 inches   Draft, 9 feet, 4 inches

NAMED FOR CAPTAIN SAMUEL CHESTER REID,
U. S. NAVY

Launched October 15, 1919, at Bethlehem Shipbuilding Corporation, Quincy, Massachusetts.

Sponsor: MRS. JOSEPH WRIGHT POWELL (Bertha Osterhout), wife of the president of the Bethlehem Shipbuilding Corporation. Mrs. Powell was sponsor for the U. S. S. "Aylwin" in 1912.

CAPTAIN SAMUEL CHESTER REID, U. S. Navy, was born in Norwich, Connecticut, in 1783. He served as acting midshipman under Commodore Truxtun. In War of 1812 commanded the privateer "General Armstrong." In September, 1814, in the harbor of Fayal, was attacked by the boats of three British men of war. Reid defeated and scattered the enemy and scuttled his own ship to prevent capture. He received the commendation of Congress for this remarkable battle. Captain Reid was appointed a sailing master in the Navy and held the position until his death. He was the son of Lieutenant John Reid of the British Navy who while a prisoner resigned and espoused the American cause.

RENO

TORPEDO BOAT DESTROYER

Length, 314 feet   Beam, 30 feet, 11 inches   Draft, 9 feet, 4 inches

NAMED FOR LIEUTENANT COMMANDER WALTER E. RENO,
U. S. NAVY

Launched January 22, 1919, at Bethlehem Shipbuilding Corporation, San Francisco, California.

Sponsor: MISS KATHRYN BALDWIN ANDERSON, daughter of Mr. Alden Anderson, Lieutenant Governor of California.

LIEUTENANT COMMANDER WALTER E. RENO, United States Navy, was born in Iowa, 1881. Appointed midshipman, 1902; commissioned lieutenant commander, May 23, 1917. Drowned while commanding the U. S. S. "Chauncey" on November 19, 1917. The "Chauncey" was rammed by the British merchant ship "Rose," of Glasgow, while convoying a merchant fleet through the danger zone.

RENSHAW

TORPEDO BOAT DESTROYER

Length, 314 feet   *Beam, 30 feet, 11 inches*   *Draft, 9 feet, 2 inches*

NAMED FOR COMMANDER WILLIAM B. RENSHAW, U. S. NAVY

Launched September 21, 1918, at Bethlehem Shipbuilding Corporation, San Francisco, California.

Sponsor: MRS. FRANK JOHNSON (Grace Coomer), wife of Lieutenant Frank Johnson, C. C., U. S. Navy, on duty at the shipbuilding plant.

COMMANDER WILLIAM B. RENSHAW, U. S. Navy, born in Brooklyn, New York, 1816; killed in battle January 1, 1863. Appointed midshipman 1831; commander 1861. Sea duty: 1847–1848 in the "Warren," Pacific Squadron. Took part in operations on the Pacific side in the War with Mexico. Civil War, commended by Admiral Farragut for "the handsome manner in which he managed his vessel," the "Westfield," in operations with the Mortar Fleet below New Orleans and on the Mississippi River, 1862–1863. Refused to surrender to the Confederate forces, Galveston Harbor, January 1, 1863, setting fire to his vessel to prevent her falling into their hands, and was killed in the explosion of the vessel which followed.

NAMING THE U.S. SUBMARINE "R-26"

RICHMOND (3D.)

LIGHT CRUISER

Length, 555 feet   *Beam, 55 feet*   *Draft, 14 feet, 3 inches*

NAMED FOR THE CITY OF RICHMOND,
THE CAPITAL OF VIRGINIA

Launched September 29, 1921, at William Cramp & Sons' Shipbuilding Company, Philadelphia, Pennsylvania.

Sponsor: MISS ELIZABETH STROTHER SCOTT, daughter of Mr. Frederick W. Scott, a prominent citizen of Richmond, Virginia.

THE first "Richmond" was a frigate of 200 tons, purchased at Norfolk in 1798.

The second "Richmond" was a steamer of 2700 tons, launched in 1860.

RINGGOLD

TORPEDO BOAT DESTROYER

Length, 314 feet   *Beam, 30 feet, 11 inches*   *Draft, 9 feet, 2 inches*

NAMED FOR REAR ADMIRAL CADWALLADER RINGGOLD,
U. S. NAVY

Launched April 14, 1918, at Bethlehem Shipbuilding Corporation, San Francisco, California.

Sponsor: MRS. DAVID W. FARQUHAR (Grace T.), mother of Lieutenant Francis P. Farquhar, U. S. N. R. F., on duty at the shipbuilding works.

REAR ADMIRAL CADWALLADER RINGGOLD, United States Navy, was born in Washington County, Maryland, 1802; died 1867. Appointed midshipman 1819; commissioned rear admiral 1866. Commanded Ringgold expedition in the Pacific; received the thanks of Congress for daring and skill displayed by him while in command of the sailing ship "Sabine" in the rescue of a battalion of marines at sea, in a steamer on the lee shore, and the search for and rescue of the line-of-battleship "Vermont."

RIZAL

TORPEDO BOAT DESTROYER

Length, 314 feet   *Beam, 30 feet, 11 inches*   *Draft, 9 feet, 2 inches*

NAMED FOR JOSE RIZAL

Launched September 21, 1918, at Bethlehem Shipbuilding Corporation, San Francisco, California.

Sponsor: SENORA JAIME C. DEVEYRA, wife of Senor DeVeyra, Filipino delegate to Congress.

JOSE RIZAL was born 1861 in Luzon, Philippine Islands; executed December 30, 1896. Filipino doctor of medicine, author, patriot. Imprisoned by Spanish Government for "carrying on an antireligious and antipatriotic campaign education" in the Philippines; tried before a military court, denied the right of counsel, found guilty and ordered to be shot, as "the principal organizer and the soul of the insurrection in the Philippines." The U. S. S. "Rizal" now on duty with the Asiatic fleet, has two distinct peculiarities. One is its foreign-sounding name, the "Rizal," and the other is the fact that it is manned by a crew of 96 Filipinos, only its officers and chief petty officers being American. The reason for this departure is that the new war craft is a present to the United States from the Philippine Islands.

ROBIN

MINE SWEEPER

Length, 187 feet   *Beam, 35 feet*   *Draft, 9 feet, 9 inches*

NAMED FOR THE BIRD ROBIN

Launched June 17, 1918, at Todd Shipyard Corporation, New York.

Sponsor: MISS BESSIE VERONICA CALLAHAN, daughter of a foreman of the shipyard.

ROBINSON

TORPEDO BOAT DESTROYER

Length, 314 feet   *Beam, 30 feet, 11 inches*   *Draft, 9 feet*

[196]

NAMED FOR CAPTAIN ISAIAH ROBINSON,
U. S. NAVY

Launched March 27, 1918, at Bethlehem Shipbuilding Company, San Francisco, California.

Sponsor: MISS EVELYN TINGEY SELFRIDGE, a great-granddaughter of Rear Admiral T. O. Selfridge, U. S. Navy.

CAPTAIN ISAIAH ROBINSON, United States Navy, commissioned captain by Continental Congress October 10, 1776; in command of the "Andrea Doria" in December, 1776; captured off Porto Rico the British ship "Race Horse" and one smaller vessel; November, 1777, took part in the defense of the Delaware River; burned his ship to prevent capture by the British.

RODGERS (2D)

TORPEDO BOAT DESTROYER

Length, 314 feet   *Beam, 30 feet, 11 inches*   *Draft, 9 feet, 4 inches*

NAMED FOR COMMODORE JOHN RODGERS,
U. S. NAVY

Launched April 26, 1919, at Bethlehem Shipbuilding Corporation, Fore River, Massachusetts.

Sponsor: MISS HELEN THEODOSIA RODGERS, granddaughter of Commodore John Rodgers, U. S. Navy.

COMMODORE JOHN RODGERS, United States Navy, was born in 1771. Entered the Navy as lieutenant in 1798. Was executive officer of the "Constellation" when she captured the French frigate "L'Insurgente" in 1799, for which he and the other officers received a silver medal and thanks of Congress. In the War with Tripoli, distinguished himself in command of the "John Adams" and the "Congress." In 1805 became commander of the squadron against Tripoli. In War of 1812 — service in command of a squadron in 1812 and 1813.

In 1814 he organized the defense of Baltimore against

the combined attack of army and navy, and the repulse of the enemy before Baltimore was acknowledged at the time as his deed. In 1815 he became President of the newly organized Board of Navy Commissioners, which office he held until his death in 1837 except for two years, 1825–1827, when he was Commander-in-Chief in the Mediterranean.

ROPER

TORPEDO BOAT DESTROYER

Length, 314 feet   *Beam, 30 feet, 11 inches*   *Draft, 9 feet*

NAMED FOR LIEUTENANT COMMANDER JESSE M. ROPER, U. S. NAVY

Launched August 17, 1918, at William Cramp & Sons' Company, Philadelphia, Pennsylvania.

Sponsor: MRS. HARRIET H. ROPER, widow of Lieutenant Commander Jesse M. Roper, U. S. Navy.

LIEUTENANT COMMANDER JESSE MIMS ROPER, United States Navy, was born in Glasgow, Missouri, 1851; died at Cavite, Philippine Islands, March 31, 1901. Appointed a midshipman 1868; commissioned a lieutenant commander 1899. In 1901, while on the "Petrel," lost his life in an heroic effort to save the life of one of his men. He was the first man to descend into the hold of the vessel when a fire was discovered; and, while endeavoring to rescue seaman Patrick Tower, he was overcome by suffocation and lost his life.

ROWAN (2D)

TORPEDO BOAT DESTROYER

Length, 315 feet   *Beam, 29 feet, 11 inches*   *Draft, 9 feet, 6 inches*

NAMED FOR VICE ADMIRAL STEPHEN CLEGG ROWAN, U. S. NAVY

Launched March 23, 1916, at Fore River Shipbuilding Company, Quincy, Massachusetts.

[198]

U. S. TORPEDO BOAT DESTROYER "REID" GOING FULL SPEED

Sponsor: MISS LOUISE MCLEAN AYRES, daughter of Doctor Stephen C. Ayres, and great-niece of Vice Admiral Stephen Clegg Rowan, U. S. Navy.

ADMIRAL STEPHEN C. ROWAN, United States Navy, was born in Ireland in 1805. Was appointed midshipman in the U. S. Navy in 1826. Took active part in the War with Mexico and in the acquisition of California. In 1861, in command of the "Pawnee," took part in the capture of forts at Hatteras Inlet. In 1862 performed conspicuous services in command of a flotilla in Sounds of North Carolina, and in the attack of Army and Navy on Roanoke Island. For his brilliant achievements he was promoted to the rank of Commodore. Commanded Naval forces at the fall of Newbern and participated at Forts Wagner, Gregg and Moultrie. Commanded "New Ironsides" off Charleston. In 1870 was made Vice Admiral of the Navy in recognition of distinguished service, by special Act of Congress, being the first officer in our Navy to hold this rank.

Dimensions of Submarines S–1 to S–3 inclusive are:

Length, 219 feet   *Beam, 20 feet, 8 inches*   *Draft, 15 feet, 10 inches*

S–1

SUBMARINE

Launched October 26, 1918, at Bethlehem Shipbuilding Corporation, Quincy, Massachusetts.

Sponsor: MRS. EMORY S. LAND (Elizabeth Stiles), wife of Commander E. S. Land, C. C., U. S. Navy.

S–2

SUBMARINE

Launched February 15, 1919, at Lake Torpedo Boat Company, Bridgeport, Connecticut.

Sponsor: MRS. PHILIP B. BRILL (Chrystie Knox), wife of the General Manager of the Company.

[199]

S–3
SUBMARINE

Launched December 21, 1918, at Navy Yard, Portsmouth, New Hampshire.

Sponsor: MRS. WILLIAM L. HILL (Katherine Sweetser), wife of Lieutenant W. L. Hill, U. S. Navy, on duty at the Navy Yard.

Dimensions of Submarines S–4 to S–17 inclusive are:
Length, 231 feet   *Beam, 21 feet, 10 inches*   *Draft, 13 feet*

S–4
SUBMARINE

Launched August 27, 1919, at Navy Yard, Portsmouth, New Hampshire.

Sponsor: MRS. HERBERT SEYMOUR HOWARD (Mary Morris), wife of Commander H. S. Howard, C. C., U. S. Navy, constructor of the submarine.

S–5
SUBMARINE

Launched November 10, 1919, at Navy Yard, Portsmouth, New Hampshire.

Sponsor: MRS. GLENN S. BURRELL (Geraldine Boush), wife of Lieutenant Commander G. S. Burrell, C. E. C., U. S. Navy, and daughter of Rear Admiral Clifford J. Boush, in command of the Navy Yard.

S–6
SUBMARINE

Launched December 23, 1919, at Navy Yard, Portsmouth, New Hampshire.

Sponsor: MISS ELEANOR WESTCOTT, step-daughter of Captain L. S. Adams, C. C., U. S. Navy, Industrial Manager of the Navy Yard.

S-7
SUBMARINE

Launched February 5, 1920, at Navy Yard, Portsmouth, New Hampshire.

Sponsor: MRS. HENRY LAKE WYMAN (Margaret Myers), wife of Captain H. L. Wyman, U. S. Navy, on duty at the Yard.

S-8
SUBMARINE

Launched April 21, 1920, at Navy Yard, Portsmouth, New Hampshire.

Sponsor: MRS. ROY W. RYDEN (Garnett Rainey), wife of Commander R. W. Ryden, C. C., U. S. Navy, on duty at the Yard.

S-9
SUBMARINE

Launched June 17, 1920, at Navy Yard, Portsmouth, New Hampshire.

Sponsor: MRS. JAMES EDWARD PALMER, (Anna Key) wife of Commander J. E. Palmer, U. S. Navy, Engineer Officer at the Navy Yard.

S-10
SUBMARINE

Launched December 9, 1920, at Navy Yard, Portsmouth, New Hampshire.

Sponsor: MISS MARIAN KINGSBURY PAYNE, step-daughter of Captain F. T. Arms, U. S. Navy, Supply Corps.

S-11
SUBMARINE

Launched February 7, 1921, at Navy Yard, Portsmouth New Hampshire.

Sponsor: MISS ANNA ELEANOR ROOSEVELT, daughter of Franklin D. Roosevelt, former Assistant Secretary of the Navy.

S–12
SUBMARINE

Launched August 4, 1921, at Navy Yard, Portsmouth, New Hampshire.

Sponsor: MRS. GORDON WOODBURY (Charlotte Woodbury) wife of former Assistant Secretary of the Navy, Gordon Woodbury.

S–13
SUBMARINE

Launched October 20, 1921, at Navy Yard, Portsmouth, New Hampshire.

Sponsor: MISS MARY HOWE, daughter of Mr. L. McH. Howe, Assistant to the Assistant Secretary of the Navy during the World War.

S–14
SUBMARINE

Launched October 22, 1919, at Lake Torpedo Boat Company, Bridgeport, Connecticut.

Sponsor: MRS. GEORGE T. PARKER (Kathryn Randall), wife of Mr. G. T. Parker, President of the Federal Underwriters of Washington, D. C.

S–15
SUBMARINE

Launched March 8, 1920, at Lake Torpedo Boat Company, Bridgeport, Connecticut.

Sponsor: MRS. SIMON LAKE (Margaret Vogel), wife of the Inventor of the Lake type Submarine and the founder of the Company.

S–16
SUBMARINE

Launched December 23, 1919, at Lake Torpedo Boat Company, Bridgeport, Connecticut.

Sponsor: MRS. ARCHIBALD W. McNEIL (Ann Orr), wife of Senator A. W. McNeil, Jr., of Bridgeport.

U.S. SCOUT CRUISER "RICHMOND", MAKING A RECORD RUN

S-17
SUBMARINE

Launched May 22, 1920, at Lake Torpedo Boat Company, Bridgeport, Connecticut.

Sponsor: MRS. RAYMOND G. THOMAS (Louise Timanus), wife of Lieutenant Commander R. G. Thomas, U. S. Navy, Inspector of Machinery for the Navy at the works.

Dimensions of Submarines S-18 to S-41 inclusive are:
Length, 219 feet   Beam, 20 feet, 8 inches   Draft, 15 feet, 10 inches

S-18
SUBMARINE

Launched April 29, 1920, at Bethlehem Shipbuilding Corporation, Quincy, Massachusetts.

Sponsor: MISS VIRGINIA BELLE JOHNSON, daughter of Senator E. S. Johnson.

S-19
SUBMARINE

Launched June 21, 1920, at Bethlehem Shipbuilding Corporation, Quincy, Massachusetts.

Sponsor: MISS GENEVIEVE KITTINGER, daughter of Commander T. A. Kittinger, U. S. Navy, Inspector of Ordnance at the works.

S-20
SUBMARINE

Launched June 9, 1920, at Bethlehem Shipbuilding Corporation, Quincy, Massachusetts.

Sponsor: MISS ANNE CLAGGETT ZELL, daughter of Lieutenant Edward M. Zell, U. S. Army.

S-21
SUBMARINE

Launched August 18, 1920, at Bethlehem Shipbuilding Corporation, Quincy, Massachusetts.

Sponsor: MRS. THOMAS BAXTER (Gladys Moffett), wife of Lieutenant Commander T. Baxter, U. S. Navy, Inspector of Machinery for the Navy at the Quincy works.

S-22
SUBMARINE

Launched July 15, 1920, at Bethlehem Shipbuilding Corporation, Quincy, Massachusetts.

Sponsor: MRS. MARK C. BOWMAN (Nannie Rice), wife of Lieutenant Commander M. C. Bowman, U. S. Navy, submarine assistant to Bureau of Steam Engineering.

S-23
SUBMARINE

Launched October 27, 1920, at Bethlehem Shipbuilding Corporation, Quincy, Massachusetts.

Sponsor: MISS BARBARA SEARS, daughter of Hon. Russell A. Sears, formerly Mayor of Quincy.

S-24
SUBMARINE

Launched June 27, 1922, at Bethlehem Shipbuilding Corporation, Quincy, Massachusetts.

Sponsor: MRS. HERBERT B. LOPER (Eleanor Opie), wife of Lieutenant H. B. Loper, U. S. Army, and niece of Rear Admiral Herbert O. Dunn.

S-25
SUBMARINE

Launched May 29, 1922, at Bethlehem Shipbuilding Corporation, Quincy, Massachusetts.

Sponsor: MRS. ROSS P. SCHLABACH (Vera Hobart), wife of Commander R. P. Schlabach, U. S. Navy, Superintending Constructor.

S-26
SUBMARINE

Launched October 22, 1922, at Bethlehem Shipbuilding Corporation, Quincy, Massachusetts.

Sponsor: Mrs. CARLOS BEAN (Mary Baldwin), wife of Commander Carlos Bean, U. S. Navy, on duty at the works.

S-27
SUBMARINE

Launched October 18, 1922, at Bethlehem Shipbuilding Corporation, Quincy, Massachusetts.

Sponsor: Mrs. FRANK BALDWIN (Helen Golden), wife of Lieutenant Commander Frank Baldwin, U. S. Navy, Supply Corps, on duty at the works.

S-28
SUBMARINE

Launched September 20, 1922, at Bethlehem Shipbuilding Corporation, Quincy, Massachusetts.

Sponsor: Mrs. WILLIAM R. MUNROE (Katherine Johnson), wife of Lieutenant Commander W. R. Munroe, U. S. Navy, Inspector of Machinery at the works.

S-29
SUBMARINE

Launched November 9, 1922, at Bethlehem Shipbuilding Corporation, Quincy, Massachusetts.

Sponsor: Mrs. RONAN C. GRADY (Louise M.), wife of Commander R. C. Grady, U. S. Navy, Naval Inspector of Machinery at the works.

S-30
SUBMARINE

Launched November 21, 1918, at Bethlehem Shipbuilding Corporation, San Francisco, California.

Sponsor: Mrs. EDWARDS STUART STALNAKER (Marion La Tourette), wife of Lieutenant Commander E. S. Stalnaker, Supply Corps, U. S. Navy.

S-31
SUBMARINE

Launched December 28, 1918, at Bethlehem Shipbuilding Corporation, San Francisco, California.

Sponsor: MRS. GEORGE A. WALKER (Maisie Genevra), wife of Mr. G. A. Walker, Chief Clerk in Navy Construction Department at the Works.

S–32
SUBMARINE

Launched January 11, 1919, at Bethlehem Shipbuilding Corporation, San Francisco, California.

Sponsor: MISS MARGARET TYNAN, daughter of Mr. J. J. Tynan, General Manager of Union Plant.

S–33
SUBMARINE

Launched December 5, 1918, at Bethlehem Shipbuilding Corporation, San Francisco, California.

Sponsor: MRS. THOMAS M. SEARLES (Clifford B.), wife of Lieutenant Commander T. M. Searles, C. C., U. S. Navy, in charge of submarine construction at the works.

S–34
SUBMARINE

Launched February 13, 1919, at Bethlehem Shipbuilding Corporation, San Francisco, California.

Sponsor: MISS FLORENCE HELLMAN, daughter of Mr. I. W. Hellman, Jr., vice president of the Union Trust Company and Nevada National Bank.

S–35
SUBMARINE

Launched February 27, 1919, at Bethlehem Shipbuilding Corporation, San Francisco, California.

Sponsor: MISS LOUISE CAROLYN BAILEY, daughter of Mr. T. S. Bailey, Pacific Coast representative of the Electric Boat Company.

S–36
SUBMARINE

Launched June 3, 1919, at Bethlehem Shipbuilding Corporation, San Francisco, California.

NAMING THE U. S. SUBMARINE "S-15"

Sponsor: MISS HELEN M. RUSSELL, daughter of Lieutenant George L. Russell, U. S. Navy, on duty at the works at the time.

S-37
SUBMARINE

Launched June 20, 1919, at Bethlehem Shipbuilding Corporation, San Francisco, California.

Sponsor: MISS MILDRED BULGER, daughter of Mr. John King Bulger, U. S. Shipping Board Inspector for the Pacific Coast at the time.

S-38
SUBMARINE

Launched June 17, 1919, at Bethlehem Shipbuilding Corporation, San Francisco, California.

Sponsor: MRS. CORNELIUS COLLINS (Grace Danills), wife of Lieutenant C. J. Collins, U. S. Navy, Assistant Inspector of Machinery for the Navy.

S-39
SUBMARINE

Launched July 2, 1919, at Bethlehem Shipbuilding Corporation, San Francisco, California.

Sponsor: MISS CLARA M. HUBER, daughter of Lieutenant (T) Martin Huber, U. S. Navy, on duty at the works at the time.

S-40
SUBMARINE

Launched January 5, 1921, at Bethlehem Shipbuilding Corporation, San Francisco, California.

Sponsor: MRS. JOHN H. ROSSETER (Alice May), designated by Senator Phelan of California.

S-41
SUBMARINE

Launched February 21, 1921, at Bethlehem Shipbuilding Corporation, San Francisco, California.

Sponsor: MRS. JOHN F. CONNERS (Stella Standeford), wife of Mr. John F. Conners, Editor of the *Oakland Inquirer*, Oakland, California.

Dimensions of Submarines S–42 to S–47 inclusive are:
Length, 225 feet   *Beam, 20 feet, 8 inches*   *Draft, 16 feet*

S–42
SUBMARINE

Launched April 30, 1923, at Bethlehem Shipbuilding Corporation, Quincy, Massachusetts.

Sponsor: MRS. HENRY A. HUTCHINS, JR., (Barbara Kerley), wife of Lieutenant H. A. Hutchins, C. C., U. S. Navy, Assistant to the Superintending Constructor at the works.

S–43
SUBMARINE

Launched March 31, 1923, at Bethlehem Shipbuilding Corporation, Quincy, Massachusetts.

Sponsor: MRS. JOHN H. BROWN (Nellie Janvier), wife of Lieutenant J. H. Brown, U. S. Navy, Assistant Inspector of Machinery at the works.

S–44
SUBMARINE

Launched October 27, 1923, at Bethlehem Shipbuilding Corporation, Quincy, Massachusetts.

Sponsor: MRS. H. E. GRIESHABER (Eldora Corson), wife of Mr. H. E. Grieshaber, Naval Architect for the Electric Boat Company.

S–45
SUBMARINE

Launched June 26, 1923, at Bethlehem Shipbuilding Corporation, Quincy, Massachusetts.

Sponsor: MRS. CHARLES HIBBARD (Mary McQuillan), wife of Lieutenant C. Hibbard, U. S. N. C. C., Assistant to Superintending Constructor.

S-46
SUBMARINE

Launched September 11, 1923, at Bethlehem Shipbuilding Corporation, Quincy, Massachusetts.

Sponsor: MISS GRACE ROOSEVELT, daughter of Honorable Theodore Roosevelt, Assistant Secretary of the Navy.

Dimensions of Submarines S-48 to S-51 inclusive are:
Length, 240 feet   Beam, 21 feet, 10 inches   Draft, 13 feet, 6 inches

S-48
SUBMARINE

Launched February 26, 1921, at Lake Torpedo Boat Company, Bridgeport, Connecticut.

Sponsor: MRS. JAMES O. GERMAINE (Princess Tocoomwas), daughter of Mr. Lemuel M. Occom Fielding, who is Chief of the Council of the Mohegan Tribe and a descendant of Uncas I.

S-49
SUBMARINE

Launched April 23, 1921, at Lake Torpedo Boat Company, Bridgeport, Connecticut.

Sponsor: MRS. JOSEPH ELIOT AUSTIN (Mamie Wadman), wife of Lieutenant Commander J. E. Austin, U. S. Navy (Retired).

S-50
SUBMARINE

Launched June 18, 1921, at Lake Torpedo Boat Company, Bridgeport, Connecticut.

Sponsor: MRS. WILLIAM G. ESMOND (Ella Sanger), wife of the Naval Architect of the Lake Torpedo Boat Company.

S-51
SUBMARINE

Launched August 20, 1921, at Lake Torpedo Boat Company, Bridgeport, Connecticut.

Sponsor: MRS. ROY PORTER MILLS (Edith Newton), wife of an official of the Lake Torpedo Boat Company.

[209]

SACRAMENTO (2D)

GUNBOAT

Length, 226 feet   *Beam, 40 feet, 10 inches*   *Draft, 11 feet, 6 inches*

NAMED FOR THE CITY OF SACRAMENTO, THE
CAPITAL OF THE STATE OF CALIFORNIA

Launched February 21, 1914, at William Cramp & Sons' Company, Philadelphia, Pennsylvania.

Sponsor: MISS PHEBE BRIGGS, daughter of Doctor Ellery Briggs, of Sacramento, baptized the ship with Sacramento Valley champagne.

U. S. S. "Sacramento 1st" launched in 1862, was a gunboat named for Sacramento River.

SAMPSON

TORPEDO BOAT DESTROYER

Length, 315 feet   *Beam, 29 feet, 11 inches*   *Draft, 9 feet, 6 inches*

NAMED FOR REAR ADMIRAL WILLIAM T. SAMPSON,
U. S. NAVY

Launched March 4, 1916, at Fore River Shipbuilding Company, Quincy, Massachusetts.

Sponsor: MISS MARJORIE SMITH, granddaughter of Rear Admiral Sampson, U. S. Navy, and daughter of Captain Roy C. Smith, U. S. Navy.

REAR ADMIRAL WILLIAM T. SAMPSON, United States Navy, was born at Palmyra, New York, 1840; graduated midshipman 1861; master 1861; lieutenant 1862; lieutenant commander 1866; commander 1874; captain 1889; commodore July 3, 1898; rear admiral March 3, 1899; died 1902. 1861 ordered to U. S. S. "Potomac"; 1862–1863 on U. S. S. "John Adams"; 1864–1865 South Atlantic Squadron; on the ironclad "Patapsco" when she was blown up by a submarine mine in Charleston Harbor January 15, 1865; cruised in the Mediterranean and China and on duty at the U. S. Naval Academy 1866–1882; 1882-

[210]

U.S. SUBMARINE "S-42" LAUNCHED

1884 naval observatory; 1885–1886 torpedo station and member of board on fortifications and defense; 1886–1890 superintendent Naval Academy; 1893–1897 chief bureau of ordnance; commanding U. S. S. "Iowa," 1897; president of court of inquiry on the blowing up of the U. S. S. "Maine" in Havana Harbor February 15, 1898.

April 21, 1898, ordered to command North Atlantic station with the rank of rear admiral; was commander in chief of U. S. naval forces operating against Spain in the West Indies, which blockaded ports of Cuba and porto Rico and destroyed the fleet of Admiral Cervera; September, 1898, appointed one of the three commissioners to Cuba; resumed command of the North Atlantic station until detached October 1899, and ordered to the Boston Navy yard. Retired February 9, 1902.

SANDERLING

MINE SWEEPER

Length, 187 feet   *Beam, 35 feet*   *Draft, 9 feet, 9 inches*

NAMED FOR THE BIRD SANDERLING

Launched September 2, 1918, at Todd Shipyard Corporation, New York.

Sponsor: MISS DOROTHY BAINE, daughter of the General Superintendent of Tebo Yacht Basin when the vessel was built.

SANDPIPER

MINE SWEEPER

Length, 187 feet   *Beam, 35 feet*   *Draft, 9 feet, 9 inches*

NAMED FOR THE BIRD SANDPIPER

Launched April 28, 1919, at Navy Yard, Philadelphia, Pennsylvania.

Sponsor: MISS EDITH V. TAWRESEY, daughter of Captain J. G. Tawresey, C. C., U. S. Navy, Construction Officer of the Navy Yard.

[211]

SANDS

TORPEDO BOAT DESTROYER

Length, 314 feet   Beam, 30 feet, 11 inches   Draft, 9 feet, 4 inches

NAMED FOR REAR ADMIRAL BENJAMIN F. SANDS, U. S. NAVY, AND REAR ADMIRAL JAMES H. SANDS, U. S. NAVY

Launched October 28, 1919, at New York Shipbuilding Corporation, Camden, New Jersey.

Sponsor: MISS JANE McCUE SANDS, granddaughter of Rear Admiral Benjamin F. Sands, U. S. Navy.

REAR ADMIRAL BENJAMIN F. SANDS, United States Navy, was born 1811; died 1883. Appointed midshipman 1828; rear admiral 1891; 1830–1846 cruised in the Brazil, West India, and Mediterranean squadrons; 1847 attached to the home squadron, took part in the Mexican War at Tobasco and Tuxpan; 1863 commanded the "Dacotah," North Atlantic blockading squadron, and participated in the engagement with Fort Caswell; in command of the "Fort Jackson" 1864–1865 and took part in attacks on Fort Fisher December 24–25 and January 13–15, 1865. Commanded division on the blockade of Texas from February to June, 1865, and took formal possession of Galveston and hoisted the United States Flag over that city. Retired 1874.

REAR ADMIRAL JAMES H. SANDS, United States Navy, son of Rear Admiral B. F. Sands, was born 1845; died 1911. Appointed midshipman 1859; rear admiral 1902. Civil War, served with North Atlantic blockading squadron on the U. S. S. "Tuscarora" and the U. S. S. "Shenandoah." Took part in both attacks on Fort Fisher, December, 1864, and January, 1865, and was recommended for distinguished gallantry. 1865–1868, attached to the "Hartford," East India Squadron; commended for gallantry in skirmishes with savages at Formosa. 1869-1870, European Station. 1871–1872, commanded "California,"

Pacific Station. 1898, commanded the U. S. ships "Columbia" and "Minneapolis." Superintendent of the Naval Academy 1905–1907.

SATTERLEE

TORPEDO BOAT DESTROYER

Length, 314 feet   Beam, 30 feet, 11 inches   Draft, 9 feet, 4 inches

NAMED FOR CAPTAIN CHARLES SATTERLEE,
U. S. COAST GUARD

Launched December 21, 1918, at Newport News S. B. & D. D. Company, Newport News, Virginia.

Sponsor: MISS REBECCA ELOISE SATTERLEE, niece of Captain Charles Satterlee, U. S. Coast Guard.

CAPTAIN CHARLES SATTERLEE, United States Coast Guard, was born in Connecticut, 1875. Appointed a cadet in the Revenue Service 1895; promoted to captain in the Coast Guard 1915. In 1908 he was assigned as supervisor of anchorages at Sault Ste. Marie, Michigan, which duty included the command of the cutter "Mackinac." In 1909 he was ordered to the "Tahoma," for a cruise to the Pacific. From 1910 to 1913 he was assistant inspector of life-saving stations. On September 26, 1918, while in command of the "Tampa," which was escorting a convoy of vessels in Bristol Channel, England, she was sunk by an enemy torpedo and all hands were lost.

SCHENCK

TORPEDO BOAT DESTROYER

Length, 314 feet   Beam, 30 feet, 11 inches   Draft, 9 feet, 4 inches

NAMED FOR REAR ADMIRAL JAMES FINDLEY SCHENCK,
U. S. NAVY

Launched April 23, 1919, at New York Shipbuilding Corporation, Camden, New Jersey.

Sponsor: MISS MARY JANET EARLE, daughter of Rear Admiral Ralph Earle, U. S. Navy, and great-granddaughter of Rear Admiral James F. Schenck, U. S. Navy.

[213]

Rear ADMIRAL JAMES FINDLEY SCHENCK, United States Navy, was born in Ohio, 1807. Appointed midshipman 1825; rear admiral 1868. He was highly commended for service during the Mexican War, under Commodore Stockton, at Santa Barbara, San Pedro, Los Angeles, Guaymas, and Mazatlan. In 1846, with his own hands, he hoisted at Santa Barbara the first American flag in California. He took command on the "Saginaw" July, 1859, and saw service in Cochin, China, silencing the forts at Quim-hon Bay, June 1861. At the outbreak of the Civil War was in command of the "Saginaw," which had been pronounced unseaworthy. Commander Schenck proceeded home without waiting for orders. He was at once given command of the "St. Lawrence," May 3, 1862, joining the West Gulf Blockading Squadron. He took a prominent part in the two attacks on Fort Fisher, and was mentioned for gallantry in action in the report of Rear Admiral Porter, then commanding the North Atlantic Blockading Squadron. He died 1882.

SCHLEY

TORPEDO BOAT DESTROYER

Length, 314 feet   *Beam, 30 feet, 11 inches*   *Draft, 9 feet, 1 inch*

NAMED FOR REAR ADMIRAL WINFIELD SCOTT SCHLEY, U. S. NAVY

Launched March 28, 1918, at Bethlehem Shipbuilding Corporation, San Francisco, California.

Sponsor: MISS ELEANOR MARTIN, daughter of Mr. Walter S. Martin, a prominent citizen of San Francisco.

Rear ADMIRAL WINFIELD SCOTT SCHLEY, United States Navy, was born at Frederick, Maryland, 1839; died 1911. Appointed midshipman, 1856; commissioned lieutenant, 1862; commander, 1874; commodore, February 6, 1898; rear admiral, March 3, 1899. Served: 1860–1861, frigate "Niagara," East India Squadron; Civil War, 1861–1865. In the West Gulf Blockading Squadron, 1862, under Admiral Farragut, took part in en-

INDIAN PRINCESS SPONSOR FOR THE SUBMARINE
"S-48" WITH HER PARTY

gagements on the Mississippi River. Particularly mentioned for gallantry at the capture of Port Hudson. 1864–1865 on duty in the Pacific Squadron. 1865 landed with U. S. Forces at LaUnion, San Salvador, to protect American interests. 1869–1872, Asiatic Station. Took part in capture of Korean Forts on Salee River. 1876–1879 Brazil Station. 1884 commanded the expedition that rescued General Greely and survivors of his party near Cape Sabine, Grinnell Land, and brought them to the United States. Personally thanked by President Arthur for this service. 1884–1889 Chief of Bureau of Equipment. In the war with Spain, with the "Brooklyn" as flagship, commanded the Flying Squadron until June 1, 1898, and from that date commanded the second Squadron of the North Atlantic Fleet which took a prominent part in the destruction of Cervera's fleet, on July 3, 1898; 1899–1901 commanded South Atlantic Squadron.

SEA GULL

MINE SWEEPER

Length, 187 feet   *Beam, 35 feet*   *Draft, 9 feet, 9 inches*

NAMED FOR THE BIRD SEA GULL

Launched December 24, 1918, at Consolidated Shipbuilding Corporation, New York City.

Sponsor: MRS. CLEMENT GOULD AMORY (Louise Mathews), wife of the Treasurer of the Corporation.

SELFRIDGE

TORPEDO BOAT DESTROYER

Length, 314 feet   *Beam, 30 feet, 11 inches*   *Draft, 9 feet, 4 inches*

NAMED FOR REAR ADMIRAL THOMAS O. SELFRIDGE, U. S. NAVY

Launched July 25, 1919, at Bethlehem Shipbuilding Corporation, San Francisco, California.

Sponsor: MRS. FREDERIC G. KELLOND (Katherine Selfridge), granddaughter of Rear Admiral Thomas O. Selfridge, U. S. Navy.

REAR ADMIRAL THOMAS O. SELFRIDGE, United States Navy, was born in Boston, Massachusetts, 1804; died 1902. Appointed midshipman 1818; rear admiral, retired, 1866; served on exploring expedition of 1829; commanded the U. S. S. "Columbus," flagship of the East India Squadron. Early in 1847 the authorities of Mulje having refused to make an apology for an insult to the United States flag, he landed with a force of marines and seamen to enforce his demands. In November, 1847, he landed with about 70 men from the "Dale" and put a force of about 400 Mexicans to flight. During the Civil War, 1861, in command of the "Mississippi, was actively engaged in blockading off Mobile Bay and Passes of the Mississippi. Subsequently held important positions ashore.

SEMMES

TORPEDO BOAT DESTROYER

Length, 314 feet   *Beam, 30 feet, 11 inches*   *Draft, 9 feet, 4 inches*

NAMED FOR COMMANDER RAPHAEL SEMMES, U. S. NAVY

Launched December 21, 1918, at Newport News S. B. & D. D. Company, Newport News, Virginia.

Sponsor: MRS. JOHN H. WATKINS (Anne Spencer), granddaughter of Commander Raphael Semmes, U. S. Navy.

COMMANDER RAPHAEL SEMMES, United States Navy, was born in Charles County, Maryland, 1809; died in 1877. Appointed a midshipman, 1826; commissioned commander, 1855. At the beginning of the war with Mexico, he was made flag lieutenant under Commodore David Conner, commanding the squadron in the Gulf, and in the siege of Vera Cruz was in charge of a naval battery on shore. April 28, 1847, ordered into the interior of Mexico on a special mission, and went to the city of Mexico with the Army as aid to Gen. Worth. He served for several years as inspector of lighthouses on the Gulf coast, and in 1858 became secretary of the Lighthouse Board at Washington.

(At the outbreak of the Civil War resigned. He commanded the "Sumter" and "Alabama," Confederate States Navy, and commanded James River Squadron with rank of Rear Admiral. A brilliant and daring officer.)

SHARKEY

TORPEDO BOAT DESTROYER

Length, 314 feet   *Beam, 30 feet, 11 inches*   *Draft, 9 feet, 4 inches*

NAMED FOR LIEUTENANT WILLIAM J. SHARKEY, U. S. NAVY

Launched August 12, 1919, at Bethlehem Shipbuilding Company, Squantum, Massachusetts.

Sponsor: MRS. MARY E. SHARKEY, widow of Lieutenant William J. Sharkey, U. S. Navy.

LIEUTENANT WILLIAM J. SHARKEY, United States Navy (junior grade) (T), was born in Auburn, New York, 1885; appointed ensign (T) March 15, 1918; detailed to the U. S. S. O–5; appointed lieutenant (junior grade) September 21, 1918; killed by an explosion of the U. S. S. O–5, October 5, 1918. He was promoted from the ranks, and at the time of the explosion was assisting his commanding officer in averting the danger of an explosion, the imminence of which had been discovered.

SHAW

TORPEDO BOAT DESTROYER

Length, 315 feet   *Beam, 29 feet, 11 inches*   *Draft, 9 feet, 5 inches*

NAMED FOR CAPTAIN JOHN SHAW, U. S. NAVY

Launched December 9, 1916, at Navy Yard, Mare Island, California.

Sponsor: MRS. LYMAN C. MILLARD (Virginia Lynch), great-great-granddaughter of Captain John Shaw, U. S. Navy.

CAPTAIN JOHN SHAW, United States Navy, was born in Ireland, 1773. Commissioned Lieutenant, U. S. Navy, August 3, 1798; promoted Master Commandant (Commander), 1804; Captain, 1807; died, 1823.

Commanded U. S. S. "Enterprise" 1798–1800 and captured 8 vessels from the French in the West Indies. Recaptured 11 American vessels. His engagement with "Le Flambeau" and "La Pauline," both of which he captured, was counted one of the most gallant actions of the Naval War with France.

1801 commanded the "George Washington," carried tribute from the United States to the Dey of Algiers and brought home many Americans that had been made prisoners (from merchant vessels) by the Dey. 1804 commanded the "John Adams," Mediterranean Squadron. During the years 1806 and 1807 superintended the construction of gunboats building at New Orleans. In 1808 commanded Norfolk Navy Yard. 1810–1813 commanded New Orleans Naval Station. 1814 transferred to the commands of the vessels lying in the Thames, above New London; was blockaded there by the British fleet. From 1815 to 1817 commanded the Mediterranean Squadron, and in 1818–1823 commanded Boston Navy Yard and Naval Station at Charleston, South Carolina.

SHENANDOAH

RIGID AIRSHIP

Length, 680 feet *Height, 93 feet* *Diameter, 78 feet, 9 inches*
Volume, 2,100,000 cubic feet

NAMED SHENANDOAH, AN INDIAN NAME MEANING "DAUGHTER OF THE STARS"

Launched October 10th, 1923, at Lakehurst, New Jersey.

Sponsor: MRS. EDWIN DENBY (Marion Thurber), wife of the Secretary of the Navy.

THIS first American rigid airship christened and commissioned in the naval service was afterwards piloted by the sponsor for an hour and a half. Among those present

U.S. AIRSHIP "SHENANDOAH" MOORED TO MAST ON U.S.S. "PATOKA,"
AIRSHIP TENDER, THE FIRST VESSEL OF ITS KIND

at the ceremonies were Secretary of the Navy Edwin Denby, Rear Admiral Moffett, Rear Admiral Scales, and officers from the Philadelphia Navy Yard, and Mrs. Russell C. Langdon, President of the Society of Sponsors.

Washington Herald: "With martial music, fluttering flags, blare of trumpets and impressive ceremony, the Navy's new "ZR-1" was christened "Shenandoah" this afternoon and formally commissioned in the service. At the christening Mrs. Denby, standing in front of the control car, pulled a line which released a flock of carrier pigeons which wheeled about and then flew out of the hangar. Two dozen pigeons were released to fly to Washington, Anacostia, Hampton Roads and Dahlgren, Virginia. Two pigeons bore messages to President Coolidge in aluminum cartridges announcing the commissioning of the ship. Mrs. Denby pronounced the words "I name thee 'Shenandoah'" as the ship, lightened of ballast, rose upward in the shed. Small balloons were also released by the party in the forward car. The national anthem was then played and the ship hauled down and secured. Secretary Denby and Rear Admiral Moffett, Chief of the Bureau of Aeronautics, then delivered addresses and placed the ship in commission. Acceptance was made by Commander McCrary, first commander of the "Shenandoah." The crew, following the exercises, shifted into flight uniforms and prepared the ship for her first commissioned flight."

SHIRK

TORPEDO BOAT DESTROYER

Length, 314 feet   *Beam, 30 feet, 11 inches*   *Draft, 9 feet, 4 inches*

NAMED FOR COMMANDER JAMES W. SHIRK, U. S. NAVY

Launched June 20, 1919, at Bethlehem Shipbuilding Corporation, San Francisco, California.

Sponsor: MISS IDA LAWLOR DUNNIGAN, daughter of Mr. John S. Dunnigan, clerk of the Board of Supervisors, San Francisco.

[219]

COMMANDER JAMES W. SHIRK, United States Navy, was born in Pennsylvania 1832; died 1873. Appointed midshipman 1849; commander 1866. During the Civil War he was especially distinguished for service in the Mississippi Squadron. At Shiloh, April 6, 1862, his vessel the "Lexington," in company with the "Tyler," prevented the enemy from crossing and saved the army from defeat. He was later thanked by the Secretary of the Navy for this service. During the siege of Vicksburg, while in command of the "Tuscumbia," he was constantly under fire from May 19 to the time of surrender July 4, 1863. Commander July 25, 1866.

SHUBRICK (2D)

TORPEDO BOAT DESTROYER

Length, 314 feet   *Beam, 30 feet, 11 inches*   *Draft, 9 feet, 4 inches*

NAMED FOR REAR ADMIRAL WILLIAM BRANFORD SHUBRICK, U. S. NAVY

Launched December 31, 1918, at Bethlehem Shipbuilding Corporation, Quincy, Mass.

Sponsor: MRS. THOMAS F. BAYARD (Mary Clymer), granddaughter of Rear Admiral W. B. Shubrick, U. S. Navy, and widow of Honorable Thomas F. Bayard, Secretary of State, under President Cleveland.

REAR ADMIRAL WILLIAM BRANFORD SHUBRICK, United States Navy, was born in South Carolina 1790; died 1874. Appointed midshipman in 1806. He was a lieutenant on the "Constitution" when she captured the "Cyane" and "Levant" in 1815. Active in the War with Mexico and captured the town of Mazatlan and other Mexican ports. Rear admiral (retired) July 16, 1862; awarded medal for service in War of 1812; commanded Pacific Squadron in 1847 during the Mexican War.

SICARD

TORPEDO BOAT DESTROYER

Length, 314 feet   *Beam, 30 feet, 4 inches*   *Draft, 9 feet, 4 inches*

SPONSOR PULLING THE CORD TO BREAK THE
BOTTLE WHEN NAMING THE AIRSHIP
"SHENANDOAH"

NAMED FOR REAR ADMIRAL MONTGOMERY SICARD,
U. S. NAVY

Launched April 20, 1920, at Bath Iron Works, Bath, Maine.

Sponsor: MRS. MONTGOMERY H. SICARD (Adelaide Ireland), daughter-in-law of Rear Admiral Montgomery Sicard, U. S. Navy.

REAR ADMIRAL MONTGOMERY SICARD, U. S. Navy. Born in New York 1836; died 1900. Appointed midshipman, 1857; rear admiral, 1897; retired 1898. Served in the Home and East India Squadrons, 1855–1861; Civil War, 1861–1865, in the West Gulf Blockading Squadron. Commanded the "Oneida," 1863; 1864–1865 commanded the "Ticonderoga," South Atlantic Blockading Squadron. Took part in attacks on Fort Fisher, December 24 and 25, 1864, and in the land and naval assault on Fort Fisher, January 15, 1865. Chief of Bureau of Ordnance, 1881–1890; 1897–1898, in command of the North Atlantic Squadron. Placed in charge of Board of Strategy, and while on this board took an important part in the conduct of the war with Spain. He was considered a distinguished ordnance expert.

SIGOURNEY

TORPEDO BOAT DESTROYER

Length, 314 feet   *Beam, 30 feet, 11 inches*   *Draft, 9 feet, 2 inches*

NAMED FOR MIDSHIPMAN JAMES BUTLER SIGOURNEY,
U. S. NAVY

Launched December 16, 1917, Bethlehem Shipbuilding Corporation, Fore River, Massachusetts.

Sponsor: MRS. GRANVILLE W. JOHNSON (Jeannette Fallon), wife of Mr. Granville Johnson of Boston, Massachusetts.

MIDSHIPMAN JAMES BUTLER SIGOURNEY, United States Navy, was born in Boston. Appointed midshipman, 1809; served on "Wasp" under Capt. T.

Robinson and Capt. James Lawrence; was sailing master of "Nautilus" and was captured in her shortly after commencement of War of 1812; after his exchange was placed in command of the "Asp," a schooner fitted out for defense of Chesapeake Bay; July 14, 1813, was attacked by three British barges but succeeded in driving them off; on a second attack the "Asp" was boarded and Sigourney was killed at his post on deck.

SIMPSON

TORPEDO BOAT DESTROYER

Length, 314 feet *Beam, 30 feet, 11 inches* *Draft, 9 feet, 4 inches*

NAMED FOR REAR ADMIRAL EDWARD SIMPSON, U. S. NAVY

Launched April 28, 1920, at William Cramp and Sons' Company, Philadelphia, Pennsylvania.

Sponsor: MISS CAROLINE STERETT SIMPSON, daughter of Rear Admiral Edward Simpson, U. S. Navy.

REAR ADMIRAL EDWARD SIMPSON, U. S. Navy, was born in New York, 1824; died 1888. Appointed midshipman, 1840; rear admiral, 1884; 1840–1843 attached to line of battleship "Independence"; 1845 "Congress," Brazil Station. War with Mexico: 1845 attached to the "Vixen" and took part in the attack on forts of Alvarado, Tobasco, and Tuxpan. The "Vixen" covered the landing of our Army at the siege of Vera Cruz and took part with the mosquito fleet in the bombardment of that city; 1856–1857 lieutenant on the "Portsmouth," East India Station; took part in the bombardment of the Barrier Forts in the Canton River, China. Civil War: Commanded monitor "Passaic" 1863–1864 in attacks on Forts Wagner, Sumter, Moultrie, and Battery Bee in Charleston Harbor; 1864 commanded "Isonomia," East Gulf Blockading Squadron; 1865 fleet captain West Gulf Blockading Squadron and engaged in operations against Mobile from March 27 to April 12, 1865, when the city capitulated; 1867–1868 commanded the "Mohican," North Pacific Squadron. He was sent on a special mission to Europe, and was later in charge of the Torpedo Station, Newport, Rhode Island, and Commandant at the Naval Station, New London. He was considered an authority on naval ordnance.

SINCLAIR

TORPEDO BOAT DESTROYER

Length, 314 feet   *Beam, 30 feet, 11 inches*   *Draft, 9 feet, 4 inches*

NAMED FOR CAPTAIN ARTHUR SINCLAIR,
U. S. NAVY

Launched June 2, 1919, at Bethlehem Shipbuilding Corporation, Quincy, Massachusetts.

Sponsor: MRS. GEORGE BARNETT (Lelia Sinclair Montague), great-granddaughter of Captain Arthur Sinclair, U. S. Navy, and wife of Major General Barnett, U. S. M.C.

CAPTAIN ARTHUR SINCLAIR, United States Navy, was born in Virginia; died at Norfolk, Virginia, 1831. Appointed midshipman 1798. Served on the "Constellation" in 1799. Commissioned lieutenant 1804; master commandant 1812; captain 1813. In 1807–1809 on duty at Norfolk; 1809–1811 in command of the "Nautilus"; 1811–1813 in command of the "Argus"; 1813 Sackett's Harbor; 1814 Erie, Pennsylvania; 1817 in command of the "Congress"; 1818 ordered to Washington; 1819 to command Naval Station at Norfolk. Took part in many brilliant engagements of the War of 1812; commanded the "Niagara" on Lake Huron in 1814 and captured a number of the enemy's vessels. Captain Sinclair exerted himself for some time to get a nautical school established for the instruction of midshipmen, and the first nautical school commenced on board the frigate "Guerriere" at Norfolk on December 3, 1821, under the direction of Captain Sinclair, by orders of Secretary of the Navy Smith Thompson.

SLOAT

TORPEDO BOAT DESTROYER

Length, 314 feet   *Beam, 30 feet, 11 inches*   *Draft, 9 feet, 4 inches*

NAMED FOR REAR ADMIRAL JOHN DRAKE SLOAT, U. S. NAVY

Launched May 14, 1919, at Bethlehem Shipbuilding Corporation, San Francisco.

Sponsor: MRS. EDWIN A. SHERMAN (Adaline Dodd), wife of Major Sherman, biographer of Rear Admiral John Drake Sloat, U. S. Navy, and largely instrumental in planning the monument to Rear Admiral Sloat at Monterey, California.

REAR ADMIRAL JOHN DRAKE SLOAT, United States Navy, was born in Sloatbury, New York, 1781; died 1867. Appointed midshipman 1800; rear admiral on the retired list 1866. Was sailing master of the "United States" under Commodore Decatur and was promoted to lieutenant for conspicuous gallantry in the engagement with H. B. M. S. "Macedonian" and her capture October 25, 1812; was wounded during the fight but remained on deck; was included in the thanks of Congress to officers who took part in the engagement and awarded a silver medal. Commanded the Pacific Squadron 1844–1846, during the Mexican War. Under his direction the American flag was hoisted July 7, 1846, in Monterey, California, and possession of that part of California was taken by the United States. Many important commands on shore and made the plans of Mare Island Navy Yard.

ROBERT SMITH

TORPEDO BOAT DESTROYER

Length, 314 feet   *Beam, 30 feet, 11 inches*   *Draft, 9 feet, 4 inches*

NAMED FOR SECRETARY OF THE NAVY
ROBERT SMITH

Launched September 19, 1919, at Bethlehem Shipbuilding Corporation, San Francisco, California.

Sponsor: MISS JANE COOPER, daughter of Mr. Oscar Cooper, prominent citizen of San Francisco.

SECRETARY OF THE NAVY ROBERT SMITH was born in Lancaster, Pennsylvania, November, 1757; died 1842. He was graduated from Princeton University in 1781; was admitted to the bar, and settled in Baltimore; 1793 became State senator from Maryland and was a member of the House of Delegates from 1796–1800. On January 26, 1802, he became Secretary of the Navy and held that office until he was appointed Secretary of State in 1809.

SOMERS

TORPEDO BOAT DESTROYER
Length, 314 feet   Beam, 30 feet, 11 inches   Draft, 9 feet, 4 inches

NAMED FOR LIEUTENANT RICHARD SOMERS, U. S. NAVY

Launched December 28, 1918, at Bethlehem Shipbuilding Corporation, San Francisco, California.

Sponsor: MISS ANNA MAXWELL JAYNE, daughter of Rear Admiral Joseph L. Jayne, U. S. Navy.

LIEUTENANT RICHARD SOMERS, United States Navy, was born at Somers Point, New Jersey, 1778; killed by an explosion on the "Intrepid" in the harbor of Tripoli, September 4, 1804. Appointed midshipman April 30, 1798. On September 4, 1804, he took the bomb vessel "Intrepid" into the harbor of Tripoli to destroy the enemy's fleet. The vessel had a quantity of powder on it and when fired upon it exploded, blowing it to atoms and killing all on board.

SOUTHARD

TORPEDO BOAT DESTROYER
Length, 314 feet   Beam, 30 feet, 11 inches   Draft, 9 feet, 4 inches

NAMED FOR SECRETARY OF THE NAVY SAMUEL LEWIS SOUTHARD

Launched March 31, 1919, at William Cramp & Sons' Company, Philadelphia, Pennsylvania.

Sponsor: Miss Francesca Lewis Stewart, great-granddaughter of Secretary of the Navy Samuel Lewis Southard.

SECRETARY OF THE NAVY SAMUEL LEWIS SOUTHARD was born in Basking Ridge, New Jersey, 1787; died 1842. He was graduated at Princeton in 1804; became associate justice of the State supreme court in 1815, was a presidential elector in 1820, and was chosen to the United States Senate as a Whig in place of James J. Wilson, who had resigned, serving from February 16, 1821, until March 3, 1823. In September, 1823, he became Secretary of the Navy and served until March 3, 1829, acting also as Secretary of the Treasury from March 7 until July 1, 1825, and taking charge of the portfolio of War for a time. In 1829, he became attorney general of New Jersey, and in 1832 was elected governor. United States Senator again in 1833, and served until his resignation on May 3, 1842. In 1841, on the death of President Harrison and the consequent accession of John Tyler, he became President of the Senate.

SPROSTON

TORPEDO BOAT DESTROYER

Length, 314 feet   *Beam, 30 feet, 11 inches*   *Draft, 9 feet, 2 inches*

NAMED FOR LIEUTENANT JOHN G. SPROSTON, U. S. NAVY

Launched August 10, 1918, at Bethlehem Shipbuilding Corporation, San Francisco, California.

Sponsor: Mrs. George J. Denis (Alberta Johnston), Los Angeles, California.

LIEUTENANT JOHN G. SPROSTON, U. S. Navy, was born in Maryland, and was killed in action June 8, 1862. Appointed midshipman 1846. Pacific station during war with Mexico. On November 1, 1861, at the Battle of Port Royal, South Carolina, he fired nearly all the 11-inch shells with his own hand. He took active part in operations of the South Atlantic blockading squadron on the coast and up

[226]

the rivers of South Carolina, Georgia, and Florida. Was
killed while on a boat expedition in St. Johns River, Florida.
Was commended in a letter from Rear Admiral S. F. du
Pont as "an able, brave, and devoted officer from the State
of Maryland."

STANSBURY

TORPEDO BOAT DESTROYER

Length, 314 feet   *Beam, 30 feet, 11 inches*   *Draft, 9 feet, 2 inches*

NAMED FOR LIEUTENANT JOHN STANSBURY, U. S. NAVY

Launched May 16, 1919, at Bethlehem Shipbuilding
Corporation, San Francisco, California.

Sponsor: MISS MARY ELEANOR TREVORROW, daughter
of Lieutenant William J. Trevorrow, U. S. Navy, (Retired),
Assistant Inspector of Machinery at Union Works.

LIEUTENANT JOHN STANSBURY, U. S. Navy, was
born in Baltimore, Maryland; killed in action September 11,
1814. Midshipman with Decatur in the capture of the
"Macedonian" by the "United States" October 25, 1812;
lieutenant on the "Ticonderoga" at the battle of Lake
Champlain, during which battle he was killed.

STEVENS

TORPEDO BOAT DESTROYER

Length, 314 feet   *Beam, 30 feet, 11 inches*   *Draft, 9 feet, 2 inches*

NAMED FOR CAPTAIN THOMAS HOLDUP STEVENS, U. S. NAVY

Launched January 13, 1918, at Bethlehem Shipbuilding
Corporation, Quincy, Massachusetts.

Sponsor: MISS MARIE CHRISTIE STEVENS, great-granddaughter of Captain Thomas Holdup Stevens, U. S. Navy.

CAPTAIN THOMAS HOLDUP STEVENS, U. S. Navy,
was born in Charleston, South Carolina, 1795; died January
22, 1841; appointed midshipman January 16, 1809; at
beginning of War of 1812 he volunteered for service on the

Great Lakes, and was assigned to the Niagara frontier, where he rendered splendid service and at the attack on Black Rock; commander of the "Trippe" in the battle of Lake Erie; 1823–1824 commanded vessels in the West Indies in the suppression of piracy. Died in command of the Washington Navy Yard.

STEWART (2D)

TORPEDO BOAT DESTROYER

Length, 314 feet   *Beam, 30 feet, 11 inches*   *Draft, 9 feet, 4 inches*

NAMED FOR REAR ADMIRAL CHARLES STEWART, U. S. NAVY

Launched March 4, 1920, at William Cramp & Sons' Company, Philadelphia, Pennsylvania.

Sponsor: MRS. ROBERT MACGREGOR STEVENS (Margaretta Parnell Stewart), granddaughter of Rear Admiral Charles Stewart, U. S. Navy, and sister of Miss Frances Rodney Stewart, sponsor for U. S. S. "Stewart 1st," in 1902.

REAR ADMIRAL CHARLES STEWART, U. S. Navy, was born in Philadelphia, Pennsylvania, 1778; died 1869. Lieutenant March 9, 1808; senior flag officer, 1859; rear admiral, retired list, 1862. Distinguished in Naval War with France, 1798–1801. Took part in operations against Tripoli, 1802–1805. Commanded the U. S. S. "Constitution" 1813–1815, War of 1812; captured "Pictou" and merchant vessels; February 20, 1815, captured H. B. M. S. "Cyane" and "Levant." 1820–1824, commanded Pacific squadron. 1830–1832, Navy commissioner, included in thanks of Congress for gallant conduct in the war with Tripoli, and awarded a sword. Thanks of Congress and gold medal for service in War of 1812. By special act of Congress, in recognition of his distinguished service, commissioned senior flag officer of the United States Navy.

STOCKTON (2D)

TORPEDO BOAT DESTROYER

Length, 315 feet   *Beam, 30 feet, 8 inches*   *Draft, 8 feet, 4 inches*

NAMED FOR COMMODORE ROBERT F. STOCKTON,
U. S. NAVY

Launched July 17, 1917, at William Cramp & Sons' Company, Philadelphia, Pennsylvania.

Sponsor: MISS ELLEN EMELIE deMARTELLY, cousin of Mrs. Harold M. Whiteway, a granddaughter of Commodore Stockton.

COMMODORE ROBERT FIELD STOCKTON, U. S. Navy, was born in Princeton, New Jersey, 1795; died 1866. He was appointed midshipman 1811; captain 1838. He took part in the defense of Alexandria, Virginia, and Baltimore, Maryland, during the War of 1812; served in War with Algiers in 1815; commanded Mexican Squadron 1846–1847, Mexican War, and established provisional government of California; designed and superintended the building of the steam frigate "Princeton," and was wounded by the bursting of one of the large guns of that vessel; resigned from the Navy May 28, 1850; United States Senator from New Jersey 1851–1852; was engineer of the Delaware & Raritan Canal.

STODDERT

TORPEDO BOAT DESTROYER

Length, 314 feet   *Beam, 30 feet, 11 inches*   *Draft, 9 feet, 4 inches*

NAMED FOR SECRETARY OF THE NAVY BENJAMIN STODDERT

Launched January 8, 1919, at Bethlehem Shipbuilding Corporation, San Francisco, California.

Sponsor: MRS. GAVIN McNAB (Wilma Davidson), wife of Mr. Gavin McNab, a prominent citizen of San Francisco, California.

HONORABLE BENJAMIN STODDERT, Secretary of the Navy 1798–1801, was born in Charles County, Maryland, 1751; died 1813. In 1776, as captain of Cavalry in the Continental Army, he was so severely wounded as to unfit him for active service. In May, 1798, he was appointed Secretary of the Navy, being the first to hold the post, and so remained till March 4, 1801. He was Acting Secretary of War after the resignation of James Henry until his successor, Samuel Dexter, took charge. When the Navy Department was created in 1798, the frigates "Constitution," "Constellation," and "United States" constituted the bulk of the American Navy. By the latter part of 1799, five frigates and 23 sloops of war were in commission. Mr. Stoddert's experience in the mercantile marine, coupled with his tact, industry, and judgment, were valuable in the formation of this naval force.

STRIBLING

TORPEDO BOAT DESTROYER

Length, 314 feet   *Beam, 30 feet, 11 inches*   *Draft, 9 feet, 2 inches*

NAMED FOR REAR ADMIRAL CORNELIUS K. STRIBLING, U. S. NAVY

Launched May 29, 1918, at Bethlehem Shipbuilding Corporation, Quincy, Massachusetts.

Sponsor: MISS MARY CALVERT STRIBLING, daughter of Mr. Cornelius Stribling, and granddaughter of Rear Admiral Cornelius K. Stribling, U. S. Navy.

REAR ADMIRAL CORNELIUS K. STRIBLING, U. S. Navy, was born in Pendleton, South Carolina, 1795; died January 17, 1880. Appointed midshipman January 18, 1812; rear admiral July 25, 1866; served in War of 1812 on U. S. S. "Mohawk," squadron on Lake Ontario; 1848, commanding ship of the line "Ohio" during Mexican War; superintendent Naval Academy, 1851–1853; special examining board, 1861; Lighthouse Board, 1862; commanded Philadelphia Navy Yard, 1863–1864; commanding East Gulf Blockading Squadron, 1865 (Civil War); Lighthouse Board, 1866–1872.

STRINGHAM (2D)

TORPEDO BOAT DESTROYER

Length, 314 feet   *Beam, 30 feet, 11 inches*   *Draft, 9 feet, 2 inches*

NAMING U.S. TORPEDO BOAT DESTROYER "STEWART 2D"

NAMED FOR REAR ADMIRAL SILAS HORTON STRINGHAM,
U. S. NAVY

Launched March 30, 1918, at Bethlehem Shipbuilding Corporation, Quincy, Massachusetts.

Sponsor: MRS. EDWARD B. HILL (Leslie Farwell), wife of Mr. Edward B. Hill, Treasurer of Fore River Shipbuilding Corporation.

REAR ADMIRAL SILAS HORTON STRINGHAM, U. S. Navy, was born in Middletown, Connecticut, 1798; died 1876; appointed midshipman 1810; rear admiral 1862; War of 1812, on U. S. S. "President" in engagements with H. B. M. S. "Little Belt" and "Belvidere"; war with Barbary States, attached to the "Spark," and took part in operations against Algiers and capture of Algerine vessels; captured pirate schooner "Moscow" in the West Indies while attached to "Hornet"; commanded "Ohio" in Mexican War, and took part in attack on Vera Cruz; Civil War, in command of Atlantic squadron.

STURTEVANT

TORPEDO BOAT DESTROYER

Length, 314 feet   Beam, 30 feet, 11 inches   Draft, 9 feet, 4 inches

NAMED FOR ENSIGN ALBERT D. STURTEVANT,
U. S. NAVAL RESERVE FORCE

Launched July 29, 1920, at New York Shipbuilding Corporation, Camden, New Jersey.

Sponsor: MRS. CURTIS RIPLEY SMITH (Ruth Sturtevant), only sister of Ensign Albert D. Sturtevant, U. S. Navy.

ENSIGN ALBERT D. STURTEVANT, U. S. Naval Reserve Force, was born in Washington, D. C., May 2, 1894; commissioned ensign in the United States Naval Reserve Force, March 26, 1917; naval aviator May 1, 1917; ordered overseas Sept. 10, 1917; detailed to duty at Felixstowe, England, November 26, 1917; shot down February 15, 1918, when attacked by a squadron of German airplanes.

[231]

SUMNER

TORPEDO BOAT DESTROYER

Length, 314 feet   *Beam, 30 feet, 11 inches*   *Draft, 9 feet, 4 inches*

NAMED FOR CAPTAIN ALLEN SUMNER,
U. S. MARINE CORPS

Launched November 24, 1920, at Bethlehem Shipbuilding Corporation, San Francisco, California.

Sponsor: MISS MARGARET SUMNER, daughter of Captain Allen Sumner, U. S. Navy.

CAPTAIN ALLEN M. SUMNER, U. S. Marine Corps; born in Boston, Massachusetts, 1882; died in action in France, July 19, 1918; appointed second lieutenant in the Marine Corps, March 15, 1907; served continuously until January 1, 1914, when he resigned; appointed first lieutenant March 22, 1917; sailed for duty in France August 5, 1917; killed in action by enemy shell fire during the advance on Tigny July 19, 1918; buried on the field; posthumously awarded croix de guerre with gilt star. During the advance from Viercy he accompanied one of his platoons to the front, keeping all his men under cover while he alone watched for signals for the advance. In so doing he saved the lives of many of his men without regard for his own safety.

SWALLOW

MINE SWEEPER

Length, 187 feet   *Beam, 35 feet*   *Draft, 9 feet, 9 inches*

NAMED FOR THE BIRD SWALLOW

Launched July 4, 1918, at Todd Shipyard Corporation, New York.

Sponsor: MISS SARA V. BRERETON, daughter of a foreman of the company.

SWAN

MINE SWEEPER

Length, 187 feet   *Beam, 35 feet*   *Draft, 9 feet, 9 inches*

NAMED FOR THE BIRD SWAN

Launched July 4, 1918, at Alabama D. D. & S. B. Co., Mobile, Alabama.

Sponsor: MISS HAZEL DONALDSON, daughter of Mr. W. S. Donaldson, Hull Superintendent of the company.

SWASEY

TORPEDO BOAT DESTROYER

Length, 314 feet   *Beam, 30 feet, 11 inches*   *Draft, 9 feet, 4 inches*

NAMED FOR LIEUTENANT CHARLES H. SWASEY, U. S. NAVY

Launched May 7, 1919, at Bethlehem Shipbuilding Corporation Quincy, Massachusetts.

Sponsor: MISS MARY LOVERING SWASEY, grandniece of Lieutenant Charles H. Swasey, U. S. Navy, and daughter of the vice president of the Herreshoff Manufacturing Company.

LIEUTENANT CHARLES H. SWASEY, United States Navy, was born in Massachusetts. Appointed midshipman 1854; lieutenant 1861. He served on the "Varuna" in the engagement with the steamer "Governor Moore" below New Orleans, April 24, 1862; and as executive officer of the "Sciota," West Gulf Blockading Squadron, he fell mortally wounded during an engagement with the Confederates near Donaldsonville, Louisiana, October 4, 1862, and died the same day.

T–1

SUBMARINE

Launched July 25, 1918, at Bethlehem Shipbuilding Corporation, Fore River, Massachusetts.

Sponsor: MRS. ALVIN HOVEY-KING (Lilian Hovey-King), wife of Lieutenant Commander Hovey-King, P. C., U. S. N., on duty at the works.

[233]

T-2
SUBMARINE

Launched September 6, 1919, at Bethlehem Shipbuilding Corporation, Quincy, Massachusetts.

Sponsor: MISS MADELINE EVERETT, fiancee of Lieutenant Commander Ames Loder, U. S. Navy, Assistant Inspector of Machinery, at the works.

T-3
SUBMARINE

Launched May 24, 1919, at Bethlehem Shipbuilding Corporation, Quincy, Massachusetts.

Sponsor: MRS. JOHN N. JORDAN (Lilian Terhune), wife of Commander J. N. Jordan, P. C., U. S. Navy, on duty at the works.

TALBOT

TORPEDO BOAT DESTROYER

Length, 314 feet   *Beam, 30 feet, 11 inches*   *Draft, 9 feet*

NAMED FOR CAPTAIN SILAS TALBOT, U. S. NAVY

Launched February 20, 1918, at William Cramp & Sons' Company, Philadelphia, Pennsylvania.

Sponsor: MISS ELIZABETH DALY MAJOR, daughter of Representative Major of Missouri, and a descendant of Captain Silas Talbot, U. S. Navy.

CAPTAIN SILAS TALBOT, United States Navy, was born in Dighton, Massachusetts, 1751; died 1813. Commissioned captain by the State of Rhode Island in 1776; assigned to duty in charge of the boats in the Hudson River, and for gallantry in an attempt to destroy vessels of the British fleet in New York Harbor was promoted by the Continental Congress to major October 10, 1776, and received its thanks. September 17, 1779, he was appointed a captain in the Continental Navy and ordered to command an armed naval force for the protection of the coast of Long Island Sound. Later he was twice made prisoner.

[234]

J. FRED TALBOTT

TORPEDO BOAT DESTROYER

Length, 314 feet   *Beam, 30 feet, 11 inches*   *Draft, 9 feet*

NAMED FOR REPRESENTATIVE J. FRED C. TALBOTT

Launched December 14, 1918, at William Cramp & Sons' Company, Philadelphia, Pennsylvania.

Sponsor: MRS. ROBERT LEE BATES (Laura Talbott Bosley), niece of Honorable J. Fred C. Talbott.

REPRESENTATIVE J. FRED C. TALBOTT, was born near Lutherville, Maryland, 1843. Admitted to the bar September 6, 1866. In 1871 he was made prosecuting attorney for Baltimore County. In 1877 was first elected to Congress, and served in the Forty-sixth, Forty-seventh, Forty-eighth, Fifty-third, Fifty-eighth, Fifty-ninth, Sixtieth, Sixty-first, Sixty-second, Sixty-third and Sixty-fourth Congresses. He served 25 years on the Naval Affairs Committee, and worked untiringly in his efforts to secure a greater number of ships and increase in personnel.

TANAGER

MINE SWEEPER

Length, 187 feet   *Beam, 35 feet*   *Draft, 9 feet, 9 inches*

NAMED FOR THE BIRD TANAGER

Launched March 2, 1918, at Staten Island S. B. Company, New York.

Sponsor: MRS. GEORGE H. BATES (Elizabeth M.), wife of the Secretary Treasurer of the Staten Island S. B. Company.

TARBELL

TORPEDO BOAT DESTROYER

Length, 314 feet   *Beam, 30 feet, 11 inches*   *Draft, 9 feet*

NAMED FOR CAPTAIN JOSEPH TARBELL, U. S. NAVY

[235]

Launched May 28, 1918, at William Cramp & Sons' Company, Philadelphia, Pennsylvania.

Sponsor: MISS VIRGIE TARBELL, collateral descendant of Captain Joseph Tarbell, U. S. Navy.

CAPTAIN JOSEPH TARBELL, U. S. Navy, was born about 1780, and died 1815. He was appointed a midshipman 1798; captain, 1813. Served on the "Constitution" and other vessels of the Mediterranean Squadron 1800–1804, in the operations against Tripoli. June 19–23, 1813, commanded boat expedition against ships of the British squadrons off Craney Island, and in the James River. Commanded a flotilla of 15 boats, which after an action of an hour and a half drove off the enemy, sunk three of his boats and took 43 prisoners. Capt. Tarbell was highly commended by Commodore Cassin and the officers of the Army commanding forces ashore for his gallantry and assistance in the defense of Craney Island. He was included in the thanks of Congress to the officers and men of Commodore Preble's Squadron before Tripoli, 1804, and presented with a sword in recognition of his services.

TATTNALL

TORPEDO BOAT DESTROYER

Length, 314 feet   *Beam, 30 feet, 11 inches*   *Draft, 9 feet, 4 inches*

NAMED FOR CAPTAIN JOSIAH TATTNALL, U. S. NAVY

Launched September 5, 1918, at New York Shipbuilding Corporation, Camden, New Jersey.

Sponsor: MISS SARAH CAMPBELL KOLLOCK, cousin of Captain Josiah Tattnall, U. S. Navy, whose father and brother are named for Captain Tattnall, U. S. Navy.

CAPTAIN JOSIAH TATTNALL, United States Navy, was born in Savannah, Georgia, 1795; died 1871. Appointed midshipman, 1812; commissioned captain, 1850. 1812 ordered to the "Constellation." Served in the seamen's battery on Craney Island which drove off the boats of the

[236]

SPONSOR AND PARTY OF U.S. TORPEDO BOAT DESTROYER "STURTEVANT"

British squadron and captured several barges attempting to land June 22, 1813. Took part in the sinking of the barge "Centipede." Commanded a force of the employees of the Washington Navy Yard and took part in the Battle of Bladensburg, August 24, 1814. In 1814, ordered to the "Epervier," fitting out for the Mediterranean Squadron, and took part in the operations against the Algerines. 1822–1824 attached to the Mosquito Fleet, under Commodore David Porter, in the West Indies for the suppression of piracy. 1831 commanded the "Grampus," West India Squadron. Captured the Mexican war schooner "Montezuma," which had illegally boarded and robbed an American schooner on the high seas, and took his 67 prisoners into Pensacola, Florida. Took prominent part in the attacks on Vera Cruz, San Juan d'Ulloa, Tuxpan, and other Mexican fortresses. Was presented with a sword by the State of Georgia for gallantry at Vera Cruz; was wounded in the arm at Tuxpan while leading in a division of boats. (At the outbreak of the Civil War he resigned. Commanded the C. S. S. "Merrimac" in Hampton Roads March 8, 1862, in battle with "Monitor.")

TAYLOR

TORPEDO BOAT DESTROYER

Length, 314 feet   *Beam, 30 feet, 11 inches*   *Draft, 9 feet*

NAMED FOR REAR ADMIRAL HENRY CLAY TAYLOR, U. S. NAVY

Launched February 14, 1918, at Mare Island Navy Yard, California.

Sponsor: MISS MARY GORGAS, daughter of Lieutenant-Commander Miles Gorgas, U. S. Navy.

REAR ADMIRAL HENRY CLAY TAYLOR, U. S. Navy, was born in Washington, D. C., 1845; died 1904. Appointed midshipman, 1860; rear admiral, 1901; advanced five numbers for eminent and conspicuous conduct in battle during the war with Spain; served in the North Atlantic Blockading Squadron (Civil War), 1863–1865; president

[237]

Naval War College, 1893–1896; commanded battleship "Indiana," Spanish-American War; chief of Bureau of Navigation from April 29, 1902, until his death, July 26, 1904.

TEAL

MINE SWEEPER

Length, 187 feet   *Beam, 35 feet*   *Draft, 9 feet, 9 inches*

NAMED FOR THE BIRD TEAL

Launched May 25, 1918, at Sun Shipbuilding Company, Chester, Pennsylvania.

Sponsor: MISS AGNES M. HAIG, daughter of the vice president of the Sun Shipbuilding Company.

TENNESSEE (5TH)

BATTLESHIP

Length, 624 feet   *Beam, 97 feet, 3½ inches*   *Draft, 30 feet, 3 inches*

NAMED FOR THE STATE OF TENNESSEE
(Admitted to the Union in 1796)

Launched April 30, 1919, at Navy Yard, New York, N. Y.

Sponsor: MISS HELEN LENORE ROBERTS, daughter of Governor A. H. Roberts, of Tennessee.

THE maids of honor were: Miss Evelyn Todd, Murfreesboro, daughter of Lieutenant Governor; Miss Grace Humphreys, Lebanon; Miss Lura Celeste Hale, Murfreesboro; Miss Cornelia Bratten, Watertown; Miss Geraldine Ford, Gallatin; Miss Mary Elizabeth Maxwell, Cookeville; Miss Christine Maxwell, Cookeville; Miss Alix Field, Knoxville; Miss Mildred Welch, Nashville; Miss Ruth Welch, Nashville; Miss Clara Wrenne Sumpter, Nashville; Miss Virginia Bryson, Fayetteville, and Miss Mamie D. Long, Springfield.

The Sponsors' "Prayer for our Navy" was offered by Chaplain Isaacs, U. S. Navy.

[238]

Governor Roberts of Tennessee and a large party of officials were on the launching stand, together with Lieutenant Governor Todd:

General M. C. McGannon, Nashville; General L. D. Smith, Knoxville; Colonel L. B. Humphreys, Lebanon; Colonel Caeser Thomas, Watertown; Colonel M. M. Ford, Gallatin; Colonel T. W. Wrenne, Nashville; Colonel A. G. Maxwell, Cookeville; Colonel Eli Riddleshimer, Nashville; Colonel J. M. Bracken, Dyersburg; Colonel S. E. Cleage, Knoxville; Colonel G. C. Davis, Knoxville; Colonel F. L. Pittman, Union City; Major Walter Hale, Murfreesboro; Captain George Welch, Jr., Nashville, and Colonel C. H. Bacon, London.

The delegation from the Society of Sponsors were Mrs. Reynold T. Hall, Miss Ruth Lawrence, Mrs. Julia Long Knapp, Mrs. Russell C. Langdon, Mrs. Arthur T. Sutcliffe, Mrs. Daniel T. Worden, Mrs. Albert Mathews, Mrs. Sylvie De Long Mills and Mrs. George H. Rock.

The armistice having been signed, war time instructions were revoked and an enormous concourse of people joyfully cheered as the battleship went down the ways, many Navy and Army officers and men recently returned from the war being present.

The battleship "Tennessee" is the 5th to bear the name.

"Tennessee 4th" later renamed "Memphis" was an armored cruiser launched in 1904.

"Tennessee 3rd" was a steam sloop of war launched in 1865 as "Madawaska" and name changed to "Tennessee."

"Tennessee 2d" was an ironclad ram built in 1864 and captured from the Confederates by Admiral Farragut's fleet.

"Tennessee 1st" was a side-wheel steamer blockade runner built in 1853, captured from the Confederates by Admiral Farragut's fleet and converted into a vessel of war.

TERN

MINE SWEEPER

Length, 187 feet   *Beam, 35 feet*   *Draft, 9 feet, 9 inches*

NAMED FOR THE BIRD TERN

[239]

Launched March 22, 1919, at Consolidated Shipbuilding Corporation, New York City.

Sponsor: MRS. BRUCE SCRIMGEOUR (Anastasia Miller), wife of the General Manager of the corporation.

THATCHER

TORPEDO BOAT DESTROYER

Length, 314 feet   *Beam, 30 feet, 11 inches*   *Draft, 9 feet, 2 inches*

NAMED FOR REAR ADMIRAL HENRY KNOX THATCHER, U. S. NAVY

Launched August 31, 1918, at Bethlehem Shipbuilding Corporation, Quincy, Massachusetts.

Sponsor: MISS DORIS BENTLEY, grandniece of Rear Admiral Henry Knox Thatcher, U. S. Navy.

REAR ADMIRAL HENRY KNOX THATCHER, U. S. Navy, was born in Thomaston, Maine, 1806; died 1880. Appointed a midshipman 1823; rear admiral 1866. 1823–1862 cruised on the Pacific, Mediterranean, African, and Pacific stations and held important positions at various shore stations. 1862–1863, commanded the U. S. S. "Constellation." 1864–1865, commanded the U. S. S. "Colorado" and a division of the North Atlantic Blockading Squadron in the attacks on Fort Fisher, December 24–25, 1864, and January 13–15, 1865. After the fall of Fort Fisher he was appointed to command the West Gulf squadron and co-operated with the Army against Mobile, which surrendered with the forts and batteries on the 12th of April, 1865. On May 10, 1865, the Confederate forces in the waters of Alabama surrendered to Admiral Thatcher; the only remaining fortified points on the Gulf coast, Sabine Pass and Galveston, capitulated on the 25th of May and 2nd of June, 1865.

THOMAS

TORPEDO BOAT DESTROYER

Length, 314 feet   *Beam, 30 feet, 11 inches*   *Draft, 9 feet, 3 inches*

U.S. TORPEDO BOAT DESTROYER "TATTNALL."
TAKING THE WATER

NAMED FOR LIEUTENANT CLARENCE CASE THOMAS,
U. S. NAVY

Launched July 4, 1918, at Newport News Shipbuilding &
Dry Dock Company, Newport News, Virginia.

Sponsor: MRS. EVELYN MARTIN THOMAS, widow of Lieutenant Clarence Case Thomas, U. S. Navy.

LIEUTENANT CLARENCE CASE THOMAS, U. S.
Navy, was born at Grass Valley, California, 1886; died at
sea April 28, 1917. Appointed midshipman in 1904; commissioned lieutenant August 29, 1916; lost his life while in
command of the armed guard crew of the steamship "Vacuum" when that vessel was torpedoed by a German submarine on April 28, 1917; was the first United States Naval
officer to lose his life in the War with Germany.

THOMPSON

TORPEDO BOAT DESTROYER

Length, 314 feet   *Beam, 30 feet, 11 inches*   *Draft, 9 feet, 4 inches*

NAMED FOR SECRETARY OF THE NAVY
RICHARD W. THOMPSON

Launched January 15, 1919, at Bethlehem Shipbuilding
Corporation, San Francisco, California.

Sponsor: MRS. HERBERT H. HARRIS (Florence Knowles),
wife of the Marine Superintendent of the Company.

HONORABLE RICHARD WIGGINTON THOMPSON,
Secretary of the Navy, 1877–1881. Born in Virginia 1809.
He was admitted to the bar in 1834, began to practice in
Bedford, Indiana, and served in the lower house of the legislature in 1834–1836, and in the upper house 1836–1838. He
was for a short time president pro tempore of the State
Senate, and acting lieutenant governor. Served in Congress
from 1841–1843, and 1847–1849. In 1867–1869 he was
judge of the eighteenth circuit court of the State. On March
12, 1877, he became Secretary of the Navy, resigning in 1881
to become chairman of the American committee of the Panama Canal Company.

[241]

SMITH THOMPSON

TORPEDO BOAT DESTROYER

Length, 314 feet   Beam, 30 feet, 11 inches   Draft, 9 feet, 4 inches

NAMED FOR SECRETARY OF THE NAVY
SMITH THOMPSON

Launched July 14, 1919, at William Cramp and Sons' Company, Philadelphia, Pennsylvania.

Sponsor: MRS. EDWARD LLOYD (Kate Everett Thompson), granddaughter of Secretary of the Navy Smith Thompson.

SECRETARY OF THE NAVY SMITH THOMPSON was born in Stanford, Dutchess County, New York, 1768; died 1843; was graduated from Princeton College in 1788; associate justice of the Supreme Court of the State of New York 1802–1814; chief justice 1814–1818, when he was made Secretary of the Navy. He was later appointed Associate Justice of the Supreme Court of the United States, which position he held at the time of his death. He was one of the earliest men to suggest and work for a Naval Academy.

THORNTON

TORPEDO BOAT DESTROYER

Length, 314 feet   Beam, 30 feet, 11 inches   Draft, 9 feet, 4 inches

NAMED FOR CAPTAIN JAMES SHEPARD THORNTON,
U. S. NAVY

Launched March 22, 1919, at Bethlehem Shipbuilding Corporation, Quincy, Massachusetts.

Sponsor: MISS MARCIA T. DAVIS, great-niece of Captain James Shepard Thornton, U. S. Navy.

CAPTAIN JAMES SHEPARD THORNTON, U. S. Navy, was born in Merrimack, New Hampshire, 1826; died 1875. Appointed midshipman 1841; captain 1872; during the Civil War he served on the "Bainbridge"; was executive officer of the flagship "Hartford" at the passage of the forts and batteries below New Orleans and had charge of the steam gunboat "Winona" in engagements at Mobile, where a reconnaissance of Fort Gaines in sounding approaches under fire was made and several Confederate steamers were destroyed.

THRUSH

MINE SWEEPER

Length, 187 feet   *Beam, 35 feet*   *Draft, 9 feet, 9 inches*

NAMED FOR THE BIRD THRUSH

Launched September 15, 1918, at Pusey and Jones Company, Gloucester, New Jersey.

Sponsor: MRS. JOHN EDWARD SNYDER (Minnie Webb), daughter of Commander W. H. Webb, U. S. Navy.

TILLMAN

TORPEDO BOAT DESTROYER

Length, 314 feet   *Beam, 30 feet, 11 inches*   *Draft, 9 feet*

NAMED FOR UNITED STATES SENATOR
BENJAMIN RYAN TILLMAN

Launched July 7, 1919, at Navy Yard, Charleston, South Carolina.

Sponsor: MISS MARY Y. TILLMAN, granddaughter of Senator Benjamin Ryan Tillman.

HON. BENJAMIN RYAN TILLMAN was born in Edgefield County, South Carolina, in 1847; died in Washington, D. C., July 3, 1918. Elected Governor of South Carolina by the Democratic party in 1890 and re-elected 1892. Was elected U. S. Senator for four terms 1895–1918. Chairman of the Naval Committee since 1913, and a most ardent advocate and promoter of a "big Navy."

TINGEY (2D)

TORPEDO BOAT DESTROYER

Length, 314 feet   *Beam, 30 feet, 11 inches*   *Draft, 9 feet, 4 inches*

[243]

NAMED FOR CAPTAIN THOMAS TINGEY,
U. S. NAVY

Launched April 24, 1919, at Bethlehem Shipbuilding Corporation, Quincy, Massachusetts.

Sponsor: MISS MARY VELORA ARRINGDALE, daughter of Mr. Jere Arringdale, Inspector of Construction at Squantum Works.

CAPTAIN THOMAS TINGEY, U. S. Navy, was born in London, England, 1750; died 1829. Upon the reorganization of the Navy in 1794 the President made him a captain, his commission being dated September 3, 1798, and was assigned to the command of the "Ganges," which, with three other ships, formed a squadron to cruise in the West Indies during the War with France, 1798–1799; in 1800 he was called to Washington to establish the Washington Navy Yard, of which he became commandant, holding that position until his death.

TOUCEY

TORPEDO BOAT DESTROYER

Length, 314 feet   Beam, 30 feet, 11 inches   Draft, 9 feet, 4 inches

NAMED FOR SECRETARY OF THE NAVY ISAAC TOUCEY

Launched September 5, 1919, Bethlehem Shipbuilding Corporation, Squantum, Massachusetts.

Sponsor: MISS ELIZABETH ALDEN ROBINSON, great-great-grandniece of Secretary of the Navy, Isaac Toucey.

SECRETARY OF THE NAVY ISAAC TOUCEY. Born in Newton, Connecticut, 1796; died 1869. Was admitted to the bar in 1818 at Hartford, where he afterwards practised; appointed Attorney General of the United States, serving from June 21, 1848, to March 3, 1849. Was also for part of this time Acting Secretary of State. He was a member of the State Senate in 1850 and of the State house of representatives in 1852; was elected United States Senator from Connecticut on May 14, 1852, serving until 1857; be-

U.S. BATTLESHIP "TENNESSEE" LEAVING NEW YORK NAVY
YARD FULLY COMPLETED

came Secretary of the Navy on March 6, 1857, and served until March 3, 1861.

TRACY

TORPEDO BOAT DESTROYER

Length, 314 feet   Beam, 30 feet, 11 inches   Draft, 9 feet, 4 inches

NAMED FOR SECRETARY OF THE NAVY
BENJAMIN FRANKLIN TRACY

Launched August 12, 1919, at William Cramp & Sons' Company, Philadelphia, Pennsylvania.

Sponsor: MRS. FRANK BRODHEAD TRACY (Elizabeth Cornell), daughter-in-law of Secretary Benjamin Franklin Tracy.

SECRETARY OF THE NAVY BENJAMIN FRANK-LIN TRACY was born in Oswego, New York, 1830; died in 1915. Was admitted to the bar in 1851. In 1861 he was a member of the State assembly; 1862 he recruited the One Hundred and Ninth and One Hundred and Thirty-seventh New York Volunteers and became colonel of the former. For his gallantry in the Battle of the Wilderness he received the congressional medal of honor in 1895. At the close of hostilities he was brevetted brigadier general of volunteers. From 1866 to 1873 he was United States district attorney of New York, and from 1881 to 1883 was associate judge of the State Court of appeals. Secretary of the Navy, 1889–1893.

TRENTON (2D)

LIGHT CRUISER

Length, 555 feet   Beam, 55 feet   Draft, 14 feet, 3 inches

NAMED FOR THE CITY OF TRENTON, CAPITAL OF NEW JERSEY

Launched April 16, 1923, at William Cramp & Sons' Ship-building Company, Philadelphia, Pennsylvania.

Sponsor: MRS. JOHN M. HAULENBECK (Katherine Donnelly), daughter of Honorable Frederick W. Donnelly, Mayor of Trenton.

[245]

AMONG those on the launching stand were Mayor Donnelly, Mrs. Donnelly, Mayor Moore, of Philadelphia, Rear Admiral and Mrs. Scales, Captain and Mrs. Robert, Mrs. Russell Langdon, President Society of Sponsors, and officers of the Naval Station.

The first "Trenton" was a sloop of war of 2300 tons, launched in 1876.

TREVER

TORPEDO BOAT DESTROYER

Length, 314 feet   Beam, 30 feet, 11 inches   Draft, 9 feet, 4 inches

NAMED FOR LIEUTENANT COMMANDER GEORGE A. TREVER, U. S. NAVY

Launched September 15, 1920, at Navy Yard, Mare Island, California.

Sponsor: MRS. BESS MCMILLAN TREVER, widow of Lieutenant Commander George A. Trever, U. S. Navy.

LIEUTENANT COMMANDER GEORGE A. TREVER, United States Navy, was born in Waupun, Wisconsin, June 11, 1885; appointed midshipman, 1905; ensign, 1911; lieutenant (junior grade), 1914; lieutenant, 1917; lieutenant commander, 1918, in command of the U. S. S. O–5; died October 5, 1918, while engaged in preventive measures to avert an explosion.

TRUXTUN (3D)

TORPEDO BOAT DESTROYER

Length, 314 feet   Beam, 30 feet, 11 inches   Draft, 9 feet, 4 inches

NAMED FOR COMMODORE THOMAS TRUXTUN, U. S. NAVY

Launched September 28, 1920, at William Cramp & Sons' Company, Philadelphia, Pennsylvania.

Sponsor: MISS ISABELLE TRUXTUN BRUMBY, great-great-granddaughter of Commodore Truxtun. The sponsor's mother was the sponsor for U. S. S. "Truxton (2D)" in 1901.

COMMODORE THOMAS TRUXTUN, United States Navy, was born on Long Island, 1755; died 1822. Entered the merchant service at the age of 12. Impressed on an English frigate. Offered a midshipman's appointment — declined it. Returned to America. Commanded several privateers during the War of the Revolution, was successful in making prizes. June 4, 1794, commissioned captain in the United States Navy. Ordered to the "Constellation"; cruised the West Indies in the War with France, 1798–1800. Engaged and captured the French frigate "L'Insurgente," of 50 guns, February 9, 1799, and captured two other vessels. February 2, 1800, fought to a surrender the French frigate "La Vengeance," also of 50 guns, but she escaped in the darkness during a heavy squall. The mainmast of the "Constellation" having fallen overboard she could not pursue her prize. For his distinguished service Truxtun was awarded a gold medal and received the thanks of Congress.

TUCKER

TORPEDO BOAT DESTROYER
Length, 315 feet   *Beam, 29 feet, 11 inches*   *Draft, 9 feet, 4½ inches*

NAMED FOR CAPTAIN SAMUEL TUCKER, U. S. NAVY

Launched May 4, 1915, at Fore River Shipbuilding Company, Quincy, Massachusetts.

Sponsor: MRS. WILLIAM GARTY (Mary Hinds), great-great-granddaughter of Captain Samuel Tucker, U. S. Navy.

CAPTAIN SAMUEL TUCKER, United States Navy, was born in Marblehead, Massachusetts, in 1747. At the outbreak of the Revolutionary War received his first commission from George Washington, placing him in command of the armed schooner "Franklyn." In 1777 commissioned captain in the Navy and given command of the U. S. frigate "Boston" in which he was commissioned by Congress to convey John Quincy Adams as our envoy to France. His whole career was crowned by deeds of valor and courage, and as his biographer has said, "Samuel Tucker took more prizes, fought more sea fights and gained more victories, with a few exceptions, than any naval hero of the age," but it remained for a later day to honor his memory, the national government giving his name to the U. S. Destroyer "Tucker."

TULSA
GUNBOAT
Length, 241 feet   *Beam, 41 feet*   *Draft, 11 feet, 4 inches*
NAMED FOR TULSA, OKLAHOMA

Launched August 25, 1922, at the Navy Yard, Charleston, South Carolina.

Sponsor: MISS DOROTHY VERA McBIRNEY, daughter of Mr. James H. McBirney, a leading citizen and banker of Tulsa and selected by the Mayor of Tulsa as being one-sixteenth Creek Indian.

TURKEY
MINE SWEEPER
Length, 187 feet   *Beam, 35 feet*   *Draft, 9 feet, 9 inches*
NAMED FOR THE BIRD TURKEY

Launched April 30, 1918, at Chester Shipbuilding Company, Pennsylvania.

Sponsor: MRS. WILLIAM T. SMITH (Gertrude Hammond), wife of the first vice president of the Shipbuilding Company.

TURNER
TORPEDO BOAT DESTROYER
Length, 314 feet   *Beam, 30 feet, 11 inches*   *Draft, 9 feet, 4 inches*
NAMED FOR CAPTAIN DANIEL TURNER, U. S. NAVY

Launched May 17, 1919, at Bethlehem Shipbuilding Corporation, Quincy, Massachusetts.

Sponsor: MRS. LEIGH C. PALMER (Bessie Draper), wife

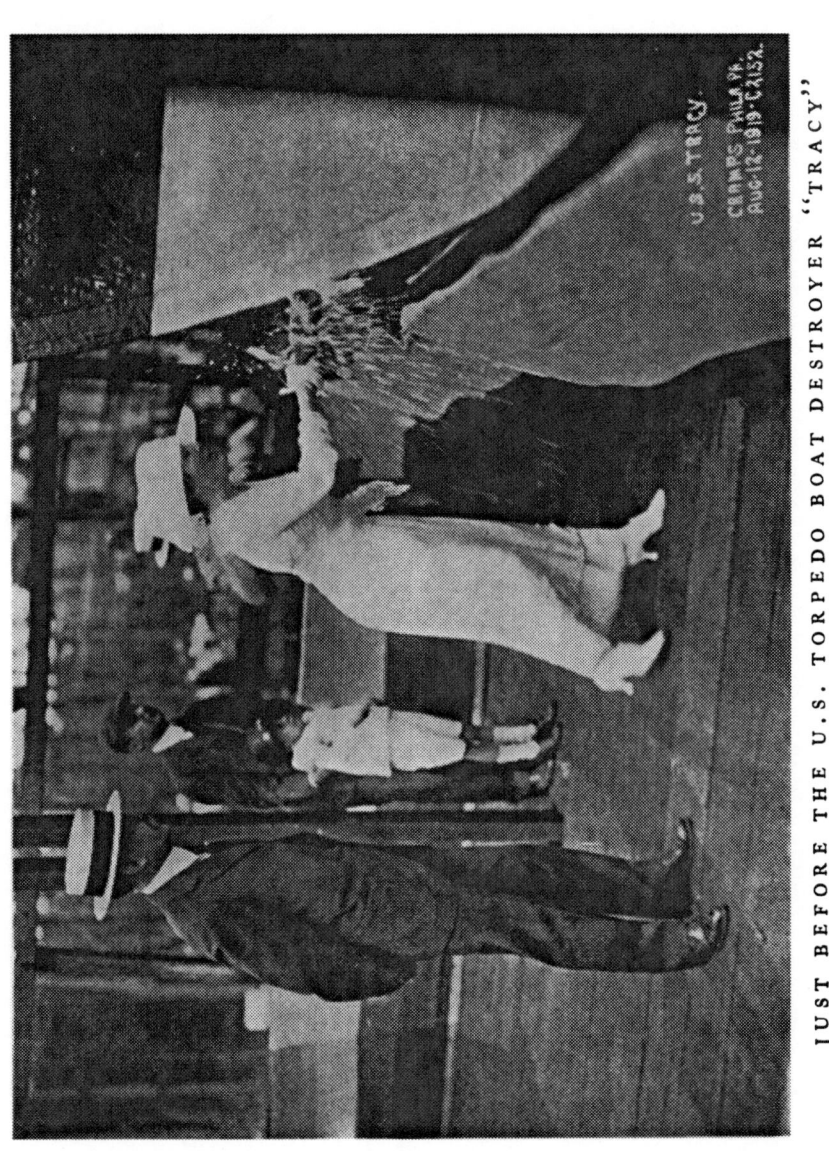

JUST BEFORE THE U.S. TORPEDO BOAT DESTROYER "TRACY"
STARTED DOWN THE WAYS

of Captain L. C. Palmer, U. S. Navy, Chief of Bureau of Navigation at the time.

CAPTAIN DANIEL TURNER, United States Navy, was born in New York; died 1850. Appointed midshipman 1808. Captain, 1835. Commanded the "Caledonia" in the battle of Lake Erie, September 10, 1813, and was commended for the good management of his vessel. In 1815 was with Commodore Perry in the Mediterranean. Held various important positions ashore. Was included in the thanks of Congress to Commodore Perry, and was awarded a silver medal for distinguished service on the Lakes.

TWIGGS

TORPEDO BOAT DESTROYER

Length, 314 feet   *Beam, 30 feet, 11 inches*   *Draft, 9 feet, 4 inches*

NAMED FOR MAJOR LEVI TWIGGS, U. S. MARINE CORPS

Launched September 28, 1918, at New York Shipbuilding Corporation, Camden, New Jersey.

Sponsor: MISS LILLIE S. GETCHELL, granddaughter of Major Levi Twiggs, U. S. M. C.

MAJOR LEVI TWIGGS, U. S. Marine Corps, was appointed second lieutenant November 10, 1813. He was killed in battle September 13, 1847, at the storming of the castle of Chapultepec in the Mexican War. Major Twiggs served during the War of 1812, and commanded the Marines on the U. S. S. "President" during the engagement between that vessel and the British ships "Majestic," "Endymion," "Pomona" and "Tenedos" in January, 1815. He served with the Marines, co-operating with the Army in the campaigns against the Indians in Georgia and Florida in 1836 and 1837. Major Twiggs was in command of the volunteer division of General Scott's Army, which with a pioneer party of seventy, under command of Capt. J. G. Reynolds, also of the Marines, were placed at the head of the column which stormed the castle of Chapultepec, Major Twiggs being killed while leading the assault.

[249]

UPSHUR

TORPEDO BOAT DESTROYER

Length, 314 feet   *Beam, 30 feet, 11 inches*   *Draft, 9 feet*

NAMED FOR REAR ADMIRAL JOHN H. UPSHUR,
U. S. NAVY

Launched July 4, 1918, at William Cramp & Sons' Company, Philadelphia, Pennsylvania.

Sponsor: MRS. ALEXANDER GUSTAVUS BROWN (Kate Upshur), granddaughter of Rear Admiral John Henry Upshur, U. S. Navy.

REAR ADMIRAL JOHN HENRY UPSHUR, U. S. Navy, was born in Northampton County, Virginia, 1823; died 1917. Appointed a midshipman 1841; rear admiral 1884. From 1842 to 1847 on the "St. Mary's" in the Gulf of Mexico took part in the expedition against Tampico, and was with the naval battery at the bombardment of Vera Cruz March 10–25, 1847, War with Mexico. He was actively employed in the Mediterranean, East India, and African Squadrons; on ordnance duty Washington Navy Yard and United States Naval Academy from 1848 to 1861; was passed midshipman on the "Supply" with Commodore Perry's expedition to Japan, 1853–1856; during the Civil War took part in the capture of the forts at Hatteras Inlet and operations in the Sounds of North Carolina, 1861; served as executive officer of the frigate "Wabash" at the capture of Port Royal, South Carolina; served in the South Atlantic blockading squadron and took part in operations against Charleston, South Carolina, 1862–1863; participated in engagements of December, 1864, and January, 1865, resulting in the capture of Fort Fisher, North Carolina; commanded the Pacific Squadron 1882–1884.

ABEL P. UPSHUR

TORPEDO BOAT DESTROYER

Length, 314 feet   *Beam, 30 feet, 11 inches*   *Draft, 9 feet*

NAMED FOR SECRETARY OF THE NAVY
ABEL P. UPSHUR

Launched February 14, 1920, at Newport News S. B. & D. D. Company, Newport News, Virginia.

Sponsor: MRS. GEORGE J. BENSON (Elizabeth Upshur), great-great-niece of Secretary Abel P. Upshur.

SECRETARY OF THE NAVY ABEL P. UPSHUR was born in Northampton County, Virginia, 1790; killed on the U. S. S. "Princeton" February 28, 1844. He was admitted to the bar in 1810; elected to the State Legislature of Virginia in 1826; judge of the general court in 1829. On September 13, 1841, he was appointed Secretary of the Navy and held that position until July 23, 1843, when he became Secretary of State. On February 28, 1844, he accompanied a party of distinguished persons down the Potomac on the "U. S. S. "Princeton" to witness some experiments in firing a new iron gun of unusual size. On the return trip the gun was fired a third time and burst, killing six and wounding a number of those on board.

VIREO

MINE SWEEPER

Length, 187 feet   *Beam, 35 feet*   *Draft, 9 feet, 9 inches*

NAMED FOR THE BIRD VIREO

Launched May 26, 1919, at Philadelphia Navy Yard, Philadelphia, Pennsylvania.

Sponsor: MISS ELIZABETH STARK ROBERT, daughter of Captain William P. Robert, C. C., U. S. Navy, Construction Officer of the Yard.

WADSWORTH

TORPEDO BOAT DESTROYER

Length, 315 feet   *Beam, 29 feet, 11 inches*   *Draft, 9 feet, 3 inches*

NAMED FOR COMMODORE ALEXANDER S. WADSWORTH,
U. S. NAVY

Launched April 29, 1915, at Bath Iron Works, Bath, Maine.

Sponsor: MISS JUANITA DOANE WELLS, granddaughter of Commodore Alexander S. Wadsworth, U. S. Navy.

COMMODORE ALEXANDER SCAMMELL WADSWORTH, United States Navy, was born in Portland, Maine, 1790; died 1851. Appointed midshipman 1804; captain 1825. Served as 2d lieutenant on the "Constitution" during her escape from the British fleet, and in the engagement with the "Guerriere," August 19, 1812. Received a silver medal and thanks of Congress. April 27, 1816, was promoted to Master Commandant (Commander) for gallant service during the War of 1812. Served in the Mediterranean, West Indian and Pacific Squadrons. Navy Commissioner 1837–1840. Inspector of Ordnance 1841–1850.

WAINWRIGHT

TORPEDO BOAT DESTROYER

Length, 315 feet   *Beam, 29 feet, 11 inches*   *Draft, 9 feet, 8 inches*

NAMED FOR COMMANDER RICHARD WAINWRIGHT, U. S. NAVY

Launched June 12, 1915, at New York Shipbuilding Company, Camden, New Jersey.

Sponsor: MISS EVELYN WAINWRIGHT TURPIN, great-granddaughter of Commander Richard Wainwright, U. S. Navy.

COMMANDER RICHARD WAINWRIGHT, United States Navy, was born in Charlestown, Massachusetts, 1817; died in New Orleans, Louisiana, August 10, 1862. Appointed midshipman, May 11, 1831; commissioned lieutenant, September 8, 1841; commander, April 24, 1861. Served: On the Coast Survey and Home Station from 1841 to 1857. Cruised in the steam frigate "Merrimack," special service, 1857–1860. Civil War: 1861, ordered to command the "Hartford," Admiral Farragut's flagship, West Gulf

Blockading Squadron. April 24–25, 1862, during the passage of the forts below New Orleans rendered conspicuous, gallant service in extinguishing the fire on the "Hartford," caused by a Confederate fire-raft, while continuing the bombardment of the forts. Wainwright participated in the operations of the fleet below Vicksburg until taken ill with fever. Highly commended by Admiral Farragut.

WALKER

TORPEDO BOAT DESTROYER

Length, 314 feet   *Beam, 30 feet, 11 inches*   *Draft, 9 feet, 1 inch*

NAMED FOR REAR ADMIRAL JOHN GRIMES WALKER, U. S. NAVY

Launched September 14, 1918, at Bethlehem Shipbuilding Company, Fore River, Massachusetts.

Sponsor: MRS. JOHN J. THOMAS (Frances Walker), daughter of Rear Admiral John Grimes Walker, U. S. Navy.

REAR ADMIRAL JOHN GRIMES WALKER, U. S. Navy, was born in Hillsborough, New Hampshire, 1835; died 1907. Appointed acting midshipman 1850; rear admiral 1894. During the Civil War served with distinction on board the U. S. S. "Connecticut," "Winona," "Baron De Kalb," and "Saco," which vessels were engaged in operations on the Mississippi River and along the Atlantic coast. In 1862 was present at engagements with Forts Jackson and St. Philip and Chalmette batteries at the capture of New Orleans, and took part in the operations against Vicksburg, including the passage of the batteries both ways. In 1862–1863 participated in the operations against Haines Bluff, Arkansas Post; took part in the Yazoo Pass expedition, the attack on Fort Pemberton, and the capture of Yazoo City. During the siege of Vicksburg was in command of naval battery with Fifteenth Army Corps.

WARBLER

MINE SWEEPER

Length, 187 feet   *Beam, 35 feet*   *Draft, 9 feet, 9 inches*

NAMED FOR THE BIRD WARBLER

Launched July 30, 1919, at U. S. Navy Yard, Philadelphia, Pennsylvania.

Sponsor: MISS ALICE KEMPFF, daughter of Captain C. S. Kempff, U. S. Navy, Inspection Officer at the Navy Yard.

AARON WARD

TORPEDO BOAT DESTROYER

Length, 314 feet   *Beam, 30 feet, 11 inches*   *Draft, 9 feet*

NAMED FOR REAR ADMIRAL AARON WARD, U. S. NAVY

Launched April 10, 1919, at Bath Iron Works, Bath, Maine.

Sponsor: MRS. WASHINGTON LEE CAPPS (Edna Ward), daughter of Rear Admiral Aaron Ward, U. S. Navy, and wife of Rear Admiral W. L. Capps, C. C., U. S. Navy.

REAR ADMIRAL AARON WARD, United States Navy, was born in Philadelphia, Pennsylvania, 1851; died July 5, 1918. Entered the Navy as midshipman in 1867; ordered to the Pacific station, serving on the "California" from 1871 to 1873. He then served on the "Brooklyn" in the West Indies until 1874 and on the "Franklin" on the European station from 1875 to 1876. Then followed a tour of duty at the Naval Academy from 1876 to 1879; service on the "Constitution," training squadron, from 1879 to 1882; and, from 1882 to 1885, professional duty of various kinds at the torpedo station at Newport and the New York Navy Yard. From 1885 to 1888 he served on the "Hartford" and "Monongahela" on the Pacific station. In 1889–1892, attaché at Paris, Berlin, and St. Petersburg; 1893–1894 he served on the "New York" in the West Indies and Brazil; and in 1894–1896 on the "San Francisco" in the Mediterranean. During the Spanish-American War he commanded the "Wasp," and as a result of his gallantry he was recommended and received promotion for "eminent and conspicuous conduct in battle."

U.S. CRUISER "TRENTON 2D" — SPONSOR BREAKING THE BOTTLE

WARD

TORPEDO BOAT DESTROYER

Length, 314 feet　　　　*Beam, 30 feet, 11 inches*　　　　*Draft, 9 feet*

NAMED FOR COMMANDER JAMES HARMAN WARD,
U. S. NAVY

Launched June 1, 1918, at Mare Island Navy Yard, California.

Sponsor: MISS DOROTHY HALL WARD, great-granddaughter of Commodore James Harman Ward, U. S. Navy.

COMMANDER JAMES HARMAN WARD, U. S. Navy, was born 1806 in Hartford, Connecticut; killed in action June 27, 1861, the first officer of the United States Navy during the Civil War. Appointed midshipman 1823; commander 1853. On April 22, 1861, he proposed to the Navy Department the creation of a "flying flotilla" to operate in the opening of the Potomac River. He was appointed to fit out this flotilla and command it. On May 20, 1861, with the converted steamboat "Thomas Freeborn" and three other improvised gunboats, he attacked and silenced the Confederate batteries at Aquia Creek, Virginia, the first naval engagement of the Civil War. On June 27, 1861, he planned a landing expedition against Matthias Point, Virginia, and was killed during the bombardment while in the act of sighting one of the guns.

WASHINGTON (5TH)

BATTLESHIP

Length, 624 feet　　　*Beam, 97 feet, 3 inches*　　　*Draft, 30 feet, 6 inches*

NAMED FOR THE STATE OF WASHINGTON
(Admitted to the Union in 1889)

Launched Sept. 1, 1921, at New York Shipbuilding Company, Camden, New Jersey.

Sponsor: MISS JEAN SUMMERS, daughter of Representative John W. Summers, member of Congress from Washington.

[255]

THE "Washington" was baptized with commingled water from the rivers of Washington State.

The sponsors' "Prayer for our Navy" was offered just before the ship was launched. Among those on the launching stand were Rear Admiral Thomas Washington, representing the Navy Department; Rear Admiral Nulton, commandant of the Navy Yard; Rear Admiral T. R. Hall, and other officials. The Society of Sponsors was represented by Mrs. Russell Langdon, president, Mrs. Henry Beates and others.

The first "Washington," named for George Washington, was a galley with eight guns and eighty men. She was captured by the British in a fight on Lake Champlain in 1776.

The second "Washington" was a ship of 32 guns, built at Philadelphia in 1776.

The third "Washington" was a ship of 2250 tons, launched in 1814.

The fourth "Washington" was an armored cruiser named for the state of Washington and launched in 1905, renamed "Seattle" in 1916.

WASMUTH

TORPEDO BOAT DESTROYER
Length, 314 feet   *Beam, 30 feet, 11 inches*   *Draft, 9 feet, 4 inches*

NAMED FOR HENRY WASMUTH, U. S. MARINE CORPS

Launched September 15, 1920, at Mare Island Navy Yard, California.

Sponsor: MISS GERTRUDE ELIZABETH BENNET, stepdaughter of Major Russell H. Davis, U. S. M. C.

HENRY WASMUTH, United States Marine Corps, saved the life of "Fighting Bob" Evans at the attack on Fort Fisher at the risk of his own and was killed during the engagement.

[256]

WATERS

TORPEDO BOAT DESTROYER

Length, 314 feet   *Beam, 30 feet, 11 inches*   *Draft, 9 feet*

NAMED FOR CAPTAIN DANIEL WATERS,
U. S. NAVY

Launched March 9, 1918, at William Cramp and Sons' Company, Philadelphia, Pennsylvania.

Sponsor: MISS MARY BORLAND THAYER, daughter of Captain George C. Thayer, Captain of the Philadelphia City Troop, and formerly an official of the Shipbuilding Company.

CAPTAIN DANIEL WATERS, U. S. Navy; appointed January, 1776, to command the schooner "Lee," and captured several valuable transports. In 1778, commanding the privateer "Thorn" he engaged the British ship "Governor Tryon" and the "Sir William Erskine," and after an engagement of two hours captured both, and a few days later captured the "Sparlin." He was appointed by Congress a captain of the Navy March 15, 1777, upon the recommendation of Gen. Washington, by whom he had been employed, and who wrote of him in terms of high approbation.

WELLES

TORPEDO BOAT DESTROYER

Length, 314 feet   *Beam, 30 feet, 11 inches*   *Draft, 9 feet, 4 inches*

NAMED FOR SECRETARY OF THE NAVY
GIDEON WELLES

Launched May 8, 1919, at Bethlehem Shipbuilding Corporation, Quincy, Massachusetts.

Sponsor: MISS ALMA FREEMAN WELLES, granddaughter of Secretary of the Navy Gideon Welles.

HON. GIDEON WELLES, Secretary of the Navy, 1861 to 1869. Born in Glastonbury, Connecticut, 1802; died 1878; 1827–1835 was a member of the State legislature; 1835,

[257]

1842, and 1843 was State comptroller, serving as postmaster of Hartford in the intervening years. From 1846 until 1849 he was Chief of the Bureau of Provisions and Clothing in the Navy Department. In his first report as Secretary of the Navy he announced the increase of the effective naval force from 42 to 82 vessels; this and the subsequent increase in a few months to more than 500 vessels was largely due to his energy.

WEST VIRGINIA (2D)

BATTLESHIP

Length, 624 feet   *Beam, 97 feet, 3½ inches*   *Draft, 30 feet, 6 inches*

NAMED FOR THE STATE OF WEST VIRGINIA

(Became a separate State in 1863)

Launched November 19, 1921, at Newport News Shipbuilding and Drydock Co., Newport News, Virginia.

Sponsor: MISS ALICE WRIGHT MANN, daughter of Mr. Isaac T. Mann, prominent citizen of West Virginia. Maids of honor were Miss Eleanor Williams, and Miss Mary Hellen.

AMONG those present on the launching stand were Governor E. F. Morgan of West Virginia, Congressman Goodykoontz, Mr. John Marshall, Brigadier General Hersey, U. S. A., Rear Admiral Philip Andrews and officers of the Norfolk Navy Yard, Mrs. Hall, President of the Society of Sponsors, Mr. Watters Martin, Mr. Homer Ferguson, President of the Shipbuilding Company. Hampton Roads was filled with craft of every description, laden with people eager to view the impressive spectacle. The housetops and surrounding land were a mass of cheering humanity.

The first "West Virginia" was an armored cruiser launched in 1903 and renamed "Huntingdon" for Huntingdon, West Virginia.

WHIPPLE (2D)

TORPEDO BOAT DESTROYER

Length, 314 feet   *Beam, 30 feet, 11 inches*   *Draft, 9 feet, 4 inches*

NAMED FOR CAPTAIN ABRAHAM WHIPPLE, U. S. NAVY

BREAKING THE BOTTLE ON THE BOW OF U.S.S. "TRUXTON 3D"

Launched November 6, 1919, at William Cramp & Sons' Company, Philadelphia, Pennsylvania.

Sponsor: MISS GLADYS V. MULVEY, great-great-great-granddaughter of Captain Abraham Whipple, U. S. Navy.

CAPTAIN ABRAHAM WHIPPLE, U. S. Navy, was born in Providence, Rhode Island, 1733; died 1819. In the French War, 1759–1760, he won distinction in command of the "Game Cock"; captured 23 prizes. June 18, 1772, he commanded the party of volunteers who captured and burned the British revenue schooner "Gaspee," which ran ashore while in chase of the Providence packet "Hannah." This was considered the first overt act of resistance against Great Britain by the colonies. June, 1775, Rhode Island sent out two vessels under Whipple, who captured and brought in the "Rose." December 22, 1775, Congress appointed Capt. Whipple third on the list of captains in the Continental Navy and gave him command of the "Columbus." August of this same year, off the northeast coast of America, Capt. Whipple captured the "Royal Exchange," with valuable cargoes. The "Columbus" was chased ashore on Point Judith and burned April 1, 1778. Upon the rearrangement of the officers of the Continental Navy, October 10, 1776, Whipple was placed No. 12 on the list and the "Providence" assigned to him. In her he made many prizes, and was captured on her at Charleston, South Carolina, May 12, 1780, and kept a prisoner until the close of the war.

WHIPPOORWILL

MINE SWEEPER

Length, 187 feet   *Beam, 35 feet*   *Draft, 9 feet, 9 inches*

NAMED FOR THE BIRD WHIPPOORWILL

Launched January 28, 1919, at Alabama Dry Dock & Shipbuilding Company, Mobile, Alabama.

Sponsor: MISS MARGARET INEZ EVANS, daughter of Mr. W. M. Evans, vice president of the company.

[259]

WHITNEY

DESTROYER TENDER

Length, 483 feet   *Beam, 61 feet*   *Draft, 21 feet*

NAMED FOR SECRETARY OF THE NAVY
WILLIAM C. WHITNEY

Launched at Navy Yard, Boston, Massachusetts, October 12, 1923.

Sponsor: MRS. RODERICK TOWER (Flora Whitney), granddaughter of Secretary of the Navy William C. Whitney.

HONORABLE WILLIAM C. WHITNEY was Secretary of the Navy, 1885–1889. Born in Conway, Massachusetts, in 1841; was educated at Yale and Harvard and settled in New York City, where he was admitted to the bar. As corporation counsel of the City of New York, 1875–1882, he completely reorganized and simplified the work of this office, thereby effecting great economy. In 1885 he became Secretary of the Navy and was a powerful advocate of naval expansion. He advocated that the ships of our Navy should equal the best in the world and under his administration great progress was made in the building of the new Navy. Two battleships, the "Maine" and "Texas" were authorized; also one armored cruiser, four gunboats; one practice vessel, one ram, one torpedo boat and one dynamite cruiser. He changed the Washington Navy Yard to the Naval Gun Factory. He died in 1904.

WICKES

TORPEDO BOAT DESTROYER

Length, 314 feet   *Beam, 30 feet, 11 inches*   *Draft, 9 feet*

NAMED FOR CAPTAIN LAMBERT WICKES,
U. S. NAVY

Launched June 25, 1918, at Bath Iron Works, Bath, Maine.

Sponsor: MISS ANN ELIZABETH YOUNG WICKES, daughter of Doctor Walter Wickes, a relative of Captain Lambert Wickes, U. S. Navy.

CAPTAIN LAMBERT WICKES, United States Navy, was born in Kent County, Maryland, about 1735; lost at sea, off the coast of Newfoundland, October, 1777. Appointed by Continental Congress December 22, 1775, and commissioned captain October 10, 1776; commanded "Reprisal" in 1776, and being ordered to West Indies for arms and ammunition captured four merchant vessels on the voyage. In 1776 conveyed Benjamin Franklin to France, capturing two brigs on the voyage and was the first Man of War to appear in European waters. June to August, 1777, cruised around Ireland, capturing 15 vessels in five days; on return voyage to the United States the "Reprisal" foundered off the coast of Newfoundland.

WIDGEON

MINE SWEEPER

Length, 187 feet   *Beam, 35 feet*   *Draft, 9 feet, 9 inches*

NAMED FOR THE BIRD WIDGEON

Launched May 5, 1918, at Sun Shipbuilding Corporation, Chester, Pennsylvania.

Sponsor: MISS MILDRED MOYER, selected by Lieutenant Raymond Bitzer, U. S. Navy, on duty at the works.

WILKES (2D)

TORPEDO BOAT DESTROYER

Length, 315 feet   *Beam, 29 feet, 11 inches*   *Draft, 9 feet, 5¾ inches*

NAMED FOR REAR ADMIRAL CHARLES WILKES,
U. S. NAVY

Launched May 18, 1916, at Williams Cramp & Sons' Company, Philadelphia, Pennsylvania.

Sponsor: MISS CARRIE McIVER WILKES, great-granddaughter of Rear Admiral Charles Wilkes, U. S. Navy.

REAR ADMIRAL CHARLES WILKES, United States Navy, was born in New York in 1801. Appointed midshipman in 1818. In 1838–1842 commanded the wonderfully successful exploring expedition that went around the world. Author of "Meteorology," "Western America" and "Theory of the Winds." In 1861, in command of the "San Jacinto," took from the English passenger steamer "Trent" the Confederate commissioners to England, Mason and Slidell. Was complimented by the Secretary of the Navy, although the prisoners had to be given up. In 1862 commanded the James River Flotilla. In 1863 commanded Special Blockade Squadron in the West Indies.

WILLETT

MINE SWEEPER

Length, 187 feet   *Beam, 35 feet*   *Draft, 9 feet, 9 inches*

NAMED FOR THE BIRD WILLETT

Launched September 11, 1919, at U. S. Navy Yard, Philadelphia, Pennsylvania.

Sponsor: MISS CAROLINE CHANTRY, daughter of Commander A. J. Chantry, C. C., U. S. Navy, on duty at the Navy Yard.

WILLIAMS

TORPEDO BOAT DESTROYER

Length, 314 feet   *Beam, 30 feet, 11 inches*   *Draft, 9 feet, 2 inches*

NAMED FOR CAPTAIN JOHN FOSTER WILLIAMS

Launched July 4, 1918, at Bethlehem Shipbuilding Corporation, San Francisco, California.

Sponsor: MRS. HARRY GERARD LEOPOLD (Mary Downey), wife of Commander H. G. Leopold, U. S. Navy.

CAPTAIN JOHN FOSTER WILLIAMS, U. S. Navy, was born in Boston, Massachusetts, October 12, 1743; died June 24, 1814. Appointed a captain in the Massachusetts State Navy, commanding the "Hazard" in 1779 he captured the "Active"; 1780, commanding the "Protector," he fought the letter of marque "Admiral Duff," which blew up after a spirited engagement of an hour and a half.

Photo by New York Shipbuilding Corporation

U.S. TORPEDO BOAT DESTROYER "WAINWRIGHT"
LEAVING THE WAYS

WILLIAMSON

TORPEDO BOAT DESTROYER

Length, 314 feet   Beam, 30 feet, 11 inches   Draft, 9 feet, 4 inches

NAMED FOR LIEUTENANT COMMANDER WILLIAM PRICE
WILLIAMSON, U. S. NAVY

Launched October 16, 1919, at New York Shipbuilding Corporation, Camden, New Jersey.

Sponsor: MRS. WILLIAM PRICE WILLIAMSON (Florence Bean), widow of Lieutenant Commander William Price Williamson, U. S. Navy.

LIEUTENANT COMMANDER WILLIAM PRICE WILLIAMSON, United States Navy, was born in Norfolk, Virginia, 1884; appointed midshipman, 1903; ensign, 1908; lieutenant (junior grade), 1910; lieutenant, 1914; lieutenant commander, 1917. Served, 1907–1909, battleship "Kansas," Atlantic Fleet; 1910–1911, duty in the Bureau of Ordnance (instruction); 1912–1914, battleship "Utah," flagship, Atlantic Fleet; 1915–1916, inspection duty, Bureau of Ordnance; 1916–1917, ordnance duty, Olongapo; 1918, April 4, ordered to duty in connection with the fitting out of the "Orizaba," and when the vessel was commissioned became her executive officer. He was killed instantly by explosion of a depth charge on that vessel August 17, 1918.

WINSLOW (2D)

TORPEDO BOAT DESTROYER

Length, 305 feet   Beam, 30 feet   Draft, 9 feet, 5½ inches

NAMED FOR REAR ADMIRAL JOHN A. WINSLOW,
U. S. NAVY

Launched February 11, 1915, at William Cramp & Sons' Company, Philadelphia, Pennsylvania.

Sponsor: MISS NATALIE EMELIE WINSLOW, daughter of Rear Admiral C. McR. Winslow, U. S. Navy, a cousin of Rear Admiral John A. Winslow, U. S. Navy.

Rear ADMIRAL JOHN A. WINSLOW, United States Navy, was born in North Carolina in 1811. Appointed midshipman in 1827. Served gallantly in Mexican War. For gallantry at Tobasco was commended by Commodore Perry. In the Civil War was in command of the Mississippi Flotilla, 1861–1862. Commanded the "Kearsarge" when she sank the "Alabama," June 19, 1864, in the famous fight off Cherbourg. For this action Captain Winslow was promoted to the rank of Commodore.

WOOD

TORPEDO BOAT DESTROYER

Length, 314 feet   *Beam, 30 feet, 11 inches*   *Draft, 9 feet, 4 inches*

NAMED FOR MEDICAL DIRECTOR WILLIAM MAXWELL WOOD, U. S. NAVY

Launched May 28, 1919, at Bethlehem Shipbuilding Corporation, San Francisco, California.

Sponsor: MRS. GEORGE KIRKHAM SMITH (Lisa Wood), granddaughter of Medical Director William Maxwell Wood, U. S. Navy.

MEDICAL DIRECTOR WILLIAM MAXWELL WOOD, U. S. Navy, was born in Baltimore, Maryland, in 1809; died 1880. Appointed assistant surgeon 1829; medical director 1871. Took active part in the Mexican War and received the commendation of Commodore Sloat for bringing him valuable information "at the risk of his life," which induced the commodore to take possession of California; was commended by the chairman of the Naval Commitee of the Senate for services rendered on this occasion. Civil War, 1861–1865, served in the North Atlantic Blockading Squadron. Held position of Chief of Bureau of Medicine and Surgery 1870–1871.

WELBORN C. WOOD

TORPEDO BOAT DESTROYER

Length, 314 feet   *Beam, 30 feet, 11 inches*   *Draft, 9 feet, 4 inches*

NAMED FOR ENSIGN WELBORN C. WOOD,
U. S. NAVY

Launched March 6, 1920, at Newport News S. B. &
D. D. Company, Newport News, Virginia.

Sponsor: MISS VIRGINIA MARY TATE, daughter of Congressman Farish Carter Tate, was selected by the family of
Ensign Welborn C. Wood to name the ship.

ENSIGN WELBORN C. WOOD, U. S. Navy, was born
in Georgia, 1876; killed in action September 17, 1899, at
Orani, Philippine Islands. Appointed naval cadet 1895;
graduated from the Naval Academy in January, 1899. On
September 17, 1899, while commanding the gunboat "Urdaneta," engaged in patrolling the Orani River, Manila
Bay, for the purpose of preventing the introduction of supplies of food and materials of war to the insurgent Filipinos, the vessel went aground in the mud and was attacked
by a band of insurgents. In the engagement which followed Ensign Wood was killed and all under his command
were either killed or captured.

WOODBURY

TORPEDO BOAT DESTROYER

Length, 314 feet   *Beam, 30 feet, 11 inches*   *Draft, 9 feet, 4 inches*

NAMED FOR SECRETARY OF THE NAVY
LEVI WOODBURY

Launched February 6, 1919, at Bethlehem Shipbuilding
Corporation, San Francisco, California.

Sponsor: MISS CATHERINE MUHLENBERG CHAPIN,
daughter of Mr. W. W. Chapin, publisher of the *"Oakland Enquirer."*

HON. LEVI WOODBURY was born in Francestown,
New Hampshire, 1789; died 1851. After graduation with
the highest honors at Dartmouth, entered the Litchfield,
Connecticut, law school. Admitted to the bar in 1812. In
1817 he was appointed a judge of the supreme court of the

State and in 1819 removed to Portsmouth, where he practiced law, after serving as governor of New Hampshire in 1823–1824. He was speaker of the State house of representatives in 1825 and was elected to the United States Senate as a Democrat, serving from December 5, 1825, until March 3, 1831, when he was appointed Secretary of the Navy and held that office until 1834, when he was made Secretary of the Treasury, serving until 1841.

WOODCOCK

MINE SWEEPER

Length, 187 feet   *Beam, 35 feet*   *Draft, 9 feet, 9 inches*

NAMED FOR THE BIRD WOODCOCK

Launched May 12, 1918, at Chester Shipbuilding Company, Pennsylvania.

Sponsor: MRS. LEWIS THAYER KNISKERN (Vera Culver), wife of the General Manager of the Merchant Shipbuilding Company.

WOOLSEY

TORPEDO BOAT DESTROYER

Length, 314 feet   *Beam, 30 feet, 11 inches*   *Draft, 9 feet*

NAMED FOR CAPTAIN MELANCTHON TAYLOR WOOLSEY,
U. S. NAVY

Launched September 17, 1918, at Bath Iron Works, Bath, Maine.

Sponsor: MRS. HEWITT WELLS (Elise Campau), great-granddaughter of Captain Melancthon Taylor Woolsey, U. S. Navy.

CAPTAIN MELANCTHON TAYLOR WOOLSEY, United States Navy, was born in New York 1782; died 1838; appointed midshipman 1800; captain 1816; superintended construction of vessels on Great Lakes in 1808; laid keel of "Oneida," first naval vessel built on the lakes; in 1809 made first display of American ensign in waters of

U.S. TORPEDO BOAT DESTROYER "WATERS" CAMOUFLAGED DURING THE WORLD WAR

Niagara River; served under Commodore Chauncey in War of 1812; July 19, 1812, landed part of his battery and repelled a British attack by five vessels; participated in attack on Kingston, November, 1813, and operations off False Rocks.

WORDEN (2D)

TORPEDO BOAT DESTROYER

Length, 314 feet   *Beam, 30 feet, 11 inches*   *Draft, 9 feet*

NAMED FOR REAR ADMIRAL JOHN LORIMER WORDEN, U. S. NAVY

Launched October 24, 1919, at Bethlehem Shipbuilding Corporation, Squantum Works.

Sponsor: MRS. DANIEL T. WORDEN (Emilie Neilson), daughter-in-law of Rear Admiral John Lorimer Worden, U. S. Navy. Mrs. Worden was sponsor for the first torpedo boat destroyer "Worden," August 15, 1901.

REAR ADMIRAL JOHN LORIMER WORDEN, United States Navy, was born 1818, Westchester County, New York; died 1897. Appointed midshipman 1834; promoted to lieutenant 1846, and served in Pacific, Mediterranean, and Home Squadrons. At the outbreak of the Civil War ordered to Washington, D. C., for special duty. January 16, 1862, ordered to command the U. S. S. "Monitor," and on March 9, 1862, fought the battle with the Confederate ironclad "Merrimac" in Hampton Roads; promoted to the rank of rear admiral November 20, 1872, and received the thanks of Congress for his skill and gallantry.

WRIGHT

AIR CRAFT TENDER

Length, 448 feet   *Beam, 58 feet*   *Draft, 23 feet, 7 inches*

NAMED FOR WILBUR WRIGHT, AMERICAN INVENTOR

Launched April 28, 1920, at Tietjen and Lang Dry Dock Company, Hoboken, New Jersey.

Sponsor: MRS. ROLAND M. COMFORT, wife of Lieutenant Commander R. M. Comfort, U. S. Navy, a personal friend of the Wright brothers.

WILBUR WRIGHT, American Inventor; born in Millville, Indiana, 1867. Died May 30, 1913. Educated in the high schools of Richmond, Indiana, and Dayton, Ohio. From 1903, with his brother Orville, he devoted time to heavier than air flying machines, patented by the Wright brothers in the leading countries of the world. He made numerous flights in the United States and abroad. He was awarded a medal by the French Academy of Science in 1909, also many other medals.

YARBOROUGH

TORPEDO BOAT DESTROYER
Length, 314 feet　　*Beam, 30 feet, 11 inches*　　*Draft, 9 feet, 4 inches*

NAMED FOR FIRST LIEUTENANT GEORGE H. YARBOROUGH, U. S. MARINE CORPS

Launched June 20, 1919, at Bethlehem Shipbuilding Corporation, San Francisco, California.

Sponsor: MISS KATE BURCH, fiancee of the late Lieutenant George H. Yarborough, U. S. M. C., for whom the ship was named.

FIRST LIEUTENANT GEORGE H. YARBOROUGH, JR., United States Marine Corps, was born in Roxboro, North Carolina, October 14, 1895; died in France from wounds received in action June 23, 1918. Served in France with the Fifth Regiment and was posthumously awarded the distinguished-service cross for extraordinary heroism in the Bois de Belleau, France. After being wounded by an exploding shell he refused aid until he saw that the wounded men with him had been treated and removed to shelter. He died later from his wounds.

YARNALL

TORPEDO BOAT DESTROYER

Length, 314 feet   *Beam, 30 feet, 11 inches*   *Draft, 9 feet*

NAMED FOR LIEUTENANT JOHN JOLIFFE YARNALL, U. S. NAVY

Launched June 19, 1918, at Wm. Cramp & Sons' Company, Philadelphia, Pennsylvania.

Sponsor: MRS. DAVID WORTH BAGLEY (Marie Harrington), wife of Commander D. W. Bagley, U. S. Navy.

LIEUTENANT JOHN JOLIFFE YARNALL, U. S. Navy, was born in Wheeling, West Virginia, in 1786. Appointed midshipman January 11, 1809; lieutenant July 24, 1813. Cruised in the "Chesapeake" and "Revenge" 1809–1812. He was first lieutenant of the "Lawrence" in the engagement on Lake Erie, September 10, 1813; was wounded several times but refused to leave the deck. Left in command of the "Lawrence" when Perry went on board the "Niagara"; after the victory he was ordered to take the "Lawrence" with the wounded of Perry's Squadron to Erie. Commended by Commodore Perry for his ability and bravery, he was included in the thanks of Congress and awarded a medal for his gallantry at the Battle of Lake Erie. On the "Guerriere" June 17, 1815, took part in capture of the Algerine cruiser "Mahouda"; wounded during the engagement. Commended by Commodore Stephen Decatur. He was transferred to the "Epervier" for return to the United States, being bearer of dispatches. The "Epervier" was lost with all on board.

YOUNG

TORPEDO BOAT DESTROYER

Length, 314 feet   *Beam, 30 feet, 11 inches*   *Draft, 9 feet, 4 inches*

NAMED FOR CAPTAIN JOHN YOUNG, U. S. NAVY

Launched May 8, 1919, at Bethlehem Shipbuilding Corporation, San Francisco, California.

Sponsor: MRS. JOHN I. NOLAN (Mae Hunt), wife of Congressman John I. Nolan, of San Francisco.

CAPTAIN JOHN YOUNG, U. S. Navy, was born in Philadelphia; lost at sea 1781; commissioned captain October 10, 1776. July 5, 1777, ordered to proceed to Nantes in the "Independence." February 15, 1778, Captain Young sailed the "Independence" through the French fleet (having on board John Paul Jones), saluted the French flag with 13 guns, received 9 guns in return. May 20, 1781, Capt. Young sailed in the "Saratoga" with French and American ships from Cape Francois. Soon separated from her consorts and was never seen again; supposed to have foundered at sea.

ZANE

TORPEDO BOAT DESTROYER

Length, 314 feet   *Beam, 30 feet, 11 inches*   *Draft, 9 feet, 4 inches*

NAMED FOR MAJOR RANDOLPH T. ZANE,
U. S. MARINE CORPS

Launched August 12, 1919, at Mare Island Navy Yard, California.

Sponsor: MISS MARJORIE ZANE, daughter of Major Randolph T. Zane, U. S. Marine Corps.

MAJOR RANDOLPH T. ZANE, U. S. Marine Corps, was born in Philadelphia, Pennsylvania, August 12, 1887; died from wounds he received in action with the Sixth Regiment in France. He was awarded the distinguished service cross for conspicuous bravery and coolness in holding the town of Bouresches, June 7, 1918, where he successfully resisted a heavy attack by machine guns and infantry. He died later from wounds received in this engagement. He was also awarded the Navy Cross for the same engagement.

LAUNCHING PARTY OF U.S. TORPEDO BOAT DESTROYER
"WHIPPLE 2D"

ZEILIN

TORPEDO BOAT DESTROYER

Length, 314 feet   *Beam, 30 feet, 11 inches*   *Draft, 9 feet, 4 inches*

NAMED FOR BRIGADIER GENERAL JACOB ZEILIN,
U. S. MARINE CORPS

Launched May 28, 1919, at Bethlehem Shipbuilding Corporation, San Francisco, California.

Sponsor: MRS. WILLIAM P. LINDLEY (Frances Smith), wife of Lieutenant Commander W. P. Lindley, U. S. N. R. F., Assistant Inspector of Machinery for the Navy at Union Works.

BRIGADIER GENERAL JACOB ZEILIN, U. S. Marine Corps, was born in Philadelphia, Pennsylvania, July 16, 1806; died in 1880. Commissioned second lieutenant 1831; first lieutenant 1836. Was brevetted major for gallantry in action at crossing San Gabriel River, January 9, 1847. Was military commandant at San Diego in 1847. Was marine officer in the flagship "Mississippi" in Commodore Perry's expedition to Japan in 1852. In 1864 took command of marine barracks at Portsmouth, New Hampshire. Appointed colonel commandant of the Marine Corps in 1864. Commissioned brigadier general commandant, 1867.

The Society of Sponsors
of the
United States Navy

Organized 1908
Incorporated 1920

INSIGNIUM

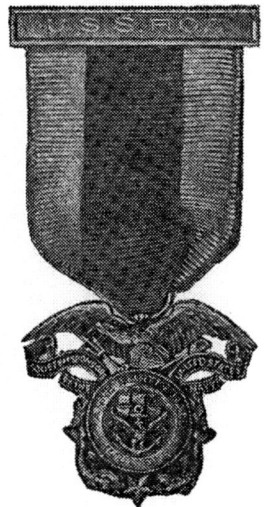

The name of the ship is engraved on the bar.
The insignium is fitted with a brooch pin, so that it can be worn separately from the ribbon when desired, in which case the ribbon ring is invisible.

BY-LAWS

I.

The name of the organization is SOCIETY OF SPONSORS OF THE UNITED STATES NAVY.

II.

THE OBJECTS OF THE SOCIETY ARE:

1. The securing to its members of those benefits which would accrue from an acquaintance and association of women residing in different parts of the Union.

2. The cultivation of a love of our country and its form of government. Remembering the occasion which gives membership in the Society, it is expected that the members will take pride in the achievements of the Navy, and will, within their proper spheres, be interested in the promotion of a healthy, popular sentiment for the development and support of the United States Navy.

3. The undertaking of such benevolent work as the Society may determine.

III.

Any woman who shall have bestowed the name, or been a sponsor for a man-of-war, or other vessel connected with the United States Navy, as one of its fighting craft, shall be eligible to membership in the Society; provided, however, that she shall file an application for membership with the Board of Trustees of the Society, and at least three-fourths of the Board vote to admit such applicant.

IV.

The management of the Society's affairs, except when it is in meeting assembled, shall be under the supervision of a Board of Trustees, to be composed of seven members, one of whom shall be the President of the Society, who shall be ex-officio Chairman of the Board. The officers, besides the Board of Trustees, shall consist of a President, a First Vice-President, a Second Vice-President, a Treasurer and a Secretary. The office of Secretary and Treasurer may be combined and held by one person. The said officers shall be elected to serve until the next annual meeting following their election and until their successors are elected and qualified.

V.

1. There shall be an annual meeting of the Society held at Washington on some date to be named by the Board of Trustees or by the President at least thirty days before the meeting and in the month of January or February of each year.

2. Special meetings of the Society may be held when called by the Board of Trustees or by the President.

3. Special meetings of the Board of Trustees may be held when called by the President. A majority shall constitute a quorum.

VI.

If, from any cause, officers shall not be chosen at the annual meeting, such officers, including members of the Board of Trustees, may be chosen at a regularly called special meeting.

VII.

Vacancies in the Board of Trustees, or in any office, may be filled by the Board of Trustees until the next annual or special meeting of the Society.

VIII.

The board of Trustees shall consist of seven members, one of whom shall be the President of the Society, and such Board shall, except when the Society is in annual or special meeting, be vested with the management and control of the Society's affairs.

IX.

The President is ex-officio a member of the Board of Trustees, and Chairman thereof, and is entitled to vote on matters before the Board.

X.

In the absence of the President, a Vice-President shall discharge her duties, but in case of a vacancy in the office of President, it must be filled by the Board of Trustees, the member so elected to serve for the unexpired term.

XI.

The Secretary shall keep a record of the proceedings of the Society and the Board of Trustees, and shall preserve in a well-bound book the names and addresses of the members. She shall mail notices of meetings to the several members at their addresses shown on the record, and she shall perform such other duties as the Board of Trustees shall prescribe.

XII.

The Treasurer shall keep safely the funds of the Society, disburse the same as directed by the Society or the Board of Trustees, and take proper receipt therefor. She shall make a full report of receipts and disbursements at each annual meeting, and at such other times as the Board of Trustees may require, and it shall be a part of her duty to notify the members who are in arrears and to request payment. The Board of Trustees may remove the Treasurer and designate another to discharge the duties of the office for the balance of the term.

Thirty days prior to the annual meeting the accounts of the Treasurer shall be audited.

XIII.

The term of office of the several officers shall be one year, and until their successors are elected.

XIV.

Prior to each annual meeting the Board of Trustees shall designate a committee of three to be known as an Entertainment Committee, who shall have charge of functions provided by the Society for the entertainment of the members.

XV.

The annual dues of membership are three dollars.

XVI.

If any member of the Society fails to pay dues within three

months after the Treasurer has sent notice that dues for the current year are now payable, a second notice shall be sent, saying that it repeats the notice previously given on such-and-such a date. At the expiration of two years members in arrears for dues, having received due and proper notice of such arrears, shall be notified that their names will be dropped from the rolls of the Society and printed unless they signify their intention to pay such dues.

XVII.

The Society shall have a seal which shall be in the custody of the Secretary.

XVIII.

₮ A certificate of membership in the Society, of such form as the Board of Trustees may prescribe, shall be furnished each member applying therefor, and the same shall be signed by the President and countersigned by the Secretary, who shall affix the seal.

XIX.

A badge or other insignia of the Society may be adopted by the Board of Trustees, and when adopted shall not be changed.

XX.

The motto of our Society shall be: "Don't give up the ship."

XXI.

The insignium of a member who resigns or is dropped shall be returned by such member to the Treasurer and her rights therein are made void. The Treasurer shall refund to her the amount of value appraised by the maker of the insignium.

XXII.

Notice of voting upon any proposed amendment to a By-Law shall be sent to every member of the Society at least thirty days before the meeting, requesting a signed ballot. The adoption of amendment shall require the affirmative vote of two-thirds of those voting.

SPONSORS PRESENT AT ORGANIZATION MEETING IN 1908

From left to right, Upper Row: Mrs. Angela Turner Toland, Sponsor for U.S.S. Juniata; Mrs. Roberta Wright Pels, U.S.S. Denver; Mrs. Daisy Ainsworth Morgan, U.S.S. Oregon 2d; Miss Helen Deshler, U.S.S. Ohio 3d; Mrs. Mary Drake Sturdivant, U.S.S. Iowa; Miss Lorna Pinnock, U.S.S. Salem; Miss Harriet E. Rankin, U.S.S. Wilkes.

Lower Row: Miss Dorothy W. Sproul, U.S.S. Chester; Miss Ida May Schieren, U.S.S. Brooklyn 2d; Miss Minnie Conrad, U.S.S. Montana; Miss Mary Campbell, U.S.S. Birmingham; Miss Annie Keith Frazier, U.S.S. Tennessee 4th; Mrs. Christine Bradley South, U.S.S. Kentucky; Miss Eleanor Gow, U.S.S. B-2.

PRAYER FOR OUR NAVY

O Eternal God, Creator of the Universe and Governor of Nations: Most heartily we beseech thee with thy favor to behold and bless thy servant, the President of the United States, and all the officers of our Government, and so replenish them with the grace of thy Holy Spirit that they may always incline to thy will and walk in thy way. Bless the Governors of the several States, and all who are in authority over us; give them Grace to execute justice and maintain truth that peace and happiness, religion and piety, may be established among us for all generations.

May the vessels of our navy be guarded by thy gracious Providence and care. May they not bear the sword in vain, but as the minister of God, be a terror to those who do evil and a defense to those who do well.

Graciously bless the officers and men of our navy. May love of country be engraven on their hearts and may their adventurous spirits and severe toils be duly appreciated by a grateful nation; may their lives be precious in thy sight, and if ever our ships of war should be engaged in battle, grant that their struggles may be only under an enforced necessity for the defense of what is right.

Bless all nations and kindreds on the face of the earth and hasten the time when the principles of holy religion shall so prevail that none shall wage war any more for the purpose of aggression, and none shall need it as a means of defense.

All of which blessings we ask through the merits of Jesus Christ our Lord. Amen.

This prayer is offered at the launching of Navy battleships and at meetings of the Society of Sponsors of the U. S. Navy. It is an adaptation of a prayer offered by the Reverend Doctor Suddards at the launching of a Navy ship at the Philadelphia Navy Yard in 1843, and is the only instance of prayer at a Navy launching discovered in examined records 1798–1914.

The full text of the original prayer was discovered in research work for the book "Ships of the U. S. Navy and their Sponsors" and was sent to Washington by Mrs. Reynold T. Hall, President of the Society of Sponsors, with the suggestion that the adapted prayer be offered at future launchings of battleships. The suggestion was favorably received by Secretary of the Navy Josephus Daniels and was adopted at the launching of the battleship Oklahoma at Philadelphia March 12, 1914, and thereafter at launchings of battleships. During the war with Germany the prayer was sent to ministers and was offered in churches as the prayer for Our Navy.

Officers of the Society of Sponsors of the United States Navy since its Organization, 1908–1923

HONORARY LIFE PRESIDENT

Mrs. Mary Campbell Underwood

PRESIDENTS

Miss Mary Campbell, 1908
Miss Minnie D. Coates, 1909, 1910
Mrs. John G. South, 1911
Mrs. Reynold T. Hall, 1912–1921
Mrs. Russell C. Langdon, 1922, 1923

VICE-PRESIDENTS

Miss Minnie Conrad, 1908
Miss Keith Frazier, 1908
Mrs. Roy Hearne, 1909
Mrs. Lewis Nixon, 1909, 1923
Mrs. Charles W. Mac Quoid, 1910
Mrs. Robert Toland, 1910
Miss Anna Cahall, 1911
Miss Anna M. Yeiser, 1911
Mrs. John R. Pels, 1912
Mrs. George Cameron, 1912
Miss Ruth Lawrence, 1913
Mrs. John R. Burke, 1913
Mrs. Josephus Daniels, 1914–1921
Mrs. William R. Sands, 1914, 1915
Mrs. Russell C. Langdon, 1916–1921
Mrs. Larz Anderson, 1922, 1923

Mrs. Frederick C. Hicks, 1922

SECRETARIES

Mrs. John G. South, 1908
Mrs. William W. Kitchen, 1909, 1910
Miss Edith Benham, 1911–1918
Mrs. Goldsborough Adams, 1919
Miss Nannie D. Barney, 1920
Mrs. Louisa W. Turpin, 1921–1923

TREASURERS

Miss Ida May Schieren, 1908
Miss Mira O'Brien, 1909
Mrs. John R. Pels, 1910, 1911
Mrs. Charles W. Mac Quoid, 1912
Mrs. Goldsborough Adams, 1913, 1919
Miss Edith Benham, 1914–1918
Miss Nannie D. Barney, 1920
Mrs. Louisa W. Turpin, 1921–1923

BOARD OF CONTROL 1913–1920

Mrs. Lewis Louer, 1913
Mrs. Helen W. Chapin, 1913

Miss Elizabeth L. Fleming, 1913
Mrs. Josephus Daniels, 1913
Mrs. DeWitt Coffman, 1913, 1914
Mrs. Russell C. Langdon, 1913–1915
Mrs. Henry Beates, 1914–1918
Mrs. William B. Beekman, 1914–1917
Mrs. Frank W. Brooks, 1914
Miss Ruth Lawrence, 1914, 1915
Mrs. Charles V. Ferguson, 1915, 1916
Mrs. E. Stuart Cottman, 1915
Mrs. Albert H. Mathews, 1916, 1919
Mrs. Goldsborough Adams, 1916, 1917
Mrs. William Garty, 1916, 1917
Miss Elsie Calder, 1916–1918
Mrs. Elsie Calder Lee, 1919
Miss Lorna Burrows, 1917, 1918
Mrs. John R. Pels, 1918
Mrs. Bertram Greene, 1918, 1919
Miss Edith Benham, 1919, 1920
Mrs. Arthur T. Sutcliffe, 1919
Mrs. Sylvie de L. Mills, 1919

INCORPORATORS 1920

Anne Martin Hall,
Mary W. C. Bayard,
Addie W. B. Daniels,
Edith Wallace Benham,
Helen A. Colhoun,
Elizabeth Davis,
Adria M. Semple Langdon.

TRUSTEES
1920–1923

Miss Edith Benham, 1920
Mrs. Edith Benham Helm, 1921
Mrs. Robert Corwin Lee, 1920–1923
Mrs. Arthur T. Sutcliffe, 1920–1923
Mrs. Goldsborough Adams, 1920–1923
Miss Helen A. Colhoun, 1920
Mrs. George Barnett, 1920
Mrs. Reynold T. Hall, 1922, 1923
Mrs. Frederick C. Hicks, 1921
Mrs. Brooke Lee, 1921
Mrs. Emory S. Land, 1922
Miss Virginia L. Hunt, 1922, 1923
Mrs. Albert W. Stahl, 1923

CHAIRMAN OF CHAPTERS
1913–1923
Northeastern Chapter

Miss Minnie D. Coates, 1913
Miss Agnes Herreshoff, 1914
Mrs. Arthur T. Sutcliffe, 1915–1918
Mrs. Larz Anderson, 1919–1921
Mrs. Albert H. Mathews, 1922, 1923

[281]

Southeastern Chapter

Mrs. I. B. Beard, 1913
Mrs. Robert N. Somerville, 1914
Mrs. William C. Bitting, 1915–1918
Mrs. Frank P. Hamilton, 1919–1921
Mrs. Josephus Daniels, 1922, 1923

Northwestern Chapter

Mrs. Dean H. Lightner, 1913
Mrs. A. John Schubert, 1914, 1915

Mrs. Thomas Ruhm, 1916–1918
Mrs. Wilbur B. Joyce, 1919–1923

Southwestern Chapter

Mrs. H. Clifford More, 1913
Miss Anna B. Dickie, 1914, 1915
Miss Esther Ross, 1916–1918
Miss Lorena Cruce, 1919–1922
Mrs. Lorena Cruce Norris, 1923

MISS MINNIE DARLINGTON COATES
1909-1910

MRS. JOHN G. SOUTH
1911

MRS. MARY CAMPBELL UNDERWOOD
1908
Honorary Life President

MRS. REYNOLD THOMAS HALL
1912-1921

MRS. RUSSELL CREAMER LANGDON
1922-1923

PRESIDENTS OF THE SOCIETY OF SPONSORS OF
THE UNITED STATES NAVY SINCE ITS
ORGANIZATION

U. S. NAVAL INSTITUTE, ANNAPOLIS, MD.

· THE BAPTISM OF SHIPS

By Robert G. Skerrett

Just once so often during the upbuilding of our modern navy there is agitation anent the particular form that the launching ceremony should take; and the special rock upon which there is a split is over the use of wine or water. There are some good souls intensely insistent, in the name of temperance, that water shall be spilled upon the vessel's bow at the time of naming, while there are others, probably unconsciously subscribing more closely to tradition, who urge with equal vim that wine shall be the element in the baptismal ceremony. Both of these partisans are more or less right, but all of them have commonly lost sight of the derivation and the real significance of the performance. The whole question is primarily a religious one, while the popular attitude to-day is one of tolerance toward a surviving superstition.

From the very beginning of primitive man's venture upon the water — perhaps because of the frail character of his craft, he recognized the risks he ran and in his superstitious awe sought the protection of the hidden powers that ruled the wind and the waves. Through all the devious paths of developing religions, early man strove to placate opposing deities and to propitiate the favoring gods who, to him, became more or less personal. As his religion became more concrete his gods took the material shape of idols, and that they might be always with him he first fashioned some part of his vessel more or less after the manner in which he pictured them, and never launched his craft until after he had made tribute by word or act to his protecting deity. Later on, his idols ceased to be the grotesque semblance of animals and demons and became benignant and human-like, and for these he made a special place within his vessel and sanctified that place of keeping.

It is quite impossible to follow chronologically the evolution of the launching ceremony, but enough can be found here and

[283]

there to point to a reasonable sequence, and for a probable survival of the most ancient practices we must naturally turn to the customs still remaining among primitive peoples. Ellis, in his "Polynesian Researches," tells us that the Samoans and the Fijians used to make human sacrifices to their shark deities who ruled the waters. In Tahiti, it was the custom to shed human blood when a new canoe was built or launched. Again, Mariner, in "Tonga," tells us that men were sometimes sacrificed in order to wash a new canoe's deck with blood, and that it was likewise the practice to use men as living rollers on which to launch the craft. In this there is a strange likeness to the ancient Norse habit of attaching human victims to the rollers upon which they launched their ships; and in the Eddas this ceremony is referred to under the name of "hlun-rod" or roller-reddening. Among the Tonga islanders it is the custom to-day still to offer kava and oil to the sea gods, and in all of these ceremonies the native priest plays a conspicuous part if the ancient rites prevail. These votive offerings or oblations are still made among the primitive peoples of many parts of the world, and in this particular they show the persistent permanence with which such practices are handed down from the ages past.

So far as actual records go, the earliest account of a votive offering to the gods upon the completion of a ship dates back twenty-one hundred years before Christ, and it seems that even then man dared not venture upon the sea until he had thus propitiated the gods. On an Assyrian tablet, found some years ago by Professor Schiel, we have a Babylonian account of the Deluge and of the building of the Ark, and of the religious ceremony at its completion. Rendered into English, the story reads, in part, as follows:

> Eighthly, its interior I examined.
> Openings to the water I stopped;
> I searched for cracks and the wanting parts I fixed;
> Three sari of bitumen I poured over the outside;
> Three sari of bitumen I poured over the interior;
> Three sari of men bearers who carried chests on their heads.
> I kept a saros of chests for my people to eat.
> Two sari of chests I divided among the boatman.
> To the gods I caused oxen to be sacrificed.

To the Chinese belongs the palm for pioneer work in breasting the tempestuous sea and in carrying their explorations into far lands — their commerce reaching at a very remote period as far west as the Persian Gulf. Probably no existing country has held with more faithfulness of detail to its ancient religious practices in most of their forms. In "A Discourse of the Navigation of the Portuguese," translated into English in 1579, is found this fairly full account of the Chinese practices at the launching of their ships: "When they launched their ships into the sea at the first making, the priests go apparelled with long garments, being very rich of silk, to make their sacrifices in the poops of them, where the place of prayer is, and they offered painted figures, and they cut and burned them before their idols with certain ceremonies that they make, and sing songs with an unorderly tone, sounding certain little bells. They worship the devil, where they have him painted in the fore-part of the ship, because, as they say, he should do no hurt to the ships. In all this discourse they are eating and drinking at discretion."

Among the Chinese these ceremonies have since undergone no substantial change, and in every large junk there is a shrine in honor of the goddess Tien-how, who is the tutelary deity of sailors. In addition to the goddess Tien-how, the Chinese sailors particularly engaged in the river traffic are devotees of the goddess Loong-moo or the Dragon's Mother. In honor of this latter deity the master of every river junk makes tribute at the beginning of a voyage. Prior to weighing anchor, he takes his place at the bow, which, agreeably to Chinese tradition, is the most sacred part of the ship, and there proceeds to propitiate the Dragon's Mother. Before him on a small temporary altar are placed three cups containing Chinese wine or "saki." With a live fowl in one hand, the master performs the Kow-tow, and raising the cups one after the other from the altar he elevates them above his head before emptying them upon the deck by way of a libation. Next he cuts the throat of the fowl with a sharp knife and sprinkles the deck immediately about him with the blood of the sacrifice. One of the crew now presents the master with several pieces of silver paper, which in turn are sprinkled with the sacrificial blood and then fastened to the door-posts and lintels of the captain's cabin. This is suggestively like one of the rites of the Jewish Passover.

The Bible tells us of the glories of the fleets of Tyre, and history records as well much of the religious pomp and ceremony associated with the ships of ancient Egypt. The mythology of ancient Egypt is full of the part played by its deities in watching over its hardy mariners, and there can be no doubt whatever that some form of priestly ceremony and blessing was a part of the launching of the ships of the state at least, if the records of

Du Sein and other historians are to be trusted. At the battle of Salamis, the Greeks went into the fight just after the conclusion of religious ceremonies, which consisted of sacrifices offered to all the gods and the pouring of a special libation to Zeus, the Protector, and to Poseidon, Ruler of the Seas. In those days, it was the common custom among the Greeks to name their vessels after goddesses, and as a further propitiation the launching was made the occasion of a religious ceremony which Virgil described as follows:

> Ipse caput tonsae foliis evinctus olivae,
> Stans procul in prova, pateram extaque salsos
> Porricit in fluctus, ac vina liquentia fundit. —Æneid.

Here we see the part that wine played in the early days. Appian also described the religious aspect of the blessing of the ancient ships: "On the shores of the sea altars were erected where their bases might be washed by the waves. In a semi-circle the ships of the fleet were drawn about near by, their crews the while maintaining a profound silence. The priests in boats rowed three times round the fleet . . . adding prayers to the gods that illluck should not befall the vessels. Then returning to the shore, they immolated bulls or calves, the blood of which reddened the sea and the shore."

The use of water in the ancient ritual dates back to the Greek ceremony of lustration and to the later Roman practice of using water not only as a token of purification but also as an element in the act of priestly blessing. Here we have the pre-Christian practice of baptism. Like other pagan customs, wine and water were given place in Christian ceremonials, but not infrequently with a modified or deeper meaning. It was thus that wine and water became elements of the sacrament of the Christian Church, while water alone remained the token of purification and a part of the blessing at the time a person was brought into the church, named, and placed under the protection of a particular patron saint.

During the Middle Ages, religious zeal and its derivative superstitions led to the custom of naming ships after saints, as the more ancient craft had been named after pagan gods and goddesses; and this practice was carried to the extremity of saintly image-worship — no craft being sent to sea without its shrine and an imposing array of attendant images. Thus began the practice that subsequently led to the evolution of the figurehead and the effigies placed in the niches about the stern galleries of more modern vessels. Guerin, in his history of the French Navy, tells us that the ships of Louis IX, when he sailed for the Holy Land in 1248, were provided with every facility for conducting mass, each ship having an altar and priestly retinue. These altars were situated in the after part of the ships — just as the Greeks and Romans reared their shrines there in their own days, and the index of the antiquity of the practice survives in the name of the "poop" deck — the highest aftermost deck of the older type of modern vessels. This name is derived from the Latin term "puppis," which was the name the ancients gave to the honored after deck where they kept their "pupi" or doll-like images of their tutelary deities and where they offered before them libations and sacrifices.

As Taylor has told us in his "Primitive Customs," "Some religious ceremonies are marvels of permanence, holding substantially the same form and meaning through age after age, and far beyond the range of historic record." In proof of this, remembering what has been recorded of ancient Greece, it is instructive to know that at the launching of a modern Greek vessel her bow is decorated with flowers, and at the instant the ship takes the water her captain raises a jar of wine to his lips and then empties the rest of it upon the deck of his craft. Among the Turks, the launching of a vessel is of religious significance, and a priest attends asking the blessing of Allah and praying that the ship may have a prosperous and a successful career and ride safely over the waves in all weather. Sheep are sacrificed just as the vessel starts for the water, and the flesh is subsequently given to the poor. No wine is spilt upon the vessel's bow, but a feast is afterwards given to the participating officials and the invited guests.

In Russia, when a naval vessel is launched, the Greek Church participates in a very imposing manner. The service includes the blessing of the ship in detail — the officiating priest and his attendant acolytes and choristers marching through all the decks, burning incense, carrying lighted candles, and sprinkling the craft everywhere with holy water — all the while prayers are read and chants are sung. When the ship has thus been blessed the crew are assembled before an altar especially reared for the occasion within the vessel, and, after the craft's colors are blessed, each member steps forward to the altar, kisses the priest's hands, and receives the benediction of the church. This carries us back directly to the practice among the Egyptians of purifying their ships by lighted torches, of burning sulphur, and of the breaking of eggs by the priests within their vessels, and later to the very

[287]

similar custom among the Greeks leading to what generally became known as "the purification of the ship." Combined with the subsequent libations, we see in the present ceremony of the Greek Church a survival of the ancient practice which had for its purpose the driving out of evil spirits, the purifying of the body, the propitiation of the deities, and the beginning of a new life. In Russia, to-day, wine does not enter into the ritual of the church at the launching of ships, the breaking of a bottle of wine at the actual naming of the vessel being a secular performance entirely apart from ecclesiastical participation. In this we see the reflex of the practice among other nations introduced into Russia only within the recent period of her advent upon the sea.

During the days of Venetian dominance upon the Adriatic and the Mediterranean, the church took a conspicuous part in the launching functions of all official craft. It was then the custom to espouse the Adriatic at the time of the floating of the vessel, and this was done with much significant pomp, the ceremony closing by the Doge or some other high official throwing a bridal ring into the sea. In the Museum at Venice to-day there are a number of these rings, and in recognition of that old custom a pretty revival of it was practiced at the launching of the submarines recently built for the Italian Government.

In 1488, when the "Sovereign" was launched at Humble — England's foremost dockyard of mediæval times, in the presence of Henry VII, we are told the ship was formally renamed and the renovated vessel blessed with all the ceremonial display customary in England in pre-Reformation times — "A mitred prelate with attendant train of priests and choristers, crosier in hand, with candle, book, and bell, and holy water stoup" performing the benediction. With the coming of the Reformation under Henry VIII, the official participation of the Church of Rome disappeared in England upon such occasions. The same, too, is true of Protestant Europe during the same period, although we are told the Lutherans practiced a baptismal ceremony at the launching of their vessels while they attach no importance to the observance. In the early part of the seventeenth century, in England, the launching of government vessels was entirely devoid of religious significance so far as the church was concerned, and what did survive of ancient custom was more strictly a remnant of the far-away pagan libation. The ship "Prince Royal" was launched at Woolwich in 1610, and the launching function was performed by Prince Henry in the manner described as follows by Phineas Pette, one of the master shipwrights of James I:

"The noble Prince, himself, accompanied with the Lord Admiral and the great lords, were on the poop, where the standing great gilt cup was ready filled with wine to name the ship so soon as she had been afloat, according to ancient custom and ceremony performed at such times, and heaving the standing cup overboard. His Highness then standing upon the poop with a selected company only, besides the trumpeters, with a great deal of expression of princely joy, and with the ceremony of drinking in the standing cup, threw all the wine forwards toward the half-deck, and solemnly calling her by the name of the 'Prince Royal,' the trumpets sounding the while, with many gracious words to me, gave the standing cup into my hands."

During the same century, in the Catholic parts of Europe, the Church of Rome still participated. In 1675, Henry Teonge, Chaplain in the British Navy, visited Malta in His Majesty's Ship "Assistance," where he witnessed the launching of a Maltese craft, which he describes in this manner: "This day we saw a great deale of solemnity at the launching of a new bryganteen of 23 oares, built on the shoare, very neare the water. They hoysted 3 flaggs in her yesterday, and this day by 12 they had turned her head neare the water. When as a greate multitude of people gathered together, with severall of their knights and men of quality, and a clowd of fryars and churchmen. They were at least 2 howers in their benedictions, in the nature of hymns or anthems, and their other ceremonys; their trumpetts and other music playing often. At last 2 fryars and an attendant went into her, and kneeling downe prayed halfe an howre, and layd their hands on every mast, and other places of the vessell, and sprinkled her all over with holy water. Then they came out and hoysted a pendent to signify she was a man of warr; and then at once thrust her into the water." Malta was given to the Knights Hospitalers by the Catholic Emperor Charles V in 1530, and being an island and under its own particular government, we see that the ceremony had escaped the immediate influence of the Reformation.

In Catholic France in the eighteenth century and at the beginning of the nineteenth century, especially among the merchant craft and fishing vessels, the launching ceremony was closely analogous to the baptismal ritual at the time of christening an infant. The custom was one that lay close to the hearts of the common people, and the parish priest, a god-father and a god-mother chosen for the occasion were the principal participants — the god-parents not infrequently being children. The ceremony was very simple and lovely. The god-father carried a bouquet which he duly presented to the god-mother, and with this done, both sponsors then pronounced the name chosen for the new vessel, and the priest repeating it so declared the vessel named — finishing the ceremony with the sprinkling of holy water upon the bow of the boat and with a benediction. To-day, the official ceremony at the launching of naval vessels carries out in spirit this older practice save that there is more pomp and churchly parade. There is a god-father and also a god-mother. Should the ship be named after a national hero or a famous officer, one of the sponsors is generally a descendant. A priest high in the dignity of the church leads in the formalities accompanied by acolytes and choristers. He blesses not only the ship, herself, but also, in accordance with ancient custom, sprinkles holy water upon the launching ways and gives them the benediction of the church. No wine is spilled upon the ship's bow, but the distinguished guests are invited to what is termed a "vin d'honneur" where champagne flows freely and a bountiful repast is served. This is a very old custom that has existed for many centuries — especially among the fishermen of Europe, and to decline either the food or the drink then offered was formerly considered an omen of misfortune.

It was not until the early part of the nineteenth century that either a layman or a woman took any part in the official ceremony at the launching and naming of a British man-o'-war. Prior to that time, if the formalities were not conducted by a member of the royal family, the naming was done by some high functionary of the port or dockyard staff. The present Queen of England is said to have originated the religious service now a part of the launching of British ships of war; and the occasion when the practice was thus instituted was at the launching of the "Alexandria" — named after her — in 1875. Since then a full choral service has been prescribed, which includes extracts from the 107th Psalm — beginning with the twenty-third verse — together with a special prayer of great beauty. The benediction is in accordance with the ritual of the Church of England and therefore does not include the use of holy water. The civil ceremony which follows consists of the usual naming of the vessel by a fair sponsor, after which a bottle of wine is smashed upon the vessel's bow. This blessing of a British ship carries us back by actual record of the fourteenth century, when in 1390, so the monk of St. Denys tells us, referring to the Duke of Bourbon's expedition to Genoa under the Earl of Derby, that "According to ancient custom and to ensure success, the ships were blessed by the priests"; and again, in July of 1418, the Bishop of Bangor was sent to Southampton to give a benediction to the King's ship lately built there — called the "Grace Dieu," and was an occasion of much imposing ceremony: the worthy bishop being paid five pounds for his trouble. William Laird Clowes, in his history of "The Royal Navy," tells us that there is no trace in the British records of ship-baptism with wine in the fifteenth century.

In the latter part of the eighteenth century and during a considerable period in the first half of the nineteenth century, it was the custom in France to remove all impediments to the launching of their ships but a single beam or heavy timber which is commonly known among the shipwrights as the "dog-shore." This beam was canted against the stern post of the vessel in such a manner as to keep her from voluntarily sliding toward the water, and when everything was in readiness this shore was chopped through and knocked out of the way. This task was hazardous in the extreme and a volunteer for the work was commonly chosen from among the convicts in the galleys. Clothed in red, this man would take his place between the launching ways and under the shadow of the juggernaut-like craft that towered ponderously above him. At the proper signal, he would begin to chop with his axe into the dog-shore, and if alert and quick enough he was able to drop into the pit dug for him before either his timber fell or the ship rushed down upon him crushing out life or fearfully wounding him. Not infrequently the man was killed and very often he was wounded and blood flowed, thus seeming to perpetuate the sacrificial offerings of the ancient Norsemen and the similar primitive practices among some of the South Sea Islanders. If the convict escaped with his life, freedom was the reward for his perilous undertaking.

In our own country, tradition does not carry us very far back so far as we are immediately concerned — our ceremonies naturally following the customs prevailing in England at the time our forebears landed here; and so far as the records examined go to show, there was no religious significance given to this function by us.

It has been said that water was used at the launching of the "Constitution," in 1797; but if this be so, it was broken upon the bow of that ship at one or the other of the two unsuccessful efforts first made to get that vessel overboard. When the "Constitution" was finally launched at the third effort, the late Rear-

Admiral George H. Preble tells us in his manuscript history of the Boston Navy Yard, that "Commodore James Sever stood at the heel of the bowsprit, and, according to time-honored usage, baptized the ship with a bottle of choice old Madeira, from the cellar of the Honorable Thomas Russell, a leading Boston merchant." No one can question the fighting merits of the "Constitution," nor belittle that abundant glory that she reflected upon our flag in the days when every victory counted with especial weight. Let those that attach a superstitious value to either wine or water bear this fact in mind.

In 1858, the U. S. S. "Hartford" was launched at Boston, her launching sponsors being three in number. One was the daughter of Commodore Downes, one the daughter of Commodore Stringham, and the other was then Lieutenant George H. Preble of the navy. As she touched the water, Miss Stringham broke a bottle of Connecticut River water across the ship's figurehead, Miss Downes smashed a bottle of Hartford Spring water, and Lieutenant Preble concluded the formalities by emptying a bottle of sea water upon the vessel's bow. The particular significance of each bottle of water is too plain to call for explanation; and, again, the performances of the "Hartford" are too fresh to need present point. In each case, however, it is quite evident that neither the wine nor the water had anything to do with the fighting efficiencies and the enduring good fortune of those famous vessels. . . .

Addenda to Ships of the United States Navy and Their Sponsors, 1797-1913

ADIRONDACK

STEAM SLOOP

Length, 205 feet   *Beam, 38 feet*

NAMED FOR ADIRONDACK MOUNTAINS

Launched February 22, 1862, at Navy Yard, New York.

Sponsor: MISS MARY PAULDING, daughter of Rear Admiral Hiram Paulding, U. S. Navy, then commanding New York Naval Station.

BROOKLYN (1ST)

STEAM SLOOP

NAMED FOR CITY OF BROOKLYN, NEW YORK

Launched July 27, 1858, at Brooklyn, New York.

Sponsor: MISS EMMA WESTERVELT, daughter of Commodore Jacob Westervelt, U. S. Navy.

PROMINENT among a bevy of young ladies out upon the forepeak was Miss Westervelt. By her side stood her friend, Miss McKay, who was to assist her in the ceremony. Miss Westervelt dashed the bottle of champagne over the head rail of the ship when settled into the water "from her working ways."

CHATTANOOGA (1ST)

SCREW STEAMER

Length, 315 feet   *Beam, 46 feet*

NAMED FOR CHATTANOOGA RIVER

Launched October 13, 1865, at William Cramp & Sons' Company, Philadelphia, Pennsylvania.

Sponsor: MISS JESSIE TURNER (Mrs. Henry W. Biddle), daughter of Rear Admiral Thomas Turner, U. S. Navy, commanding Philadelphia Navy Yard.

AMONG those present was Gideon Welles, Secretary of the Navy, and William Cramp, founder of the shipbuilding company.

CIMARRON

WOODEN GUNBOAT

Length, 205 feet   *Beam, 35 feet*   *10 guns*

NAMED FOR CIMARRON, NEW JERSEY

Launched March 16, 1862, at Shipyard of D. S. Mershon, Bordentown, New Jersey.

Sponsor: MISS ELEANOR V. NEWELL, daughter of Congressman William A. Newell of New Jersey and former Governor of New Jersey, saying "I christen thee Cimarron — in honor of the State of New Jersey."

CONGRESS

WOODEN GUNBOAT

Length, 290 feet   *Beam, 41 feet*

NAME CHANGED TO "CONGRESS" FROM PUSHMATAKA, AN INDIAN NAME

Launched July 3, 1867, at Philadelphia Navy Yard.

Sponsor: MISS ANNA P. DRAKE, daughter of Senator Charles D. Drake, of Missouri.

CYCLOPS

FUEL SHIP

Length, 542 feet   *Beam, 65 feet*   *Draft, 27 feet, 8 inches*

NAMED FOR "CYCLOPS," IN HESIODIC LEGEND A TITAN WHO FORGED ZEUS' THUNDERBOLTS

LAUNCHING PARTY OF U.S.S. "CHATTANOOGA 1ST," OCTOBER 13, 1865

Miss Jessie Turner, Sponsor, Secretary of the Navy Gideon Welles (with shawl) Charles H. Cramp, founder of the Shipbuilding Company.

Launched May 7, 1910, at William Cramp & Sons', Philadelphia, Pennsylvania.

Sponsor: MRS. WALTER H. GROVE (Mabel Richardson), daughter-in-law of Mr. H. S. Grove, president of the ship-building company.

MARCH 4, 1918, the "Cyclops" sailed from Barbados, West Indies, for Baltimore, Maryland, and was never heard from again. Her fate is one of the mysteries of missing ships.

INTREPID

GUNBOAT

Length, 170 feet   *Beam, 35 feet*

NAMED FOR THE KETCH "INTREPID," FAMOUS AT TRIPOLI

Launched March 5, 1874, at Navy Yard, Charlestown, Massachusetts.

Sponsor: MISS H. EVELYN FROTHINGHAM POOKE, daughter of Naval Constructor Pooke, U. S. Navy.

JASON

FUEL SHIP

Length, 536 feet   *Beam, 65 feet*   *Draft, 27 feet*

NAMED FOR JASON, IN GREEK LEGEND
THE LEADER OF THE ARGONAUTS

Launched November 16, 1912, at Maryland Steel Company, Sparrows Point, Maryland.

Sponsor: MISS MARGARET WINANS WATERS, appointed at the suggestion of Senator John W. Smith of Maryland.

KENOSHA

GUNBOAT

Length, 283 feet   *Beam, 38 feet*

INDIAN NAME AFTERWARDS CHANGED TO PLYMOUTH
FOR THE CITY OF PLYMOUTH

Launched August 8, 1868, at the Navy Yard, New York. *Sponsor:* MISS MARY E. WOOD (Mrs. Eugene de F. Heald), daughter of Engineer in Chief W. W. W. Wood, U. S. Navy, stationed at the Navy Yard.

THE sponsor and party were on board and launched with the vessel. The bottle of champagne was tied to the wrist of the sponsor to prevent dropping it when it was broken over the bow as the vessel touched the water. Among those on board were Admiral Sylvanus Gordon, commander of the Navy Yard, Captain Trenchard, Naval Constructor B. J. Delano, Engineer in Chief Wood, Captain Cushman and a large company of Naval officers and ladies.

KINEO

SCREW STEAMER
Length, 138 feet   *Beam, 28 feet*

NAMED FOR MOUNT KINEO, MAINE

Launched October 9, 1861, at Shipyard of J. P. Dyer, Portland, Maine.

Sponsor: MISS EUNICE C. DYER (Mrs. Henry Inman), daughter of the builder.

MARS

FUEL SHIP
Length, 403 feet   *Beam, 53 feet*   *Draft, 24 feet, 8 inches*

NAMED FOR "MARS," IN ROMAN MYTHOLOGY
THE GOD OF WAR

Launched April 10, 1909, at Maryland Steel Company, Sparrows Point, Maryland.

Sponsor: MISS JULIANA KEYSER, daughter of Mr. R. Brent Keyser, a prominent business man of Baltimore, Maryland.

NEPTUNE

FUEL SHIP

Length, 542 feet   *Beam, 65 feet*   *Draft, 27 feet, 8 inches*

NAMED FOR "NEPTUNE," OF ROMAN MYTHOLOGY,
THE OLD ITALIC GOD OF THE SEA

Launched January 21, 1911, at Maryland Steel Company,
Sparrows Point, Maryland.

Sponsor: MISS DOROTHY LOUD, daughter of Congressman George A. Loud from Michigan, Member of the Naval Committee of the House of Representatives.

ORION

FUEL SHIP

Length, 536 feet   *Beam, 65 feet*   *Draft, 27 feet*

NAMED FOR ORION, GREEK MYTHOLOGICAL HUNTER
OF GIGANTIC SIZE AND STRENGTH

Launched March 23, 1912, at Maryland Steel Company,
Sparrows Point, Maryland.

Sponsor: MISS EVELYN V. TAYLOR, daughter of Naval Constructor Charles V. Taylor, U. S. Navy, Superintendent of Construction at the works.

PROTEUS

FUEL SHIP

Length, 522 feet   *Beam, 62 feet*   *Draft, 27 feet*

NAMED FOR PROTEUS, IN GREEK MYTHOLOGY,
OLD MAN OF THE SEA

Launched September 14, 1912, at Newport News S. B Company, Newport News, Virginia.

Sponsor: MISS LUCY DAY MARTIN, daughter of United States Senator Thomas S. Martin of Virginia.

[297]

SUSQUEHANNA

STEAM FRIGATE

Length, 250 feet   *Beam, 45 feet*

NAMED FOR SUSQUEHANNA RIVER

Launched April 6, 1850.

Sponsor: MORTON McMICHAEL, Mayor of Philadelphia and proprietor of the *Philadelphia North American.*

"THE noble steamship "Susquehanna" made her entry into the world of waters with a grace and beauty that called forth the plaudits of the spectators thronging the adjacent wharves. Morton McMichael, Esq., was seated in the bow with the bottle of Susquehanna prepared to perform the christening ceremony. He failed, however, in breaking the bottle, and at last it went spinning over-board unbroken. The naming, however, was complete in all other respects, the following being the words made use of: "I name this good ship "Susquehanna" and predict that in time of peace she will be an ornament and in time of war a pride and honor to our naval service."

VULCAN

FUEL SHIP

Length, 403 feet   *Beam, 53 feet*   *Draft, 24 feet, 8 inches*

NAMED "VULCAN," OF ROMAN MYTHOLOGY, THE GOD OF FIRE, OF FORGING AND SMELTING

Launched May 15, 1909, at Maryland Steel Company, Sparrows Point, Maryland.

Sponsor: MISS MARY ELEANOR DYSON, daughter of Commander Charles W. Dyson, U. S. Navy.

WORCESTER

SCREW STEAMER

Length, 290 feet   *Beam, 41 feet*

NAMED FOR WORCESTER, MASSACHUSETTS

Launched August 25, 1866, at Navy Yard, Charlestown, Massachusetts.

Sponsors: MISS MARY ADDISON AND MISS ROSA SANDS.

"FOUR or five hundred ladies and gentlemen were aboard and the number of spectators estimated at 4000. The band of the Yard played 'Hail Columbia' as the vessel slipped down the ways. The christening ceremony was performed by Miss Mary Addison and Miss Rosa Sands, the former a niece and the latter a daughter of Commodore Benjamin Franklin Sands, U. S. Navy. Captain Clitz had charge of the operations." — *Army and Navy Journal.*

In the sponsor's own words:

"I think the only reason for the Admiral's choice of me as sponsor was the fact that I was a southerner and at that time a most rancourous hater of Admiral Farragut, who so short a time before had taken possession of my native city, New Orleans. It was a most graceful act of propitiation. That the propitiation was complete was shown by the fact that then and there I met for the first time my husband, Commander Gibson, U. S. Navy."

Errata Volume I

Page xiii. Read 1908 instead of 1898.

Page 27. Under "Brandywine," line 7, read *1825* for 1819.

Page 93. Under "Kearsarge," for Miss Margaret Eastman, read *Miss Mary Truxtun Eastman.*

Page 95. Under "Lamson," "was born in Missouri," read "was born in *Iowa.*"

Page 152. "Princeton," footnote, for "1884" read "*1844.*"

Page 174. "Stringham," Rear Adm. J. *Blakeley* Creighton, instead of J. Berkeley Creighton.

Page 200. Under "Wyoming," paragraph beginning U. S. S. "Wyoming," read *Shimonoseki, Japan,* in place of Manila.

Index of Sponsors

Volume I

1797-1913

NOTE. — For convenient reference the known married names of maiden sponsors are also given, under their initial letters, with maiden name in brackets.

SPONSOR	WARSHIP
ABERCROMBIE, MRS. B. T. (WATERS)	Maryland
ADAMS, MRS. ELIZABETH GOLDSBOROUGH	Paul Jones
ADAMS, MISS NORVELLE	Mayrant
ADDISON, MISS MARY	Worcester
AGNUS, MISS ELSIE	Rodgers
AINSWORTH, MISS DAISY	Oregon
ALLEN, MRS. CHARLES F.	Marblehead
AMIDON, MRS. KATHERINE HERRESHOFF	Cushing
ANDERSON, MRS. LARZ (PERKINS)	Perkins
ANDERSON, MISS MARY PREBLE	Maine 2d
ANDREWS, MISS ETHEL	Ammen
ANDREWS, MISS LINA	Reid
ANSEL, MISS FREDERICA	South Carolina
ASHE, MISS ELIZABETH	Farragut
ASTON, MISS ANNE	Bennington
BACKUS, MRS. M. F.	F-3 and F-4
BAILEY, MISS FLORENCE BEEKMAN	Bailey
BAINBRIDGE, COMMODORE WILLIAM	Independence
BALCH, MISS GRACE	Balch
BALLIN, MISS GERTRUDE	Goldsborough
BARNES, MISS CHARLOTTE ADAMS	Barry
BARNEY, MISS ESTHER NICHOLSON	Barney
BARNEY, MRS. JOSEPH N. (DORNIN)	Colorado 1st
BASSETT, MRS. F. B. (THOMAS)	Sangamon
BATTLES, MRS. DONALD RAYMOND	E-1
BAURY, MISS	Pequot
BEARD, MRS. I. B. (ADAMS)	Mayrant
BEATES, JR., MRS. HENRY (Agnes Barrington)	Cummings
BECKWITH, MRS. J. L. (LINCOLN)	Atlanta
BEEKMAN, MRS. WILLIAM B. (PARKER)	Trenton
BELL, COMMANDER C. H.	San Jacinto
BELL, MISS JENNIE	Vermont
BELMONT, MRS. O. H. P.	Nicholson
BENHAM, MISS EDITH WALLACE	Benham and San Francisco
BENSON, MISS NELLIE	Amphitrite
BENTON, MISS MARY	North Dakota
BIDDLE, MISS EMILY B.	Biddle
BIDDLE, COMMANDER JAMES	Pennsylvania 1st

INDEX

SPONSOR	WARSHIP
BISHOP, MRS. HENRY (MALLORY)	*Pensacola*
BITTING, MRS. WILLIAM C. (SMITH)	*St. Louis*
BLALOCK, MRS. WILLIAM (KIENE)	*Ericsson*
BLEECKER, MISS MARY	*Sonoma*
BOUSH, MISS EULALIE	*Alliance*
BOUTELLE, MISS ANNIE	*Newark*
BOUTELLE, MISS GRACE	*Tonopah*
BOWLES, MISS CATHERINE S. H.	*D-2*
BRADFORD, MISS ELISE	*Severn*
BRADFORD, MISS MINNIE	*Mackinaw*
BRADLEY, MISS CHRISTINE	*Kentucky*
BRECKINRIDGE, MISS ELEANOR	*Vesuvius*
BROOKS, MRS. FRANK W. (NEWBERRY)	*Michigan 2d*
BROWN, MRS. CHARLES EDWARD (DESHLER)	*Ohio*
BROWN, MISS LUCIE S.	*Wheeling*
BRUMBY, MRS. FRANK H. (TRUXTUN)	*Truxtun*
BRYANT, MISS SALLIE	*Shamrock*
BURKE, MRS. JOHN H. (STEELE)	*Helena*
BURROWS, MISS LORNA D.	*Burrows*
CAHALL, MISS ANNA	*Delaware*
CALDER, MISS ELSIE	*New York*
CAMERON, MRS. GEORGE (DE YOUNG)	*Intrepid*
CAMERON, MISS MARY	*Yorktown*
Campbell, MRS. COLIN (LEITER)	*Illinois*
CAMPBELL, MISS MARY	*Birmingham*
CARUSI, MISS HELEN CASSIN	*Cassin*
CASE, MISS	*Wampanoag*
CHALKLEY, MRS. LYMAN (BRECKINRIDGE)	*Vesuvius*
CHAMBLISS, MISS LILIAN N.	*Chattanooga*
CHANDLER, MRS. WILLIAM E.	*Shawmut*
CHASE, MRS.	*Housatonic*
CHILDS, MRS. E. H.	*Newport*
CHURCHMAN, MRS. CHARLES WEST (BIDDLE)	*Biddle*
CLARK, MISS DOROTHY	*Duncan*
CLARKE, MRS. JOHN ALEXANDER (MCLANE)	*New Hampshire*
CLEBORNE, MISS EDITH	*Chicago*
COATES, MISS MINNIE D.	*Concord*
COCKE, MRS. PAUL LEE	*Stewart*
COCKRELL, MISS MARION	*Missouri*
COFFMAN, MRS. DE WITT (BOUSH)	*Alliance*
COLBY, MISS JANE C.	*Housatonic*
COLWELL, MRS. J. C.	*Albany*
COMSTOCK, MISS NELLIE	*Weehawken*
CONRAD, MISS MINNIE	*Montana*
CONVERSE, MISS LILIAN	*Dupont*
COOPER, MISS PAGE	*Lackawanna*
CORSON, MRS. ALLAN (UPDIKE)	*Princeton*
COUDERT, MRS. FREDERIC R. (WILMERDING)	*Maine 1st*
CRAVEN, MISS ANNA T.	*Tingey*
CRAVEN, MISS AMY	*T. A. M. Craven*

INDEX

SPONSOR	WARSHIP
CREIGHTON, MISS EDWINA S.	*Stringham*
CREIGHTON, MRS. JAMES B. (STRINGHAM)	*Hartford*
CUTTING, MRS. WALTER (MAYO)	*Decatur*
DAHLGREN, MRS. JOHN VINTON	*Dahlgren*
DANIELS, MRS. JOSEPHUS	*Bagley*
DAVIS, MISS MARY THORNTON	*Thornton*
DAVISON, MRS. GREGORY C.	*D–1*
DECATUR, MISS MARIA	*Algoma*
DELANO, MISS	*Madawaska*
DE LAMATER, MISS	*Dictator*
DESHLER, MISS HELEN	*Ohio*
DE YOUNG, MISS HELEN	*Intrepid*
DICKIE, MISS ANNA BELLE	*Olympia*
DORNIN, MISS NANNIE SEDDON	*Colorado 1st*
DORR, MISS EMILY	*Genesee*
DOW, MRS. J. B.	*Canandaigua*
DOWNES, MISS CARRIE	*Hartford*
DRAKE, MISS ANNA P.	*Congress*
DRAKE, MISS MARY LORD	*Iowa*
DRAYTON, MISS EMMA GADSDEN	*Drayton*
DRURY, MISS HELEN	*Boxer*
DUMAINE, MRS. F. C.	*Rhode Island*
DYER, MISS EUNICE C. (MRS. H. INMAN)	*Kineo*
DYSON, MISS MARY ELEANOR	*Vulcan*
FALES, MISS	*Puritan*
FERGUSON, MRS. CHARLES VAUGHAN (RANKIN)	*Wilkes*
FITZGERALD, MISS	*D–3*
FLEMING, MISS ELIZABETH L.	*Florida*
FRANCIS, MRS. ARTHUR M. (PAGE)	*Saratoga*
FRAZIER, MISS ANNA K.	*Tennessee*
FROST, MRS. E. B.	*A–6*
FROTHINGHAM, MISS H. EVELYN	*Intrepid*
FROTHINGHAM, MISS MARY C.	*Wachusett*
GAITHER, MRS. WALTER T. (BROWN)	*Wheeling*
GALLAUDET, MRS. EDSON (COCKRELL)	*Missouri*
GETES, MRS. ROY (PATTERSON)	*Fox*
GILLIS, MISS CAROL	*Galena*
GITTINGS, MISS DOROTHY R.	*Sterett*
GLENN, MISS REBEKAH	*North Carolina*
GLOVER, MRS. HENRY W. B. (CLEBORNE)	*Chicago*
GOODING, MISS LOUISE	*Idaho*
GOODLOE, MRS. GREEN CLAY (WILSON)	*Washington*
GOW, MISS ELEANOR	*B–2*
GRACE, MRS. H. P.	*Tioga*
GRAY, MISS ANNA B.	*Wilmington*
GREGORY, MISS MARY	*Manhattan* and *Montauk*
GREENE, MRS. BERTRAM (HOFF)	*Bainbridge*
GRICE, MISS MARY FLORIDA	*Wyoming 1st*

[303]

SPONSOR	WARSHIP
GRICE, MISS PENNSYLVANIA	Wabash
GROVE, MRS. HENRY S.	Lamson
GROVE, MRS. WALTER H.	Cyclops
GUILD, MISS MARIA	Nashville
GUNN, MISS KATE C.	Monterey
HALE, MISS LUCY H.	Shawmut
HALL, MRS. REYNOLD THOMAS (MARTIN)	Roe
HAMILTON, MRS. FRANK P. (FLEMING)	Florida
HAND, MRS. HENRY W.	Parker
HANNA, MISS RUTH	Cleveland
HARMONY, LIEUTENANT COMMANDER DAVID B.	Quinnebaug
HARRIS, MISS JULIA M.	Tacoma
HARTT, MISS EMMA	Alaska, Guerriere, Nantasket, Octorora
HATTON, MRS. RICHARD (COTTMAN)	Warrington
HAWES, MRS. ALICE GOULD	Hopkins
HAY, MRS. MARLEY F.	A-3
HAYWOOD, MRS. ALFRED W. (HOLT)	Raleigh
HAZEL, MISS E. H.	Winslow
HEARNE, MRS. ROY W. (WILLIAMS)	San Marcos
HEBB, MRS. CLEMENT D. (LAMBERT)	Sassacus
HENRIQUES, MRS. (SCOTT)	Nipsic
HERBERT, MISS LEILA	Massachusetts
HERREID, MISS GRACE	South Dakota
HERRESHOFF, MISS AGNES M.	Porter
HERRESHOFF, MISS KATHERINE B.	Cushing
HICHBORN, MISS MARTHA	Castine and Terror
HILLMAN, CHARLES	Mackenzie
HOCH, MISS ANNA	Kansas
HOFF, MISS BAINBRIDGE	Bainbridge
HOFFMAN, MRS. DANIEL ENGLE (GLENN)	North Carolina
HOOVER, MISS EMILY V.	Monongahela
HOPPER, MRS. A. M.	Indiana
HOY, MRS. JAMES (DOWNES)	Hartford
HUDSON, MISS SUE	Housatonic
HULL, MISS GRACE	Alaska
HULL, MISS MABEL	Hull
HUMRICHOUSE, MRS. W. H. (WARDWELL)	McKee
HUTCHINSON, MRS. J. H. (INGERSOLL)	Miami
HYDE, MISS ETHEL	Machias
HYDE, MRS. JOHN	Trippe
INGERSOLL, MISS ANN	Miami
IRWIN, MISS LULU	Monadnock
JENKINS, MISS ALICE THORNTON	Jenkins
JOHNSON, MRS. EDWARD D. (BRADFORD)	Severn
JOHNSON, MISS ESTHER	Swatara
JOHNSON, MRS. HARRIET LANE (LANE)	Lancaster

INDEX

SPONSOR   WARSHIP

JONES, MISS ANNE SEYMOUR......................*Nereus*
JONES, MISS BOBBIE NEWTON....................*Ozark (Arkansas)*
JOYCE, MRS. WILBUR B. (SCHALLER)...............*Minnesota 2d*

KANE, MISS CONSTANCE HENLEY.................*Henley*
KEYSER, MISS JULIANA..........................*Mars*
KIENE, MISS CARRIE............................*Ericsson*
KINNEY, MRS. WILLIAM B........................*New Jersey*
KITCHEN, MRS. WILLIAM W. (MONEY).............*Mississippi*
KNIGHT, MISS DOROTHY EUNICE..................*Wyoming*
KNOWLES, MISS MARY...........................*Yantic*
KNOX, MISS JEAN...............................*Jarvis*

LA FARGE, MISS FRANCES.......................*Newport*
LAKE, MISS MARGARET V.........................*G-1*
LA LANDE, MISS JUANITA........................*Louisiana*
LAMBERT, MISS WILHELMINA.....................*Sassacus*
LANE, MISS HARRIET............................*Lancaster*
LANGDON, MRS. RUSSELL CREAMER (MOALE)........*Rowan*
LARDNER, MISS MARGARET.......................*Tuscarora*
LAWRENCE, MRS. CHESTER B. (BAILEY)............*Bailey*
LAWRENCE, MISS RUTH...........................*Lawrence*
LEHR, MRS. HARRY SYMES (DAHLGREN).............*Dahlgren*
LEITER, MISS NANCY............................*Illinois*
LENTHALL, MISS JENNIE........................*Guerriere*
LIGHTNER, MRS. DEAN (HERREID).................*South Dakota*
LINCOLN, MISS JESSIE..........................*Atlanta*
LITTLE, MISS MARGARET N.......................*E-2*
LOUD, MISS DOROTHY............................*Neptune*
LOUER, MRS. LEWIS (MACOMBER).................*Des Moines*
LYON, MISS CLAUDIA............................*Texas 2d*

MCALPINE, MRS. KENNETH.......................*Fanning*
MCCLELLAN, MISS ANNIE........................*Kansas 1st*
MCCORMICK, MRS. MEDILL (HANNA)..............*Cleveland*
MCFARLAND, MRS...............................*Ossipee* and *Kearsarge 1st*
MCLANE, MISS HAZEL E.........................*New Hampshire 2d*
MCLEAN, MRS. JOHN R. (BEALE).................*Beale*
MACDONOUGH, MISS LUCY T.......................*Macdonough*
MACOMBER, MISS ELSIE.........................*Des Moines*
MACON, MISS MARY LOUISE......................*Arkansas*
MAC QUOID, MRS. CHARLES W. (MILLER)..........*Bancroft*
MAGOUN, MISS KATHERINE.......................*Preston*
MALLORY, MISS MARGARET MORENO...............*Pensacola*
MALSTER, MISS FLORENCE.......................*Detroit*
MANN, MISS SUSAN L............................*Minnesota*
MARCHAND, MISS KITTY.........................*Omaha*
MARTIN, MISS LUCY DAY........................*Proteus*
MATHEWS, MRS. ALBERT H. (SCHIEREN)..........*Brooklyn*
MAYO, MISS MARIA DECATUR.....................*Decatur*
MAYNADIER, MRS. G. B. (SLEEPER)...............*Winooski*

INDEX

SPONSOR	WARSHIP
McMichael, Honorable Morton	Susquehanna
Meakins, Miss Lesley Jean	H-1
Mickey, Miss Mary Nain	Nebraska
Miller, Miss Jessie	Indiana
Miller, Mrs. Josephus (Comstock)	Weekawken
Mills, Mrs. Sylvie DeLong	DeLong
Moale, Mrs. Edward	Rowan
Monaghan, Miss Ellen R.	Monaghan
Money, Miss Mabel Clare	Mississippi
Montague, Miss Mathilde Gay	Virginia
Montgomery, Miss May	Tallapoosa
Moore, Miss Mary Frances	Bancroft
More, Mrs. H. Clifford	Marietta
Morgan, Mrs. John E. (Stephenson)	Wisconsin
Morgan, Miss Mary	Alabama
Morgan, Mrs. Percy T. (Ainsworth)	Oregon
Morton, Miss Helen	Columbia
Morton, Miss Pauline	Cumberland
Mosby, Miss Stella	Cincinnati
Murray, Mrs. David (Gillis)	Galena
Nally, Miss Marylee	Jouett
Newberry, Miss Carol B.	Michigan
Newell, Miss Eleanor V.	Cimarron
Newell, Mrs. Emerson Root	Galveston
Nelson, Mrs. Valentine	Omaha
Nicoll, Miss Alice	C-5
Nixon, Mrs. Lewis	Tallahassee and Holland
Oakley, Mrs. Owen H. (Craven)	Tingey
O'Brien, Miss Mira	O'Brien
O'Conner, Miss Maud	Perry
O'Donnell, Miss Annie C.	Niagara
Offley, Miss Katherine H.	Ticonderoga
O'Neil, Mrs. Charles (Frothingham)	Wachusett
Page, Miss Helen	Saratoga
Pardee, Miss Florence	California
Parker, Miss Katherine	Trenton
Pascoe, Miss Selina	Shenandoah
Patterson, Miss Georgeanne Pollock	Patterson
Patterson, Miss Vera	Fox
Paulding, Master Hiram	Miantonomah
Paulding, Miss Emma	Nyack and Paulding
Paulding, Miss Mary	Adirondack
Peabody, Miss Cora	Colorado 2d
Pearsall, Mrs. Paul (Hichborn)	Castine and Terror
Pels, Mrs. John R. (Wright)	Denver
Pershing, Mrs. John J. (Warren)	Cheyenne
Pinnock, Miss Lorna	Salem
Pope, Miss Elsie	Whipple

SPONSOR	WARSHIP
PORTER, MISS GEORGIA	Annapolis
POWELL, MRS. JOSEPH WIGHT	Aylwin
PREBLE, LIEUTENANT G. H.	Hartford
PREBLE, MISS ETHEL	Preble
PRICE, MISS LAURA	Foote
QUAY, MISS CORAL	Pennsylvania 2d
RADFORD, MRS. GEORGE STANLEY	B-3
RAMBO, MRS. PRESTON (TATE)	Georgia
RAMSEY, MRS. EDWARD P. (SMITH)	Montgomery
RANKIN, MISS HARRIET E.	Wilkes
READE, MRS. CHARLES (MACDONOUGH)	Macdonough
REAKIRT, MRS. EDWIN R. (LARDNER)	Tuscarora
RHETT, MISS HELEN	Charleston 2d
RICE, MRS.	A-4
RICHARDSON, MRS. EDWARD BRIDGE	Smith
ROBB, MISS	Richmond
ROCK, MRS. GEORGE H.	Terry
ROGERS, MRS. JAMES G. (PEABODY)	Colorado 2d
ROLPH, MISS ANNETTE RIED	F-2
RUGGE, MRS. GEORGE C. (POPE)	Whipple
SANDS, MISS ROSA	Worcester
SANDS, MRS. WILLIAM RANNEY	H-2
SAVAGE, MRS. EUGENE T. (BOUTELLE)	Tonopah
SCHIEREN, MISS IDA MAY	Brooklyn
SCHALLER, MISS ROSE MARIE	Minnesota 2d
SCHLEY, MISS VIRGINIA	Petrel
SCHUBERT, MRS. ADAM J. (GOODING)	Idaho
SCOTIA, MRS. JOHN B. (TYLER)	Pawnee
SCOTT, MISS ALICE	Charleston 1st
SCOTT, MISS REBECCA	Nipsic
SEALEY, MISS ELLA	Galveston
SEAMAN, MISS LILIAN	Enterprise
SEDGWICK, MISS SALLIE	Onondaga
SEVER, JAMES CAPTAIN	Constitution
SHUBRICK, MISS CAROLINE	Shubrick
SIMONS, MRS. THEODORE J. (RHETT)	Charleston 2d
SLEEPER, MISS MARY R.	Winooski
SMITH, MRS. ALICE SCOTT	Charleston 1st
SMITH, MISS GLADYS B.	St. Louis
SMITH, MRS. J. HOPKINS (MORTON)	Cumberland
SMITH, MISS SOPHIA	Montgomery
SOLEY, MISS UNA	Katahdin
SOMERVILLE, MRS. ROBERT N. (FRAZIER)	Tennessee
SOUTH, MRS. JOHN G. (BRADLEY)	Kentucky
SPEAR, MRS. LAWRENCE Y.	B-1
SPROUL, MISS DOROTHY W.	Chester
SPRY, MISS ALICE	Utah
STEELE, MISS AGNES BELLE	Helena
STEPHENSON, MISS ELIZABETH	Wisconsin

SPONSOR	WARSHIP
STEVENS, MISS ELIZABETH	*C-2*
STEWART, COMMODORE CHARLES	*New Ironsides*
STOCKTON, MISS KATHERINE	*Stockton*
STONE, MRS. J. W.	*Canandaigua*
STRINGHAM, MISS LIZZIE	*Hartford*
STURDIVANT, MRS. GEORGE W. (DRAKE)	*Iowa*
TATE, MISS STELLA	*Georgia*
TAUSSIG, MISS GRACE ANNA	*G-4*
TAYLOR, MISS EVELYN V.	*Orion*
THEISS, MISS KATHERINE	*C-3*
THOMAS, MISS FANNIE	*Sangamon*
TILTON, MRS.	*Sacramento*
TODD, MRS. MAE C. STANTON	*Chauncey*
TOLAND, MRS. GEORGE (TURNER)	*Juniata*
TOMB, MRS. JAMES HARVEY (DRURY)	*Boxer*
TOWNSEND, MRS. JULIUS C.	*C-4*
TREDWAY, MISS MARGARET	*Dubuque*
TROWBRIDGE, MISS	*Vicksburg*
TRUXTUN, MISS ISABELLA	*Truxtun*
TURNER, MISS ANGELA	*Juniata*
TURNER, MISS JESSIE (MRS. H. W. BIDDLE)	*Chattanooga 1st*
TURPIN, MRS. WALTER S.	*A-7*
TYLER, MISS GRACE	*Pawnee*
TYNAN, MISS JOSEPHINE	*F-1*
UNDERWOOD, MRS. LEWIS (CAMPBELL)	*Birmingham*
UPDIKE, MISS MARGUERETTA	*Princeton*
VANDERBILT, MISS ANNA M.	*Pawtuxet*
VIRDEN, MISS GENEVIEVE	*Flusser*
WAINWRIGHT, MRS.	*A-2*
WALTER, MISS MILDRED W.	*Walke*
WARBURTON, MRS. BARCLAY (WANAMAKER)	*Philadelphia 1st*
WARDWELL, MISS	*McKee*
WARDWELL, MISS ERNESTINE	*A-1*
WARREN, MISS HATTIE	*Cheyenne* formerly *Wyoming*
WASHBURN, MISS ELIZABETH	*Minneapolis*
WATERS, MISS JENNIE SCOTT	*Maryland*
WATERS, MISS MARGARET WINANS	*Jason*
WEBSTER, MISS FRANCES	*C-1*
WELLS, MISS ALICE	*Connecticut 4th*
WESTBROOK, MRS. JOHN D. (GUILD)	*Nashville*
WESTERVELT, MISS EMMA	*Brooklyn 1st*
WHITE, MISS KATHERINE V.	*West Virginia*
WHITE, MISS NELLIE M.	*Blakeley*
WHITNEY, MRS. C. W.	*Keokuk*
WILLIAMS, MISS MADGE H.	*San Marcos* formerly *Texas*

SPONSOR	WARSHIP
WILLETS, MISS JESSIE	McCall
WILMERDING, MISS ALICE TRACY	Maine 1st
WILSON, MISS HELEN S.	Washington
WILSON, MRS. JOSEPH D. (OFFLEY)	Ticonderoga
WILSON, MISS MARY H.	Dale
WILSON, MRS. THEODORE D.	Baltimore
WINSLOW, MRS. HERBERT	Kearsarge
WOLFE, MRS. W. H. (WHITE)	West Virginia
WOLFF, MISS HELEN	Davis
WOOD, MISS MARY	Kenosha
WOOD, MISS SALLY	Tallahassee
WORDEN, MRS. DANIEL F.	Worden
WORTLEY, MRS. RALPH M. S. (SCHLEY)	Petrel
WRIGHT, MRS. HAMILTON	Minneapolis
WRIGHT, MISS ROBERTA W.	Denver
YEISER, MISS ANNA MAY	Paducah
ZAHM, MRS. FAANK B.	A-5

Index of Sponsors of U. S. Naval Vessels
1913-1923

SPONSOR	WARSHIP
ADAMS, MRS. L. S. (CORA ISABEL)	O-1
ADAMS, MISS MARGARET ARLETTA	O-13
ALLEN, MISS DOROTHEA DIX	Allen
AMORY, MRS. CLEMENT G. (LOUISE MATHEWS)	Sea Gull
AMORY, MRS. JOHN J. (MARY S.)	Osprey
ANDERSON, MISS KATHRYN BALDWIN	Reno
ANDERSON, MRS. MAGNUS A. (MAUDE LANE)	Hogan
ANNEAR, MRS. JOHN A. (RAY EITEL)	Chase
ATKINS, MRS. LEW M. (CHARLOTTE STEELE)	L-3
ARMES, MRS. GEORGE A. (KATHERINE M.)	Harding
ARRINGDALE, MISS MARY V.	Tingey (2d)
AUSBURN, MRS. DELLA E.	Ausburn
AUSTIN, MRS. JOSEPH E. (MAMIE WADMAN)	S-49
AYRES, MISS LOUISE McLEAN	Rowan (2d)
BABBITT, MISS SARAH A.	Hopkins (2d)
BAGLEY, MRS. ADELAIDE WORTH (ADELAIDE WORTH)	Bagley (2d)
BAGLEY, MRS. DAVID WORTH (MARIE HARRINGTON)	Yarnall
BAGLEY, MISS ETHEL	Paul Jones (4th)
BAILEY, MRS. JOHN E. (BERTHA MARTIN)	O-10
BAILEY, MISS LOUISE CAROLYN	S-35

SPONSOR	WARSHIP
BAILEY, MISS ROSALIE FELLOWS	Bailey (2d)
BAINE, MISS DOROTHY	Sanderling
BALDWIN, MRS. FRANK (HELEN GOLDEN)	S–27
BALLARD, MISS ELOISE	Ballard
BANCROFT, MISS MARY W.	Bancroft (2d)
BARKER, MRS. ALBERT S. (ELLIN)	Barker
BARNETT, MRS. GEORGE (LELIA MONTAGUE)	Sinclair
BARNETT, MRS. J. WALTER (MARY SERPELL)	R–26
BARNEY, MISS NANNIE DORNIN	Barney (2d)
BARRY, MISS EDITH	Nicholas
BARUCH, MRS. BERNARD M. (ANNE GRIFFEN)	O–11
BASS, MRS. IVAN E. (FLORENCE BOUCHÉ)	R–7
BATCHELDER, MISS DOROTHY	R–11
BATES, MRS. GEORGE H. (ELIZABETH M.)	Tanager
BATES, MRS. ROBERT L. (LAURA BOSLEY)	J. Fred Talbott
BAXTER, MISS HEATHER PATTERSON	L–9
BAXTER, MISS MARGARET CUNNINGHAM	Quail
BAXTER, MRS. THOMAS (GLADYS MOFFETT)	S–21
BAYARD, MRS. THOMAS F. (MARY CLYMER)	Shubrick (2d)
BEALE, MRS. WILLIAM R. (LUCY PRESTON)	Preston (2d)
BEAN, MRS. CARLOS (MARY BALDWIN)	S–26
BEATTIE, MISS NAN MCARTHUR	Auk
BELKNAP, MISS FRANCES GEORGIANA	Belknap
BENNETT, MISS DOROTHY	Kanawha
BENNET, MISS GERTRUDE ELIZABETH	Wasmuth
BENSON, MRS. GEORGE J. (ELIZABETH UPSHUR)	Abel P. Upshur
BENSON, MRS. WILLIAM S. (MARY WYSE)	Pope
BENTLEY, MISS DORIS	Thatcher
BERNADOU, MISS CORA WINSLOW	Bernadou
BEVANS, MRS. GEORGE E. (IDA MILLER)	N–5
BILLINGSLEY, MISS IRENE	Billingsley
BISSETT, MRS. GUY A. (HELEN CAPERTON)	Pyro
BLACKMUR, MISS VIRGINIA	Dyer
BLAIR, MISS VIRGINIA	Fox (2d)
BLAKELEY, MRS. CHARLES A. (VIRGINIA LYONS)	Blakeley
BORDER, MRS. LEE S. (CHETANNA NESBITT)	Palos (2d)
BORIE, MISS PATTY	Borie
BOWMAN, MRS. MARK C. (NANNIE RICE)	S–22
BOYD, MRS. THALES (LILLIAN MARTIN)	R–15
BRACEY, MRS. BESSIE EDSALL	Edsall
BRANCH, MISS LAURIE O'BRIEN	Branch
BRAYTON, MRS. HARRY R. (ANNE FALES)	Mallard
BRECKINBRIDGE, MISS GENEVIEVE D.	Breckinbridge
BRERETON, MISS SARA V.	Swallow
BRIGGS, MISS PHEBE	Sacramento (2d)
BRILL, MRS. PHILIP B. (CHRYSTIE KNOX)	S–2
BROOME, MISS MARY JOSEPHINE K.	Broome
BROWN, MRS. ALEXANDER G. (KATE UPSHUR)	Upshur
BROWN, MISS DOROTHY	Israel
BROWN, MRS. JOHN H. (NELLIE JANVIER)	S–43
BROWN, MISS KATHERINE	Putnam

SPONSOR	WARSHIP
BRUCE, MRS. FRANK (ANNIE)	*Bruce*
BRUMBY, MISS ISABELLE TRUXTUN	*Truxtun (3d)*
BRYAN, MRS. HENRY F. (ELIZABETH BADGER)	*Badger*
BULGER, MISS MILDRED	*S-37*
BULMER, MISS ANITA POOR	*Bulmer*
BURCH, MISS KATE	*Yarborough*
BURG, MRS. ROBERT A. (ALICE CLAIRE)	*O-8*
BURLIN, MISS LUCILLE	*Babbitt*
BURRELL, MRS. GLENN S. (GERALDINE BOUSH)	*S-5*
BUSH, MISS JOSEPHINE T.	*Bush*
BUSHNELL, MISS ESCULINE W.	*Bushnell*
BUTTRICK, MISS HELEN BAGLEY	*Concord (3d)*
CABLE, MRS. FRANK T. (NETTIE HUNGERFORD)	*O-5*
CADY, MRS. FRANCIS E. (LEILA FOOTE)	*Foote (2d)*
CALDWELL, MISS CHARLOTTE M.	*Caldwell*
CALLAHAN, MISS BESSIE V.	*Robin*
CAMPBELL, MISS MARCIA BRADBURY	*O'Brien (2d)*
CAPPS, MRS. WASHINGTON L. (EDNA WARD)	*Aaron Ward*
CARTER, MRS. ANDREW F. (AUGUSTA HEACOCK)	*Monocacy (2d)*
CASE, MISS HELENA DE ST. PIERRE	*Case*
CHANDLER, MISS FANNY BEMIS	*R-13*
CHANDLER, MRS. LLOYD H. (AGATHA EDSON)	*Chandler*
CHAPIN, MISS CATHERINE M.	*Woodbury*
CHEW, MRS. FRANCIS T. (MARY HOGE)	*O-2*
CHILDS, MRS. EARLE W. F. (GERTRUDE B.)	*Childs*
CHILD, MRS. WARREN G. (JULIE McGUIRE)	*K-5*
CHRYSTIE, MISS ELIZABETH LUDLOW	*Ludlow*
COGHLAN, MRS. GRAHAM (ELIZABETH B.)	*Coghlan*
COLE, MRS. EDWARD B. (MARY WELSH)	*Cole*
COLHOUN, MISS HELEN A.	*Colhoun*
COLLINS, MISS AMY WHIPPLE	*Dent*
COLLINS, MRS. CORNELIUS J. (GRACE DANILLS)	*S-38*
COLLINS, MRS HARRY E. (HESTER BORDEN)	*Lea*
COLT, MISS J. EDITH CONVERSE	*Converse*
COMFORT, MRS. ROLAND M.	*Wright*
CONNERS, MRS. JOHN F. (STELLA STANDEFORD)	*S-41*
CONOVER, MRS. JOHN STEVENS (MARY GREENE)	*Greene*
COOKE, MRS. CHARLES M. (SARAH BLEECKER)	*R-2*
COOKE, MISS LOUISE ABBOT	*Abbot*
COONTZ, MISS BERTHA	*N-3*
COOPER, MRS. HENRY O'B. (KATHRINE LOW)	*O'Bannon*
COOPER, MISS JANE	*Robert Smith*
CORRY, MRS. WILLIAM M. (SARAH WIGGINS)	*Corry*
COTTMAN, MRS. VINCENDON L. (ELIZABETH KLINK)	*H-9*
COTTON, MRS. PERCY J. (HENRIETTA MACDONALD)	*Mackenzie (2d)*
COUZENS, MISS MADELEINE	*Detroit (4th)*
CRITTENDON, MRS. JEROME P. (PAULINE JONES)	*Jacob Jones*
CROSE, MISS JANET	*Maumee*
CRUCE, MISS LORENA JANE	*Oklahoma*
CUMMINGS, MRS. HOMER S. (MARGUERITE OWINGS)	*O-12*

INDEX

SPONSOR	WARSHIP
Cusachs, Miss Georgiana Porter	Porter (2d)
Cushing, Miss Marie L.	Cushing (2d)
Dabney, Mrs. Charles W. (Lucy Russell)	Macdonough (3d)
Daniels, Mrs. Josephus (Adelaide Bagley)	Preston, Bell, Bagley (1st)
Daniels, Miss Mary Cleaves	Clemson
Danner, Miss Anna M.	Peacock
Dashiell, Mrs. George W. (Margaret Rowe)	R-1
Daubin, Mrs. Freeland A. (Elizabeth Scott)	L-1
Davis, Miss Elizabeth	Davis (2d)
Davis, Miss Emily Crowninshield	Crowninshield
Davis, Mrs. Guy E. (Mabel Matheson)	N-1
Davis, Miss Marcia T.	Thornton (2d)
Davis, Mrs. Ralph O. (Anita Cresap)	H-4
DeBaca, Miss Margaret C.	New Mexico
DeMartelly, Miss Ellen E.	Stockton (2d)
Dempsey, Miss Ethel H.	Henshaw
Denby, Mrs. Edwin (Marion Thurber)	Shenandoah
Denis, Mrs. George J. (Alberta Johnston)	Sproston
DeVeyra, Senora Jaime C.	Rizal
Dew, Miss Bertha Francis	R-17
Dickson, Mrs. George L. (Alma Hodges)	O-3
Dickerson, Mrs. John S. (Amelia Wagner)	Dickerson
Diederich, Miss Elsa	Conner
Dinger, Mrs. Henry C. (Gertrude Mack)	McCook
Dodd, Miss Ruth Rebecca	Owl
Doll, Mrs. Chauncey R. (Martha Brandlein)	Bittern
Donaldson, Miss Hazel	Swan
Dorsey, Mrs. Vernon M. (Sarah Alden)	Alden
Doughten, Mrs. Cazenove (Florence Jones)	Jacob Jones (2d)
Doyen, Miss Fay Elizabeth	Doyen
Drake, Mrs. Whitford (Evelyn R.)	N-2
Dunnigan, Miss Ida L.	Shirk
DuPont, Miss Constance Simons	DuPont (2d)
Earle, Miss Mary Janet	Schenck
Edwards, Mrs. John D. (Mae Marshall)	John D. Edwards
Eklund, Mrs. Erick A. (Agnes Simpson)	R-22
Elliott, Miss Dorothy Hastings	N-4
Elliot, Mrs. Richard McCall (Joan Packard)	Elliot
Ely, Miss Catherine	H-6
Esmond, Mrs. William G. (Ella Sanger)	S-50
Essner, Mrs. Eugene F. (Dora T.)	Kennedy
Evans, Mrs. Joseph (Hannah Martin)	Marblehead (3d)
Evans, Miss Margaret Inez	Whippoorwill
Everett, Miss Madeline	AA-2 (T-2)
Fairweather, Mrs. J. Stewart (Rachel Hovey)	Farenholt
Farquhar, Mrs. David W. (Grace T.)	Ringgold
Field, Miss Julia	H-7

INDEX

SPONSOR	WARSHIP
FILMER, MISS MARION	*Howard*
FINN, MISS TERESA MARION	*Ortolan*
FISHER, MRS. HARRY H. (ELIZABETH OSBORNE)	*Osborne*
FLEECE, MRS. GRANVILLE S. (PAULINE BRIDGE)	*Bridge*
FOGERTY, MRS. WILLIAM B. (SARAH LLOYD)	*L–7*
FORD, MISS FLORENCE FAITH	*John D. Ford*
FORT, MRS. GEORGE H. (EDYTHE NEVINS)	*Mugford*
FOSTER, MRS. ARNOLD (MAUD BEATRICE)	*R–20*
FOSTER, MISS MAY LOUISE	*R–27*
FRY, MISS EDNA MAE	*Gannet*
GARDNER, MISS FLORENCE LOOMIS	*R–14*
GARDNER, MRS. STEPHEN A. (FLORENCE LOOMIS)	*L–4*
GARNEY, MISS EMILY P.	*Cowell*
GARTY, MRS. WILLIAM (MARY HINDS)	*Tucker*
GEORGE, MISS ELIZABETH	*Fairfax*
GERMAINE, MRS. JAMES OCCOM (PRINCESS TOCOOMWAS)	*S–48*
GETCHELL, MISS LILLIE S.	*Twiggs*
GILL, MISS NANCY	*L–8*
GLEAVES, MISS EVELINA PORTER	*Greer*
GOFF, MRS. NATHAN (KATHRINE PENNEY)	*Goff*
GOLDSBOROUGH, MISS LUCETTA PENNINGTON	*Goldsborough (2d)*
GORGAS, MISS MARY	*Taylor*
GRACE, MRS. EUGENE G. (MARION BROWN)	*McDermut*
GRADY, MRS. RONAN C. (LOUISE M.)	*S–29*
GRAHAM, MISS LOIS	*Brant*
GRAY, MRS. RUSSELL (AMY HEARD)	*L–2*
GREENE, MISS JULIET E. BERTRAM	*Bainbridge (3d)*
GRIESHABER, MRS. H. E. (ELDORA CORSON)	*S–44*
GRIFFIN, MISS HELEN	*Neches*
GUNN, MRS. ALFRED S. (ESTHER ROBERTS)	*Ingraham*
GUTHRIE, MISS ALICE S.	*Murray*
GYGAX, MRS. FELIX X. (ESTELLE ISE)	*Chew*
HAIG, MISS AGNES M.	*Teal*
HALE, MISS MARY CAMERON	*Hale*
HALL, MISS ALICE LEE	*Mullany*
HAMLIN, MISS ANNA	*Maury*
HARRIS, MRS. HERBERT H. (FLORENCE KNOWLES)	*Thompson*
HARRIS, MISS RUTH JANE	*R–23*
HASCAL, MISS RUTH	*Boggs*
HATCH, MISS ELEANOR NORTON	*O–14*
HAUGH, MRS. J. EDMOND (HELEN BROOKS)	*Hatfield*
HAULENBECK, MRS. JOHN (KATHERINE DONNELLY)	*Trenton (2d)*
HAWKINS, MISS DOLLIE HAMILTON	*Hamilton*
HEATHCOTE, MISS GRACE	*Anthony*
HELLMAN, MISS FLORENCE	*S–34*
HERNDON, MISS LUCY TAYLOR	*Herndon*
HIBBARD, MRS. CHARLES (MARY MCQUILLAN)	*S–45*
HILL, MRS. EDWARD B. (LESLIE FARWELL)	*Stringham (2d)*
HILL, MISS KATHARINE LANGDON	*R–6*

[313]

SPONSOR	WARSHIP
HILL, MRS. WILLIAM L. (KATHERINE SWEETSER)	S-3
HILLIARD, MRS. ROBERT B. (GRACE POWELL)	Palmer
HINCAMP, MRS. C. N. (FRANCES MILLER)	Maddox
HOLT, MRS. RALPH W. (FAY SLY)	H-8
HOOPES, MISS MARY	H-5
HOWARD, MRS. HERBERT S. (MARY MORRIS)	S-4
HOWE, MRS. CHARLES M. (VIRGINIA N.)	McLanahan
HOWE, MISS MARY	S-13
HUBBARD, MISS ANNA S.	Pecos
HUBER, MISS CLARA M.	S-39
HUGHES, MISS LOUISA	McFarland
HULBERT, MRS. HENRY L. (VICTORIA AKELYTIS)	Hulbert
HULL, MISS ELIZABETH	Hull (3d)
HUMPHREYS, MISS LETITIA A.	Humphreys
HUNT, MISS VIRGINIA LIVINGSTONE	Hunt
HUTCHESON, MRS. GROTE (ROSALIE ST. GEORGE)	Hopewell
HUTCHINS, MRS. HENRY A. (BARBARA KERLEY)	S-42
IMBACH, MISS FRANCES VIRGINIA	Avocet
INGRAM, MRS. N. E. (BETTY)	Ingram
IRVINE, MRS. ROBERT L. (JANET KLINK)	R-19
JACKSON, MISS EVELYN H.	Gamble
JAMES, MRS. H. H. (LOUISA DOBBIN)	Dobbin
JAYNE, MISS ANNA MAXWELL	Somers
JOHNSON, MRS. FRANK (GRACE COOMER)	Renshaw
JOHNSON, MRS. GRANVILLE W. (JEANNETTE FALLON)	Sigourney
JOHNSON, MISS VIRGINIA BELLE	S-18
JOHNSTONE, MISS ETHEL MURRAY	Kidder
JONES, MRS. ANDREW (JULIA WOOD)	Montgomery (2d)
JORDAN, MRS. JOHN N. (LILIAN TERHUNE)	AA-3 (T-3)
KAHN, MRS. JULIUS (FLORENCE PRAG)	James Francis Burnes
KALK, MRS. FRANK G. (FLORA STANTON)	Kalk
KANE, MISS FLORENCE BAYARD	Kane
KAUTZ, MRS. AUSTIN (LOUISE HOVEY)	Hovey
KELLOGG, MRS. FRANK W. (FLORENCE SCRIPPS)	Claxton
KELLOND, MRS. FREDERIC G. (KATHERINE SELFRIDGE)	Selfridge
KEMPFF, MISS ALICE	Warbler
KEYES, MRS. GEORGE S. (EMMA REED)	Brooks
KIMBERLEY, MISS ELSIE S.	Kimberley
KING, MRS. FRANK R. (ALLENE A.)	King
KING, MRS. ALVIN HOVEY (LILIAN)	AA-1 (T-1)
KISSICK, MRS. JOHN A. (IRENE GAUTHIER)	N-6
KITTINGER, MISS GENEVIEVE	S-19
KNAPP, MRS. JULIA LONG	Long
KNISKERN, MRS. LEWIS T. (VERA CULVER)	Woodcock
KOLB, MISS ELIZABETH	Pennsylvania (5th)
KOLLOCK, MISS SARAH CAMPBELL	Tattnall
LAIZURE, MRS. DALLAS (MAY MORGAN)	R-21,
LAKE, MRS. SIMON (MARGARET VOGEL)	S-15

INDEX

SPONSOR	WARSHIP
LAMBERTON, MISS ISABEL STEDMAN	*Lamberton*
LAND, MRS. EMORY S. (ELIZABETH STILES)	*S-1*
LANE, MISS NANCY	*La Vallette*
LANSDALE, MRS. PHILIP V. (ETHEL SIDNEY SMITH)	*Lansdale*
LARGE, MISS MARGARET LARDNER	*Lardner*
LATIMER, MISS MARY RICHARDS	*L-11*
LAWRENCE, MISS RUTH	*Lawrence (3d)* and *Lawrence (4th)*
LEARNED, MRS. FRANK (ELLIN CRAVEN)	*T. A. M. Craven (2d)*
LEARY, MRS. C. FREDERIC (MARY HOCKEN)	*Leary*
LEAVERTON, MISS DOROTHY	*Oriole*
LEBRETON, MISS MARGUERITE S.	*McDougal*
LEE, MRS. BROOKE (ELIZABETH WILSON)	*Maryland (3d)*
LEOPOLD, MRS. HARRY (MARY DOWNEY)	*Williams*
LEWIS, MRS. JOHN W. (LEONORE MUSTO)	*K-8*
LINDLEY, MRS. WILLIAM P. (FRANCES SMITH)	*Zeilin*
LITCHFIELD, MRS. JOHN R. (MARTHA D.)	*Litchfield*
LLOYD, MRS. EDWARD (KATE THOMPSON)	*Smith Thompson*
LOGUE, MRS. J. WASHINGTON (MARY BARRY)	*Ericsson (2d)*
LOPER, MRS. HERBERT B. (ELEANOR OPIE)	*S-24*
LOUD, MISS DOROTHY	*Neptune*
LYSOLM, MISS MAREN	*Eider*
MACK, MISS HELEN	*R-12*
MACLEISH, MISS ISHBEL M.	*MacLeish*
MACNEE, MRS. FORREST (ELLEN BRECK)	*Breck*
MAHAN, MISS ELLEN K.	*Mahan*
MAJOR, MISS ELIZABETH DALY	*Talbot*
MANN, MISS ALICE WRIGHT	*West Virginia (2d)*
MARCUS, MRS. ARNOLD (HELEN COWLES)	*Marcus*
MARSHALL, MRS. ALBERT W. (MABEL FLINN)	*K-1*
MARTIN, MISS ELEANOR	*Schley*
MARTIN, MRS. SHELTON E. (CHARLOTTE BARNES)	*Barry (2d)* and *(3d)*
MAYFIELD, MRS. IRVING H. (JULIET BORDEN)	*O-16*
McBEATH, MISS CAMILLE	*Mississippi (3d)*
McBIRNEY, MISS DOROTHY VERA	*Tulsa*
McCARTHY, MISS EILEEN DOLORES	*Mervine*
McCAWLEY, MISS ELEANOR LAURIE	*McCawley*
McCAY, MISS CAROLINE HEWES	*Partridge*
McCORD, MRS. CHARLES G. (FLORENCE CHRISTIAN)	*R-3*
McCORMICK, MISS KATHERINE	*McCormick*
McENTEE, MISS RUTH CHAMBERLAIN	*K-2*
McGRATH, MISS JUSTINE	*Paul Hamilton*
McGREGOR, MISS KATIE-BEL	*K-7*
McGUIRE, MRS. M. J. (MARY M.)	*Crane*
McILVAINE, MRS. GILBERT (ELIZABETH BREESE)	*Breese*
McKEAN, MRS. JOSIAH S. (JULIE McHAWXHURST)	*Decatur (3d)*
McKINSTREY, MISS LAURA LIVINGSTON	*Melvin*
McMICHAEL, HONORABLE MORTON	*Susquehanna (1st)*
McNAB, MRS. GAVIN (WILMA DAVIDSON)	*Stoddert*
McNEIL, MRS. ARCHIBALD W. (ANN ORR)	*S-16*

SPONSOR	WARSHIP
McRitchie, Mrs. Ernest P. (Isabel R.)	William Jones
Meade, Miss Annie Paulding	Meade
Means, Miss Agnes	Dorsey
Melville, Mrs. Max (Ruth Nicholson)	Colorado (3d)
Meredith, Mrs. William F. (Julia D.)	Meredith
Micou, Mrs. Benjamin (Ella Herbert)	Herbert
Miles, Mrs. Alfred H. (Elizabeth Gilmer)	Gilmer
Millard, Mrs. Lyman C. (Virginia Lynch)	Shaw
Miller, Mrs. Elizabeth McCalla	McCalla
Miller, Mrs. Frank (Anne Hallock)	N-7
Miller, Miss Marjorie Freeland	G-2
Mills, Miss Emma DeLong	DeLong (2d)
Mills, Mrs. Roy P. (Edith Newton)	S-51
Mohun, Miss Marjorie	Laub
Moody, Miss Mary E.	Moody
Morehead, Mrs. Albert H. (Bianca Noa)	Noa
Morgan, Mrs. Robert (Elizabeth Mahan)	Rail
Moritz, Miss Fanny Chandler	Flamingo
Moyer, Miss Mildred	Widgeon
Mull, Miss Malinda Bennett	Rathburne
Mulvey, Miss Gladys V.	Whipple (2d)
Munroe, Mrs. William R. (Katherine Johnson)	L-6, S-28
Murphy, Mrs. J. J.	O-15
Murray, Miss Helen Irving	Gillis
Neitzel, Miss Marian Louise	Hazelwood
Neel, Miss Helen Woolston	Melville
Nelson, Miss Isabella	Cardinal
Nolan, Mrs. John I. (Mae Hunt)	Young
Norton, Mrs. Edmund R. (Elizabeth Knowles)	R-24
Noyes, Mrs. Boutelle (Charlotte Luce)	Luce
Noyes, Miss Julia Edwards	Edwards
Nutting, Mrs. Daniel C. (Priscilla Dew)	Hart
Oddie, Mrs. Clarence M. (Alice Treanor)	K-3
Offley, Miss Margaret	Cuyama
Olding, Mrs. James P. (Ethelyn Hofer)	K-4
Overton, Mrs. Margaret C.	Overton
Palmer, Miss Alice H.	Burns
Palmer, Mrs. James E. (Anna Key)	S-9
Palmer, Mrs. Leigh C. (Bessie Draper)	Turner
Parker, Mrs. George T. (Kathryn Randall)	S-14
Parrott, Miss Julia Bizzell	Parrott
Parslow, Mrs. William J. (Cora Pendleton)	Falcon
Patterson, Miss Elizabeth Bache	Pelican
Paulding, Miss Mary Hubbard	James K. Paulding
Payne, Miss Marion Kingsbury	S-10
Peabody, Mrs. Frederick G. (Gertrude Douglas)	Finch
Peters, Mrs. Andrew J. (Martha Phillips)	Dale (3d)
Pfeil, Mrs. Rudolph (Josephine Schultz)	Milwaukee (3d)

SPONSOR	WARSHIP
PHILIP, MRS. BARRETT (MAZIE F.)	*Philip*
PIERCE, MRS. JOSIAH (ULRICA DAHLGREN)	*Dahlgren (2d)*
PLAGEMANN, MRS. FRED A. (NELLIE CLOAK)	*Red Wing*
POE, MRS. BURNS (ELSIE GRUMBLING)	*Medusa*
POOKE, MISS EVELYN	*Intrepid*
POTTER, MISS PENELOPE	*R-8*
POTTS, MRS. TEMPLIN M. (MARIE CHARLIER)	*Farragut (2d)*
POWELL, MRS. JOSEPH W. (BERTHA OSTERHOUT)	*Reid (2d)* and *Alwyn*
PROCTOR, MISS JENNIE M.	*Raleigh (3d)*
PROVANCE, MRS. JOSEPH B.	*Pigeon*
PRUITT, MRS. BELLE	*Pruitt*
RADFORD, MISS MARY LOVELL	*Radford*
RAE, MISS LILLIAN	*Penguin*
RAMSAY, MISS MARY VIRGINIA	*Ramsay*
RANSOM, MRS. PHILIP C. (MARY SHEAFE)	*R-10*
REED, MRS. JAMES (LAURA MALTBY)	*Farquhar*
REYNOLDS, MISS ALYNE	*Asheville*
RHODES, MRS. GERTRUDE CAROL	*Curlew*
RICHARDSON, MISS HELEN LANGDON	*Pillsbury*
RINER, MISS ELIZABETH	*Kennison*
ROBERT, MISS ELIZABETH STARK	*Vireo*
ROBERTS, MISS HELEN L.	*Tennessee (5th)*
ROBERTS, MISS SARA DEAN	*M-1*
ROBERTS, MRS. THOMAS G. (ETHEL TROWBRIDGE)	*K-6*
ROBINSON, MISS ELIZABETH ALDEN	*Toucey*
ROBINSON, MISS ELISE BIDDLE	*Biddle (2d)*
ROBINSON, MRS. RICHARD H. M. (ROSALIND SMITH)	*R-25*
ROBINSON, MISS ROSALIND	*L-5*
RODGERS, MRS. CHRISTOPHER R. P. (ALICE MEYER)	*Meyer*
RODGERS, MISS HELEN THEODOSIA	*Rodgers (2d)*
ROLPH, MISS ANNETTE R.	*Lamson (2d)*
ROLPH, MISS GEORGINA H.	*Champlin*
ROOSEVELT, MISS ANNA ELEANOR	*S-11*
ROOSEVELT, MRS. GEORGE E. (JULIA ADDISON)	*Morris*
ROOSEVELT, MISS GRACE GREEN	*S-46*
ROPER, MRS. JESSE M. (HARRIET H.)	*Roper*
ROSS, MISS ESTHER	*Arizona (3d)*
ROSSETER, MRS. JOHN H. (ALICE MAY)	*S-40*
RUHM, MRS. THOMAS (EDANA COLLINS)	*Jupiter*
RUNDQUIST, MISS ASTRID	*Heron*
RUSH, MISS CATHERINE	*L-10*
RUSSELL, MISS HELEN M.	*S-36*
RUSSELL, MISS MARION SOLEY	*R-18*
RYDEN, MRS. ROY W. (GARNETT RAINEY)	*S-8*
SANDS, MISS JANE McCUE	*Sands*
SATTERLEE, MISS REBECCA ELOISE	*Satterlee*
SCHLABACH, MRS. ROSS P. (VERA HOBART)	*S-25*
SCHLEGEL, MISS AGNES FORSHEW	*Lapwing*
SCOTT, MISS ELIZABETH STROTHER	*Richmond (3d)*

INDEX

SPONSOR	WARSHIP
SCRIMGEOUR, MRS. BRUCE (ANASTASIA MILLER)	*Tern*
SCUDDER, MISS ANNE RANDOLPH	*Perry (4th)*
SEARLES, MRS. THOMAS M. (CLIFFORD B.)	*S-33*
SEARS, MISS BARBARA	*S-23*
SEARS, MISS CONSTANCE	*O-7*
SELFRIDGE, MISS EVELYN TINGEY	*Robinson*
SEWALL, MISS DOROTHY NEVILLE	*Evans*
SEWALL, MISS DOROTHY S.	*Manley*
SHAPLEY, MISS ELIZABETH HARRISON	*Kilty*
SHARKEY, MRS. WILLIAM J. (MARY E.)	*Sharkey*
SHERMAN, MRS. EDWIN A. (ADALINE DODD).	*Sloat*
SHERMAN, MRS. FREDERICK C. (FANNY JESSOP)	*O-9*
SICARD, MRS. MONTGOMERY H. (ADELAIDE IRELAND)	*Sicard*
SIEBERT, MISS ELEANOR ANNE	*Nevada (3d)*
SIMONS, MISS HENRIETTA AMELIA	*Idaho (3d)*
SIMONS, MRS. MANLEY H. (KATHERINE NAZRO)	*Downes*
SIMPSON, MISS CAROLINE STERETT	*Simpson*
SIMS, MRS. WILLIAM S. (ANNE HITCHCOCK)	*Delphy*
SMALLWOOD, MRS. ROBERT F. (ANNIE GRAHAM)	*Graham*
SMITH, MRS. CURTIS R. (RUTH STURTEVANT)	*Sturtevant*
SMITH, MRS. GEORGE K. (LISA WOOD)	*Wood*
SMITH, MRS. JOSEPHINE T.	*Gillis*
SMITH, MISS MARJORIE	*Sampson*
SMITH, MRS. WILLIAM T. (GERTRUDE HAMMOND)	*Turkey*
SNYDER, MRS. JOHN E. (MINNIE WEBB)	*Thrush*
SPERRIN, MISS MARION	*Chewink*
STAFFORD, MRS. EDWARD (AHNIGHITO PEARY)	*Peary*
STAHL, MRS. ALBERT W. (BLANCHE VINTON)	*R-4*
STALNAKER, MRS. EDWARDS S. (MARION LA TOURETTE)	*S-30*
STANLEY, MRS. HENRY A. (GLADYS CURRY)	*Lark*
STEPHENS, MISS MABEL BEATRICE	*Haraden*
STEVENS, MISS ANNA CONYNGHAM	*Conyngham*
STEVENS, MISS MARIE CHRISTIE	*Stevens*
STEVENS, MRS. ROBERT M. (MARGARETTA STEWART)	*Stewart (2d)*
STEWART, MISS FRANCESCA LEWIS	*Southard*
STOTESBURY, MRS. EDWARD T. (EVA ROBERTS)	*Ellis*
STOWE, MRS. IRVING E. (MARY INGALLS)	*R-9*
STRAUSS, MISS HELEN LIVINGSTON	*Reuben James*
STRIBLING, MISS MARY CALVERT	*Stribling*
STRONG, MISS WATHEN DALLAS	*Dallas*
SULLIVAN, MISS GLADYS	*Fuller*
SUMMERS, MISS JEAN	*Washington (5th)*
SUMNER, MISS MARGARET	*Sumner*
SUTCLIFFE, MRS. ARTHUR T. (ALICE CRARY)	*Fulton (2d)*
SUZZALO, MRS. HENRY (EDITH MOORE)	*Nitro*
SWASEY, MISS MARY LOVERING	*Swasey*
TARBELL, MISS VIRGIE	*Tarbell*
TATE, MISS VIRGINIA MARY	*Welborn C. Wood*
TAWRESEY, MISS EDITH V.	*Sandpiper*
TAYLOR, MRS. CHARLES T. (SOPHIE DAVIS)	*Nicholson (2d)*

INDEX

SPONSOR	WARSHIP
THAYER, MISS MARY BORLAND	*Waters*
THOMAS, MRS. CLARENCE C. (EVELYN MARTIN)	*Thomas*
THOMAS, MRS. FRANCIS P. (RUTH GRIDLEY)	*Gridley*
THOMAS, MRS. JOHN J. (FRANCES WALKER)	*Walker*
THOMAS, MRS. RAYMOND G. (LOUISE TIMANUS)	*S-17*
TILLMAN, MISS MARY Y.	*Tillman*
TITTMAN, MRS. CHARLES (JEAN CROSBY)	*Crosby*
TODD, MISS DOROTHY MAE	*Chauncey (2d)*
TOWER, MRS. RODERICK (FLORA WHITNEY)	*Whitney*
TRACY, MRS. FRANK B. (ELIZABETH CORNELL)	*Tracy*
TREVER, MRS. GEORGE A. (BESS McMILLAN)	*Trever*
TREVOR, MRS. GEORGE S. (ALICE HAVEN)	*Gregory*
TREVORROW, MISS MARY ELEANOR	*Stansbury*
TUCKER, MISS SALLIE MACINTOSH	*Preble (4th)*
TUDOR, MRS. CHARLES EDGAR (LILLIE FOGG)	*Cincinnati (3d)*
TURPIN, MISS EVELYN WAINWRIGHT	*Wainwright*
TYNAN, MRS. JOSEPH J. (MARGARET McGINTY)	*McKee (2d)*
TYNAN, MISS MARGARET J.	*S-32*
VILLAIRE, MISS MARIE ELIZA	*Cormorant*
WAKEMAN, MRS. SAMUEL W. (EDITH VICKERY)	*Little*
WALKER, MRS. GEORGE A. (MAISIE GENEVRA)	*S-31*
WALLING, MRS. RALPH G. (NORMA R.)	*Isherwood*
WARD, MISS DOROTHY HALL	*Ward*
WATKINS, MRS. JOHN H. (ANNE SPENCER)	*Semmes*
WELLES, MISS ALMA FREEMAN	*Welles*
WELLS, MRS. HEWITT (ELISE CAMPAU)	*Woolsey*
WELLS, MISS JUANITA DOANE	*Wadsworth*
WESTCOTT, MISS ELEANOR VAN DYKE	*S-6*
WETHERBEE, MRS. CHARLES P. (KATHERINE BROWN)	*Buchanan*
WHITE, MISS LOUISE BUSHNELL	*Omaha (2d)*
WICKES, MISS ANN E. YOUNG	*Wickes*
WIDDOWS, MRS. RICHARD G. (ETHEL MULL)	*Alameda*
WILKES, MISS CARRIE McIVER	*Wilkes (2d)*
WILLETT, MRS. PHILIP J. (ELIZABETH SULLIVAN)	*Aulick*
WILLIAMS, MRS. HENRY (MAUD STEERS)	*Flusser (2d), O-4*
WILLIAMS, MISS MARY MASON	*Mason*
WILLIAMSON, MRS. WILLIAM P. (FLORENCE BEAN)	*Williamson*
WILLIS, MISS ELSIE JEAN	*Bobolink*
WILSON, MRS. EDWARD R. (ALICE BAER)	*R-16*
WILSON, MISS MARY BADGER	*George E. Badger*
WINSLOW, MISS NATALIE EMELIE	*Winslow (2d)*
WOOD, MISS MARGARETTA	*R-5*
WOODBURY, MRS. GORDON (CHARLOTTE WOODBURY)	*S-12*
WOODS, MRS. JAMES S. (DOROTHY DAY)	*Gwin*
WORDEN, MRS. DANIEL T. (EMILIE NEILSON)	*Worden (2d)*
WURTSBAUGH, MISS ELEANOR	*Percival*
WRIGHT, MRS. CARROLL Q. (DESSALINE SHEPARD)	*O-6*
WYCHE, MRS. THOMAS J. (PHILLIPPA LUDWELL)	*S. P. Lee*
WYMAN, MRS. HENRY L. (MARGARET MYERS)	*S-7*

SPONSOR   WARSHIP

YOUMANS, MISS EMMA GRACE......................*Grebe*

ZANE, MRS. RANDOLPH T. (BARBARA STEPHENS).........*California (3d)*
ZANE, MISS MARJORIE..............................*Zane*
ZELL, MISS ANNE CLAGGETT.........................*S–20*

CPSIA information can be obtained at www.ICGtesting.com
Printed in the USA
LVOW13*1309150114

369540LV00024B/383/A